ROMAN MANCHESTER

Aerial view of the 1972 excavation area (outlined in white) from the north. The area of the fort is shown by the hatched line.

Roman Manchester

by

Prof. G.D.B. Jones, M.A., D.Phil., F.S.A.

Editor: Miss Shelagh Grealey, B.Phil., M.A.

With contributions by:
J.D. Bestwick, Prof. E. Birley, Dr. J.D. Bu'lock, P.J. Casey, Dr. J.H. Cleland, R. Higginbottom, Dr. J. Hind, B.E.L. Long, P.S. Middleton, Miss J. Price, Mrs. J. Webster, P.V. Webster, J.H. Williams

Published for
Manchester Excavation Committee
by
John Sherratt and Son Ltd., Altrincham

First published 1974
for Manchester Excavation Committee
by John Sherratt and Son Ltd.
Park Road, Altrincham
Cheshire WA14 5QQ

ISBN 0 85427 041 8

Copies may also be obtained from
the Department of Archaeology,
The University, Manchester M13 9PL

Made and printed in Great Britain
at the St Ann's Press, Park Road, Altrincham

Foreword

I WISH to congratulate Professor G. D. B. Jones and his staff at the Department of Archaeology of the University of Manchester for their enterprise in successfully undertaking excavations on the site of the former Roman Civil Settlement in the City Centre.

It was an exciting project and I know that the City Council was only too happy not only to grant permission for the excavations to take place, but to make a contribution to assist with the financial costs.

I had the good fortune to be invited to inaugurate the 'Deansgate Dig' and was delighted to meet so many people who had volunteered to help with the project. There is little doubt that it created considerable interest throughout the City and also attracted the attention of enthusiasts from other parts of the country who offered their support to enable the work to be completed on time. This ready response has, I am sure, gained the Department of Archaeology the good will of many people keenly interested in Roman Manchester.

The 'Dig' was successful for two reasons: firstly it resulted in the discovery of a considerable amount of new information concerning the Roman Civil encampment; secondly it resulted in Manchester gaining many new friends, who I earnestly hope will return time and time again when they will always be offered a warm welcome.

As a Mancunian I have therefore great pride in the history and achievements of this great City, and am delighted that the University of Manchester has through its promotion of the excavations done so much to further enhance the good name of the City of Manchester.

EDWARD GRANT
Lord Mayor

Town Hall, Manchester
3rd May, 1973

Preface

The history and archaeology of the great industrial cities of this country is just as important for an understanding of our country's past, if perhaps less obvious, than that of the ancient cathedral cities and county towns. Unfortunately we often know very little about their earlier stages, and Manchester is a case in point. Here lies the value of the Deansgate project. It has made a notable contribution to the history of Manchester. It has also shown what is still to learn and what can still (but not much longer) be achieved. And if any justification were needed beyond a real increase in the knowledge of our past, that justification was provided by the very great interest of the people of Manchester in the whole operation. Not, I think, 'exceptional' interest, or 'astonishing'. But interest of an intensity which is being shown everywhere by ordinary people in the exploration of their country's past—provided, this is, that archaeologists live up to their responsibilities to explain and demonstrate the purpose and meaning of their work to those whose possession it is, and who in the long term foot the bill.

The Deansgate team, inspired by Professor Barri Jones's skills both as an archaeologist and a teacher, achieved an impressive success. Neither the history of Manchester, nor the attitude of its present-day citizens to archaeology, will ever be quite the same. In this book we have, rapidly and concisely set forth, the results of their project. It is an achievement made possible by the working together of archaeologists and citizens, aided by Rescue and with the support of the government through the Department of the Environment. I hope it will be widely read both for the results it contains and for the successful collaboration it reflects.

Martin Biddle
Chairman of Rescue

Contents

Line drawings in text

List of Plates

(All scales are metric except where otherwise stated)

The frontispiece and plates 1, 2 and 3 are reproduced by kind permission of Airviews (Manchester).

Acknowledgements

THE DEANSGATE EXCAVATION was made possible in the first instance by financial support from Manchester City Corporation and the Inspectorate of Ancient Monuments, Department of the Environment. To their contributions was added the results of an appeal which covered a slight shortfall on the excavation side and then succeeded in its main aim of financing the work preceding publication, particularly the creation of a Publications Officer, Miss S. Grealey. Thanks are due to her for the successful completion of the publication. The actual publication was financed partly by Granada Television Ltd., who made a film of the excavation while in progress, the Inspectorate of Ancient Monuments, Department of the Environment, and the Lyth Engraving Company Ltd. We are particularly grateful to Mr. F. Dearden and Mr. T. Hawkins of the latter firm for the care and attention that has gone into the creation of the line drawings and plates. The design is the responsibility of Mr. J. C. L. Malpass, A.M.S.A. Printing was carried out with great efficiency by John Sherratt and Son Ltd., of Altrincham.

The various committee roles are listed on page 187. Every member played a role, but in the preparatory work for the excavation it would be unfair not to mention Mrs. A. Chalmers, Mrs. V. A. Jones and Mrs. E. McPherson for their work in making preliminary arrangements. Dr. W. Brockbank, Alderman A. Logan, Mr. B. E. L. Long and Lt.-Cdr. H. F. Partridge, R.N.(rtd.), helped on the financial and organisational side.

During the excavations Dr. J. P. Wild shared the task of day-to-day direction but subsequently withdrew from the publication side. Supervisors to whom thanks are due are Miss S. D. Jones, Miss L. Alker, Mr. M. Jones and Mr. Graham Fairclough (assistant directors), Mr. P. Bennett, Mr. S. Hughes, Mr. J. Lloyd and Mr. J. Riley. Mr. Hughes was also responsible for much of the on-site photography. It is a pleasure to acknowledge the assistance from Winsford Plant Hire in the mechanical removal of demolition rubble from the site. Mr. H. F. Partridge was responsible for finance and logistics on the site.

After the excavation many hands helped with the work of drawing material for publication. Mrs. V. A. Jones was responsible for drawing the samian pottery and generally supervised the work on coarse wares. The small finds were drawn by Miss R. Adamson, Miss H. Goddard, Miss A. Metcalfe, Mrs. K. Shaw, Miss V. Taylor, Mr. P. Adams, Mr. G. Burczak and Mr. M. Snelgrove. Those plans and sections not drawn by the principal author are the work of Miss L. Alker, Mr. M. Blades, Mr. J. Dore, Mr. D. Kennedy, Mr. P. Middleton, Mr. H. F. Partridge and Mr. R. Ritchings. Several of the photographs were printed by Mr. J. Sharples. Typing was undertaken by Mrs. K. Byrne, Mrs. E. Cubie and Mrs. A. Roden. The index is the work of Miss D. Kenyon.

Abbreviations

A.A.	*Archaeologia Aeliana*, 4th series, Society of Antiquaries of Newcastle-upon-Tyne.
Ant.J.	*The Antiquaries Journal*, Society of Antiquaries of London.
Arch.J.	*The Archaeological Journal*, Royal Archaeological Institute.
Britannia	*Britannia*, Society for the Promotion of Roman Studies.
Bruton	F. A. Bruton, *The Roman Fort at Manchester*, Manchester University Press, 1909.
C & W	*Transactions of the Cumberland and Westmorland Antiquarian and Archaeological Society*, new series, Kendal.
J.R.S.	*Journal of Roman Studies*, Society for the Promotion of Roman Studies.
O. & P.	F. Oswald and T. D. Pryce, *Introduction to the Study of Terra Sigillata*, London, 1920.
P.S.A.S.	*Proceedings of the Society of Antiquaries of Scotland*, Edinburgh.
R.I.B.	R. G. Collingwood and R. P. Wright, *The Roman Inscriptions of Britain*, i, Oxford, 1965.
R.I.C.	H. Mattingley and E. A. Sydenham, *The Roman Imperial Coinage*, London, 1923ff.
T.H.S.L.C.	*Transactions of the Historic Society of Lancashire and Cheshire*, Liverpool.
T.L.C.A.S.	*Transactions of the Lancashire and Cheshire Antiquarian Society*, Manchester.
V.C.H.	*Victoria County History*, London.

Full bibliographies (with abbreviations) for the sections on coarse pottery and small finds on pp.89–91 and 119 respectively.

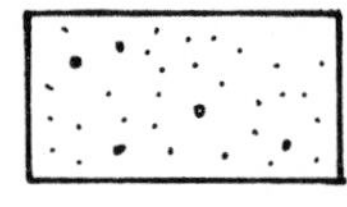
Sand

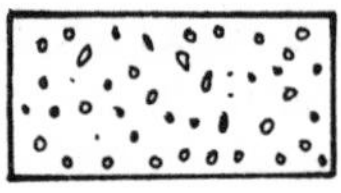
Gravel

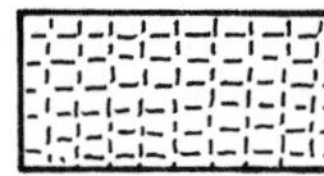
Daub

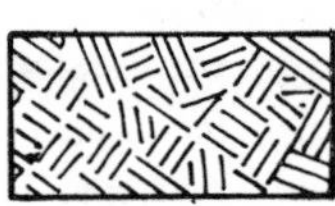
Red clay

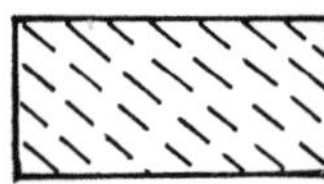
Grey clay

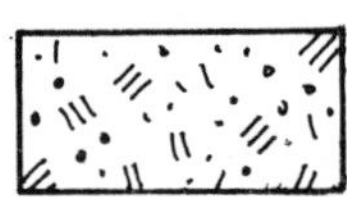
Mixed

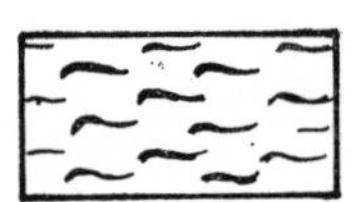
Charcoal

Silt

SOIL CONVENTIONS

A: The Background

I: The Historical Setting

G. D. B. JONES, M.A., D.Phil., F.S.A., AND SHELAGH GREALEY, B.Phil., M.A.

WHY AND WHEN was Manchester selected as the site for a Roman fort? Why did the fort and settlement, once established, develop along the lines described in this volume? To see the site in its overall development we must inevitably examine the broader history of the Roman period in the North-West.

Permanent occupation of the North-West only began at the end of the sixties of the first century A.D. following the collapse of the Brigantian buffer state.[1] None the less Roman armies had in fact penetrated the area on at least two previous occasions that are mentioned by the historian Tacitus. The first occasion was in A.D. 48 when Ostorius Scapula, the second Governor of the Roman Province, launched a campaign against the Deceangli of the Flintshire area.[2] Mention of the sea in Tacitus' text leaves little doubt that Scapula penetrated as far as the Dee estuary until halted by Brigantian unrest that threatened the stability of the politico-military alliance with Brigantia, the underpinning on which the whole of Rome's military policy was based in the initial years of conquest. Twelve years later Scapula's strategy was imitated by the famous general Suetonius Paullinus whose attack on Anglesey formed part of a policy aimed at reducing North Wales before turning attention to the problem of the Silures to the south. On that occasion the military success of Paullinus in North Wales was completely negated by the Boudiccan revolt that erupted in south-eastern England. During the campaign Paullinus must have operated from sites north of Wroxeter where a major fortress was founded by the late fifties and indeed a base at or in the vicinity of Chester in the relative safety of the Dee estuary is clearly implied by Tacitus' reference to ship-building for the attack on Anglesey.[3] These then are the two occasions on which the North-West figured directly in recorded military activity. Almost all later evidence is derived from archaeological discoveries. These have, however, to be set within a historical framework and the focus of attention where historical information is available shifts to the eastern side of the Pennines. The Brigantian buffer state survived, albeit shakily, until A.D. 69[4] when the pro-Roman elements under the hegemony of Queen Cartimandua finally lost out to the anti-Roman opposition led by her husband Venutius. Our whole interpretation of this period is bedevilled by over-generalisation and cannot be improved until we know more of the way in which the Brigantes as a nation must have been organised into various tribal septs such as the Setantii of the Fylde or the Carvetii of the Eden Valley. Indeed certain difficulties might be met by supposing that Cartimandua may have been the head of a culturally more developed group, such as the Parisi of East Yorkshire, a location that would render her early association with the Romans more explicable.[5] However that may be, during the sixties there is archaeological evidence for growing Roman involvement in and around the fringes of the Pennines. The context of the sixties forms the period when a fort was founded at Templeborough near Rotherham in the upper Don valley. The precision of the dating stems from the presence of good quality samian ware of Neronian date and kiln wasters of pottery that imitated contemporary samian forms in shape.[6] The site of Templeborough, which controls access to part of the eastern Pennines at this point, cannot have existed in military isolation. Contemporary permanent strongpoints might be expected to have occurred at strategic points in the river valleys to the south and south-west. Over the last decade there has been an increasing amount of information suggesting that this was the case. Pre-Flavian samian pottery has been found in considerable quantity west of the River Derwent at Strutts Park opposite the later fort of Littlechester, Derby, a site from which access to the southern Peak District could be controlled.[7] In addition Neronian material has been recognised to the south-west at Trent Vale,[8] a mile south-west of Stoke-on-Trent, on a hill-spur that stands at the head of the Trent valley, a few miles from the edge of the Cheshire Plain. The Neronian material, again kiln-wasters, suggests the presence of a permanent site and the site was located during recent rescue work.[9] A glance at fig. 1 will show that the site of Trent Vale lies away from the road and fort system established in the Flavian period and based on the auxiliary fort at Chesterton.[10] This at once illustrates the difficulties in obtaining any fresh insight into the manner of early Roman penetration in the North-West. Inevitably our thinking is coloured by the remains of sites and roads that have long been known. There are areas such as the East Midlands where the Roman road system appears to tally with what is known of the early pattern of military penetration. Yet by way of contrast the early military sites of Dorset bear little correlation with the eventual road system of the Roman period. Similarly in the Cheshire Plain our thinking is inevitably conditioned by the established routes, namely the road north from Wroxeter and the Chester–York arterial route. This leaves very considerable areas an apparent blank; yet there are hints of little suspected activity along the western edge of the Pennines. A record of 1744 has led to the identification of part of an extensive defended enclosure at Astbury one mile south-west of Congleton.[11] The size of the site was recorded at *c.* 60 acres in the eighteenth century. Part of its defences have been sectioned and examination of the interior has produced post-holes of flimsy timber buildings. Pending further excavation the site must remain uncertain but it none the less serves to show that some of the military movements need not have followed the patterns familiar from the eventual road system that we know. This is particularly the case because the light sandy soils of the Cheshire Plain are not conducive to the survival of field monuments; nor do they normally yield readily recognisable crop marks.

As already noted, the timber fortress at Wroxeter,[12] however large it may have been, may be assigned on the growing body of samian evidence to the late fifties while the suggested activity in the Chester area is substantiated by the location of burials with pre-Flavian pottery found beneath the site of the later legionary fortress on the south side towards the area of the Castle.[13] The distance between Wroxeter and Chester implies that there must have been some military settlement in between the two points and pre-Flavian timber buildings consisting of clay-packed construction trenches with the impression of timber uprights at the wall junctions came to light during recent excavations at Whitchurch.[14] Although adequate dating evidence for these buildings was lacking from the actual levels concerned they pre-date the later Flavian fort on the site and any interpretation must take account of the fact that they were deliberately and carefully demolished. The latter factor may well be associated with alterations in troop dispositions associated with the withdrawal of the fourteenth legion from Britain in A.D. 67. The actual period was one of considerable military upheaval in the province[15] but no details are available.

Following the advent of the Flavian dynasty* a new northern policy was initiated by the governor Petilius Cerialis in A.D. 70. His initial campaigns seem to have been concentrated in eastern Brigantia but strategically they can hardly have been conducted without some probing of the west coast as well.[16] The final conquest was, however, postponed until the mid-seventies through the necessity of finally subduing the Welsh tribes. This was achieved largely by Julius Frontinus, the second of the three Flavian governors, and completed in A.D. 78[17] by his successor Gnaius Julius Agricola, the best-known of all the governors of Roman Britain and father-in-law of the

* The Flavian dynasty covers the reigns of the Emperor Vespasian (69–79) and his two sons, Titus (79–81) and Domitian (81–96). After the brief reign of Nerva (96–98) there followed the reign of the Emperor Trajan (98–117). He in turn was succeeded by Hadrian (117–138).

historian Tacitus. In Tacitus' biography, the *Agricola*, we are fortunate to possess the one continuous account of Roman military activity in this country spanning a number of years. It is to Agricola's second campaign normally dated to A.D. 79[18] that the conquest of the North-West is usually attributed. Tacitus informs us that Agricola personally selected the sites of his auxiliary forts and reconnoitred, to use his own words, 'estuaries and forests'.[19] Admittedly this is a standard literary attribute of a successful Roman general but in the context of the situation simple geography suggests activity on the western rather than on the eastern side of the Pennines. Hence the north-western forts, Manchester amongst them, are normally assigned to an Agricolan origin. Some reservations are none the less appropriate. Despite earlier confidence, experts are now beginning to doubt the validity of distinctions made between samian pottery of the early and late seventies. Increasingly this means that, although we cannot assert that Cerialis's northern campaigns left any permanent occupation north of York, that possibility cannot be eliminated. For obvious strategic reasons it seems unlikely with the establishment of a legionary fortress at York in the early, and at Chester in the mid-, seventies, that the south-central section of the Pennines can have been left unpoliced. A mid- rather than late-seventies date for the foundation of sites such as Brough-on-Noe, the unexcavated fort at Pentrich and the newly-discovered site at Chesterfield must certainly be taken into the reckoning, together perhaps with some of the auxiliary forts on the main York–Chester arterial road.[21]

This road formed the east-west axis for the development of the North-West. The evidence surrounding the development of routes towards the northern frontier has been used to distinguish between an initial Flavian occupation established by about A.D. 80 (fig. 1) and its later development in the Flavian-Trajanic period by roughly A.D. 100[22] (fig. 2). To this we will return in a moment. To complete the picture, on the south-eastern side a defensive screen was formed by the Peak District forts of Brough, Melandra and Buxton, where Flavian samian is available from the Silverlands area. There is even the possibility of a Roman site on the southern crossing of the Mersey at Stockport.[23] Further west, Flavian auxiliary forts have recently been identified at both Northwich and Whitchurch. This information simply serves to round out the conventional picture recognised in outline many years ago. At the same time it is worth emphasising that there are anomalies in the pattern. First, abnormally short intervals separate the forts on the western edge of the Pennines and there must be a reason for this, perhaps related to the local tribal situation. Secondly, there is no doubt that the major northward-facing feature of the Cheshire plain is the line of bluffs overlooking the south side of the Mersey valley and controlling access to the limited crossing points running down to the river and the Lancashire mosses. The Chester–York road lies some way behind this but, recently, evidence has accumulated for the existence of a road running along the edge of the bluff from the Stretton area south of Warrington towards Mere near Altrincham.[24] Further work is required to establish whether the origin of this road lies in the civilian period or whether it has conceivably some strategic function. However that may be, the main focus of early military occupation clearly seems to have been provided in one direction by the Chester–York arterial road from the legionary fortress through Northwich to Manchester and so through to Castleshaw and Slack. The importance of Manchester partly lay in the fact that it was the springboard in the Flavian period for the main military route northwards ultimately to Carlisle. There is no disguising the fact that this latter road was also a difficult route, skirting the western edge of the Pennines to Ribchester and then climbing across the Forest of Bowland to Burrow-in-Lonsdale, through the Tebay gap past Low Borrow Bridge and so to Penrith and the Eden valley.

Within this framework excavation, particularly that conducted in the last few years has begun to provide a picture of the way in which this pattern of military

Fig. 1. Initial Flavian occupation of the North-West.

control developed. A growing body of evidence can be called on to support the idea that the forts associated with the two major routes already described formed the basis for the Flavian occupation that was complete in its essentials by A.D. 80. At Whitchurch, for example, excavations in 1965–6 produced the western defences of a Flavian timber fort that survived till the early years of the second century.[25] Similarly, in the area known as Castle at Northwich the line of the north rampart of an auxiliary fort was located in 1971. The topographical position suggests the presence of a fort approaching four acres in size and earlier rescue excavations (1968–70) in various areas of the interior that became accessible prior to redevelopment had already confirmed the suspicion of a military origin for the site. The most recent excavations (1973) have produced the most comprehensive picture so far by locating elements of superimposed barrack blocks that started life in the Flavian period.[26] The evidence for initial occupation at Manchester is analysed elsewhere in this volume (pp.41–47) but at Castleshaw, seen from the air in plate 3, the larger 3.7-acre fort has long been known to be a Flavian foundation.[27] To the north the fort at Ribchester has produced similar Flavian material and rescue excavation in 1970 located part of the Flavian internal buildings in a well-preserved state.[28] The site lies at the western end of the Ribble-Aire corridor and on the crest of Mellor Hill south-west of the site and visible on its skyline there lies a probable signal station. Its presence perhaps implies the existence of other such sites in the area and emphasises the strategic importance of an area where the east–west route along the Aire gap met the north–south arterial road running towards the Forest of Bowland. West of Ribchester a road ran through the northern suburbs of Preston (but well north of the site of Walton-le-Dale) to the fort site at Kirkham in the Fylde, forming one of two known outliers of the Flavian system. The site has produced Flavian samian both from casual finds and from unpublished excavations.[29] So far as it can be reconstructed, the fort lies astride Carr Hill, Kirkham, fifteen miles from Ribchester, i.e. the standard distance separating auxiliary forts, and its military character was originally indicated by the discovery of an *umbo* or boss of a shield and by the record of an auxiliary cavalryman's tombstone found in Kirkham. Excavations twenty years ago confirmed the existence of a two-period fort on the site and it may therefore be fitted into the initial pattern of Flavian conquest. Forts such as this must be viewed against a background of the possible native population. It is perhaps significant in this context that the Fylde has produced far more prehistoric material than any of the mosses south of the Ribble. Moreover, Kirkham sat astride the line of the road known as the Danes Pad that ran north-westwards from the modern town towards an unknown destination, perhaps the *portus Setantiorum* mentioned by the geographer Ptolemy.[30] Poulton-le-Fylde on the estuary of the Wyre may be a candidate for this but there is always the possibility that the site concerned has long ago disappeared through coastal erosion. Undoubtedly it was the relationship with the sea that led to the establishment of an auxiliary fort at Lancaster. The site lay astride the prominent hill now dominated by the castle and overlooking the tidal limit of the River Lune. Extensive excavation in recent years has greatly revised the picture of the early development of Roman Lancaster by showing the existence of an auxiliary fort of standard playing-card shape running along a north–south axis over the hilltop.[31] From its eastern gate a road ran down to the harbour at the tidal limit of the Lune, while the early baths have now been located at the north-eastern corner of the fort underlying the remains of the fourth-century coastal defence station known as the Wery Wall. The evidence from the western gateway in particular demonstrates that Lancaster began its life in an Agricolan context, while the fort defences appear to have been rebuilt in stone in the early years of the second century.[32]

Such then is the outline of initial Roman occupation in the North-West. It is possible to carry the argument a stage further and trace the pattern of development established in the Trajanic period, i.e. in the early years of the second century A.D.

In view of the geographical nature and political state of the North-West the pattern revealed is not surprising. Iron Age settlement in South Lancashire was always sparse, the areas of marsh to the north of the Mersey always apparently rendering the area largely inaccessible.[33] The initial programme of conquest could therefore bypass the area in the same way that Agricola ignored parts of the Lake District and for a time Galloway in his northern campaigns.[34] With the withdrawal of the second legion *Adiutrix* in the mid-eighties and the development of a Roman frontier system in Lowland Scotland, apparently in the nineties, northward communications, especially the shortening of the routes north of Chester, became of increased importance. It is therefore in the secondary phase that the development of sites and hence a communication route through the centre of the Lancashire plain became essential. Again the argument depends largely on detailed excavational evidence. The sites concerned lie along the north–south route that developed across the Cheshire plain to a Mersey crossing at Wilderspool and so north through Wigan and Walton-le-Dale to Lancaster. In the Cheshire section the behaviour of King Street in the Northwich area should have alerted archaeologists long ago to the possibility of a changing historical development for the mid-Cheshire route. As now visible, the line of King Street crosses the main Chester–Manchester route nearly two miles east of the fort—and this for no obvious topographical reason. It is not known whether any civilian site developed at the road junction but the line of the north–south route away from the known military site, the Castle area of Northwich, emphasises the different circumstances under which, it is suggested, this route developed. In supporting this thesis the extensive excavations at Middlewich conducted by Bestwick over the last few years have been of particular importance. For many years Middlewich was thought to be the site of a fort, perhaps Flavian in origin, but the modern excavations have so far served only to substantiate the idea that the site was of civilian origin and of an industrial character linked to the production of salt from the local brine. On current evidence there is pottery to suggest that the settlement began life sometime in the seventies of the first century and the site appears to have followed a pattern of ribbon development along the line of King Street at the point where it is met by an unrecognised minor road from the east.[35] The importance of Middlewich is that the evidence from a broadly spaced series of excavation sites tallies in character with that from Wilderspool, where very extensive area stripping was undertaken in excavations in 1966–7. Wilderspool, in fact, is probably the key site in the argument for the late development of the Cheshire-Lancashire plain route. Thomas May's excavations of 1885–1905 were also extensive for their time and showed that the main area represented the site of an extensive Roman settlement on the southern side of the Mersey crossing. May also located what he believed was a rampart and ditch system pre-dating most of the industrial structures on the western side of the site.[36] For many years it was generally assumed that May's features represented the remains of an early defensive system, although in reality the alleged rampart did not exceed nine feet in width and an undoubted main road ran immediately to the rear of the supposed rampart. Recent excavations by Williams (1966–7), however, have shown that May's defences did not continue either at the north-western corner or to the north-east, while the earliest buildings were demonstrated to be of industrial character dateable to the turn of the first century A.D.[37] The principal industrial phase examined by May was also shown to be largely Antonine in date with an effective end to large-scale occupation by the late second century. Thus we can see that in origin Wilderspool and Middlewich go hand-in-hand.

The next site to the north, however, remains problematical. Its name is known as Coccium from Iter X of the so-called Antonine Itinerary, a third-century list of roads and settlements, and a rationalisation of the distances suggests that the site lay at Wigan.[38] There is, in fact, nineteenth-century evidence accumulated by Watkin to suggest the presence of a settlement beneath the present town with a cemetery to

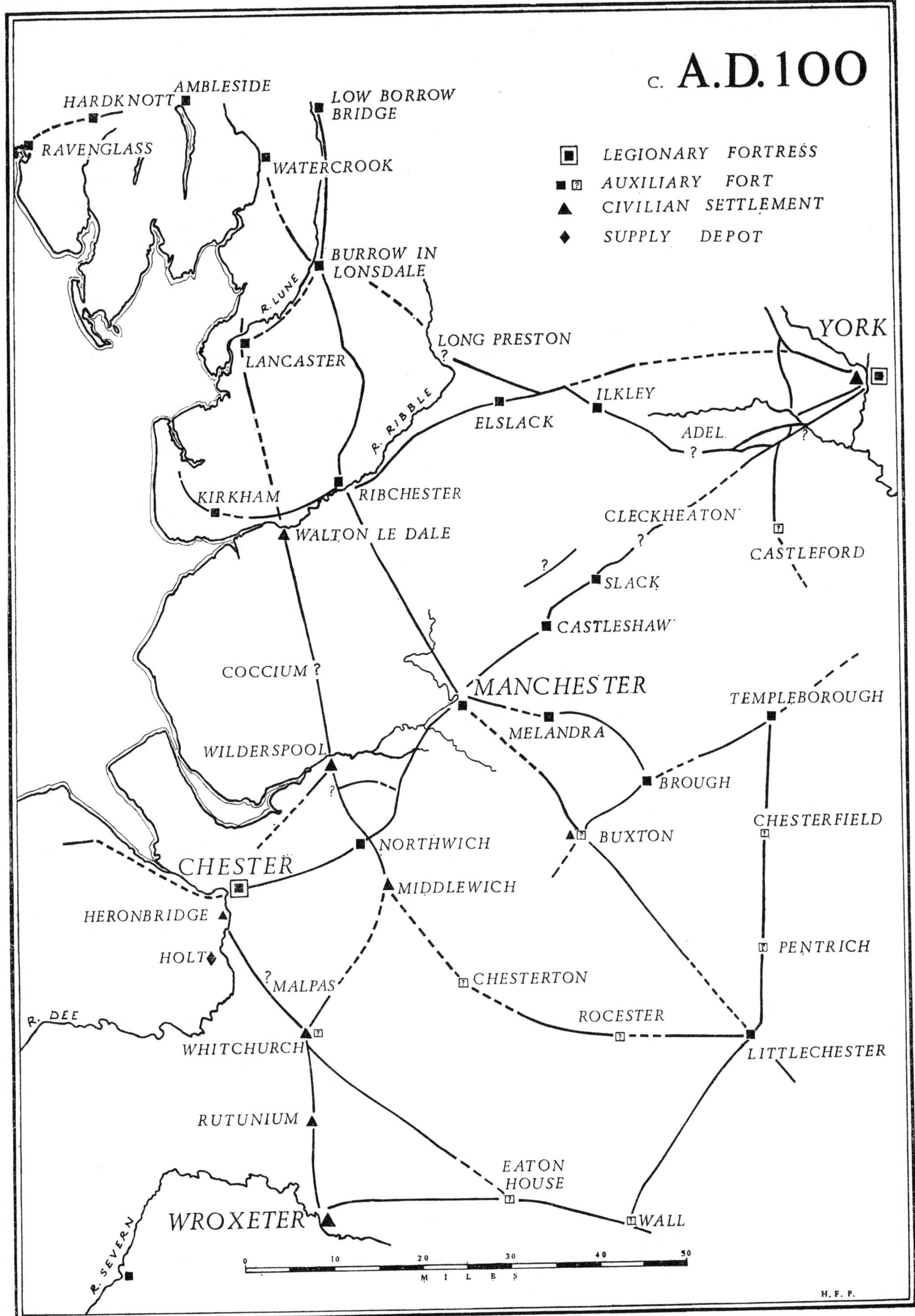

Fig. 2. Flavian-Trajanic development of the North-West.

the south-west.[39] Further clarification must, however, await excavation. This is not the case further north at Walton-le-Dale at the confluence of the rivers Ribble and Darwen. The site is marked on the Ordnance Survey map as a fortlet but in reality its character is different. Pickering's excavations in the fifties produced no satisfactory evidence for a military rampart and his timber buildings can be fitted into no known military pattern.[40] A civilian settlement seems indicated and it is significant in view of the Wilderspool evidence that the earliest pottery from the site cannot be placed earlier than A.D. 90. Wilderspool and Walton-le-Dale, therefore, both fit into a pattern of river-crossing sites along the Lancashire plain route that developed towards the turn of the first century A.D.

This then is the framework for the development of the north-west during the early years of Roman control. Information for the later periods is too scanty to permit an overall chronological development sequence to be postulated. What evidence there is relates only to individual sites and is sometimes altogether lacking. This piecemeal approach to Roman sites is at times inevitable in the development of overall historical theories from archaeological evidence. If the chronological divisions of the development sequence suggested for the north-west ultimately prove too arbitrary, then this is an inevitable hazard of any first attempt to move beyond the piecemeal approach towards an integrated history of the way in which Roman sites originated in the north-west. At the same time it is a justification for the continued examination of those sites using the best available methods to refine our understanding of the Roman heritage in our area.

NOTES

1 Tacitus, *Historiae* III, 45; for modern background accounts see S. S. Frere, *Britannia* (1967), 85ff; G. Webster, 'Military situations in Britain A.D. 43–71', *Britannia*, I(1970), 193ff; I. A. Richmond, *Roman Britain* (1963), 39ff; cf. the same author in *Journal of Roman Studies*, XLIV (1954), 43ff.

2 Tacitus, *Annales*, XII, 32.

3 Tacitus, *Ann.*, XIV, 29; *Agricola* XIV; cf. M. G. Jarrett, *Arch. J.*, CXXI (1964), 23ff.

4 Tacitus, *Ann.*, XIV, 29.

5 Tacitus, *Ann.*, XII, 40. This idea is derived from Prof. A. R. Birley whose study of Queen Cartimandua will be published shortly.

6 G. Simpson, *Britons and the Roman Army* (London, 1964), 11, fig. 1.

7 *East Midland Archaeological Bulletin*, IX (1966), 2; see later G. Webster, *op. cit.*, 190, and *Britannia*, II (1971), 256.

8 G. Simpson, *North Staffs. Journal of Field Studies*, VIII (1968), 19–38.

9 For the location of the actual site see now *Britannia*, II (1971), 259, fig. 7.

10 Excavations by F. Goodyear (forthcoming).

11 G. D. B. Jones, *Northern History*, III (1968), 3, 26; see further *Britannia*, II (1971), 255.

12 For the current state of excavations see Annual Notes in *Britannia*.

13 C. E. Stevens, *Journal of the Chester and North Wales Arch. Soc.*, XXXV, part 1 (1942), 49–52.

14 G. D. B. Jones and P. V. Webster, *Arch. J.*, CXXV (1968), 193ff.

15 *ibid.*, 213.

16 Tacitus, *Agricola*, XVII.

17 Following the conventional dating which, however, deserves further study.

18 Tacitus, *Agricola*, XX. The importance of this campaign is played down in the Tacitean account in favour of the advances into Scotland. For a different view of their importance one can, however, cite the Imperial Salutations claimed by Titus in this context and attested by the historian Cassius Dio.

19 'Aestuaria ac silvas', Tacitus, *Agricola*, XX.

20 See reports in *Derbyshire Arch. Journal*, LXXXV (1965), 123ff., and following years to 1969.

21 A slightly worn Neronian *denarius* of A.D. 68 might perhaps be used to argue for an early foundation date at Castleshaw. See F. H. Thompson's account of recent excavations *T.L.C.A.S.* (forthcoming).

22 These arguments are developed in detail by G. D. B. Jones, *Northern History*, III (1968), 1–26, and more briefly in 'Roman Lancashire', *Arch. J.*, CXXVII (1970), 237–245.

23 For Roman finds see F. H. Thompson, *Roman Cheshire* (1965), 101; the possible settlement area, whatever its character, appears to be contained by the indications of a Mediaeval wall circuit enclosing four to five acres around Market Square. Exploratory excavation is due to take place in 1974.

24 Located for instance at NGR SJ 676 845 during recent work in 1973 in advance of the M56 motorway.

25 G. D. B. Jones and P. V. Webster, *loc. cit.*, 200ff.

26 G. D. B. Jones, 'Excavations at Northwich', *Arch. J.*, CXXVIII (1972), 31–77, especially 35. 1973 excavations by P. Bennett, forthcoming.

27 F. A. Bruton, *The Roman forts at Castleshaw* (1st and 2nd reports), Manchester (1908 and 1911), *passim*; I. A. Richmond, *T.L.C.A.S.*, XL (1925), 154; F. H. Thompson, *T.L.C.A.S.* (forthcoming).

28 B. J. N. Edwards, *Ribchester*, 11; cf. *Britannia*, II, 255.

29 W. Thompson Watkin, *Roman Lancashire*, 205, records the early finds. The recent excavations were undertaken by Mr. E. Pickering and thanks are due to both him and Mr. B. J. N. Edwards for information.

30 The evidence of Ptolemy relating to Britain is most conveniently contained in the Ordnance Survey *Map of Roman Britain*, fig. 1.

31 For earlier work see I. A. Richmond, 'Excavations on the site of the Roman fort at Lancaster', *T.H.S.L.C.*, CV (1953), 1ff. See now *Britannia*, III (1972), 312, for work carried out in 1971. Major excavation took place in 1973 when rescue excavation was conducted in advance of the redevelopment of the Mitre Yard area.

32 *R.I.B.*, 604.

33 The point is well made by N. K. Chadwick, 'Early Literary contacts between Wales and Ireland', *The Irish Sea Province in Archaeology and History* (Cardiff, 1970), 68. Some indication of the constructional task involved in the provision of roads on the south side of the Mersey is shown by a massive road causeway observed at Wilderspool by May, *Warrington's Roman Remains* (Warrington, 1904), 4.

34 B. R. Hartley, *Northern History*, I (1965), 14, for the Lake District; for Galloway, see Tacitus, *Agricola*, XXII.

35 For recent excavation results at Middlewich see *Britannia*, I (1970), 282, and *Britannia*, II (1971), 255.

36 T. May, *Warrington's Roman Remains* (Warrington, 1904), *passim*. Previous detailed reports by May can be found in *T.H.S.L.C.*, XII (1896), 1; XIV (1898), 1; XVI (1900), 1.

37 *J.R.S.*, LVII (1967), 179; cf. *Northern History*, III (1968), fig. 4, and 15f.

38 B. J. N. Edwards, 'Roman Lancashire', *Britain and Rome*, ed. Dobson and Jarrett (Kendal, 1966), 95ff.

39 W. Thompson Watkin, *Roman Lancashire* (Liverpool, 1883), 200ff.

40 *T.H.S.L.C.*, CIX (1958), 1ff.

II. Roman Manchester: Exploration 1540-1972

SHELAGH GREALEY, B.Phil., M.A.

THE REMAINS of Roman Manchester, whether auxiliary fort or associated civil settlement (*vicus*), lie largely destroyed by the modern industrial city that overlies them. Most of the information in the present volume derives from excavation of that part of the civil settlement extending to either side of White Lion Street between Liverpool Road and Bridgewater Street. The process of discovery, however, goes back years, particularly to the early Industrial Revolution that gave this area of Manchester its present shape. Roman Manchester occupied an extensive area and any description must therefore take into account the information won by earlier generations, however scanty and at times misleading that might be.

The five-acre fort at Manchester occupied a rising tongue of land situated in a loop of the River Medlock a few hundred yards east of the point where that river joins the Irwell. A short distance outside the western rampart of the fort, a tract of marshy ground running up to the east bank of the Irwell must have added considerably to the strength of the defences on that side. For many centuries the open space where the fort had stood was known, appropriately, as Castlefield and the nearby canal landing stages are still called the Castlefield wharves, while the area can be approached through Castle Street which opens out from Deansgate immediately opposite Knott Mill Station.

Today the fort is completely obliterated with the exception of a small portion of the south-eastern gateway which is encapsulated within Arch number 95 of the railway viaduct leading from Central Station.[1] As far as is known, the serious gutting of the fort began during the earliest years of the nineteenth century with the construction of the Rochdale canal which cut diagonally across the site, neatly chopping off the south-eastern corner. At approximately the same period, the western and southern portions of the interior were dug away to a considerable depth, possibly in the course of gravel digging.[2] The destruction of the interior was virtually completed in the middle of the nineteenth century with the building of the railway viaduct leading west from Central Station. Like the Rochdale canal, the viaduct ran diagonally across the site, but in this instance straight through the centre of the fort. The remainder of the fort underlies the deep foundations of industrial and commercial structures and, although small sections of the rampart have become available for examination from time to time during the past sixty years, it seems certain that the 1907 excavations, undertaken by F. A. Bruton, represented the last opportunity to conduct a sizeable excavation within the site.[3]

Around the fort developed a substantial *vicus* whose extent has largely been determined by the density of chance finds which indicate that it spread out mainly in a northerly direction and developed partly along the line of the present Chester Road and partly along the line of the present Deansgate. It has been assumed that the growth of the *vicus* to west and east was impeded to an extent by the courses of the rivers Irwell and Tib but this may not have been the case as slight evidence exists to suggest that the settlement spread even to the south of the fort across the Medlock at least as far as Hulme (see below, p. 16).

No modern archaeologist has had an opportunity to examine the Manchester fort interior and only a small portion of its surrounding civil settlement seems to have been preserved in a relatively undamaged condition. We do, however, possess the records of those early antiquaries who visited the site while the walls of the fort were

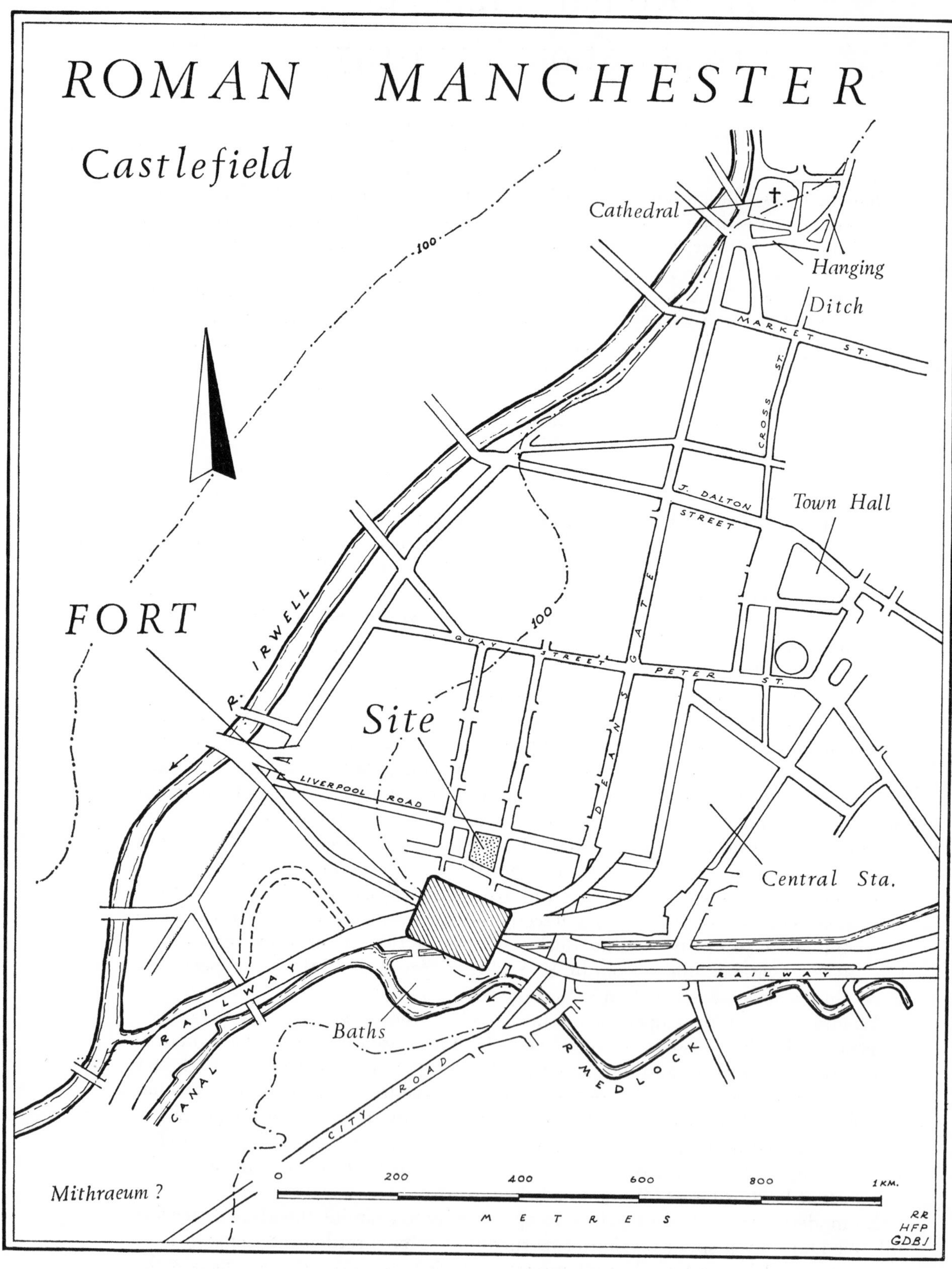

Fig. 3. General map of Roman Manchester.

still upstanding; the reports of excavators who worked on the site during the nineteenth and early twentieth centuries and the tantalising hints given by finds discovered by chance during the digging of deep foundations for buildings in the Deansgate area. From this information it is possible to build up a wider picture, however inadequate, of Manchester's Roman fort and its *vicus*.

THE EARLY ANTIQUARIES

The earliest 'modern' writer to mention the Manchester fort was Leland who, after being appointed 'King's Antiquary' by Henry VIII in 1533 spent six years touring the country during which time he visited Manchester. Writing about 1540 he said:

> 'And almost ii flyte shottes withowt the towne beneth on the same side of Irwel yet be seene the dikes and fundations of Old Man Castel yn a ground now inclosed. The stones of the ruines of this castel were translated toward making of bridgges for the towne.'[4]

Some sixty years subsequently the site was visited by Camden who remarked:

> 'In a park of the Earl of Derby in this neighbourhood called Alparc, I saw foundations of an old square tower, called Mancastle, where the river falls into the Irwell. I do not affirm this to have been the antient *Mancunium*, as it incloses but a small space, but rather some station of the Romans, &c.'[5]

The next writer of importance[6] to visit the site was Dr. Stukeley who came to Manchester about two hundred and fifty years ago and who gave a more detailed description of the remains then visible:

> 'A Roman *castrum* was on the west side, going for Chester by Stretford, and on the northern bank of the river Medlock. It is a small piece of level ground, somewhat higher than that around it. It does not cover the whole piece, but is a square, five hundred feet one way, four hundred the other; nor can it be said to be ditched about, but the ground beside it for some distance is manifestly removed into the castle, and spread along its verge, not as a regular *vallum*, but sloping inwards; by this means the area of it is higher on the sides than in the middle, and the exterior ground is lowered around to the foot of the castle, which is steep, like the side of the *vallum*. Upon this edge there has been a wall, quite round; the foundations of it are to be discovered almost everywhere, in some places large parcels of it are left, but not above ground. Now they call it the Castle Croft.'[7]

Horsley who visited the site a few years later added little to the previous accounts:

> 'When I was at Manchester, I examined with care the Roman station itself. It is about a quarter of a mile out of the town, being south or south-west from it. The station now goes by the name of *Giant's Castle* or *Tarquin's Castle*, and the field in which it stands is called *Castle Field*. The river runs near it on the south-east side. The ramparts are still very conspicuous.'[8]

Certainly the longest description of Roman Manchester contained in the works of an early antiquary is that to be found in the *History of Manchester* by the Rev. J. Whitaker[9] who, regrettably, was prone to speculative tendencies even when simply describing the remains which he noted on the ground. His general description of the fort site was as follows:

'The eastern side, like the western, is an hundred and forty (yards) in length, and for eighty yards from the northern termination the nearly perpendicular rampart still carries a crest of more than two in height. It is then lowered to form the great entrance, the *porta praetoria* of the camp; the earth there running in a ridge, and mounting up to the top of the bank about ten in breadth. Then rising gradually, as the wall falls away, it carries an height of more than three for as many at the south-eastern angle. And the whole of this wall bears a broken line of thorns above, shews the morter peeping here and there under the coat of turf, and, near the south-eastern corner, has a large buttress of earth continued for several yards along it. The southern side, like the northern, is an hundred and seventy-five in length; and the rampart, sinking immediately from its elevation at the eastern end, successively declines, till about fifty yards off it is reduced to the inconsiderable height of less than one. And about seventeen further there appears to have been a second gateway, the ground rising up to the crest of the bank for four or five at this point. . . . One on the south was particularly requisite . . . in order to afford a passage to the river; but about fifty-three yards beyond the gate, the ground betwixt both falling away briskly to the west, the rampart, which continues in a right line along the ridge, necessarily rises till it has a sharp slope of twenty in length at the south-western angle. And all this side of the wall, which was from the beginning, probably, not much higher than it is at present, as it was sufficiently secured by the river, and its banks before it, appears crested at first with an hedge of thorns, a young oak rising from the ridge and rearing its head considerably over the rest, and runs afterwards in a smooth line, nearly level for several yards with the ground about it and just perceptible to the eye, in a rounded eminence of turf. At the south-western point of the camp, the ground slopes away on the west towards the south, as well as on the south towards the west. And the third side still runs from it nearly as at first, having an even crest, about seven feet in height, an even slope of turf for its whole extent, and the wall in all its original condition below. About an hundred yards beyond the angle, was the *Porta Decumana* of the station, the ground visibly up the ascent of the bank in a large shelve of gravel, and running in a slight but perceivable ridge from it. And beyond a level of forty-five yards, that still stretches on for the whole length of the side, it was bounded by the western boundary of the British city, the sharp slope of fifty to the morass below it. On the northern and remaining side are several chasms in the original course of the rampart. And in one of them, about an hundred and twenty-seven yards from its commencement, was another gateway, opening into the station directly from the road to Ribchester. The rest of the wall still rises about five and four feet in height, planted all the way with thorns above, and exhibiting a curious view of the rampart below. Various parts of it have been fleeced of their facing of turf and stone, and now shew the inner structure of the whole, presenting to the eye the undressed stones of the quarry, the angular pieces of rock, and the round boulders of the river, all bedded in the morter, and compacted by it into one. And the white and brown patches of morter and stone, on a general view of the wall, stand strikingly contrasted with the green turf that entirely conceals the level line, and with the green moss that half reveals the projecting points of the rampart. The great foss of the British city, the Romans preserved along their northern side for more than thirty yards beyond the eastern end of it, and for the whole beyond the western. And as the present appearances of the ground intimate, they closed the eastern point of it with an high bank, which was raised upon one part of the ditch, and sloped away into the other.'[10]

Included in Whitaker's book was the earliest known plan of the Castle Field fort drawn up by Dr. Henry Clarke. Although later work has indicated that refinements could be made to Clarke's plan, in general terms, this and a plan produced by

William Green in 1794 seem to offer a reasonably accurate impression of what was visible on the ground prior to the nineteenth-century depredations.

Whitaker provided considerable, though often confused, information concerning the make-up of the rampart and about structures discovered both within and without the fort proper but this will be discussed below (p. 17) in conjunction with an examination of later excavations which took place in the area. Some points of interest, however, arise out of his general descriptive comments. The first of these concerns the 'great foss' described by Whitaker as belonging to an earlier 'British city' and clearly delineated on the plans of both Clarke and Green. It must be stated immediately that no evidence exists to indicate that an Iron Age settlement of any kind ever existed anywhere in Manchester and the suggestion of its presence was a piece of pure speculation on the part of Whitaker. The existence of the 'great foss', however, cannot be disputed. The most probable explanation of this ditch is that its presence was necessitated by the position of the fort whose siting was such as to render its northern defences most vulnerable to attack and the ditch probably represented an attempt to create defence in depth in the weakest part of the fort's defences.[11]

The other point of interest raised by the publication of Whitaker and Clarke is that apart from the 'great foss' immediately outside the north wall, no other ditches at all are indicated. Recent work, however, has shown that on the north side of the fort at least two defensive ditches protected the ramparts (see below, p. 23f.) apart from a short-lived outlying system discovered in 1972 (see below, p. 41f.). During the 1906-7 excavations of F. A. Bruton, attempts were made to pick up the ditch associated with the western rampart but the results were inconclusive,[12] and no sufficient area around the eastern and southern ramparts has ever become available to prove or disprove the presence of a ditch associated with either. In this context it is of note that Leland in 1540 refers to the '*dikes* and fundations' of the fort, while Stukeley writing nearly two hundred years later remarks that the site 'cannot be said to be ditched about'. If Leland's words can be taken to mean that the fort was encompassed by ditches then these must have been obliterated by the early eighteenth century, thus explaining their absence from the only available early plans of the fort. The question, however, must remain unresolved.

After the time of Whitaker little new information of a purely descriptive nature became available. In 1850 Mr. Edward Corbett described the site as a 'bare and grassy plain with few things ancient or modern upon it'.[13] Obviously the Industrial Revolution had taken its toll. The accounts of Baines[14] and Thompson Watkin[15] both contain descriptive references of the site but any new information contained in either was culled from the sporadic excavations which had been taking place on the site from 1828 onwards.

THE HISTORY OF DISCOVERY AND EXCAVATION

The gradual discovery and examination of various aspects of Roman Manchester has been a slow process, most information being derived from chance finds or excavations carried out under conditions which were far from ideal. As a result of the efforts of earlier workers, however, some picture—albeit hopelessly incomplete—can be gleaned of the fort and its environs.

External Buildings

Some slight information concerning several of the buildings which must have formed part of the civil settlement became available during the eighteenth century. Unfortunately, none of the structures in question was discovered during the course of organised excavation. The first of these buildings came to light in 1766 'on the slope of the bank'[16] outside the Castle Field fort and was a simple rectangular structure measuring 16 yards by 12 yards internally with 6 ft. thick walls and a door in its northern wall. The floor was paved with stone cemented by clay. Between 1765 and 1770 part of a street consisting of a stretch of small paving stones set on to the underlying bedrock and running for perhaps 30 or 40 yards was noted 'a little lower in the (same) field' and was ascribed to Roman construction.[17]

The description of one other group of three buildings is still extant. These appear to have been found in 1771 immediately to the south-west of the fort and about 25 yards from the river. The first was a small rectangular structure only 20 ft. long by 10 ft. wide with walls 2 ft. 3 ins. thick and a mortar floor. About 8 ft. to the west of this, slight traces of a second building were noted while 9 ft. to the east of it a more substantial structure, 30 ft. long and 10 ft. wide with 4 ft. thick walls incorporating dressed stones still standing to a height of 3 ft., came to light. This building had a paved floor with an underlying hypocaust system. The only account is somewhat confused but it would appear that this system, apparently quite well preserved, had been constructed over the remains of another, earlier hypocaust system, while a series of pipes intermingled with the debris of the hypocaust system probably formed part of the internal drainage system. Three Roman coins were mentioned as having been found in the third of the buildings but no description of them is available and their present location is unknown. Each building in this group is described as having produced many roofing tiles. Charles Roeder suggested at the end of the last century that the three 'buildings' thus described could well represent all that remained of the bath-house of the fort and in view of the siting and nature of the remains, his suggestion is quite plausible.[18]

No further descriptions of *vicus* buildings are available but Whitaker[19] declares the settlement to have been a town of some sixteen or seventeen acres with most of its buildings occurring to the north of the fort and running as far as the 'new Church in Camp Field',[20] and in addition he mentions the existence of a well-defined street grid. The density of stray finds indicates that his statement must be at least partially correct but as he failed to specify the grounds on which he based his estimation of the settlement's extent, his words must be treated with some caution.

With regard to the only other site in Manchester where the presence of a specific *vicus* building was certainly indicated, no structural information was ever obtained. The site in question lay along the line of the Roman road leading from Manchester to Chester, a few hundred yards south-west of the Castle Field fort but on the far side of the Medlock in what was then the township of Hulme. In 1821 while workmen were sinking a drain they came upon three large blocks of stone within the gravel about 6 ft. below ground level.[21] The first of these represented a figure about 2 ft. 6 ins. high, dressed in a flowing garment and with its arms crossed in front of its body. The head of this sculpture was broken off and later lost. The second stone took the form of a large, crudely carved head whose features and stiffly brushed-back hair showed marked Celtic influence. The most interesting sculpture, however, was undoubtedly the third which was carved on a large stone plaque (the two former having been freestanding) and showed the figure of a man dressed in a tunic with his left leg crossed before the right and a Persian cap on his head. In his right hand was held a torch pressed downwards into the ground while the left hand supported his chin. The broken edge of the panel showed clearly that it had formed the extreme right wing of a series.[22] The figure can be identified immediately as that of Cautopates, an important accessory figure connected with the worship of the Persian god Mithras whose cult attained great popularity among the legions.[23]

Undoubtedly the place of their discovery was the site of a *mithraeum* (temple of Mithras) and it is regrettable that no competent person was in the vicinity at the time to record whatever structures were associated with the stones. The loss is particularly unfortunate as the site would have been of special interest in that it is the only place south of the Medlock where a building belonging to the Roman occupation of the city can definitely be postulated.

It is evident that prior to 1972 information concerning the Manchester *vicus* was both scanty and ambiguous. The greater part of the available material was drawn together in 1900 by Charles Roeder[24] who had himself undertaken considerable research into the problems of the Manchester fort and its environs. Regrettably the bulk of Roeder's own findings were never published in detail.

Perhaps the most interesting of Roeder's published observations, however, are those suggesting the possibility of fairly intensive Roman occupation in the Cathedral area.[25] Whitaker, without any foundation, had previously suggested the existence of a second Roman fort in the region enclosed by Hanging Ditch. During the course of nineteenth-century redevelopment, fragments of rubble walls—at least in one place forming part of a rectangular structure—came to light in the area of the Cathedral and farther north around Chetham's College. In addition, portions of two paved paths presumed to be Roman were noted, while from time to time fragments of Roman pottery and glass together with coins were found in the area. Some coarse black pottery discovered in the same region was described by Roeder as 'British'. From this very inconclusive evidence, Roeder postulated the theory that Hunt's Bank, the part of the city enclosed by the junction of the Irk and Irwell and Hanging Ditch and its former artificial extension terminating in the present Todd Street, was originally the site of a pre-Roman Iron Age settlement utilised by the Romans during their initial campaigns in the area prior to the construction of the Castlefield fort. Roeder's 'British' pottery has not survived and cannot be commented upon though it must be remembered that the term 'British' was frequently applied by nineteenth-century antiquaries to pottery of Saxon origin[26] and the total lack of supporting evidence for an Iron Age settlement in Manchester as well as the unlikely siting of Hunt's Bank renders it improbable that this was ever the site of a hill fort. Equally there is no evidence for a second Roman fort in that area. More plausible is the suggestion that the suburbs of the fort straggled farther to the north than has hitherto been supposed while evidence is adduced elsewhere in this volume to suggest that the original Hanging Ditch may have encompassed the site of Dark Age Manchester (pp. 165–171).

Cemetery

As far as can be ascertained, the principal cemetery associated with Roman Manchester seems to have lain to the south-east of the fort. Again our earliest information derives from Whitaker who said[27] that in 1762 and 1765 respectively two cinerary urns were found near the eastern boundary of Castle Field and on the higher edge of the slope. Both contained bones and ashes.

In 1832 a 6 ft. long coffin made of (?) oak and enclosed in tiles was discovered on the opposite bank of the Medlock to Castle Field. This contained bones but they crumbled to dust on exposure to the air.[28]

Fairly extensive excavations took place in the cemetery during 1849 when numerous cinerary urns, both whole and fragmentary, were discovered though these have all since been lost. In addition a rock-cutting, 4 ft. deep and 18 ins. wide was exposed and found to contain charred bones.[29]

This brief summary contains all that is known of the burial-ground associated with the fort and settlement.

The Fort Defences

Our earliest information concerning the structure of the defences derives from Whitaker[30] who dug a trial section through the rampart which he described as being 7 ft. to 8 ft. thick at base and built on a foundation of boulders set in clay or clay and sand. As a result of the same test section, Whitaker was able to observe that the corners of the fort were rounded rather than sharply squared off as had been previously supposed. A further small section examined by Sir Henry Dryden in 1843–4 produced no new information.[31]

Virtually no fresh information concerning the nature of the defences came to light between 1844 and 1906 when F. A. Bruton began what was destined to be the first and last large-scale excavation of the site. During the course of 1906 and 1907 he examined both the eastern and western ramparts together with a portion of the north-western part of the interior comprising about one twenty-fifth of the total area of the camp.[32]

Information concerning the defences won by Bruton is discussed elsewhere in this volume in the light of recent knowledge (pp. 24–26). In this historical summary suffice to say that in 1907 he was able to say little more than that the visible defences enclosed an area *circa* 175 yards by 140 yards and consisted of a solid stone rampart 7 ft. to 9 ft. thick upstanding at one point to a height of 7 ft. His attempts to ascertain the presence or otherwise of ditches associated with the eastern and western ramparts proved inconclusive and, in the light of his observations, Bruton was prepared to suggest only a single-phase fort of probable second to third-century date, although more recent work has made possible a re-interpretation of his section drawings to support the theory that the fort enjoyed at least three major structural phases (this volume, p. 24).

Since the time of Bruton, several smaller-scale examinations of the fort defences have been undertaken by Phelps[33] and more recently by Petch and Frere.[34] The first of these excavations[33] established the existence of an earlier fort on the site enclosed by a turf and clay rampart with a double ditch system to the north but added little further information, rather confirming the results previously obtained by Bruton. The work undertaken by Petch and Frere in the 1950's[34] was carried out under extremely difficult conditions, but the excavators established a Flavian date for the initial fort. No stratified evidence for the stone replacement was found and Petch suggested a Severan date for the remains uncovered. In this case it was assumed that all trace of an early second century stone gateway had been obliterated.[35] The most recent excavations on the defences have established two periods of reconstruction in stone, one presumably Trajanic, the other possibly Severan on the basis of a Severan re-building inscription found in the fort interior,[36] and have shown that the stone fort discussed by earlier writers belongs to the latter phase (this volume, pp. 24–26). A re-assessment of earlier work has recently been produced by Simpson[37] who has suggested a late third- or even fourth-century date for the late fort re-building at Manchester on the basis of diagonal coursing noted by Bruton and Phelps.[38] Dr. Simpson has suggested that this military building technique was not used in Britain prior to the later part of the third century. The sample of parallels which form the basis for the proposed date, however, is really too small for the argument to be accepted without firm supporting evidence. Many major questions remain unanswered, however, and it seems probable that our knowledge of the defensive system will never now be completed.

Internal Lay-out of the Fort

Although a portion of the fort's interior was examined by Bruton during his 1906–7 excavations and further, though less comprehensive, investigations have also taken place there, remarkably little information concerning the internal lay-out has come to light. On the plan drawn up by John Swarbrick to illustrate Bruton's 1907 excavations,[39] a fragment of wall is marked as upstanding beneath archway 102 of the railway viaduct leading from Central Station and lying towards the centre of the fort. In the light of Petch and Frere's excavations during the 1950's which established the position of the gateways, thus fixing the line of the *via principalis* it seems reasonable to accept the excavator's tentative suggestion that this fragment formed part of the main *principia* wall of the Severan period fort.[40] In addition, work undertaken by Professor Donald Atkinson in 1951 established the position of barrack blocks situated under the houses in Ivy Street in the northern part of the fort and also apparently belonging to the Severan phase.[41] Unfortunately, Professor Atkinson's findings have never been published in full.

Bruton's excavations produced little further information in this regard. He was able to establish the line of streets running parallel to the western rampart in the north-western corner of the fort where he exposed two parallel streets, one with a well-preserved central drain. Perhaps the most interesting and most tantalising of Bruton's finds in the fort interior, however, take the form of what were described by him as 'the lower stones'. These lay about 50 ft. inside the western rampart and consisted of a series of medium sandstone blocks set in clay and standing in part to a height of two courses. In part, the line of the stones ran beneath the surface of the street with the central drain previously mentioned. Bruton described these stones as being 'in great profusion and confusion' but nevertheless took the trouble to plan their positions accurately. A glance at his plan[43] is sufficient to show that these stones undoubtedly formed the foundation courses of at least one fairly substantial building with a probable second building on a similar alignment to the north-east. In view of the fact that these stone foundations underlay the cobbled street presumed to belong to the Severan fort, it seems reasonable to suggest that they belonged to the Trajanic fort, the earliest stone fort on the site. Unfortunately, no further information about the nature of these structures is forthcoming and speculation about their function is pointless in view of the scanty evidence.

This meagre information represents the sum total of our knowledge of the internal layout of Manchester's Roman fort and the extent of later disturbance in the area makes it fairly certain that no further structural remains will be recovered at any future date.

THE FINDS

Although a quantity of finds are on record as having come from the Roman fort at Manchester and its neighbourhood, the majority of these took the form of stray finds chanced upon during construction work and the greater number have been mislaid over the years which have elapsed since their discovery. Although some of the finds possess individual merit, the number which can offer clues to the nature and extent of Roman occupation in the area are sadly limited.

Inscriptions

Two altars, four centurial stones, three cohort tiles, one legionary tile and a small fragment of a dedicatory inscription are known from Manchester. One of the altars was set up by a centurion of the VIth legion, the other by an officer in command of a vexillation of the *Raeti* and *Norici.* Three of the centurial stones were erected by centuries of the First Cohort of the Frisiavones, the fourth by a century of an unnamed cohort, their purpose being to record the building of a section of the rampart. One of the two surviving tile-stamps bears the mark of the XXth legion Valeria Victrix. In view of this, it is rather surprising that there is also evidence for a centurion of the VIth legion (mentioned above). It is possible that this centurion fulfilled the role of a *centurio regionarius* implied by another inscription from Ribchester (R.I.B. 587). The Ribchester inscription belongs to the mid-third century and a similar situation may have existed at Manchester. The unit that the centurion controlled is not known, but it is generally supposed that the Frisiavones, already mentioned and attested at Melandra (R.I.B. 279) as well as at Manchester were in garrison in the late first and early second centuries. There is another garrison, however, enigmatically attested by a tile-stamp bearing the words C III BR. This has been variously attested as referring to the Bracaraugustani, an Iberian unit who are known from diplomas to have served in Britain during the first half of the second century.[44] The contraction of Bracaraugustani to BR is not, however, satisfactorily attested elsewhere, and another possible candidate must lie with a detachment of the Breuci who are known to have formed the garrison at Slack and Castleshaw,[45] while their tile-producing centre has been located at Grimscar, Outlane, near Huddersfield.[46] Tiles of this unit have been found at Melandra Castle where a stamped tile similar to the Manchester example was found in the bath-house.[47] On the present evidence, certainty is unattainable.

Coins

The coin evidence from the area shows a reasonable number of first- and second-century issues, the latter remaining fairly constant over the Trajanic, Hadrianic and Antonine periods; few third-century issues have been noted, while Severan issues are almost non-existent although fourth-century issues occur in great numbers. Twelve coins found during Bruton's excavations in the fort interior ranged in date from A.D. 100 to A.D. 320, though nearly all were earlier than A.D. 220. (This volume pp. 137–40.)

Bronzes

The bronzes found during previous explorations in Manchester range in date from late first century A.D. to fourth century A.D., the majority being assignable to second century.

Pottery

The great bulk of the pottery accumulated over many years seems to belong to the second and third centuries with a few first-century pieces. Although only a very small proportion of the pottery found in the area has survived the chronology of the site could be ascertained from the ceramic evidence.

Conclusions

During the past four hundred years, various pieces of scattered evidence have been accumulated partly by chance and partly through the efforts of a small number of workers who have endeavoured to throw some light on the foundation of their city. The resulting picture is meagre in the extreme, for no aspect of it even approaches completeness, but it does provide some background view, however skimpy, of the origins of modern, industrial Manchester.

NOTES

1 This portion survives thanks to the foresight of the then landowner, Lord Ellesmere, who placed it under a preservation order in 1858.

2 F. A. Bruton, *The Roman Fort at Manchester*, M.U.P. (1909), 5. Henceforth, Bruton, *Roman Manchester*.

3 Bruton, *op. cit.*, *passim.*

4 Hearne's *Leland* (1769–70), V, 94.

5 Gough's *Camden* (1789), iii, 127.

6 Hollingworth in his *Mancuniensis* (Willis's edition, 1839) described the site but added no new information.

7 *Itinerarium Curiosum* (1776), 55.

8 *Britannia Romana* (1732), 415.

9 J. Whitaker, *History of Manchester* (2nd edition, 1773).

10 Whitaker, *op. cit.*, i, 49.

11 In this context it is worth emphasising that the 1972 Deansgate excavations immediately outside the north-eastern gateway of the fort produced evidence of a short-lived outlying ditch system some distance beyond the main defences (*infra*, p. 45).

12 Bruton, *op. cit.*, 71–2.

13 W. Thompson Watkin, *Roman Lancashire* (1883), 95.
14 E. Baines, *History of Lancashire* (1836).
15 Thompson Watkin, *op. cit.*, 92–124.
16 Whitaker, *op. cit.*, i, 33–5.
17 Whitaker, *loc. cit.*
18 C. Roeder, *Roman Manchester* (Manchester 1900), 45–9.
19 Whitaker, *op. cit.*, i, 271–2.
20 St. John's Church, founded 1769.
21 W. H. Whatton, *Gentlemen's Magazine* (1821), pt. i, 257.
22 For a full discussion of the Manchester Mithraic figures see E. L. Hicks in Bruton, *op. cit.*, 34ff.
23 C. M. Daniels, *Mithras and his Temples on the Wall* (Newcastle) with full bibliography.
24 Roeder, *op. cit.*, *passim*, especially illustration facing p. 50.
25 Roeder, *op. cit.*, 94–123.
26 J. D. Bu'lock, *T.L.C.A.S.*, LXVI (1956), 42.
27 Whitaker, *op. cit.*, i, 50.
28 Baines, *op. cit.*, ii, 360.
29 Thompson Watkin, *op. cit.*, 120.
30 Whitaker, *op. cit.*, i, 45.
31 Thompson Watkin, *op. cit.*, 98.
32 Bruton, *op. cit.*, 48–132.
33 *T.L.C.A.S.*, XXX (1913), 195–210.
34 *T.L.C.A.S.*, LXII (1953), 177–95; LXIV (1955), 27–37; LXVI (1957), 29–37.
35 For plan of north gateway see *Archaeological Journal* (1971), 238.
36 R. E. Collingwood and R. P. Wright, *The Roman Inscriptions of Britain* (R.I.B.) I, Oxford (1965), no. 581. For discussion see *Northern History* III (1968), pp. 8, 20.
37 Grace Simpson, 'Roman Manchester and Templeborough: the forts and dates reviewed', in Hawkes & Hawkes (eds.), *Greeks Celts and Romans*, I, London (1973), 75–77.
38 *T.L.C.A.S.*, XXX (1913), 200.
39 Bruton, *op. cit.*, folding plan 1.
40 *T.L.C.A.S.*, LXIV (1955), 36.
41 *J.R.S.*, 42 (1952), 91.
42 Bruton, *op. cit.*, 79–81.
43 Bruton, *op. cit.*, folding plan 2.
44 H. Williamson, 'The Inscriptions of Roman Manchester', in Bruton, *op. cit.*, 20–34.
45 P. W. Dodd and A. M. Woodward, 'Excavations at Slack 1913–1915', *Yorkshire Archaeological Journal*, XXVI, 72 and fig. 46.
46 I. A. Richmond, *Huddersfield in Roman Times*, Huddersfield (1925), 57–59.
47 Information from Dr. J. P. Wild.

III: The Northern Defences of the Roman Fort at Manchester 1965-1967

J. H. WILLIAMS, M.A.

SUMMARY

THE ROMAN fort at Manchester lies at the southern end of Deansgate near Deans-Gate Station, and within the confluence of the rivers Irwell and Medlock. Previous excavations on the site failed to establish a satisfactory chronology for the site, initially through inadequacies of early archaeological technique and more recently through the limitations of area available for excavation. With the demolition of houses in the Manor Street area it became possible to examine the northern defences; three phases of defensive work were identified but these probably represent less than the total number of phases in the fort. The initial occupation was almost certainly of Flavian date but the later chronology is uncertain. Further work is therefore required to elucidate even the basic history of the fort.

THE EXCAVATION[1]

In 1965 a 4-foot wide trench was laid out parallel to and about 6 feet away from the west wall of the mill on the corner of Bridgewater Street and Duke Street (fig. 4). The trench was at about 75 degrees to the known line of the Roman defences and extended for 65 feet from the pavement in Bridgewater Street to the boundary wall of the Bridgewater Estate. The area had been cleared of slum dwellings and fortunately the demolished houses had been founded on insubstantial foundations which little penetrated the underlying strata.

The natural subsoil was a yellow gravel and contrasted with the yellow sand recorded further east. Layer 1 comprised black ash and clinker deposited in levelling the site for use as a car-park. Layer 2 was formed of mixed soil and rubbish and was associated with the former slum property. Layer 3, composed of dark brown soil with some stone, is to be seen as a natural build-up after the Roman period. A closely packed layer of cobbles, layer 4, extended from wall foundation, layer 11, to the sandstone and clay of layer 5. This latter deposit was extremely solid and compact; sandstone blocks, many of them faced, were held firm in a matrix of hard grey clay. The light brown silty sand of layer 6 contained pebbles and some sandstone including two blocks measuring 1 foot by 1 foot 6 inches and a millstone grit voussoir measuring 9 inches by 9 inches by 1½ inches by 5½ inches.[2] Layer 7 was a yellow sand, identical in composition to that of layer 10. The grey/yellow clay forming layer 8 was almost certainly decayed turf. Layer 9 was yellow sand mixed with turf, and large cobbles, set in a stiff, plastic, pink clay formed layer 11. Layer 12 was a grey silty sediment. Some doubt existed, however, as to whether layer 9 cut through layer 6 or was sealed by it. The latter interpretation was adopted at the time. In an attempt to clarify the matter a further small section was cut in June 1967 a few feet to the east of the original section. The section was contaminated but it would appear that layer 6 was cut by layer 9. In all other respects the section was identical to that cut in 1965. No pottery or other dating evidence was found in either trench.

DISCUSSION

It seems reasonable from the evidence to argue for a defence system of at least three periods. The following arrangement is most probable:

Period I. Ditches 1 and 2, 10 feet and 12(?) feet wide respectively, formed a W-ditch arrangement, almost certainly associated with the turf and clay rampart noted by Petch.[3]

Period II. Ditch 1 was deliberately filled in with clay and turf from the period I rampart. Ditch 2 continued in use but was possibly recut to an increased width of 17 feet and depth of 3 feet 6 inches. The rampart material of period I was probably augmented by deposits of the light brown soil and stone which was later to be redeposited as layer 6. If layer 9 is sealed by layer 6 then layer 9 becomes part of the construction trench for the period II wall; if not, layer 9 becomes part of the construction trench for period III and the period II wall must lie further south. At the end of period II the rampart material, layer 6, collapsed or was pushed into ditch 2.

Period III. Period III saw the insertion of the wall foundation, layer 11, comprising boulders set in a plastic pink clay. A cobbled surface was laid in front of the wall; ditch 2 was extended northwards and the south face of the ditch revetted with sandstone and stiff grey clay. The compact composition of this layer makes it virtually imperative that this is deliberate packing rather than a rubble collapse. The recut measured 20 feet wide and 4 feet deep.

It is impossible to determine with which defensive phase ditch 3 should be associated.

Problems of stratigraphical interpretation.

Over the years several excavations have been conducted on the fort but in all instances have been hampered by the presence of the railway and other relics of Victorian industrialism overlying the site. The earlier excavations by Roeder,[4] Phelps,[5] and Bruton,[6] were the more extensive but suffered through a lack of understanding of some of the basic historical problems of the site. More recent excavations by Petch[7] have investigated some of the questions more systematically but the limited area open for excavation has been a serious handicap. The 1965 and 1967 excavations seem clear in their inferences but it is not a simple task to consolidate the findings with evidence from the previous excavations. In the 1950's Petch excavated several trenches along the line of the boundary wall of the Bridgewater Estate in the Manor Street area. The primary purposes were to locate the alignment of the north wall of the fort and establish the position of the gate. In the gate area an early turf rampart with timber corduroy was found to be cut by the foundations of a stone gateway. The similarity of the gateway with one of known Severan date at Bewcastle was noted,[8] but where were the remains of the likely Trajanic stone phase? It is quite possible that the massive 7 to 8 feet wide foundations of the late stone phase completely obliterated an earlier stone phase and Petch does, in fact, note elsewhere that there were apparently two distinct layers in the foundations.[9]

Petch only penetrated the start of the northern ditch complex but certain anomalies are present here also.

(1) The clay packing of ditch 1 was absent. This was also missing in a section cut by Phelps though cobble layer 4 was present in this latter instance.[10]

(2) Nearer the gate the inner ditch was missing but this is possibly because of changes in the ditch pattern, at different periods, adjacent to the gate.

(3) In the area where ditch 1 was missing tumbled masonry was noted in ditch 2.[11] This is not wholly consistent with the fill of ditch 2 found in 1965.

The 1965 section did, however, corroborate the multiple ditch system postulated by Roeder[12] but the actual ditch dimensions are inconsistent.

Sections through the eastern defences,[13] although recorded by Bruton in a fashion ahead of his time, present several problems, including the recurring one of the missing first phase stone wall. The sections as recorded, however, can be used to validate the thesis of a least a three-phase fort. The drawn section (fig. 5) is a schematic and composite one, based on Bruton's section AA and CC. Seated above

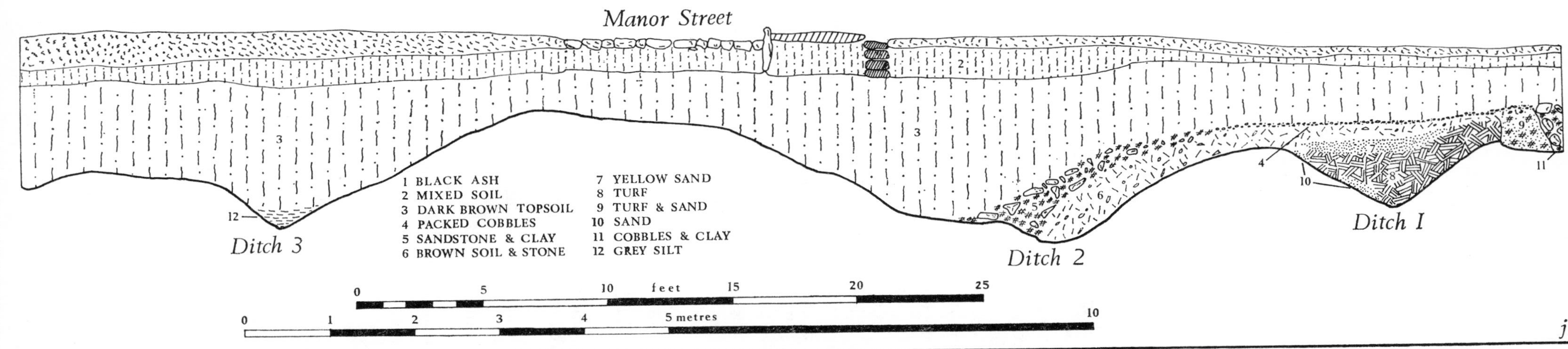

Fig. 4. Section through the northern defences (1965).

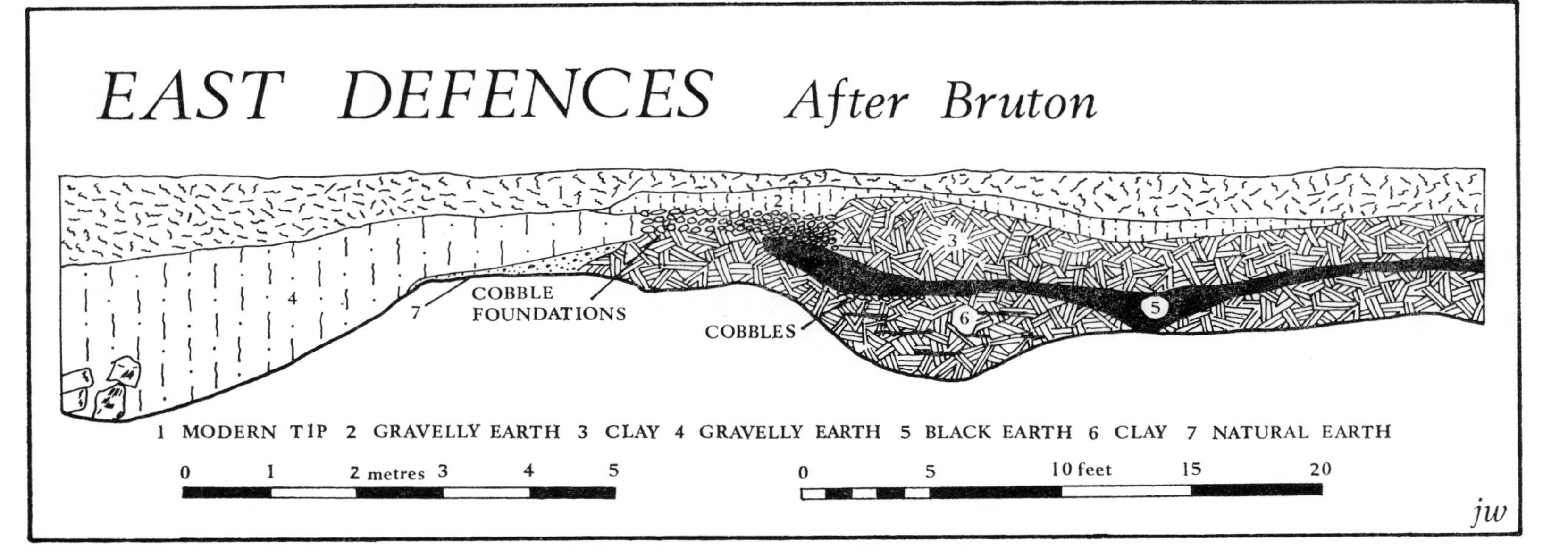

Fig. 5. Reconstructed section through the eastern defences.

the natural gravel was a hard clay layer. This was regarded as a levelling deposit by the excavators and although it is tempting to see a ditch profile cut into the natural gravel this is not substantiated by adjacent sections. The 'cobble' pavement is to be seen as the foundation for a turf revetment for the turf and clay rampart of period I and the layer of black earth is possibly a timber corduroy. The ditch is shown to be full of 'brown tip' and fallen stone presumably from the stone wall. Since, however, the cobble wall foundations cut through this layer (unless, of course, Bruton failed to differentiate various layers within layer 4) the stone must be from an earlier stone phase which again may be concealed by the massive 7 to 8 feet wide foundations. The 'brown tip' should possibly be interpreted as the rampart material of period II.

Problems of chronological interpretation.

The early defensive works are known to be of Flavian origin. It is likely, from analogy with Northwich, Chester, Ribchester and Melandra, that the fort was reconstructed in the Trajanic period. Further reconstruction in the Severan period is suggested by the similarity of the north gate with that of a gate at Bewcastle and supported by a fine Severan building inscription (R.I.B. 581).[14] The coin histogram for the site and its environs[15] shows a good quantity of first- and second-century issues with second-century coins spread fairly evenly over the Trajanic, Hadrianic and Antonine periods, a paucity of third-century issues with an almost total lack of those of the Severan period, and an abundance of fourth-century issues.[16] On this basis and on the evidence from the excavation a definitive structural chronology for the site is impossible. It is quite probable that the three phases identified represent less than the total number of phases of the fort.

[This paper was written before Dr Grace Simpson's 'Roman Manchester and Templeborough: The Forts and Dates Reviewed' (in *Greeks, Celts and Romans*, ed. by Christopher and Sonia Hawkes) was available. Dr Simpson in discussing Bruton's sections AA, CC, and EE, postulates a five phase sequence which the evidence hardly justifies. The 'ditches' of phases 1–3 seem inadequate as military works being scarcely a metre deep and of gentle and irregular profile and as such were not seriously considered by the present author. An occupation at Manchester, however, far more extensive than the three phases positively identified in the defences seems highly probable.—J.H.W., December 1973.]

NOTES

1 The excavations were undertaken by students of Manchester University under the direction of the author and Mrs J. Webster. We would like to thank Provincial Car Parks Limited (tenants of the land) and Dunlop Heywood & Co (agents of the owners) for permission to dig. Manchester City Council were extremely helpful in providing plans of amenity services which might be encountered and also supplied fencing and a mechanical shovel for backfilling. Mr F. H. Thompson and Dr G. D. B. Jones afforded much welcome advice on archaeological matters.

2 Cf. use of millstone grit for facing blocks as opposed to the more normal red sandstone: *T.L.C.A.S.*, xxx (1912), 205.

3 *T.L.C.A.S.*, xxx (1912), 205.

4 *T.L.C.A.S.*, xvii (1899), 87ff.

5 *T.L.C.A.S.*, xxx (1912), 195ff.

6 F. A. Bruton, *The Roman Fort at Manchester* (Manchester, 1909).

7 *T.L.C.A.S.*, lxvi (1956), 29; ibid., lxiv (1954), 27; ibid., lxii (1951), 177.

8 *T.L.C.A.S.*, lxvi (1956), 33.

9 *T.L.C.A.S.*, lxii (1950), 131f.

10 *T.L.C.A.S.*, xxx (1912), 204.

11 *T.L.C.A.S.*, lxvi (1956), 35.
12 *T.L.C.A.S.*, xvii (1899), 100f.
13 Bruton, 66ff.
14 Cf. also R.I.B. 576, of similar date.
15 Taken from R. S. Conway, J. McInnes and G. C. Brooke, *The Roman Coins of Manchester* bound with F. A. Bruton, op. cit.
16 See page 137ff.; cf. also the fairly continuous date range of settlement in the *vicus* as attested by the 1972 excavations.

B: The Excavations

I: The Site

i. Introduction

In a review of the world's great cities written in 1957, A. J. P. Taylor wrote that 'Manchester had a Roman foundation, though not worth lingering on. Its only standing structural remains, the fragment of wall in a goods-yard at the bottom of Deansgate, must rank as the least interesting Roman remain in England, which is setting a high standard'!

During the last decade, however, a revolution in archaeological approach has taken place, and with this has come a long overdue swing in the balance away from concentration on Roman military archaeology. In particular, there has been a welcome upsurge in the amount of information about the post-Roman history of the major towns and cities of the country. The altered emphasis has brought a change in the methods of archaeology and initiated a period characterised, one might say, by large-scale excavations in the heart of our major historical centres like Exeter, Winchester, Southampton, Gloucester, Lincoln, Colchester and York. Yet Roman archaeology in the military zone and its fringes has benefited little from the advance in techniques. Very little indeed is known about the civil settlements that grew up outside the northern forts and often, like cuckoos in the nest, went on to overshadow them and become the predecessors of many modern towns. Manchester is a case in point. The meaningless concrete mass encapsulated within an arch of the railway viaduct leading from Central Station represents all that visibly remains of the 5-acre fort at the western end of Deansgate known by tradition as Castlefield. In fact it represents what little is left of the south-eastern gateway but it is understandable that the public should think that all other tangible evidence of Manchester's Roman past was effectively lost for ever. The construction of the railway viaduct in the last century had already destroyed the core of the fort site, while subsequent industrial development severely damaged the archaeological levels in the rest of the site.

Yet this presumed loss of Manchester's historic past was not total. The speedy development of Manchester in the Industrial Revolution threw up a series of random finds from Knott Mill to Deansgate—even evidence to suggest the existence of the mithraeum at Hulme. Finds suggested that Manchester's fort was surrounded by a very substantial civil settlement that developed partly along the present Chester Road and partly along the line of the present Deansgate. Indeed the sheer size of the area in which remains were recorded in the last century, however unsatisfactorily, suggested that the civil settlement may have overshadowed the fort in size. This is not particularly surprising; for Manchester's position as the meeting place of the strategic east-west route linking the legionary bases at Chester and York with another important route striking north along the western edge of the Pennines to Carlisle must have ensured its continued importance throughout the Roman period.

How then to examine part of the civil settlement? Much of it must have been destroyed by the deep cellars of the buildings in the Deansgate area. Yet a relatively undamaged area suitable for excavation could hold the secrets both of the early layout of the civil settlement and a general guide to the history of its development. No area sufficiently large seemed likely to appear and there the matter rested until 1972. With the purpose of creating an inner relief road on the north-western side of Deansgate. Manchester City Corporation completed the demolition of White Lion Street immediately south of Liverpool Road and proposed to turn the area into a

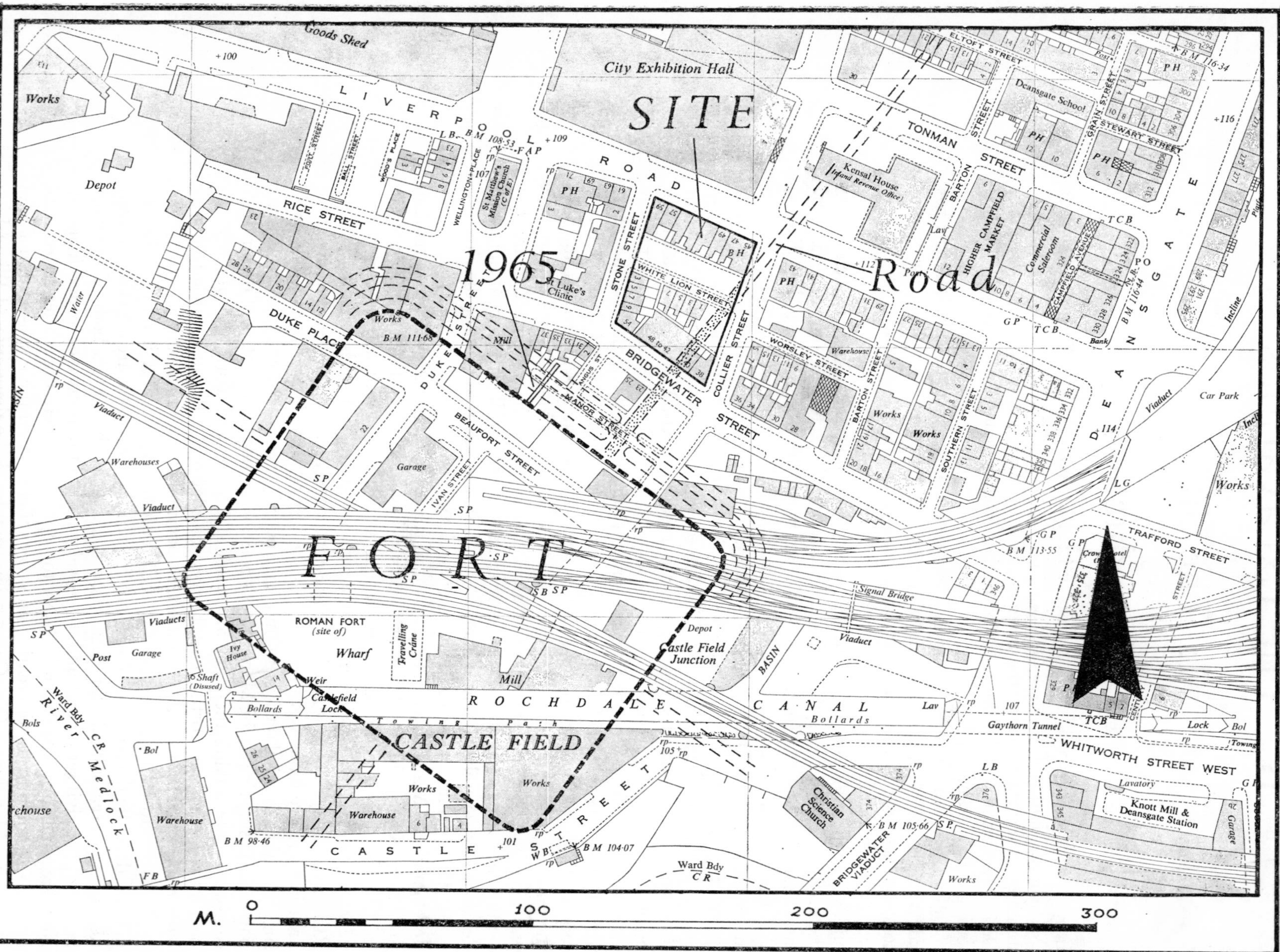

Fig. 6. The Roman fort area.

(Based upon the Ordnance Survey 50 in. map with the sanction of the Controller, Crown Copyright reserved.)

ii: The Northern Exit Road

SUMMARY

The branch-road which led from the north gate of the fort through its adjacent civil settlement to the main Roman road junction near the Cathedral followed the same line for over 300 years. During that time it was repaired regularly. Indeed, one of the most striking features of the site is the depth of road metalling, over 1.50 m. in all. The metalling was of gravel, crushed to a smooth surface by passing traffic. Each surface, varying from 5 cm. to 25 cm. in thickness, was peeled off separately by the excavators in the hope of finding material to date the various resurfacings—and there were at least ten involved. The build-up of layers alongside the road on the sidewalks and where wattle-and-daub buildings had been flattened and rebuilt kept pace with the rise in road level. It was noticeable, however, that the later road surfaces were considerably wider than the lower spreads of gravel. The uppermost surviving patches of road were examined carefully, in case they might throw light on traffic conditions in the final years of the Roman presence. While the last surface was almost 5 cm. above *modern street level outside, nineteenth-century builders had quarried most of the upper gravel away.*

THE EXIT ROAD from the north gate of the fort is described first in this report because its layout formed the axis for all subsequent buildings developed within the excavated area of the *vicus* and the northern defences. The existence of such a road in this position could be postulated once the north gate of the fort had been located during the 1950s (see p.18). The gateway was located one-third of the length of the fort from the north-eastern corner, thus determining the position of the *via principalis* and the identification of the gate as the *porta principalis sinistra*. Externally the alignment of the *via principalis* could then be projected outside the fort beneath the demolished remains of Manor Street (currently a vehicle compound), across Bridgewater Street and into the excavated area either side of White Lion Street. The overall bearing of the road's alignment ran predictably, north-east at an angle of 40°. When preparatory work began in February 1972, prior to the main summer excavation, priority was given to confirming the presence of the road in the derelict area on the south side of White Lion Street, i.e. the south-eastern corner of the eventual excavation site (=T.1). Preference was given to examining this area rather than that to the north of White Lion Street because only here was it possible to confirm the presence of buildings both east and west of the presumed exit road. In the event, the trial excavation exceeded all expectations. It was re-excavated in the summer's operations but retained its code number, MCP 1 (=Manchester preparatory trench 1), within the later excavations.

The key section revealed in its northern face no less than ten separate road surfacings spanning the period from the Flavian foundation to the fourth century (see further p.39). On the western side, late Georgian and Victorian cellars had carried away the bulk of the evidence relating to the Roman levels. To the east, however, there emerged a sequence of stratigraphy indicating the presence of timber buildings that extended in an undisturbed state to a height of 5 cm. *above* the present road level of Collier Street (see fig. 7). The earliest road was also the most clearly defined. This was because it was demarcated by two massive side ditches, MCP 1 48a and b. The actual width of the primary road was some 3.95 m. with two side ditches adding a further 1.40 m. and 0.90 m. to west and east respectively. The depth of the main ditch (0.90 m. approx.) on the western side shows that it probably served both defensive as well as drainage purposes, as one assumes was the case with rather similar arrangements outside the Roman fort at Hod Hill.[1] The road itself (46) was made up of one homogeneous dump of river pebble to a depth of 0.45 m. There was little or no differentiation between heavy and light stone in the road make-up which was set directly on the old turf-line. No ruts were available in the surface at this point although they were clear in the section further to the north (p. 37). On the eastern side of the main ditch a thin gravel spread continued for a further 1.50 m. At the point where the section was cut the northern face showed evidence of a discontinuous feature representing the sump of a stake-hole (29) infilled with a wash of gravel detritus. This isolated feature did not re-appear in the section and might best be taken to represent the remains of a defensive palisade guarding the eastern flank of the approach road to the fort, as was recently found outside the northern entrance to the auxiliary fort at Pumpsaint in Carmarthenshire. As figs. 7,10 show, the stratigraphy makes it impossible to associate stake-hole 29 with the earliest timber buildings to the east of the road. That feature (construction trench 10) is stratigraphically linked with the third road dump, as we shall see. In chronological sequence, however, the next development shown in the section in fact represented a straightforward and limited refurbishing of the exit road. On top of the modest accumulation of loose cobbles (45) a thin layer of metalling (44) was dumped to form a wedge with its thinner end to the east. On the western side, this had the effect of thinning the side ditch with detritus to a depth of 30–35 cm. (45). By this stage, in fact, the detritus in the western ditch had already reached a depth of nearly 40 cm. On the eastern side the re-surfacing showed quite clearly from its thinness that it was not designed to cross the side ditch. By the time of the third re-surfacing (42), however, this was clearly not the case. The eastern ditch had been partly filled with an unstable mass of cobbling (47) and the road was expanded eastwards by a solid dump of material (25) cut by later construction trench (23) but continuing eastward as dumps (15) and (16) to a maximum extent of 3 m. beyond the edge of the previous ditch. It was with this phase that the earliest building detected in the section was associated. It took the form of a forward construction trench (10) filled with daub (9) to a width of some 30 cm. and lying 1 m. east of the actual road edge. This feature represents the principal remains of what was designated Building H, the interior of which was indicated by a general daub-and-charcoal spread to the east up to the line of Collier Street. The construction of this building, unfortunately detected over so limited an area through reasons of space, has clear historical connotations. Like Building A, it represents the first intrusion of civilian building subsequent to the infilling and abandonment of the outer northern defences. The fuller evidence from elsewhere (discussed on pp. 45 and 49) does not require amplification here. The evidence for the construction of Building H and its stratigraphic link with the third road surface of the exit road tallies with the infilling of the outer defences and some late Flavian-Trajanic pottery including a plain samian form 27 gave a general indication of the date of this new development in accord with evidence found to the west of the exit road. The life-span of Building H was sufficiently long to allow the accumulation of a second layer of metalling (15 and 25b) on the eastern side of the road. These two cobble levels had been cut away by the principal feature associated with the next phase on the site. This was signified by a deep construction trench (28) cutting down through road surfaces at this point (i.e. 14, 15, 16, 25a, 25b and 27), and associated with occupation layer (8) that could be traced eastwards over construction trench (10) and its super-incumbent charcoal-and-daub debris (9). No other elements in this building, hereafter designated Building I, were located in the section, although an internal wall later emerged in plan. In terms of plan, trench 28 formed the front building line for the substantial structure other elements of which were located both in the southern side of MCP 1, and further north, in T.1 (see further, pp. 37 and 63). The effects of the introduction of civilian buildings were thus to broaden the exit road very considerably at this point. Instead of a military road 3.5 m. wide we can see that in the first half of the second century and perhaps in the first quarter (p. 65), the accretion of *vicus* buildings along the eastern edge of the road had the effect of broadening it to over 6.50 m. in width. This permanently displaced the centre-line of the road to the east and all subsequent re-surfacings confirm the tendency for the road centre to shift further to the east until in its final phase, represented by level (31), the road centre was actually east of the original military ditch. It was clear, however, that in the early years of the second century the original eastern military ditch was still causing problems of subsidence. During the life-span of Building I, as represented by construction trench (28), a deliberate effort was made to fill and consolidate it adequately. The tendency of the old ditch-line to act as a drainage sump clearly made the dump forming the upper ditch fill (47) unstable. With the development of Building I on the site, however, a more successful attempt was made to consolidate the road surface, this took the form of dumped metalling (41) laid across the subsidence line of the ditch and westwards on to the top of the preceding surface (42). Building I was directly associated with this building level and with the next road surfacing (39) which represented a complete re-metalling of the road over 6 m. in width. The features representing Building I were threefold. The internal floor area was marked by floor (7) which terminated 1.40 m. from the edge of the trench in construction trench (7a). As recovered in plan, the trench turned through a right-angle within the floor area of the original section (fig. 22), thus aligning the building frontage parallel to the exit road. 1.6 m. west of this construction trench, a depression containing charcoal and daub (7b) marked the line of another construction trench associated with this building and cut at a very acute angle by the excavation trench. The area in question was disrupted by construction trench (11) associated with the succeeding building (J). This was the clearest of all the structures associated with the road. A clay floor (5 and 5a) was traced for 3.25 m. away from the construction trench towards Collier Street. The lifetime of the building coincided with the development of road surface (36) which did not directly succeed road level (39) because additional dumping had taken place on the western side of the street surface (37). Although 30 cm. thick on the western side, the passage of traffic appears to have worn the road metalling (36) down to a very thin surface to the east, this explains the restricted dumping (34), (35), (33) that probably belonged to the period when the full structure associated with construction trench 11 was still in existence. Indeed a much more substantial surface, at least 3.50 m. wide (32) may also belong to this phase of the site's existence. Yet road level 32 was cut at its eastern edge by the construction trench of another building, and, although little of that building survived in recognisable form in the section, it was associated with the last defined level, namely road surface 31. Disturbance from the nineteenth-century developments on the western side meant that the surviving width of the road was no more than 3.60 m. It ran directly across to construction trench 17 and the floor of the associated building comprised the dirty mix of occupation soil (3) that terminated in its upper surface with a gravel tread forming the interior of the actual building. Above level 3 there then occurred a further 40 cm. of occupation soil but in the section, no significant occupation level could be detected, a matter of regret, as some of the latest pottery from the site was derived from the equivalent levels of the road in the next section to the north (see further p. 39). In fact the dating evidence from this section was disappointing except for its confirmation of the starting point for the *vicus* buildings in the late Flavian/Trajanic period, as previously explained. Pottery from the other levels merely confirmed the life-span of the buildings as lying within the second and early third centuries. Before describing the dating evidence further we must, however, examine the reverse side of the section MCP 1 as it was revealed in the summer excavations of 1972.

Despite disturbance to the west the original road level (46) had survived to a width of 4.2 m. between side ditches before falling away rapidly into the eastern ditch sump measuring some 1.3 m. wide by at least 45 cm. deep (fig. 10). The western ditch was 1.3 m. in width by 0.5 m. deep. Although subsequent road surfaces partly

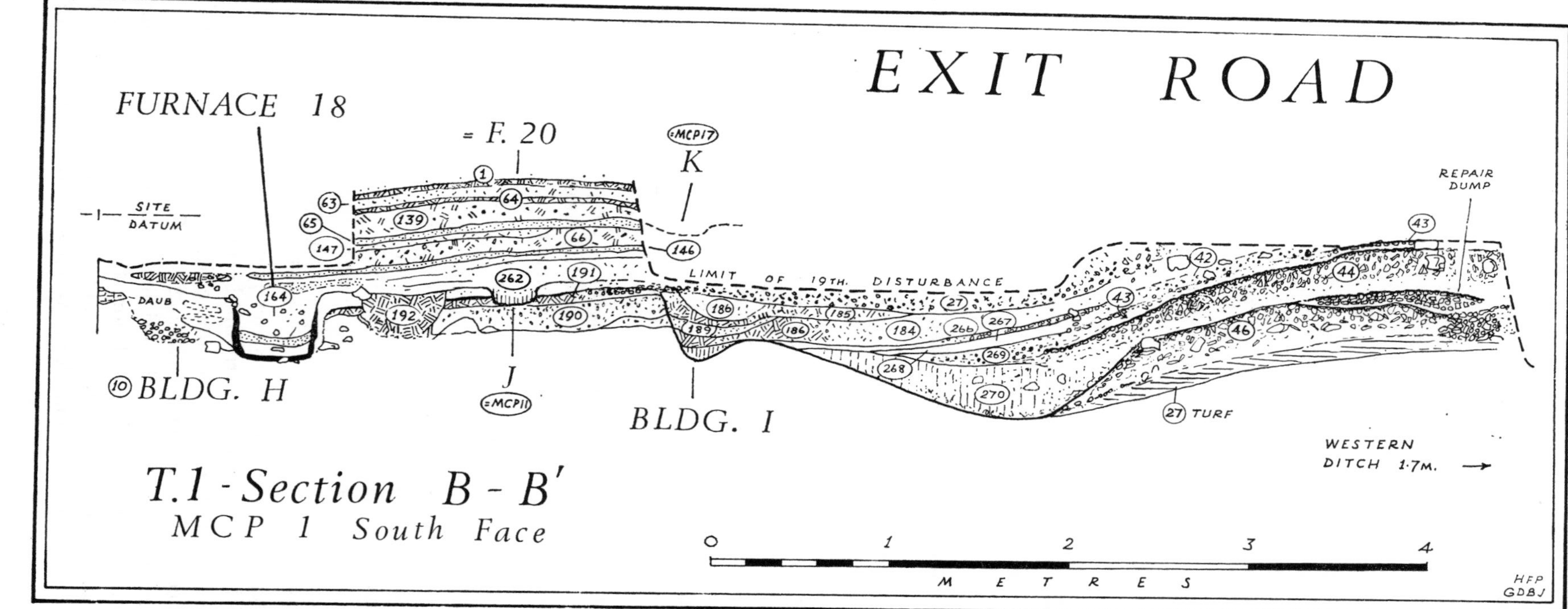

Fig. 10. MCP, south section.

obliterated the eastern ditch it was clear from the diminishing width of the road that the amount of lateral expansion was diminishing as the actual metal surfaces approached the passage through the internal defences only a matter of metres away to the south. The original road dump was some 25 cm. thick. Its successor (44) was slightly thinner (*c.* 20 cm.) but extended half-way across the ditch. Its gravel detritus (269) went a long way towards filling up the area of subsidence over the ditch line. This trend was completed by the remains of the next surface (42), the thickness of which could not be established owing to nineteenth-century disturbance. The effect of the late Georgian wall foundation in question was unfortunately to remove precise stratigraphic correlation between the middle and upper levels of the road and those to the east (see fig. 10). None the less, it was possible to establish the relationship between the early phases on both sides of the section. On the southern side, the primary building (H) appeared as a construction trench immediately east of the disturbance caused by Furnace 18 and this early phase may be associated with the build-up marked by level 190. This level was cut away by the front construction trench for Building I. Again, it was a deep sump formed by layer 186 over the packing of 189a, b, c, in the post-trench proper. The associated internal floor was represented by a thin spread (191) running eastwards until interrupted by a charcoal and clay bowl formed by 192 and the actual bowl of Furnace 2. On the north side of the section, as already described, road level 36 was associated with the next building phase (J). The same relationship was demonstrable on the south side of the trench. Road level 27 represented a considerable broadening of the actual metalled surface to cover the forward construction trench of Building I and continue for a further 60 cm. to the east. This point represented the line along which construction trench 262 was identified, the equivalent of MCP construction trench 11 and the forward edge of Building J. Its front line was traced to the south, as discussed on p. 63, and Furnace 18 is assignable to this period of building. The subsequent build-up, levels 66, 147, 65, 139 and 64, is paralleled by the less complex stratigraphy, MCP 3 and 4 to the north. They owe their complexity to the presence of the furnaces within Building J. MCP 4 represents the same level as 65 on the south side of the trench. Elements of Building K were, however, hard to identify. The reason for this was because the construction trench (17) forming the frontage of the building ran through to the south at a point where Victorian intrusions had destroyed the evidence in part. Beyond the section edge, however, construction trench 116 may be identified with MCP 17 and thus this building taken to include Furnace 20 which belongs to the highest surviving intact stratigraphy on the site excluding the latest road surfaces, to which we may now turn. Further information about the building plans is set out on p. 63.

Five metres north of the original trial examination of the exit road (which was, in part, mechanically cut) the opportunity was taken for a further examination of the road development (fig. 8, pl. 11). Accordingly, a metre-wide trench was opened across the width of the road at a point where for reasons of space it could not be related to associated buildings to the east. The lateral ditch in fact lay beyond the excavated area under the western edge of Collier Street. The western edge, however, was partly visible although over half of it had been removed by the intrusion of a nineteenth-century sewer trench. In general, the road at this point was more compact than in the section to the south. This made the archaeological examination rather simpler in that it was principally concerned with extrapolating the development within the road build-up. The sequence is here described in downward order. The latest surviving surface (Road VI), and one that remarkably enough stood to 5 cm. above the present level of Collier Street, was formed by a thin band of metalling some 4 cm. across (8). The eastern edge of the road dropped off towards a broad, shallow ditch (29) that survived beneath the superincumbent levels of the houses built in 1825–6. The uppermost surface of the underlying road (Road V) had broken

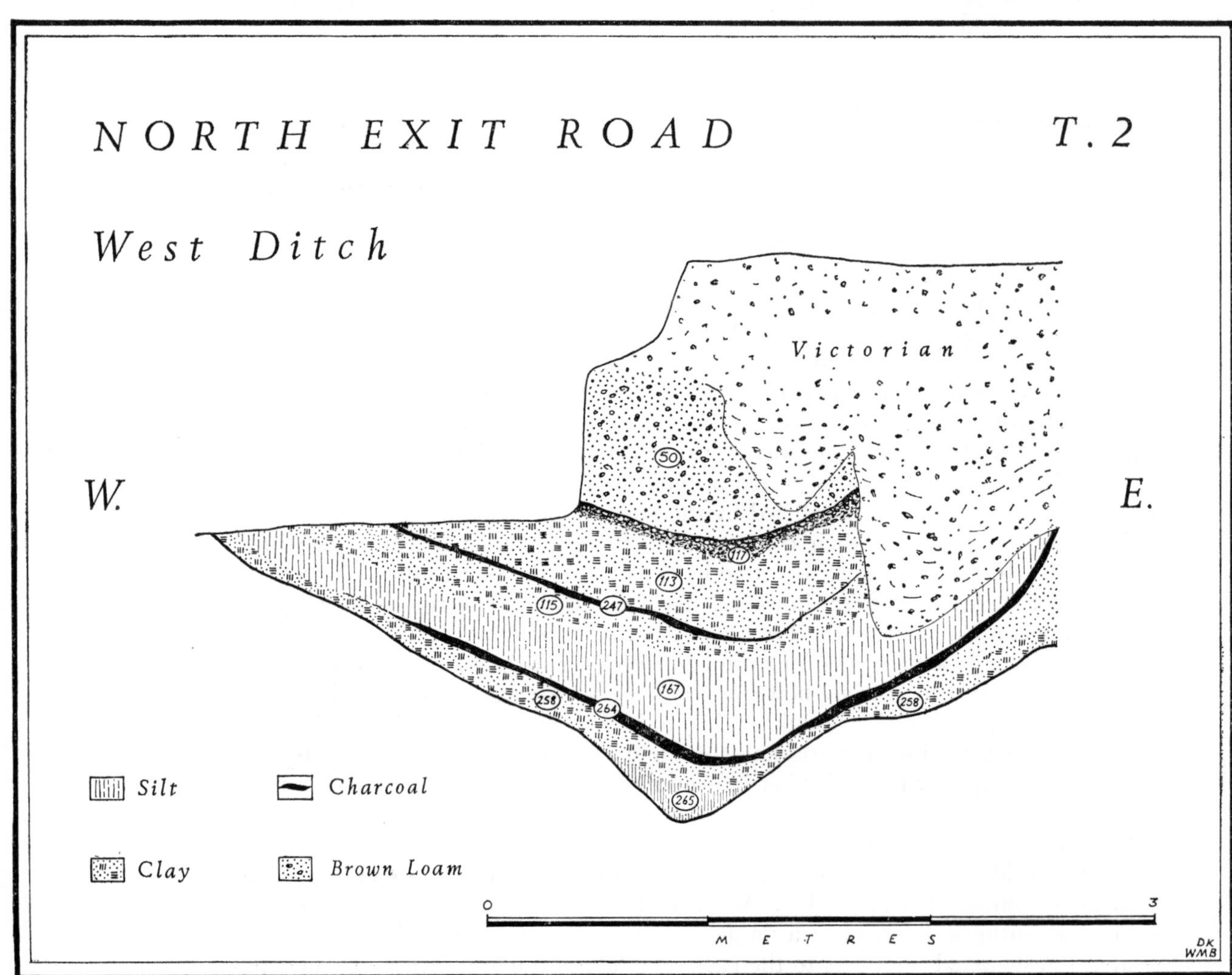

Fig. 11. Western road ditch, T2, section E–E.

up to some extent and the core of the metalling was first identified as level 6, surviving for a width of some 3.2 m. before giving way on the eastern side to a series of massive flagstones (505) forming the edge of kerbing (529) running alongside the associated ditch (502). Road IV, preceding the penultimate phase, was preserved to a somewhat smaller width 2.85 m. across. It comprised a rammed gravel pack 4–5 cm. thick (35) flanked to the east by a patch of sandstone blocks resting on the road surface (503). The bulk of the level (35) was comprised of closely-packed small pebbles that at one point (see fig. 8) showed evidence of a north–south rut. As in previous examples, the surface of the road had broken up under the pressure of passing traffic to form a supervening layer (503). The ditch was not well-defined and appears to have repeated the pattern of the road surface above with a kerb (552) flanking an associated ditch (551) that was associated with a major construction trench (28) belonging to the front wall of Building I. Along the same lines a cobble layer (512) formed the broken top-surface of the core of Road III from the top, namely level 513. This narrower band of metalling, some 2.8 m. wide and only a few centimetres thick, terminated in a boulder on the eastern side before running down to kerb 553 and its associated ditch 556. The fifth road surface down (Road II) was formed by levels 514 and 515, a massive cobble dump over 20 cm. wide at its thickest and dropping gently towards a shallow ditch on the eastern side. A 10-cm. silty agglomeration (545) intervened before the earliest levels. This may have been a way of building a road foundation because in the east-central section of the road a separate surface existed some 10–15 cm. thick (544). On the western side two thin layers of cobbling also represented early repairs. The earliest surface (Road I), however, was formed by cobbling (554) which, of course, terminated in the western flanking ditch and ran across the section for a total width of 4.8 m. towards the edge of the excavation area. The eastern flanking ditch lay beyond the trench but a rut, some 10–11 cm. wide, was very clearly preserved in this original surface 1 m. from the eastern edge of the road (see pl. 11b). The whole surface like those of the early roads in the sequence was heavily stained a reddish-orange tinge with oxidised patches. This feature no doubt related to the way in which rain-water percolated down into the road metalling from above.

The road sequence described above was more informative in general chronological terms than that uncovered in the initial trial trench (MCP). The six road levels all produced finds of pottery that do give some indication of the overall rate of development. The pottery evidence is set out on p. 111. From it it will be seen that after the initial Flavian foundation the build-up of metalling must have progressed at a fast rate. The third road surface contained material of later first and early second century date (no. 184, p.111). Naturally, a road surface like this is likely to be the context in which there is much rubbish survival but it is significant that all the material from Road IV above (i.e., levels, 35, 503, 551 of pottery, nos. 185–90, p.111) is uniformly pre-Hadrianic in character. Through the association with construction trench 28 this is important evidence for the date of Building I which probably, therefore, belongs to the second quarter of the second century (p. 65). Also of interest is the material nos. 192–196 (p. 111) associated with the penultimate phase. The important piece from a chronological standpoint is no. 194, a fragment in black calcite-gritted fabric of Gillam type 163 and belonging to the latter half of the fourth century. This undoubtedly promotes the idea that after a speedy agglomeration of road metalling into the mid-second century, occupation of the fort subsided and that there was relatively little occupation in the third century. On the other hand, the presence of this crucial pottery fragment from the drain linked with the penultimate road surface (V) shows that at least one road level (VI) can be ascribed to the period after the Pictish revolt. Thus this isolated patch of late stratified evidence can be correlated in a sense with the random, but positive, coin evidence of fourth-century occupation from within the fort area (p. 137). Due to the effects of post-Roman ploughing, however, it unfortunately was impossible to correlate these final levels with associated timber structures to the west (see further p. 59).

One further element of the northern exit road was located in T.2. This was the western side ditch examined in the east-west section at a point along the central axis of T.2 (fig. 11). The position prevented location of any part of the actual core of the exit road. As readers will find argued on p. 45, in origin this side ditch probably played a role both in defence and in drainage. The narrow sump of the original military phase side ditch was still preserved as a silty clay fill 265 and 258 cutting into natural sand 120 (fig. 11). Naturally, water action and alterations in the road to the east caused the ditch to be broadened enormously to some 3.70 m. across. The bulk of this was filled by a silty clay mixture (167) in which relatively little road gravel had accumulated. This meant that the road at this distance from the fort had either narrowed down considerably or expanded to the east rather than both to the east and west. Above the various infillings 115, 247, 113 overlying the main infill (167) only one road surface was located. This was represented by a narrow strip of metalling (117) some 6–7 cm. in thickness, that must have run down from one of the later phases of repairs to the exit road. Thus late in the life of the ditch, at a time when it was silted and its contents relatively solidified, the exit road had been expanded towards the west in such a way as to leave a metal surface overlying part of the ditch. But this development was not repeated. No further indication of road surfacing was found in layer 50, the post-Roman plough disturbance that lay directly beneath the nineteenth-century building levels.

NOTE

1 I. A. Richmond, *Hod Hill II* (1968), fig. 68, cf. pp. 2, 66; for a similar arrangement see I. A. Richmond and P. Corder (ed. M. Todd), *The Roman Fort at Great Casterton* (1968), fig. 2, p. 2.

iii: The Early Military Defences

SUMMARY

Following the results of the excavation from the lowest levels upwards it became clear that the Roman settlement in the area was built on a virgin site. There is therefore nothing from the excavations to support the idea of a prehistoric origin for Manchester. All over the four huge trenches into which the area was divided the earliest Roman levels dating from c. *A.D. 77–78 were laid directly on to the original turf overlying the sandstone beds of the subsoil. The overall layout of the site throughout its history was controlled by the alignment of the Roman road leading north-eastwards away from the rampart of the fort. In its earliest phase the road comprised a heavy cobble dump flanked by two side ditches. The road will, of course, have run out from the north-eastern gateway past the defensive ditches protecting the rampart. These are known to be at least two in number on this side but one of the most important results of the earliest period lay in the discovery of a short-lived outlying system close to the line of Liverpool Road. The double-ditch system involved ran parallel to the system closer to the fort before curving inwards to join the side ditch of the exit road. Equally important perhaps was the discovery of another ditch running off to the north from the more northerly of the two ditches already described. It was flanked to the west by a palisade trench and its alignment must have carried the feature across Liverpool Road and underneath the present City Exhibition Hall. The likeliest interpretation is that the feature represented the palisaded defence associated with a baggage park or similar feature associated with the first days of the fort's life. Certainly its topographical position would make sense in this context where protection was provided on the flank by the course of the River Irwell to the west. The outer ditch system did not enjoy a very long life. Within a few years the ditches were deliberately backfilled, partly with earth and partly with demolition debris from timber buildings. The latter was probably derived from the first renewal of timber buildings in the interior of the fort. Cartloads of wattle, daub and other debris were jettisoned in the ditches and yielded a valuable deposit of pottery from the late first century A.D. The reason for the infilling of the ditches was probably connected with the development of the first stages of the civil* vicus *in this area, because the intervening area between the discarded ditches and those close in to the fort was next given over to a series of timber buildings.*

ALL THE AVAILABLE evidence from the Deansgate site suggests that the Romans occupied a virgin site for the construction of their fort. Evidence of the original turf line was encountered in all four trenches and was clearly sealed beneath Building A (p. 49). More important in the present context, it was cut by a series of ditches that formed the outer defences of the fort in the late first century A.D. These defences were probably abandoned early in the second century, if not earlier, when for the first time civilian structures invaded the immediate perimeter of the fort, taking over the space between the outer and inner ditch systems. Before that happened, however, the outer defences formed the basis for a previously unsuspected defended enclosure. A length of palisaded ditch located in 1972 ran north across Liverpool Road underneath the Exhibition Hall in a way that suggested the presence of a baggage compound or a defended annexe extending towards the River Irwell to the north-northwest of the site. The evidence for these features fell entirely within the area of Trenches 2 and 3.

The outer ditch system was initially located most clearly in Trench 3 where the evidence was first recognised as two broad lines of grey clay and loam (143 and 148 respectively) running diagonally across the trench (pl. 6b). The contents represented deliberate backfilling of the two primary ditch systems of which the more northerly (143) was the better preserved at this point. In plan the ditches are shown in fig. 12 while their section in the eastern face of T.3 appears in fig. 13; plate 6b shows the appearance of the two main ditches prior to the removal of the clay and loam filling.

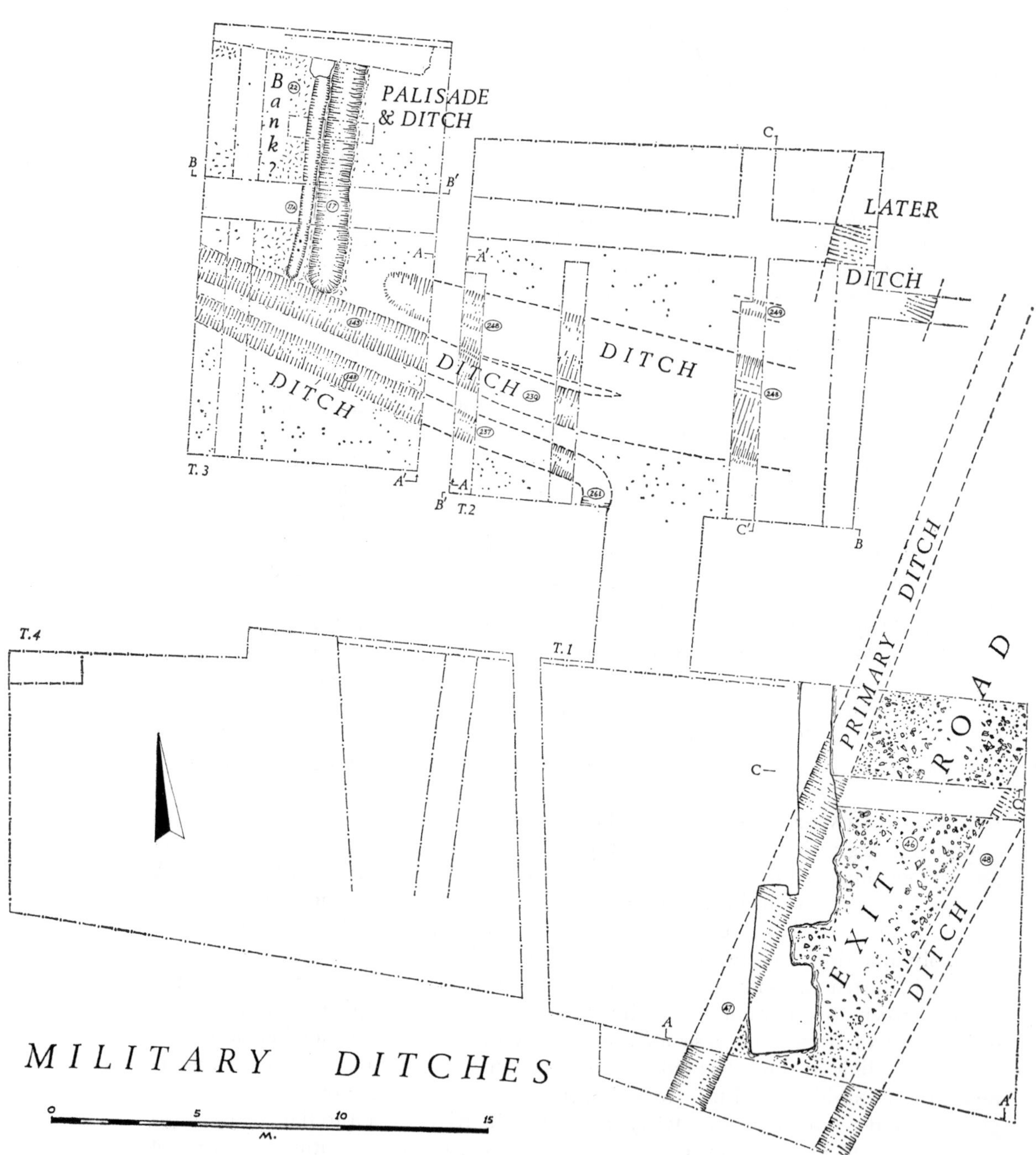

Fig. 12. Military ditch plan.

The ditches were cut directly into the natural sandy subsoil and after clearance one (143) revealed a steep V-shaped profile characteristic of the 'anklebreaker' ditch sump familiar from many military sites throughout Britain (pl. 7b). The southern ditch (148) had a rather more U-shaped profile and, so far as it was preserved, had a narrower section (*c.* 2.15 m.) than the former which was 2.35 m. wide. In section the area to the north of ditch 143 presented certain problems of interpretation in that the old ground level fell away in a rather ill-defined shallow bowl, rising gradually towards the north. Apart from some streaks of daub (143a, 143b) the filling remained the same as that in the two well-defined ditches to the south. It was apparent, therefore, that the subsoil had been cut away deliberately but the process did not become completely clear until further work in both Trench 3 and Trench 2 had clarified the issue. In Trench 3 the discovery of another ditch system hinging on the main ditch (143) and running almost at right-angles away from it underneath Liverpool Road strongly suggested the existence of an annexe at this point. At the same time in Trench 2 a section along the western baulk of the trench showed that the problematical sump in T.3 had by that stage become what was clearly the remains of the third ditch. It is to the continuation of the ditches in T.2 that we may now turn.

As stated, the section along the western edge of the baulk produced conclusive evidence for the presence of a third ditch in the system. This was confirmed by the two further sections towards the east. First, however, to deal with the evidence from the western side of the baulk (fig. 14). The features proved very similar to those already described, with evidence for a third ditch (248). Again the continuation of the central ditch (T.3 143 = T.2 230) proved to be the best defined ditch sump; it had been truncated in part during the backfilling process that had dumped a mass of clay and loam (235/233) over the whole ditch system. The sump of the southern ditch was in this case rather better defined with a V-shaped bottom (237) containing silted material (231) that continued to be sealed by the same mix (235) as the other ditches. As the approach of these ditches to the main exit road from the fort was of potential great importance two further sections were cut in the floor of the trench. The first of these lay 3.50 m. further to the east; again, it showed the same sequence of triple ditches (namely 248, 230 and 237) from north to south respectively. These were again sealed by a homogeneous filling (231) very similar to that already described and consequently given the same number (231). There was, however, by this stage evidence for a change in the alignment of the ditches on to a more north-easterly course. The southern ditch did not, however, re-appear in the third and final section 6 m. further to the east. Clearly, therefore, it must have either stopped altogether, joined the central ditch or turned away to the south. That the last hypothesis was correct appeared from the evidence contained in the southern section along the edge of T.2 (fig. 15). 4.70 m. from the south-western corner of the trench the line of the V-shaped sump appeared running roughly southwards out of the trench and beneath the line of White Lion Street. Its sump (261) sealed by the same homogeneous filling as the other examples (235) left no doubt that the ditch formed part of the same defensive system. Although time prevented the complete clearance of the presumed corner area the evidence suggested that it turned south for a few metres in much the same way as the corner of the ditch system at Hod Hill at the point where it comes in contact with the exit road from the fort.[1] In the Manchester case, however, there was no evidence to suggest that the ditch continued southwards for more than a few metres, as it was not observed in either T.1 or T.4. The onwards course of the other two ditches was only guaranteed in one instance. The third and final section (fig. 16) was cut, as already stated, 6.50 m. to the east; it showed that the central ditch had also ceased to exist by that point and that the major obstacle was presented by the northernmost ditch of the three so far described. The sump could clearly be seen (248) and its upper section (267, 263, 266, all variations on a grey clay and loam fill)

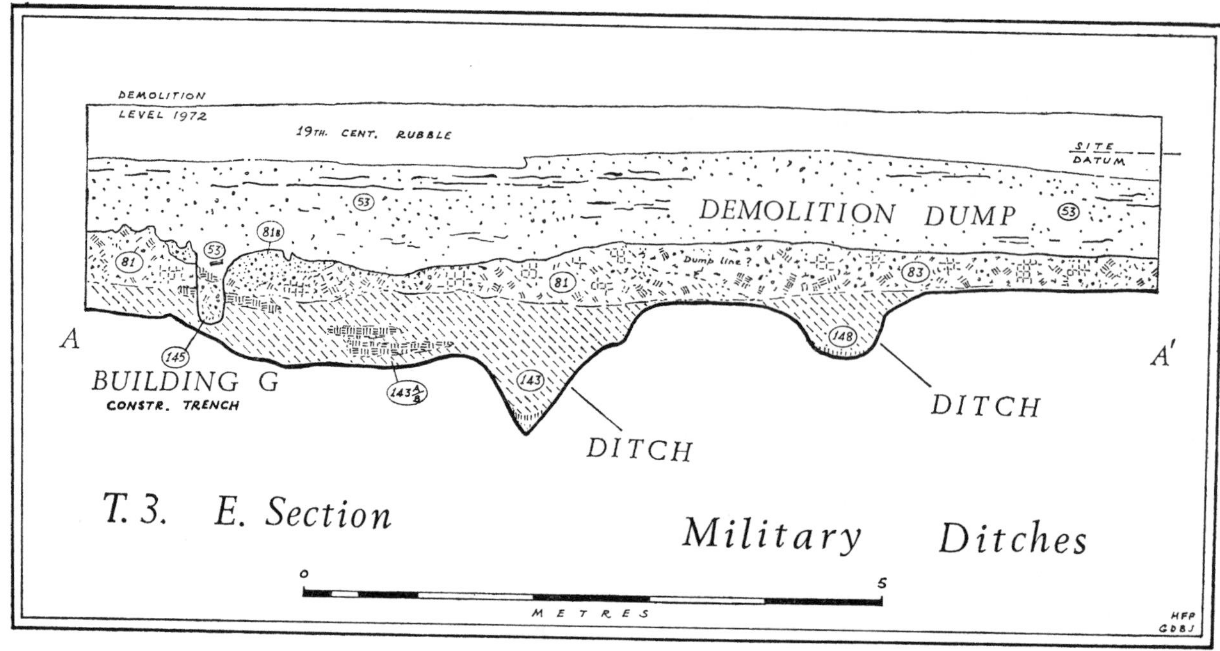

Fig. 13. Ditch section A–A[1], Trench 3, east face.

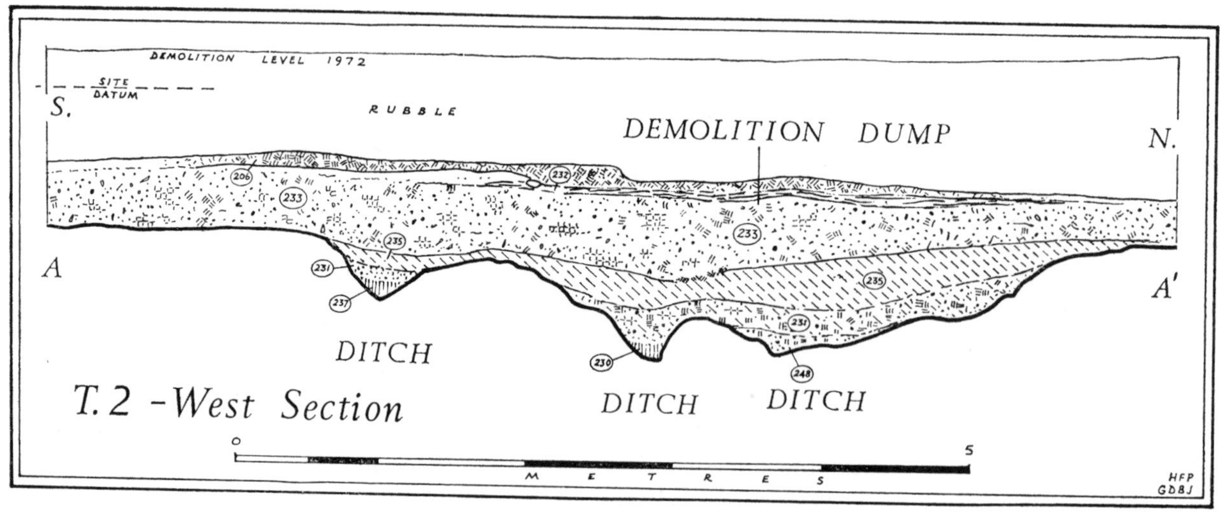

Fig. 14. Ditch section A–A[1], Trench 2, west face.

extended to such a width (5.90 m.) as to suggest that at this point the central ditch had swung into its northern neighbour in that conjunction of ditches which is becoming an increasing diagnostic of the Flavian period. The additional feature of interest was provided by the evidence for a small outer ditch (249) on the north side of the main pattern; again the sump was small, measuring 1.45 m. across, so far as its profile had survived but its place in the structural sequence was guaranteed by its being sealed beneath T.2 260, the same mixture of clay and loam that typified the deliberate infill and the levelling-up that followed the abandonment of the entire ditch system across T.2 and T.3. Further east the point of junction with the major ditch system running alongside the exit road from the fort thus shown in fig. 12 was not informative so far as the early period was concerned. The ditch must have doubled as a drain in function and consequent widening and erosion of the sides have robbed it of any value from the early chronological point of view.

The dating of the outer ditch system was, however, of crucial importance in establishing changes in the layout of the *vicus* in this area. Unfortunately, samian material from the backfill was entirely lacking except for one fragment of a Flavian form 27 from T.3 143. The sections in T.2, however, were more productive of coarse wares (p. 95). Two of the sumps (168 and 262) possessed fragments from the late first/early second century. More informative perhaps was the material from the seal itself that formed an almost uniform layer above the ditch sumps. It had clearly been derived from the demolition of timber buildings presumably within the fort itself. Daub and charcoal derived from wattle could be observed in many places particularly in the eastern section of T.2 260 and 262. The first of these produced eleven sherds that seemed to be of uniform pre-Hadrianic date and the internal fort building from which they presumably derived must fall within the period of the late first to early second century (p. 95). This pottery, therefore, formed the evidence for the date of the first major adjustment to the layout of the Roman site at the point where the *vicus* touched the fort defences. It is impossible not to conceive of the massive backfilling and levelling process employed across T.2 and T.3 as a deliberate act of policy by the commander of the fort. It implied the deliberate abandonment of the outer defensive system and the encouragement of civil buildings that ran across the backfill, as we shall see, and also occupied the hitherto untouched area between the outer and inner defensive sytems.

Before we turn to this phase of the site's history, however, we must examine one further feature of the early defences. As already stated, this was the evidence for an annexe running away from the outer ditch system in T.3 underneath Liverpool Road and presumably the City Exhibition Hall where its course may be located in future years. The position of the ditch in relation to an associated palisade slot made it clear that the projected area lay to the northwest towards the Irwell away from the Deansgate zone. The ditch is shown in pl. 8a.

The ditch in question first appeared in the east-west section cut along the line of a drain trench in T.3. While the deep sump (17) became obvious from this clearance work, the associated palisade slot (17a) to the west did not become clear until area excavation had proceeded for some time and superincumbent features such as the furnace at the northern tip of the trench (135), and the construction trench of a substantial timber building (145), had been removed. It then became clear that the sump of the ditch at its uppermost reconstructable profile was 1.20 m. in width with a deep U-shaped sump that gave it a depth of at least 1.10 m. Parallel to the inner lip of the ditch and 25–30 cm. from it, there lay a trough-like cut in the subsoil varying between 20 and 25 cm. across by approximately 25–30 cm. in depth. This, like its associated ditch, ran for approximately 7.50 m. to the junction with the central of the three defensive ditches. The curved end of both ditch and trench left no doubt that the features must be taken as sharing an integrated layout. The central portion of the ditch had, of course, been carried away by the Victorian sewer. Further to the

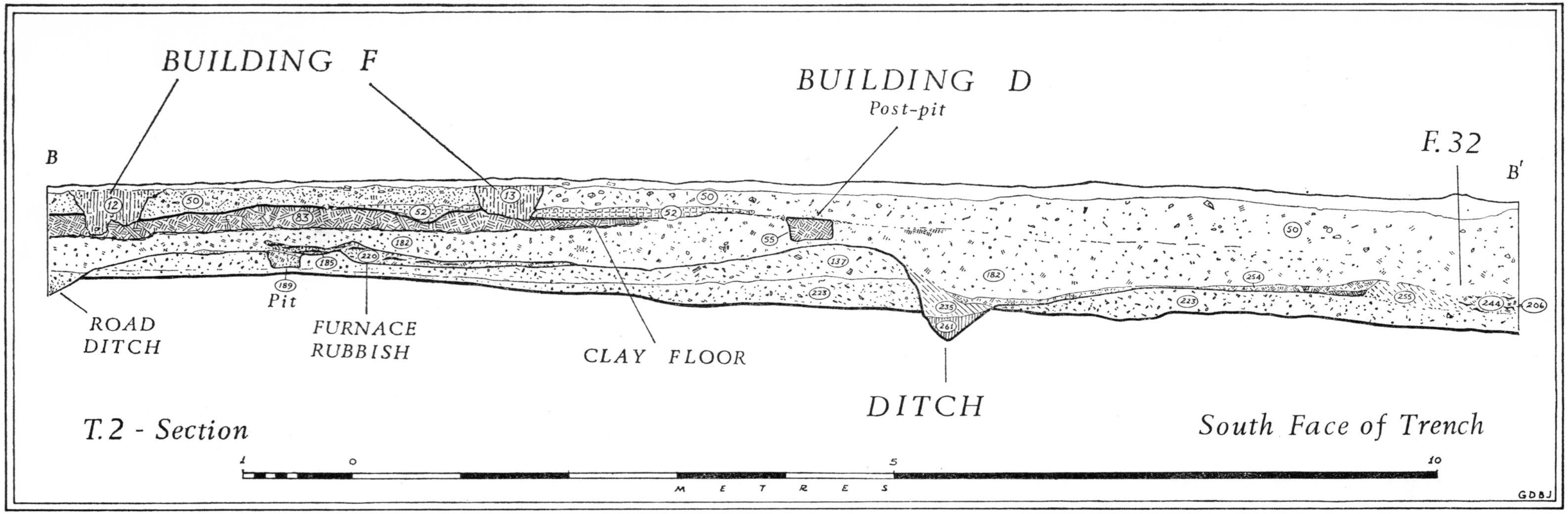

Fig. 15. T.2, south section.

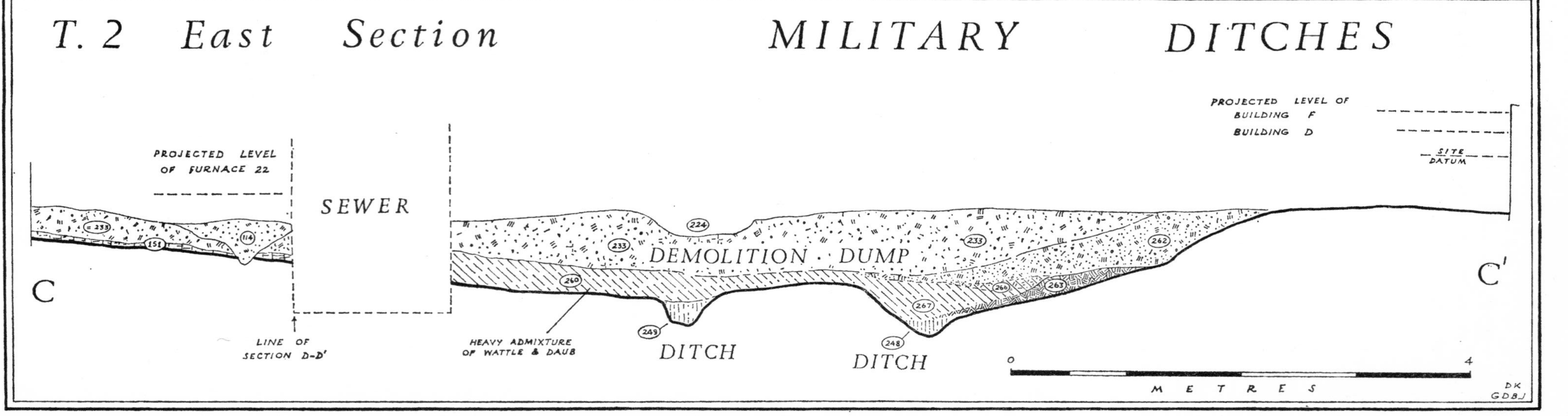

Fig. 16. T.2, east section.

north it had been considerably damaged by workings associated with the furnace features that characterised this trench in the second century. The function of the small trench was only clearly demonstrated by that portion of it that survived south of the sewer line. There, as shown in plate 8b, its bottom contained the remains of small posts set, to judge from the two surviving examples, approximately 1.25 m. apart; the effect was not that of a posthole as no chockstones were apparent but rather the impression left by stakes a few centimetres across driven into the floor of the slot. A precisely similar feature in structural terms (although with a closer spacing for the stakes) has recently been excavated at the north gate of the Roman fort at Pumpsaint[2] in South Wales. The example from Manchester seemed to represent the ditch and timber palisade forming an additional defence system, probably relating to an external annexe. In structural terms it has parallels on a larger scale in the construction trench before the toe of the earth-and-timber rampart of the legionary fortress at Lincoln.[3] Its interest here lay in the recognition of a feature of the early defensive networks beneath the mass of later occupation. Normally such features have only been recognised when the remains form upstanding features on the more remote sites of the Highland zone.

NOTES

1 See p. 40n.
2 *The Carmarthen Antiquary*, forthcoming.
3 *Journal of Roman Studies* XXXIX (1949), 57ff.; XLVI (1956), 22, fig.3.

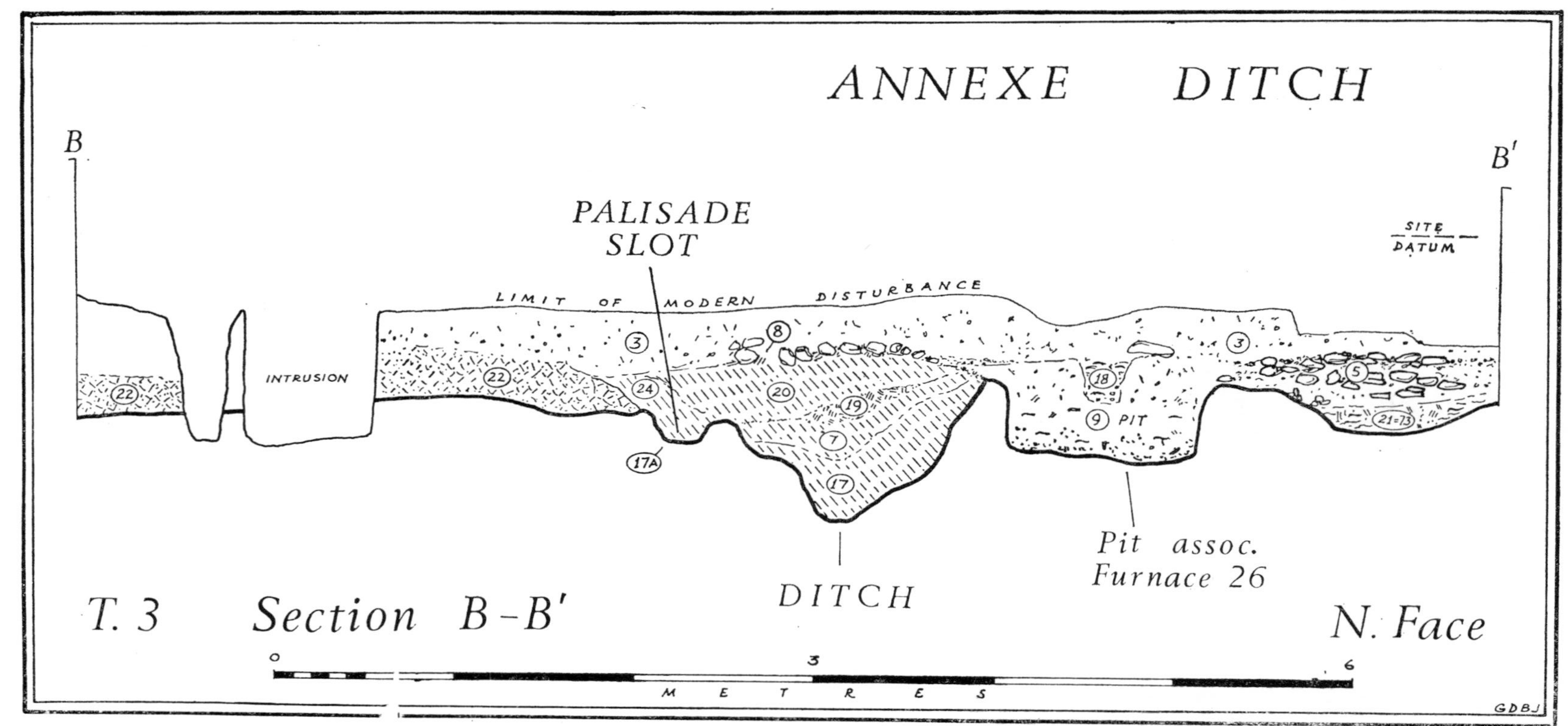

Fig. 18. Section through annexe ditch and palisade trench T.3.

iv: Buildings West of the Exit Road

(a) The Early Buildings

SUMMARY

The main road, as shown by the general plan, passed through the eastern part of the 1972 site, leaving only a small area in the far south-east corner where structures could be found. On its western side, however, trenches revealed a spread of later Roman buildings adjacent to the road, and still further west, open spaces which must have been backyards at this period. The first of these buildings (Building A), which due to subsequent Roman interference was not fully recovered in plan, was apparently a roughly square structure (8 m. × 8 m.) laid out on the western side of the exit road. As one might expect, its character was made clear by the set of gaming counters and knucklebones recovered from the debris of its floor. It was the first resort of troops outside the fort and the quantity of glass found in the building testifies to the availability of drink on the premises. The structure had a short life. Perhaps profits were high enough to allow its rapid replacement! The next structure was a more elongated building, 5m. by at least 6 m. (Building B), the front portion of which abutted more directly on to the exit road from the fort. It was more substantially constructed than its predecessor, particularly along the front, where a series of postholes were preserved in the clay-packed construction trench of its front wall. The two early buildings to the south were both later in date than Building A. They formed the remains of an open-sided shed (Building C i/ii) that was renewed along almost identical lines on a further occasion. The shed was open to catch the draught of the prevailing south-westerly wind and the individual bays contained a bewildering series of often renewed furnaces associated with metal fabrication. These in fact form the antecedents of the much larger furnaces that came to form so distinctive a feature of the site in its later phases. Across the exit road to the east, a further array of early building frontages was uncovered. Limitations of space, however, prevented extensive recovery of any of the buildings concerned in plan.

THE WESTERN SIDE of the northern exit road from the fort was lined by a series of timber structures the plans of which were recovered from the less disturbed areas of T.1. The line of the major modern sewer trench ensured that much of the stratigraphy linking the various road surfaces westwards towards their associated timber buildings had been destroyed; yet in the event, disturbance from the sewer did not substantially affect the earliest timber buildings located in the area. The situation was further helped by the removal of part of White Lion Street (largely in a successful attempt to unravel the chronological relationship of the two last timber structures in the area). The area beneath the actual road surface was almost entirely undisturbed and so the elements of the earliest buildings found at that point went a long way towards establishing both the chronology and plan of the structures concerned.

As already described, the subsoil of the site is sandy loam above pinkish-brown clay that in turn overlies sandstone beds such as those exposed in the banks of the nearby canal. Within the area concerned, inside Trench 1, the first indication of the Roman presence on the site was formed by a compressed layer of burnt charcoal and turf. This suggests that the surface vegetation between the inner and outer ditch systems had been burned or trampled down in the period of initial military occupation. The first recorded building was constructed directly on top of this burnt layer so far as it could be traced across areas of T.1. When the building (A) was constructed is a chronological problem discussed in detail further on p. 96, but the existence of an outer defensive system makes it unlikely that any such structure could have been in position between the inner and outer ditch systems. It would have affected the fort's field of fire and so can hardly have been allowed at a time when the outer ditches were still in commission. How brief a period this was will never probably be precisely defined from the small amount of datable pottery recovered from positions of stratigraphic importance. Yet the evidence of the preparatory trench (MCP. 1) shows support for the line of argument in that the original exit road does not relate to associated timber buildings. The first indication of lateral structures was linked stratigraphically to the third road surface (see previously, p. 33).

For the moment then we may turn simply to the structural remains and their relative sequence. Building A was of large proportions. It lay set back 1.70 m. from the western edge of the road and probably because of disturbance from later Roman structures built closer to the road kerb the possibility of a colonnade cannot entirely be ruled out, particularly because a furnace (no. 16=T.1.50) had destroyed the front wall to the south. The alignment of the wall, however, was perfectly clear to the north where it was observed in section in a baulk and then ran on past the point where it was bisected by the south wall of Building B (T.1 282) and so on to the trench edge. Quite clearly, therefore, the whole layout of the building was related to the axis formed by the exit road. The construction trench, when best observed, was on average 30 cm. wide and composed of the relatively clean backfill associated with primary trenches. Above and beside the construction trench proper lay areas of daub from the demolition of the walls. The wide section cut across White Lion Street was particularly important in view of the absence of any elements of this building in T.2. The White Lion Street trench (T.1/2) served to locate the main northern wall of the building (16) with hints of an eavesdrip (17) on its outer edge. By projection it was therefore possible to reconstruct the position of the north-eastern corner immediately under the southern edge of White Lion Street (see fig. 17). The position of the north-western corner could also be established by the location of the western or rearward wall in T.4. In constructional terms this formed a similar trench to those located in T.1 and in the last day of the excavation its alignment was further confirmed by the partial removal of the baulk between T.1 and T.4. Over all, the east-west dimensions of the building are 7.60 m. by at least 8.30 m. north-south. The nineteenth-century disturbance to the southern side of the building and indeed to all subsequent remains made it impossible to locate the delimiting wall on the side of the inner defences. Certainly, however, the building reflects a period when space was not at so high a premium as it later became with the intensification of occupation on the edge of the *vicus*.

If the exact plan of the building must remain in doubt, then its character was almost certainly established. Towards the north-eastern corner and close to the inside edge of the eastern wall clearance of the demolition debris uncovered a set of gaming counters made from glass paste in three different colours. Together with them were found a knucklebone and several lumps of quartz (not a local stone) suggesting that a whole set of gaming equipment had been swept aside and lost in the debris when Building A was demolished. The individual items are described in detail in the appropriate specialist reports on pp. 125 and 127. Their discovery strongly helps to identify the character of the building as a hostelry serving the soldiers and occupying the prime position on the immediate northern edge of the fort. Another object found with the gaming equipment begs a further question. It is a fine obsidian ring (probably forming part of a necklace rather than a finger ring) with a spiral inlay of millefiore glass (see further, p. 125). If it is to be associated with women's jewellery, it raises a possibility that the building served a wider range of functions. No further evidence was available to show the way in which the building had been arranged nor need any have been expected to have survived beneath the superincumbent remains of Building B and Building C.1 and 2.

Within the space available this was largely due to the superimposition of Building B over the northern end of the early structure. It had a far narrower frontage than its predecessor, presumably reflecting the growing pressure for space close to the

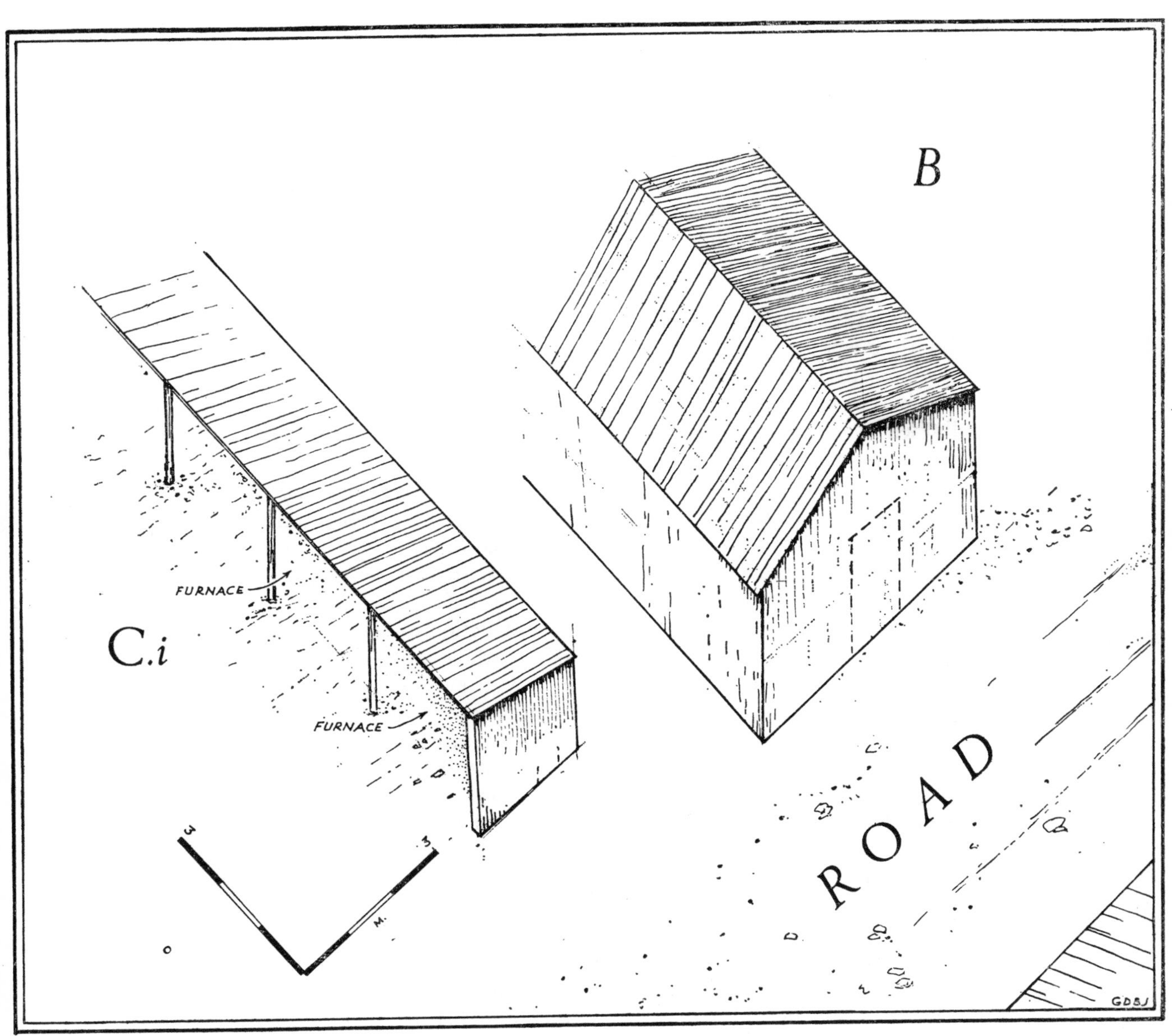

Fig. 19. Reconstruction of Buildings B and C.

exit from the fort. The front of the building represented by construction trench (282) came to within 0.60 m. of the line of the kerb, thus rendering a colonnade arrangement unlikely (figs. 17, 19). On average the construction trenches measured 30 cm. wide but the structure was more solidly built than its predecessor. This was evident from the traces of medium-sized postholes set within the construction trench and located at points in both the eastern and southern walls. In plan the building fitted into the strip pattern familiar from many stone-built equivalents among the excavated buildings of Roman towns. The eastern frontage was, however, partly lost beneath the unexcavated portion of White Lion Street. The section cut further west, however, revealed a cross wall of the building (T. 1/2 18) and in doing so established the overall width as 4.95 m. At both northern and southern ends this partition wall met the main external walls in a T-junction; this demonstrated that the building projected further west, although it was not possible to establish any overall length. On the south side the line of the construction trench disappeared beneath the baulk within 2.50 m., while the northern wall had suffered from extensive later disturbance. This leaves the dimensions for the front portion of the building as 5.30 m. long by 4.95 m. across. The chronological sequence involved in Buildings A and B is fundamental to understanding the development of the site in the late first and early second century. Both the evidence from T.1/2 and the superimposition of construction trench 282 over 283 in T.1 left no doubt as to the secondary dating of Building B. Unfortunately, however, the actual dating evidence for the overall timespan involved is limited (see further, p. 96) and for the moment we must rest content with placing both these buildings in the late Flavian-Trajanic period.

On the southern side of the built-up area lay the remains of two other structures both posterior to Building A (fig. 17). Both structures (C.1 and C.2) were interrelated by two parallel and nearly contiguous construction trenches (for C.1, T.1 271; for C.2, T.1 270 and T.4 87). Indeed at first sight there might be a tendency to treat trench 271 as the eavesdrip line from the roof supported by 270. This was made impossible not only by the steep side of construction trench 271 as it was revealed in section but, above all, by the presence of a posthole at its north-eastern corner which clearly indicated the original presence of a structural support. Thus T.1 271 and T.1 274, the construction trench representing the frontage of the building abutting on to the roadside kerb, formed two sides of a structure that had otherwise been destroyed—or so one thinks at first sight. Yet on second thoughts one is left to ask whether the whole structure was not represented by these two sides. The reason for doing so stems from unequivocal evidence in Building C.2. In that case it was clear that the construction trench T.1 270 turned through posthole 291 in a short southward extension mirrored by another arm 2 m. to the west. The other branch of the trench as it continued west (T.4 87) demonstrably terminated in a pile of stone supports. It showed no southward turn. Moreover, the purpose of the bays became clear during excavations. They served to separate a series of furnace bases. With the additional presence of Furnace 13 it became clear that a mass of superimposed furnaces was involved extending westwards into T.4 to include Furnace 10. Lacking any southern wall, the complex can be seen as designed to catch the prevailing south-westerly winds and so provide draught for the actual furnace floors. With this pattern of layout firmly established for Building C.2, then the apparent absence of a western side to Building C.1 need not call for further explanation. The building simply formed an earlier version of Building C.2. The relative chronological relationship between the two trenches was established by a small section close to the eastern baulk of T.4. The risk of fire must have been considerable and the presence of heat clearly had an adverse effect on daub-lined walls, so one would not expect Building C.1 to have enjoyed a long life; Building C.2, therefore, represented a replacement of the original structure along almost identical lines at a point in time near the middle of the second century A.D.

iv(b): Building G and the Lateral Road

SUMMARY

North of Buildings A and B the backfilled area of the outer military defences was at first used in the early second century for the operation of Furnaces 30 and 31. This phase was terminated by the construction of a lateral spur road west from the main exit road, a development that occurred in the early mid-second century. This new feature also obliterated the remains of Building G further to the west. The evidence suggests that it probably formed a substantial (at least 16.75 m. long) working shed that possibly housed Furnaces 25, 26 A–C and 29. To the south in Trench 4 the area of Furnaces 5 and 14 developed in the early second century and the main group, Furnaces 2, 3 and 4, somewhat later towards the mid-second century. Two pits (68, 69) were probably dug on the abandonment of the outer defences. The smaller was wicker-lined and perhaps served as a well, while the larger (68) became a demolition pit for military material from the fort proper.

WHAT WERE the other developments during the lifespan of Buildings A and B? The principal new feature of the area to the north was the creation of a lateral road paved with medium river gravel (165). The road was not, however, a feature that developed immediately upon demilitarisation. For obvious reasons of subsidence and instability the area over the infilled outer ditch system would not have recommended itself for building purposes. Instead the area of dump noticed in all three sections in T.2, namely levels 223, 233 and 235, was used on the working floor for various industrial activities associated with Furnace 30 (T.2.246 with fill of inner bowl, 250) and Furnace 31 (T.2.246 with associated stakehole 251) (fig. 17). To this group may be added Furnace 32 (T.2.244) but the truncated stratigraphy in the south-western corner of the trench does not allow certainty on this point. The chronological significance of this group, however, lies with the two northern examples. Furnaces 30 and 31 were obliterated by the construction of the lateral road (165). Indeed various charcoal-stained areas (106, 114 and 174) were also sealed beneath the later road make-up. The material from these levels and the associated furnaces mentioned above therefore serves as a *terminus post quem* for the construction of the road. In this respect Furnace 30 was the most informative. As shown by the associated pottery (nos. 132–6 on p. 105) the phase of industrial activity appears to have ceased by the early mid-second century, a conclusion that reinforces and lends precision to the stratigraphic sequence. Road 165, therefore, was created in the early mid-second century; further than that one cannot argue with certainty. Theoretically this event might coincide with the replacement of Building B by Building D but the point is not capable of resolution on the existing evidence.

Before discussing the road, however, other pre-road development in T.2 and T.3 requires description. While Buildings A and B were in existence similar developments were going on in the north-western corner of the site. Indeed one of the buildings there formed the clearest example of a timber structure. This was the building designated G, part of which lay beyond the area of the excavation. As shown by fig. 17 its lifespan was, like Furnaces 29 and 30, cut short by the creation of Road 165, if the building had not already ceased to exist. The visible remains were a substantial clay- and daub-filled construction trench (35 cm. wide) running for a distance of 16.75 m. through Trenches 2 and 3. The structure was first identified as a construction trench (136) in the floor of the sewer trench (39) running diagonally east-west across Trench 2. This feature showed clearly in the floor of the trench as turning through a right-angle junction in such a way that the eastern wall would have been aligned approximately west-north-west. It appears clearly in section (fig. 26) as belonging to the period subsequent to the general dumping on site associated with the backfilling of the outer defensive system. This was even clearer in Trench 3; there the westward continuation of the construction trench was marked by construction Trench 145. It ran the whole width of the trench for a distance of 8.1 m. and overlay not only two of the primary ditch systems (143, 148) but also the butt end of the palisade slot (129) and its associated ditch (139) described on p. 45. As to the date of the building, fragments of plain samian form 18 or 18/31 of south Gaulish manufacture found in the fill of the construction trench offer a *terminus post quem* in the early years of the second century, if not earlier. The material may, however, represent rubbish survival from the military phase, in which case an unequivocal *terminus ante quem* is provided, as already stated, by the superimposition of road 165 over the building in the early mid-second century. This again coincides with the overall picture of the timespan involved in the development of Buildings A and B once the outer defences had been abandoned.

Little is known of the interior of Building G. In view of the right-angle turn in T.2 the enclosed area must have lain to the north of construction trench 145. Significantly perhaps, all the earlier second-century furnaces also lie to the north, namely Furnaces 25, 26 A–C and 29. The latter, like Furnace 24, was placed to take advantage of the shallow depression left by annexe ditch 91, but all three examples abut the construction trench. Only in Furnace 25 could a direct stratigraphic link be proven but perhaps an equally strong argument is the way in which all three developments of Furnace 26, particularly the large bowls forming Furnaces 26A and B, stop just short of the line of the construction trench. The structure may, therefore, provisionally be assigned a role as a working shed in the first half of the second century.

Doubt surrounds the remains of another feature found as a single construction trench (147) terminating in one post-pit sump in Trench 3 (fig. 17). Its length was some 6.2 m. over all. Its width was 40 cm. across, terminating in a post-pit towards the south-western corner of the trench. Unfortunately the feature did not run through into Trench 2 and so our knowledge of its structure, which must have been less substantial than the previous building, must remain a matter of speculation. In general chronological terms, however, it postdates the Building G but not by a considerable period as it was in turn overlaid by Furnaces 27 and 28 of later second-century date.

To the south in T.4 developments during this phase were isolated (fig. 17). All the furnaces seem to have functioned in the open air. The earliest industrial activity appears to have developed, as one might expect behind Buildings A and B in the early years of the second century. Furnace 5, for instance, belongs to this phase but cannot be directly linked with Building C1 or C2 (for the pottery evidence see nos. 155–6, p. 107, and cf. no. 157 of the same early second-century date from Furnace 14). As space was pre-empted or rendered unusable, activity spread further west across T.4. The material from Furnace 2 (nos. 152–4) suggests that its working life lay somewhat later in the second century but not appreciably later than the second quarter. Furnaces 3 and 4 are also associated with this major furnace, and all three may therefore be taken as roughly contemporary. This is not the place for a detailed description of these, or the other furnaces; that is reserved for a later chapter where the *comparabilia* from all the furnaces are discussed. Mention must be made, however, of the largest features in T.4, two massive pits (68, 69) sunk into the bedrock sandstone. The first to be uncovered was T.4.69. It is roughly circular in shape measuring approximately 2.45 m. across east-west at the top and 1.15 m. at the bottom. With a total depth of 2.20 m. below the contemporary Roman ground surface the sides of the pit had acquired an uneven profile dependent on the relative solidity of the subsoil through which they were cut. Thus, while the sump retained much of its original profile cut into the sandstone bedrock, the central portion had become bulbous as it passed through sandy loam. A circular line of heavy charcoal material (71) apparently represents the remains of a timber or wattle revetment to cope with this problem. Despite careful examination by spits it proved impossible to make any significant subdivisions in the homogeneous sandy clay fill of the feature apart, of course, from the rapid silt at the bottom. The absence of any quantity of pottery, the relatively homogeneous fill and the suggested wickerwork around the middle and upper portions of the cone-shaped depression combine to suggest that it functioned as a well until deliberate infilling some time in the second century. It may have been excavated initially to provide material for the dump over the military ditches in the late Flavian-Trajanic period.

Certainly this is the likely explanation for the origin of its close neighbour, pit 68 (fig. 17). The elongated depression measuring 3.30 m. east-west by 1.90 m. north-south is best described, unlike 69, as a demolition pit. Its sump (140) was used as a receptacle for all kinds of rubbish that must derive from a military source, namely the fort to the south. The pottery includes a decorated samian form 29 and a stamped mortarium of Albinus (see no. 172, p. 109, and no. 173, p. 109) that would be appropriate in the Agricolan period (when the area of the pit was an open space between ditch systems) and the level yielded a series of querns in both millstone grit and Andernach lava, the latter overwhelmingly attested in military contexts. The pit, for whatever purpose excavated, was therefore used immediately for dumping demolition rubble (witness the high wattle and daub content of the super-incumbent levels 63 and 68). The pottery of the interior levels contains much material that belongs to a late first–early second century context. It is, however, only part of a very mixed collection (see nos. 158–180, p. 109) continuing until the third century in date. The pit may therefore have continued to be filled from elsewhere on the site and the redeposited material is therefore residual. The latest sherds (p. 110) may, however, derive from vessels roughly contemporary with the final infilling which may be assigned to the early third century.

iv(c): The Later Buildings

SUMMARY

It was unfortunate that a deep, wide, modern sewer-trench separated the Roman road from the buildings which accompanied it on the west. Although the problem of deciding which road surfaces were contemporary with which building-phase was made more acute because of this, the link was not completely severed. Excavation established two building-phases that were clearly later than the timber buildings of late first and early second century date described above. They were quite distinct from one another, although they followed the same general lines and may have had the same function.

The first of these (Building D) was erected at a time when very little stone was available in the area, and consisted of a long wooden building sited parallel to the western edge of the road, and set back about 2.50 m. from it. It was timber-framed, relying for stability on heavy wooden uprights which carried the main weight of the roof. The wooden posts were set into rectangular clay-packed post-pits, dug to receive them. Six pairs of post-pits were discovered, implying a building at least 12.50 m. long by 5 m. wide. The main axis of the structure was parallel to the road—not the kind of building which excavations in the civil settlements of other forts had led us to expect.

Inside the building was found a large furnace, while outside its northern gable-end occurred a large patch of reddened clay which seems to have been an iron-worker's hearth. These industrial structures indicate the function of the building, which may have been a military workshop. Certainly, the structure—even allowing for the fact that the plan may not be complete—did not resemble domestic quarters.

The building may not have lasted more than 25 years. After that, posts set in the ground would have started to rot and would have needed replacing. There is no sign, however, that they were repaired or withdrawn from their post-pits. The dilapidated building was replaced, not necessarily at once, by a more massive structure characterised by circular stone-packed post-pits (Building E). The long axis again ran parallel to the road, but the building was much broader. There were several difficulties in understanding the layout of this new building. The main uprights on the eastern side were set in pits filled with undressed stone, some of it local sandstone. These posts carried the main weight of that wall of the building. On the western side, a series of closer-set posts in similar stone-packed pits matches them. Between the principal lines of posts lay another row, also running north-south, perhaps marking an internal partition.

The building measured about 10 m. by 10 m. over all, and timbers 6 m. long would have been required to span the main hall. It may have been roofed with tile. At the north end of the building-platform, where there had earlier been a metal-working hearth, a group of post-holes forms the partial remains of another building (F) measuring 7.50 m. by 3.45 m. The principal feature of the interior was Furnace 15, a tile-floored iron carburising furnace of considerable interest in view of its date in the late second–early third century.

Although the problem of linking the surfaces of the exit road with contemporary buildings was made difficult by the presence of a nineteenth-century sewer trench, excavation established three building phases post-dating Buildings A–C. Although the three buildings involved were structurally different from one another, their layout was controlled as previously by the basic road alignment. The first of these (Building D), for reasons that will become apparent, consisted of an open shed aligned parallel to the western edge of the road. The structure was located not by an external wall but by two parallel lines of post-pits, of which the eastern row ran 2 m. from the edge of the road. The post-pits marked the points where uprights had carried the weight of the roof and each clay-packed pit contained a post-hole some 25–30 cm. across. Altogether six pairs of post-pits were located, thus indicating that the building's dimensions were at least 12.50 m. long by 5 m. wide, though the true southern end may have been lost. The yellow clay post-pits are nos. 73, 73a, 94, 32, 48 and 128 in Trench 1 together with T.1/2.5 and 6 and T.2.88. The reason why the structure did not have any side walls and thus represented an open working shed, became clear during the excavation. At least two industrial features may be associated with the interior. Furnace 15 (=T.1.90) set on burnt clay (83) belongs to this building. It lay between post-pits 73 and 73a and rested on the associated floor (80), a spread of sandy, yellow clay that could be traced through to the north as T.2.83. The furnace proper is of intrinsic interest as an iron carburising hearth and is described fully on p. 71 and fig. 27. At the same time on the south side of partition wall 121 (pl. 14a) the very substantial Furnace 16 (T.1.91.50) was also incorporated within this period. The bowl-shaped depression formed by the furnace with its charcoal fill (49) interrupts the alignment of an external wall based on the clay-packed post-holes and helps corroborate the idea that the sides of the structure were open. Some of the links across the floor area, however, were difficult to establish because of the intrusion of a nineteenth-century sewer pit (28) in this area. The relationship between the eastern side of Furnace 16 and the tiled floor (90) of Furnace 15 across partition 121 was, however, eventually established as contemporary. The building is shown in plans and reconstruction in figs. 20, 21.

In reconstruction the axis of the roof ran parallel to the road. In view of the relatively light main timber uprights the roof was probably covered with shingles rather than tiles, of which none survived save in Furnace 15. At the northern end, however, other features were identified. Outside the northern gable end, as already stated, an extensive red clay spread (83) was associated with the floor levels of Building D. The clay formed the basis into which the elaborate arrangements for Furnace 21 (p. 67) had been set. These comprised a wall (nos. 191, 192, 193 and 194) demarcating the northern edge of the furnace. Despite the difficulties caused by the presence of White Lion Street in this area, it can be seen that the north-western post-hole of this line related to post-hole 60 to the south. With two further post-holes (T.2.57, 74) the latter forms a post-hole alignment leading directly to post-pit 88, i.e. coinciding with the northern gable end of the open working shed. It is therefore treated as part of Building D. Furnace 21 evidently formed part of the building but was set, as the post-hole plan implies, in a northern extension to the shed in which the roof axis must have changed through ninety degrees to run at right-angles to the road (fig. 21).

The date of Building D is indicated by a considerable quantity of pottery (pp. 98–9), particularly that found stratified within clay floor T.2.83 demarcating the northern extent of the structure (nos. 41–49). The latter form the evidence for dating the building within the mid–late second century and the volume of pottery is perhaps itself evidence for a relatively protracted working lifespan covering some twenty to thirty years. As already stated (p. 53), it cannot be conclusively shown that the construction of Building D coincided with the creation of a lateral road (T.2.165) branching at right-angles from the exit road along the northern side of the structure. Certainly, however, both building and road must have co-existed for a time in the mid–late second century. The evidence for this, so far as the road is concerned, comes partly from the *terminus post quem* provided by pottery from features broadly contemporary with Building G (p. 54) and partly from the *terminus ante quem* of pottery found sealed within the make-up for Furnaces 22 and 23 which were superimposed on the road in the lifetime of Buildings E and G. When cleaned the road proper was found to be composed of a heavy dump of medium–small river pebble (T.2.186, 146 and 165, corporately designated road 165) as shown in plates 12a, b; see fig. 17. The nineteenth-century sewer trench running east–west across T.2 had inevitably destroyed much of the precise road edge but a row of large limestone blocks on the north side indicated the presence of deliberate kerbing in places. Unfortunately, little of the road survived further west in T.3 owing to further modern intrusion.

The date of Building D lay within the middle and later second century A.D. as discussed at length in relation to the pottery (pp. 98–102). The timber uprights would inevitably have started to rot and required replacement within twenty to thirty years at the outside. There is no sign, however, that they were replaced or withdrawn from their post-pits and so we must assume that towards the end of the second century the building fell into dilapidation. The structure was replaced by two more substantial buildings. The southern example was characterised by the use of massive stone-packed post-pits for its external walls and the employment of small double post-holes for internal partition walls. This building was designated Building E and indeed its relative position in the chronological sequence after Building D was only firmly established by the excavation of T.1/2 across White Lion Street. The reason lay in the extensive post-Roman ploughing that had the effect of shearing off all the later Roman stratigraphy. As a result both Buildings D and E survived at approximately the same actual level. By excavating T.1/2 the building sequence was finally confirmed when it was discovered that a post-hole (T.1/2.50) belonging to the north wall of Building E had been cut through the yellow clay-capped post-pit (4) belonging to Building D. The main uprights on the eastern side were set in massive post-pits almost a metre across, filled with undressed limestone (113, 61) and representing the eastern front of the building. The back wall was similarly represented by post-pits T.4.86 and T.4.85 probably to be taken with T.2.59. The internal walls were represented by post-holes 123, 215, 195 and also T.1/2.2, 3 and 7. It will be seen that the building thus measured some 9.80 × 8 m. overall and timbers 6 m. long would have been required to span the main hall, a distance that need not cause surprise.[1]

The structure (F) to the north lying principally within the area of T.2 presented greater complexities. While occurring at the same stratigraphic level as Building E, it became apparent during the course of excavation that the post-holes located in T.2 must have belonged to a separate structure. The three major eastern post-holes (T.2.59, 56, 63) do not coincide with the rear wall of Building E as marked by post-hole T.4.86, etc. Moreover, the construction of the post-holes involved was recognisably different from those of Building D, being limited in diameter to *c.*45 cm. and lacking chockstones in some cases. Of the remaining major post-holes in T.2 (after the assignment of post-holes 57, 60 and 76 to Building D, as argued above on p. 58) the northern wall of the building may be recognised as post-holes 59, 54, 93 and 191. Central roof supports were given by post-holes 53 and 66. This left the question of the southern wall. It was observed that the southern face of the trench showed evidence of a post-hole in section (13) directly coinciding with the central internal support, post-hole 53 (see fig. 21). At an equivalent stratigraphic level to the east post-hole 12 may be taken as part of the building frontage, if not the actual central support of the gable end. While the structure was not laid out with rigid rectangularity, it is clear from the post-hole layout, even as partially preserved that the roof axis ran the length of the building and at right-angles to the road. The length involved was slightly over 7.50 m. by 3.45 m. across. The central position of post-holes 53 and 56 implies a pitched roof to either side with gable ends at front and rear (figs. 20, 21).

The lifetime of this building and indeed that of Building E is shown by pottery nos. 91–113 (p. 103), belonging to the later second century or early–mid third century. As a number of pieces present (nos. 105, 109 and 112) are unlikely to have been produced prior to A.D. 210–220, Buildings E and F must have continued in use until at least that time. In view of this, wooden structure survival beyond the early–mid third century must be thought improbable. During this time, however, extensive alterations took place to the road surface on the north side of Building F. The original road (165) was obliterated as a through route by the construction of Furnaces 22 and 23 (p. 67) above the original road cobbling. This led to a build-up in levels of

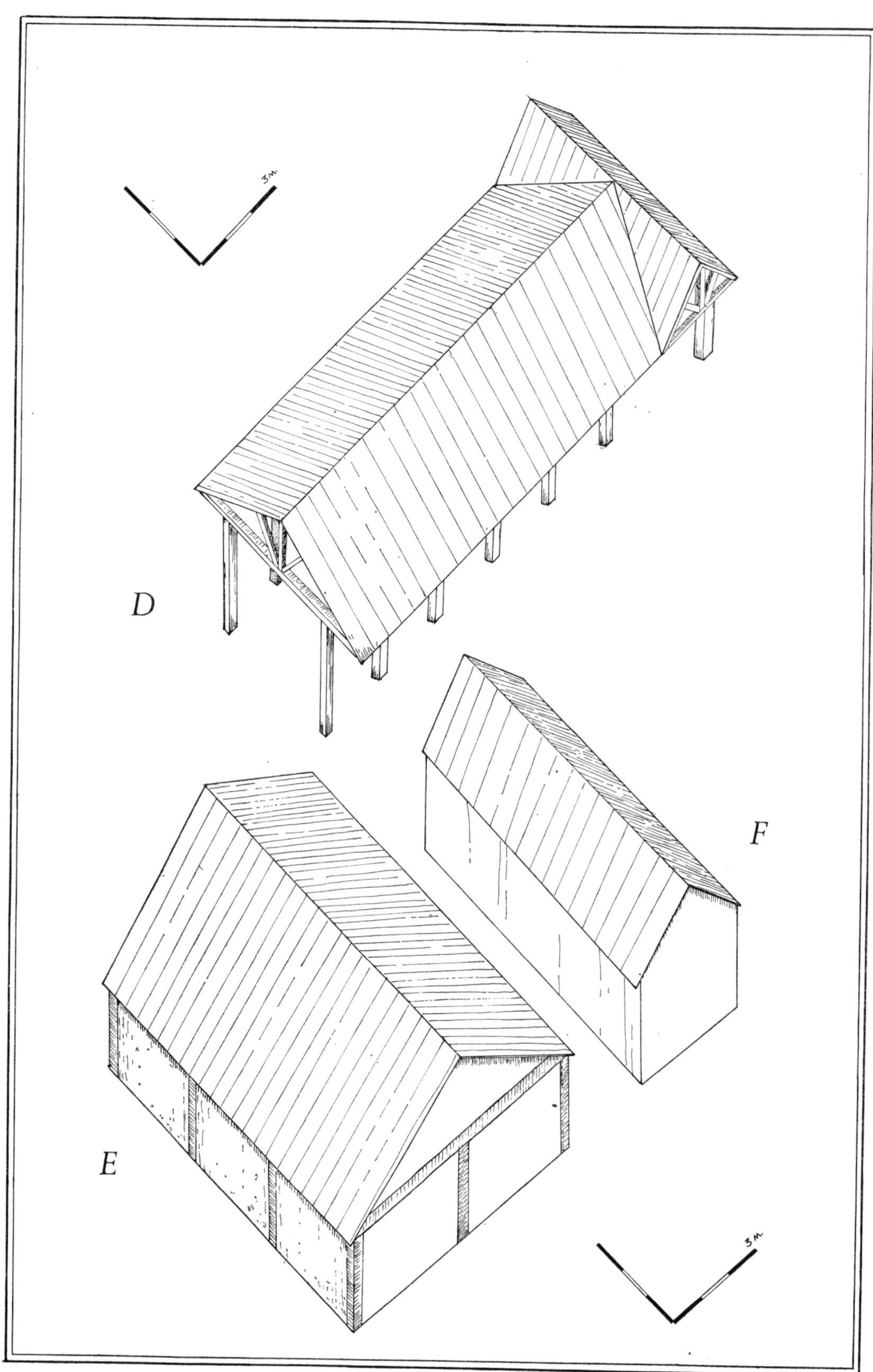

Fig. 20. Reconstruction of Buildings D, E and F.

some 10–20 cm., principally through the dumping of patches of medium cobbling (T.2.37, 45, 65, 79, 97 and 117). The effect of this was to fill in the shallow depression previously forming the southern side drain of the lateral road (165); and so to create by the late second century an untidy, roughly paved area in which the two furnaces actually functioned at one stage. The southernmost cobbling (65) was bounded by two upstanding ashlar blocks (73, 74). If these have a structural role, then their twin location opposite two post-holes (160, 162) suggests that they may have formed the protective chockstones for an open lean-to shed abutting the north wall of Building F. Indeed the charcoal line of feature 94 attests the position of a fallen timber beam on the ground surface. It was 2.55 m. long and appears to have fallen from its footing behind feature 73. Certainly the alignment between the two stone uprights (73, 74) is exactly paralleled by that between the two post-holes (162, 169) and as such might form the faint traces of an open-sided wagon shed or stall. Further west, cobbling in both T.2 (72) and T.3 (31, 35) belongs to this structural phase. The stratified levels under discussion, together with their associated Buildings E and F, form the latest structural remains of the Roman period, apart from the fourth-century resurfacing of the northern exit road. The reason for this situation is explained in a later section.

NOTE

1 *Journal of Roman Studies* LX (1970), 125.

v: Buildings East of the Exit Road: Buildings H-L

SUMMARY

Excavation produced evidence of at least five timber buildings fronting the eastern side of the northern exit road. Interpretation was made difficult by the restricted space available and the disturbance caused by the presence of furnaces. Little was uncovered of the earliest structure (H) and three of the furnaces belonged to the second, and most substantial, building on the eastern side (I). This elongated building stretched the entire length of the eastern roadside that was examined, a distance of c.*14.5 m. The subsequent building (J) was set back further from the kerb and overlay the flattened remains of the Furnaces 17, 18 and 19. Building K was identified by a line of postholes set in a construction trench that ran out of the southern end of the site and must have included Furnace 20 in the interior. Posthole 536 to the north of the excavated area provided an isolated hint of a later structural phase (L) of probable fourth century date. Otherwise the construction of Building H followed on the abandonment of the outer military defences at the turn of the first century and Building I apparently followed rapidly, early in the second century.*

As OUTLINED on p. 33, the two earliest road surfaces of the exit road from the *porta principalis sinistra* belonged to the early military phase when the outer defensive ditch system was maintained. The earliest structural evidence of buildings was associated with the third road surface and took the form of a construction trench (MCP 10) running across the floor of the original exploratory trench but destroyed on the southern side by Furnace 18 (T.1.164). No further evidence of this building (designated Building H) could be located owing to the lack of time and the overburden involved. In view of the spread of road metalling (MCP 14, 15 16) it seems likely that this particular construction trench formed the front line of the building in question. A charcoal spread to the east represented the remains of a timber floor.

The subsequent structure, Building I, formed the most obvious feature of this area of the site where shortage of space severely increased the problems of interpretation. The deep (45 cm.) construction trench originally identified as MCP 28 (a numeration retained throughout this section) continued both north and south of the original exploratory section, in the latter case beyond the southern edge of the excavation area. The trench is well shown in both sections (see figs. 7, 10, 22). The building involved was of considerable size, being at least 9.5 m. long. The structure can confidently be projected a further 5 m. because in the road section in the northern half of the trench an identical construction trench was located, associated with the third road period, as was the main construction trench (28). This means that the building was probably very substantial in length. Its function was largely industrial because stratigraphically Furnaces 17, 18 and 19 belong to this phase, while a charcoal-filled depression (236) on the eastern edge of the site probably represented the edge of another furnace. Few of the internal partitions survived in recognisable form partly through the difficulties of excavation within a restricted space. In the primary investigation part of an internal partition wall had been located as MCP (7). As excavation proceeded it became clear that the depression MCP 7B formed the line of an extension of this wall running at an acute angle towards the front of the building. Similarly, 4.3 m. further north post-socket (543A) formed the remains of a small timber upright set in a construction trench (543) running into the front wall (28).

The next building (J) identified in this corner of the site was formed by MCP 11

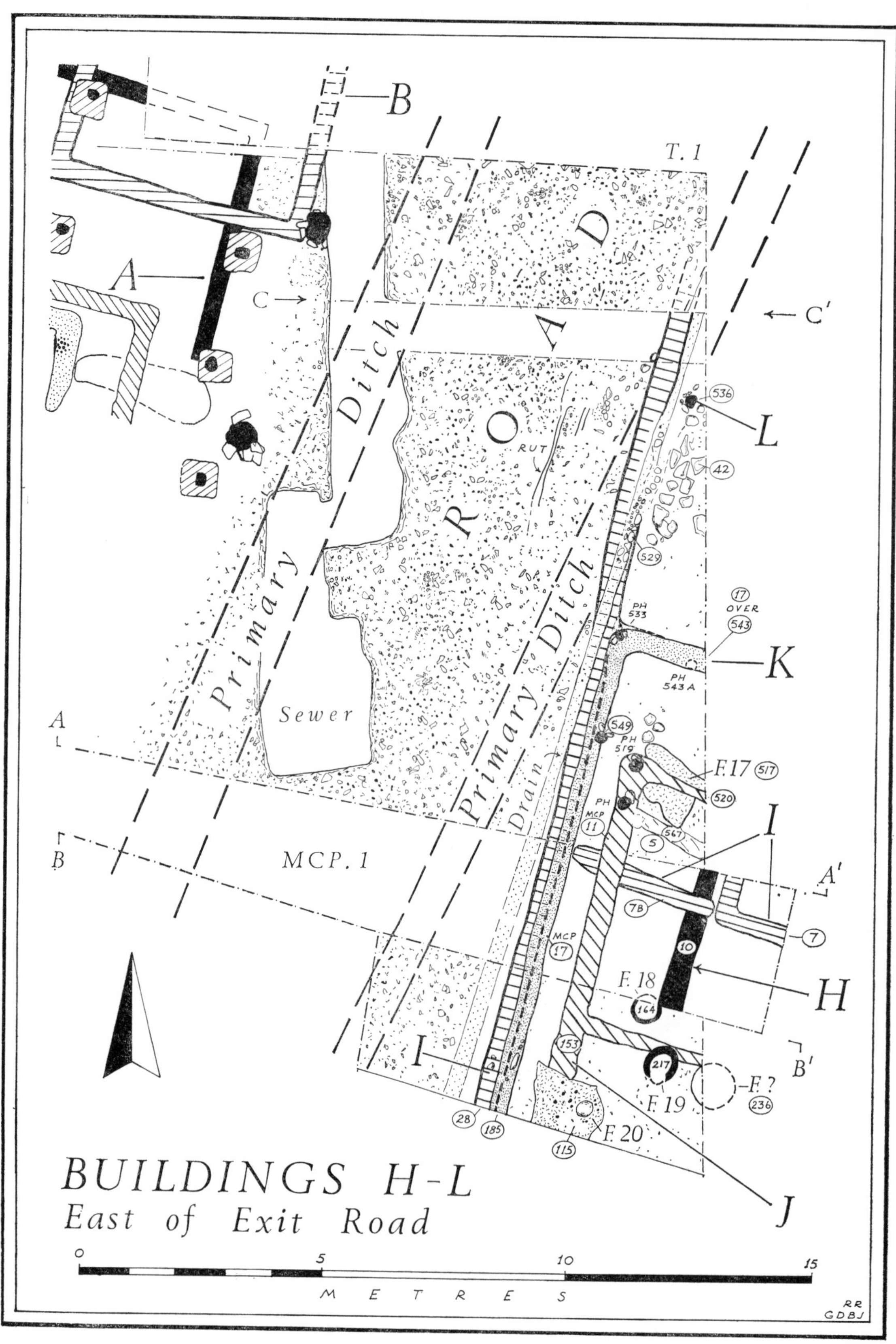

Fig. 22. Buildings east of exit road.

and its associated floor (5). On the northern side of the exploratory trench the charcoal spread across floor 5 identified the extent of the room to the north. It ran across the underlying remains of Furnace 17 (517) associated with Building I, like Furnaces 18 and 19. Into the mass of the disused furnace was cut a very obvious construction trench (520) leading towards the posthole 519. The position of this postpit in fact tallied exactly with a projection of MCP 11 and there was a hint of a partition (567) running into the front wall just 1.60 m. away. To the south the remains of the building frontage lay sealed beneath the base of Furnace 20 in the form of a charcoal and daub-filled construction trench (153). It contained a small internal partition marked by a clay line as far as Furnace 19. The stratigraphic sequence makes it possible to associate this building phase with road drain 529 in turn linked with the penultimate surviving road surface (Road V) further north (see p. 39).

At least one, and possibly two, further building phases may be identified in this area. The first of these was represented by a building frontage formed by two postholes joined by an ill-defined construction trench. In projection, however, this line led directly on to the construction trench already seen as MCP 17 and the structure is designated Building K. Little can be said of its detailed plan save that the front projected further south as a line of uprights (185), thus including Furnace 20 within the interior of the building. There remained traces of another feature possibly to be conflated in a subsequent, but otherwise unlocated, building phase (L). The sandstone blocks forming an isolated posthole (536) should stratigraphically be associated with another building but no part of its plan could be established within the extremely restricted space available. It was, however, from the equivalent of this level that pottery of post-A.D. *c.*360 was forthcoming (see p. 111). The feature was amongst the highest surviving stratified remains on the site and it is a matter of regret that the buildings of 1825–6 had removed so many of the stratigraphic links that could have made the overall layout and plan more meaningful.

In chronological terms, however, the information derived from these buildings can be associated with that from the road surfaces identified and discussed on p. 37 (see fig. 8). The most definite association is perhaps that of Building I with the third major road building phase. All the evidence from that points to the foundation of the road and its associated building by roughly the Hadrianic period, i.e. around or slightly before A.D.120. Prior to this we must posit the development of the primary Building H upon the abandonment of the outer defensive system, presumably close to the turn of the first century. The development of Building J also appears to fall in the period before the end of the second century but the date of the later buildings may considerably post-date these structures. On the evidence available, however, nothing more can be added to what has already been written on p. 39.

vi: The Furnaces and Smithing Hearths

SUMMARY

Within the excavation area thirty-three furnaces or groups of furnaces were located. This is the largest single group to be methodically studied using modern metallurgical analysis in this country. As such the furnaces and hearths have an importance that extends beyond the local scale. Three examples of early second-century date (F.16A, F.30 and F.31) functioned as smelting furnaces operating at a temperature of 1,100–1,200°C. At a similar date two furnaces (F.18 and F.19) were used for the crucible melting of lead at a temperature of c.*900°C within Building I. The most significant advance, however, probably lay in the recognition of the remaining industrial features, principally as smithing hearths for the secondary working of iron blooms at temperatures varying between 450–800°. The hearths are here described both in terms of their physical remains, function and working temperature as well as from an historical standpoint. The tile-floored Furnace 15, for instance, forms the latest surviving industrial feature. Its recognition as a probable iron-carburising furnace functioning by the very late second or early third century illustrates the way in which the evidence of improving metallurgical techniques identified on the site demonstrates one aspect of the history of technology. The fuller implications of the metallurgical evidence are discussed in a separate chapter (pp. 143–58).*

IN MUCH of the second and third centuries the area examined by the excavation outside the north gate of the fort formed an industrial zone, whether as a deliberate act of policy or not archaeology cannot tell. In this section the evidence is described as it survived without elaborate discussion of the precise technological processes involved. The latter requires a detailed exposition of firing temperatures, clinker content, etc., and is accordingly treated in a separate chapter of the work (p. 154). Briefly it is concluded that the principal process involved was not one of iron ore roasting but the smithing of iron blooms into weapons and tools. Some of the furnaces, which have been given a series of numbers 1–33, can be assigned to the building phases described above. For instance, Furnaces 18, 19 and 20 all belong within Building I. Others, however, stood to the rear of the actual building and are dated only in relative terms.

The principal type was best represented by a cluster of hearths in the extreme south-western corner of our site, that is in the backyards of Buildings A, B, C, D and E. These are represented by Furnaces 2, 3 and 4. They survived as heavy patches of clay some 15 cm. thick and over 1 m. across. The clay in each case revealed signs of heat but was not baked absolutely hard. During the excavation process small holes filled by charcoal could be detected within the clay matrix. Considerable evidence accumulated to show that these holes cannot be interpreted as vents and the most likely explanation (discussed further on p. 150) is that they represent stakeholes associated with implements used in the smithing processes discussed on p. 147. The fact that these hearths were associated with quantities of iron slag leaves no doubt as to the metal involved. Similar hearths have recently been found outside the Roman fort at Northwich (see further p. 147). The type, however, conceals two different varieties of internal arrangements. In a minority of cases, and Furnaces 1 and 2 are the only examples available in Manchester, the central area beneath the clay spread contained a charcoal-filled pit as shown in fig. 28. The great majority of the furnaces, however, consisted simply of a clay spread with no central underlying pit. This was perhaps most clearly illustrated in the furnaces such as Furnace 21 where, as shown in pl. 18a, the stakeholes cover the whole of the clay spread and in view of the lack of internal underlying arrangements cannot be regarded as ventholes. In the most elaborate form the furnaces were carefully built up above an underlying arrangement of cobbles and stone. This is shown clearly in Furnace 21 but the principle was carried to its logical extreme by the way in which Furnaces 22 and 23 took advantage of a pre-existing road surface to act as their foundation. The detailed illustration of

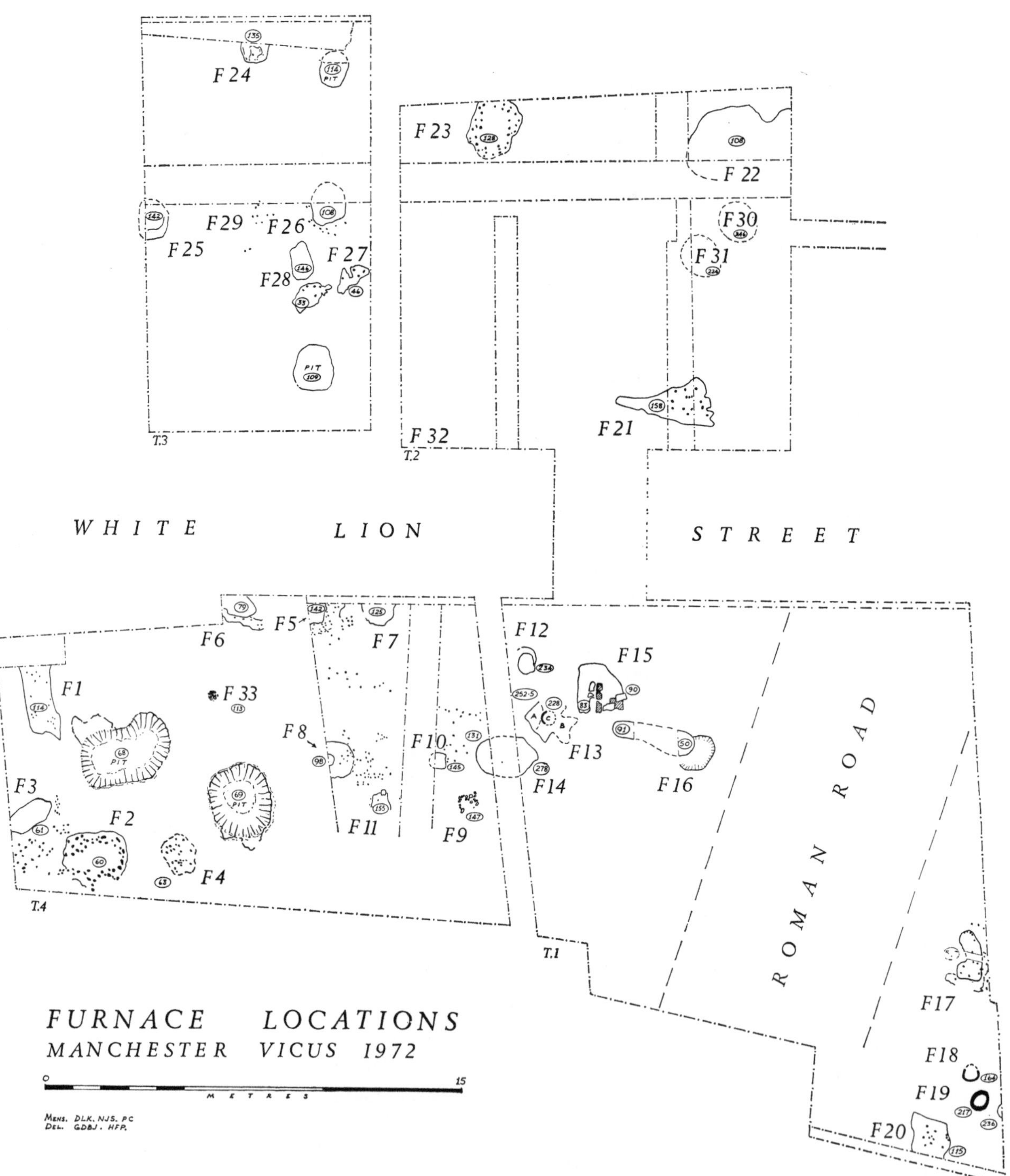

Fig. 23. General plan of furnace locations (not differentiated chronologically).

these two furnaces appears in fig. 51 and shows the way a layer of grey-brown clay (108, 128) was built up over the cobbled road surface (165) and so formed the base for the smithing processes involved.

This kind of development was at its most complex in Furnace 13 where there was evidence of four superimposed phases, suggesting a long period of use. The whole complex was built on a cobble foundation; originally the outer wall identified as 252 formed the largest of the four phases. It collapsed and the next phase was built over its fill (253) of clay and cobble. This second phase was slightly smaller as shown in fig. 51. It too collapsed to be filled with another mass of clay and cobble (255). The penultimate phase represented a complete rebuild *in situ* (256). This furnace did not collapse but received a relining (257) to show that it had at least two periods of use.

As shown on pp. 72–4, the working temperature calculated by Dr. J. Cleland of the University of Manchester Institute of Science and Technology lay in the area of 450–800°C. With the exception of Furnace 17, and possibly Furnaces 25, 26 and 29, all the smithing hearths functioned either in the open or in an open-sided shed. Details of size, associated levels and working temperatures will all be found tabulated at the end of this chapter.

The second type of furnace is better understood since many examples have been found in Roman Britain. They comprise a clay-lined, circular chamber somewhat over half a metre in diameter dug below ground level and with a short narrow flue. In the examples from the Manchester excavation splashes of lead indicate that the furnaces operating at approximately 900° C must have been used to melt lead in crucibles. Of this type Furnaces 18 and 19 were particularly well preserved (pls. 20a, 20b); several others, however, probably existed within the same early second-century building (I) and survived merely as patches of hard-baked, biscuit-yellow clay. Furnace 18 is shown in section in fig. 28 (cf. fig. 22). The area surrounding the furnace and its clay backing (pl. 20b) was burnt a brilliant red around the circular bowl measuring 41 cm. across by 34 cm. deep. The ochre-coloured furnace lining measured some 2–3 cm. in thickness and was extensively preserved, particularly on the south side. The flue had been destroyed by the mechanical cutting of the original trial trench (MCP) in February 1972.

The earliest furnaces on the site also belonged to a separate category. As described on pp. 53–4 two furnaces (30, 31) of early second-century date preceded the construction of lateral road 165. They both took the form of shallow circular bowls in the subsoil filled with charcoal, stone and heavy clinker. Analysis showed that Furnace 30 and, therefore, by implication also Furnace 31 represented the remains of actual smelting furnaces. Their importance lies in the evidence for a primary metal-working activity on the site in the early second century, a function that must have been transferred further away from the fort in later years. The earlier furnace (16A) underlying elongated Furnace 16 is probably another example of this type. A primary process was involved, whether preliminary roasting or actual iron smelting. Indeed, the area is another example of the complexities of superimposed working. In this case furnace complex 16 contains the remains of three furnaces, the first of which (175) was identifiable from traces of its burnt clay lining and associated clinker as an iron smelting or roasting hearth. It was cut into by the subsequent phase (112), a lining of dark-red clay associated with a level of charcoal (155) and an earth and stone backfill (51) apparently used to level up the site prior to the construction of Building D. Superimposed on this lay the eastern bowl of Furnace 16, an elongated double-bowled furnace (50), the orange clay lining of which was filled by charcoal-stained dark brown soil (49) forming the western extremity of the sump.

Beyond this category Furnace 15 (T.1.90) deserves separate treatment. It is composed of a floor of tiles (90) set in reddish-pink-brown clay (83) that represents the very damaged remains of a furnace with a rectangular chamber approximately 1.20 ×3.8 m. with a flue to the north-west. The position of the flue as shown in fig. 27

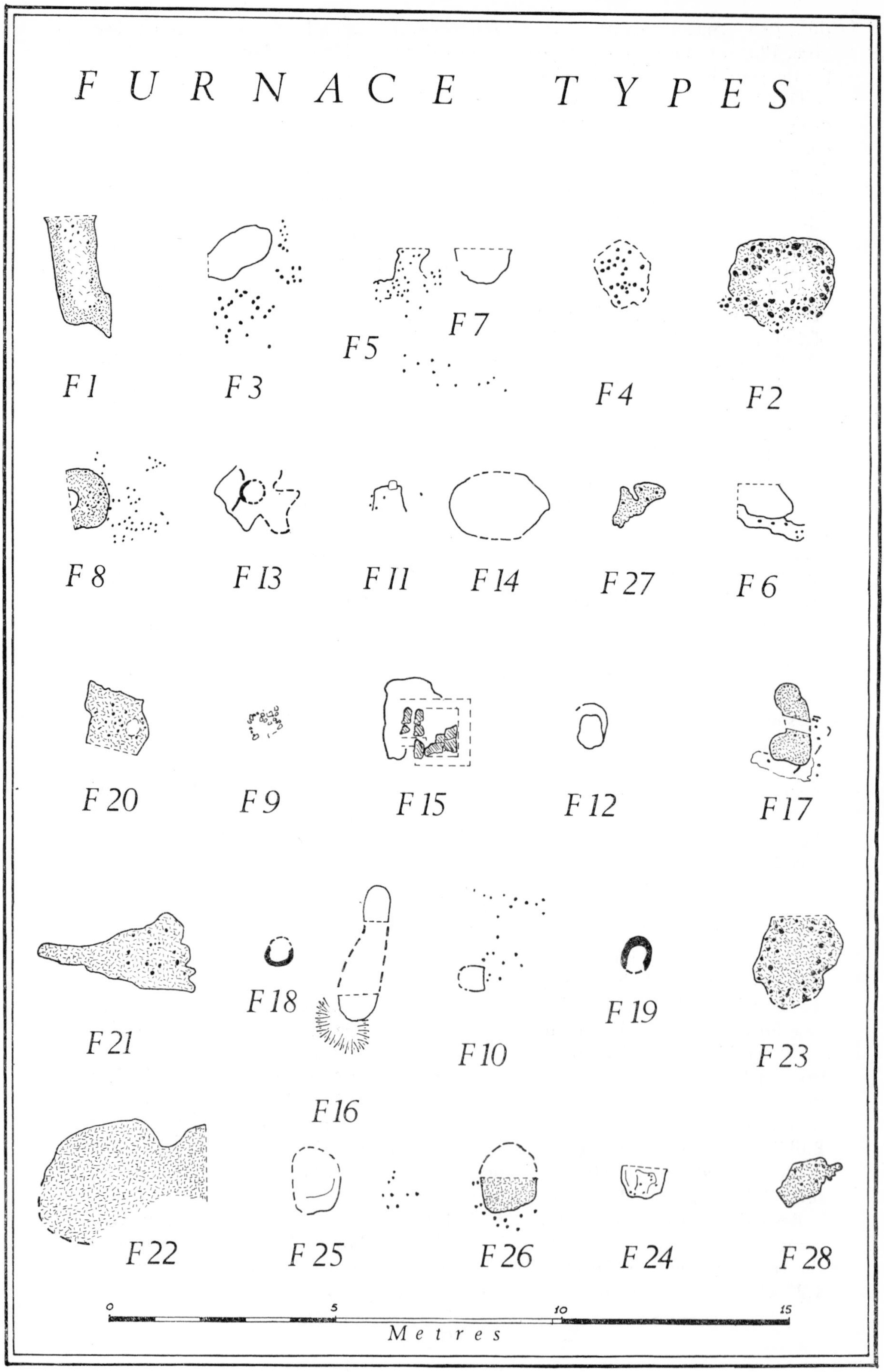

F U R N A C E   T Y P E S

F 1 F 3 F 5 F 7 F 4 F 2

F 8 F 13 F 11 F 14 F 27 F 6

F 20 F 9 F 15 F 12 F 17

F 21 F 18 F 16 F 10 F 19 F 23

F 22 F 25 F 26 F 24 F 28

0 5 10 15

Metres

Fig. 24. Furnace types.

was demonstrated by the layout of the tiles and the distribution of the heat cracks in them. On the southern side of the chamber stones were found in position to represent the original walling. Below the burnt clay was a layer of intensive charcoal and daub scatter (122/137) that was revealed by the loss of much of the northern part of the firing chamber and its clay foundation. This, the latest furnace on the site, operating at a temperature of over 800°C, is probably recognisable as an iron carburising furnace, a technological improvement that gave additional strength to the working and cutting surfaces of iron implements through tempering the metal with carbon. The date of Furnace 15, in the very late second–early third centuries, accords with what little is known of this improvement elsewhere in this country where other examples belong to the third or fourth century.[1]

The late date of the iron carburising furnace brings us naturally to the overall development pattern amongst the furnaces. The earliest examples (early second century) fall into two distinct groups. The first of these are the three iron smelting (or, in one case, possibly roasting) furnaces (F.30, 31 and 16A) described earlier on p. 69. They revealed relatively little clinker *in situ*, but that is readily explained by its suitability for incorporation in road make-up. Similarly, obvious environmental reasons explain why later smelting furnaces must have been located at a greater distance from the fort. The other early group is also small, consisting of the two lead crucible melting furnaces (F.18, 19) housed within Building I, with strong hints of a third nearby beneath the eastern baulk of T.1. As the second century developed smithing hearths began to predominate. One can see a little of their development, particularly in T.2. The smaller examples (F.5, 6, 7, 8, 9, 10 and 11) all probably belong to the first half of the century. The average size increased, with diameters consistently over 2 m. in the mid–late second century, as demonstrated by F.2, 21, 22 and 23. Interestingly, the latest smithing hearths (F.27, 28) of the late second–early third century date show a reduction in size to that of the earlier second-century examples. In the opinion of the metallurgists this rise and decline in size is less likely to reflect technological changes than increased market demand in the mid–late second century, whether from military or civilian sources. Finally the introduction of a probable iron carburising furnace (F.15) by the early third century introduced, as already discussed, an element of technological innovation.

This then is a rough description of the physical remains of the furnaces. What follows is an appendix citing the detailed dimensions of the actual furnaces together with their constituent levels. All discussion of their precise function is postponed until the chapter on metal-working when the evidence from the North-West is reviewed against that in the country as a whole. Much of the interpretation of the furnaces depends on detailed metallurgical analysis that was carried out by the University of Manchester Institute of Science and Technology in its Department of Metallurgy. Indeed, through the good offices of that Department, two of the furnaces were removed intact for further examination by sliding sheets of steel underneath them (Pl. 6a). Whatever may have been the overall character of these industrial features in relation to the fort, whether the deliberate creation of an industrial annexe or a spontaneous civilian response to the market needs of the military and their civilian satellites, by the later second century practically the whole of the excavated site was devoted to industrial activity associated with smithing. As such, the thirty-three furnaces located in this area are unique in their density and at the same time a warning on excavational method. Sampled in section these features would have been almost unintelligible apart from their bare identification as furnaces of some kind. They can only yield significant results if excavated totally through the kind of careful area stripping employed in 1972.

NOTE

1 Especially from Colsterworth, Lincs. See I. C. Hannah, The Roman Blast Furnace in Lincolnshire, *Ant. J.* XII (1932), 262–8; The Colsterworth Iron Furnace, Grantham Public Library and Museum, Tenth Ann. Rep. 1931–2, 15.

APPENDIX

Furnace	*Trench*	*Assoc. Levels*	*Type (for categories of smithing hearths see p. 148)*	*Dimensions*	*Working Temperature*	*Date*	*Other Features*
1	4	114	Smithing hearth PIA				
2	4	41 and 60	Smithing hearth PIII	2.35m × 2m	*c.*600°C	mid-2nd century	Cobble foundations. Contains pit (see fig. 50, pl. 18b).
3	4	61	PIV	1.20m × 0.80m	*c.* 600°C	mid-2nd century	
4	4		Smithing hearth PIV	1.20m × 1.45m	*c.* 600°C	mid-2nd century	Possibility of demolished earlier version on western side.
5	4	142	Smithing hearth PIV	1.50m × 1m	*c.* 600°C	early 2nd century	
6	4	79	Smithing hearth PIII	1.20m × 0.75m	*c.* 600°C	early 2nd century	
7	4	125	Smithing hearth	1.55m × 0.75m	*c.* 600°C	early 2nd century	(see pl. 23b)
8	4	98	Smithing hearth PIII	0.90m × 1.25m	*c.* 450°C	early-mid 2nd century	(see pl. 23a)
9	4	147	Smithing hearth	0.75m × 0.60m	not known (very damaged)	early-mid 2nd century	Cobble foundation.
10	4	145	Smithing hearth PIII	0.60m × 0.55m	*c.* 550°C	early-mid 2nd century	Heavy clay base (see fig. 25, pl. 9b) truncated by sewer trench.
11	4		Smithing hearth	0.70m × 0.60m	not known	early-mid 2nd century	
12	1	234	Smithing hearth	0.65m × 1m	*c.* 800°C	early 2nd century	?Associated with Building C.
13A,B,C	1	228 252 255 263	Smithing hearth	1.90m × 1.45m	*c.*800°C	early-mid 2nd century	Assoc. with Building C2 (fig. 51). Enclosed within open shed.
14	1/4	T1 278 T4 131	Smithing hearth	2.20m × 1.35m	*c.* 800°C	early-mid 2nd century	Assoc. with Building C2. Enclosed within open shed.
15	1	83 90	Iron carburising furnace with assoc. tiled area	Rectangular chamber reconstructed as approx. 1.20m × 3.8m with a flue to the north-west	*c.* 800°C+	very late 2nd century early 3rd century	Assoc. with Building D. Enclosed within open working shed.
16A, B	1	A 50 91 B 112 truncated by modern disturbance	A bowl smithing hearth or roasting hearth B Elongated double bowl hearth	A1.60m diam. B2.95m × 0.95m	A*c.*800°C+ B no greater than *c.*600°C	A early 2nd century B mid-late 2nd century	B cobble in clay lining.

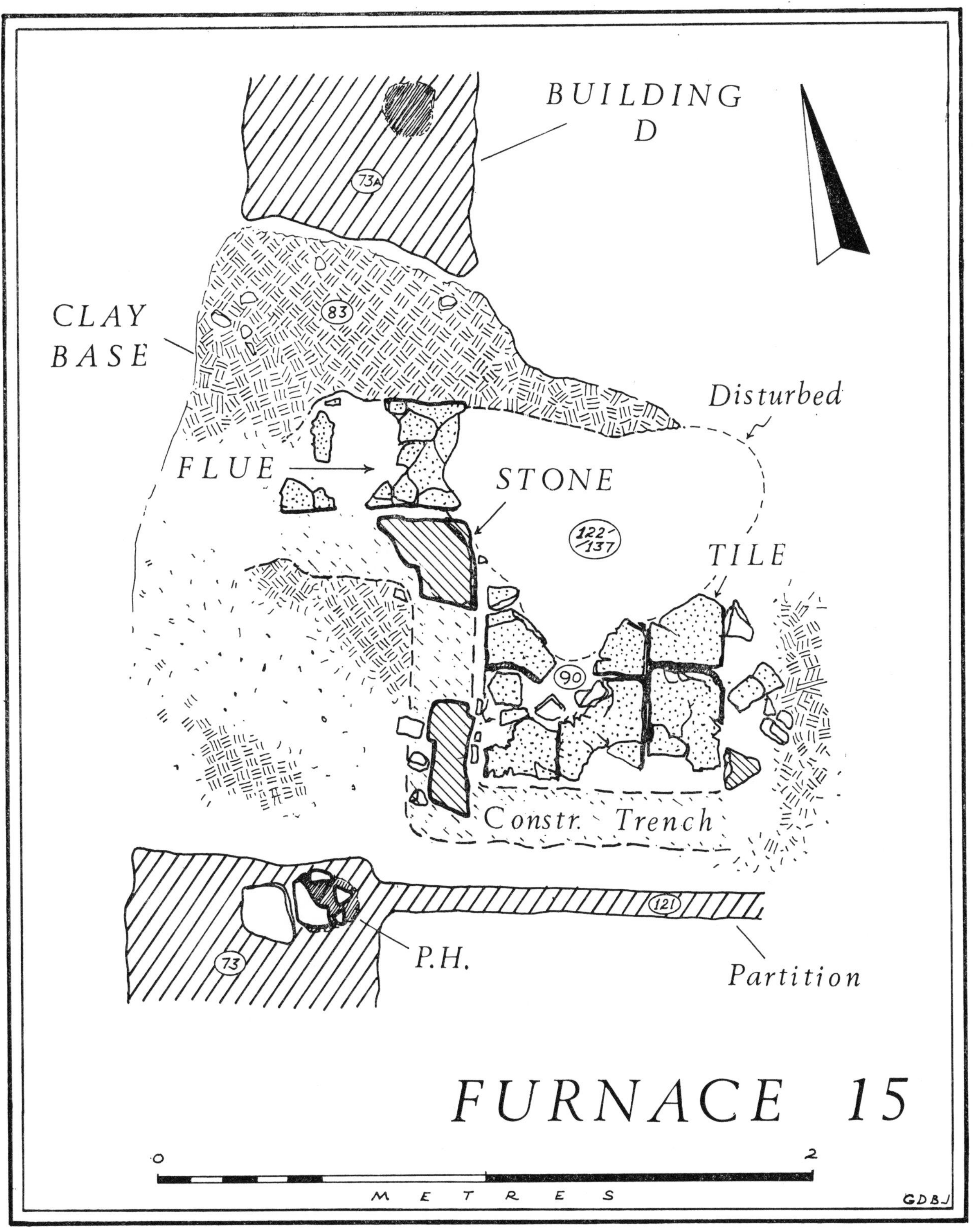

Fig. 27. Plan of Furnace 15.

Furnace	*Trench*	*Assoc. Levels*	*Type (for categories of smithing hearths see p. 148)*	*Dimensions*	*Working Temperature*	*Date*	*Other Features*
17	1	517	Smithing hearth PII	1.70m × 0.85m	*c.* 450°C	first quarter of 2nd century	Enclosed within north room of Building I. Evidence of demolished earlier version (see pl. 22b).
18	1	164	Furnace for crucible melting of lead	0.70m × 0.70m	*c.* 850°C	first quarter of 2nd century	Enclosed in south room of Building I. Cobble in wall exterior. Furnace lining preserved. Well-constructed (pl. 20b, 21a).
19	1	217 236	Furnace for crucible melting of lead	0.68m × 0.80m	*c.* 850°C	first quarter of 2nd century	Enclosed in south room of Building I. Further furnace to east (pl. 20a).
20	1	115		1.90m in diam. bowl 45cm diam.	*c.* 850°C	late 2nd-early 3rd century	Within Building K. Substantial river pebble base (pl. 21b).
21	2	158 185 220	Smithing hearth PIA	3.55m × 1.65m	*c.* 750°C	mid-late 2nd century	Assoc. with but external to Building D.
22	2	108 107	Smithing hearth	3.70m × 2.35m	*c.*500°C	late 2nd century	Uses road 165 as foundation (pl. 22a).
23	2	128 99 156	Smithing hearth PIC	1.75m × 2m	*c.* 500°C	late 2nd century	Uses road 165 as foundation.
24	3	135	Smithing hearth PIV	1m × 0.65m	*c.* 400°C	early 2nd century	Inserted within annexe ditch cf. F.29.
25	3	142	Smithing hearth	1.10m × 1.35m	not known	early 2nd century	Within Building F.
26	3	108	Smithing hearth PIII	1.25m × 1.45m	*c.*400°C	early 2nd century	Evidence for two earlier demolished versions. ?Within Building F.
27	3	46	Smithing hearth PIA	1.30m × 0.90m	*c.* 800°C	late 2nd-early 3rd century	Very heavy cobble base.
28	3	33	Smithing hearth PIC	1.50m × 0.80m	*c.*800°C	late 2nd-early 3rd century	Very heavy cobble base.
29	3		Smithing hearth		*c.* 400°C	early 2nd century	Inserted into annexe ditch. Poss. within Building F.
30	2	246	Smelting furnace	1.60m × 1.50m	1,100–1,200°C	early 2nd century	
31	2		Smelting furnace	approx. 2.00m × 2.30m	1,100–1,200°C	early 2nd century	
32	2	244	?	?	?	prob. early 2nd century	
33	4	113	?	0.52m across	?	prob. early 2nd century	pl. 15c.

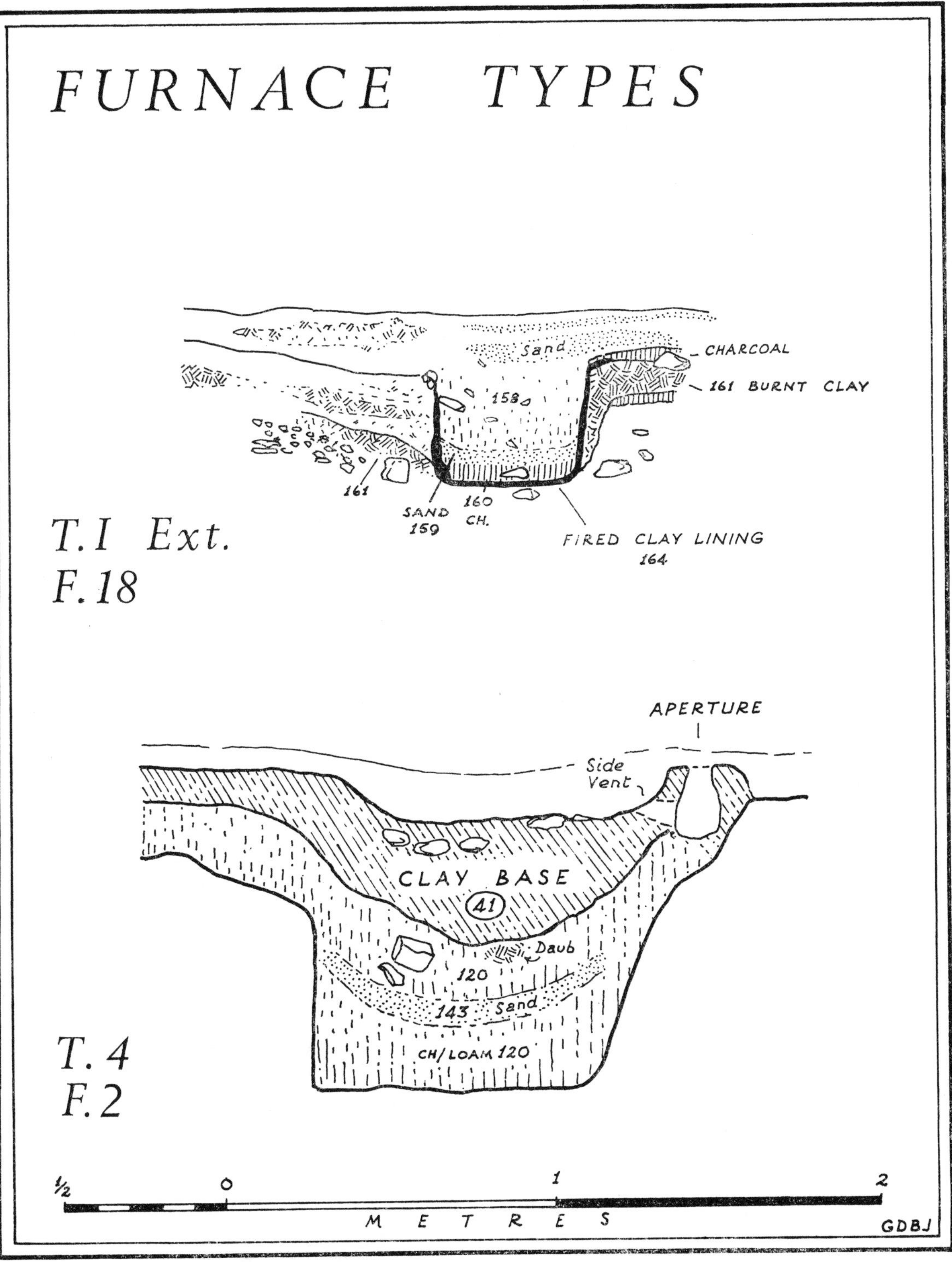

Fig. 28. Plan of furnaces 18 and 2.

vii: The post-Roman Period

ONE of the most potentially intriguing aspects of the Deansgate excavation lay in the possibility of archaeological levels surviving from the post-Roman and pre-Georgian period. The historical background that led to this possibility centred on the location of the Mercian *burgh*, known to have been established somewhere in Manchester in the ninth century. The details are discussed elsewhere in this volume (p. 165ff). Broadly speaking, prior to the excavation there appeared to be two main possibilities. The site of the Roman fort might have been re-utilised in the same way that another Mercian *burgh* was established within the defences of the hill-fort at Eddisbury in Cheshire. To support this line of thinking prior to excavation one might have argued from the record of nine Saxon *sceattae* found beneath the area of the City Exhibition Hall in the last century, and marked on one of Roeder's plans of central Manchester.[1] The late Roman coin evidence[2] leaves little doubt that the fort continued in existence into the fourth century and the early antiquaries quoted in an introductory chapter[3] attest the upstanding nature of the remains at Castlefield as late as the sixteenth century, i.e. the site did not become rapidly levelled and degraded. Against this must be set the evidence for the growth of early mediaeval Manchester. It is little understood in precise topographical terms but, as shown on p. 169, the mediaeval core grew up in the area of the Cathedral at the northern end of Deansgate, presumably within the defensive circuit known as the Hanging Ditch and Hunt's Bank, although little definitive can be said of these features which have never been met during development in this century, let alone subjected to archaeological investigation by modern methods.

With these considerations in mind, the examination of the uppermost levels of the excavation site was carried out in a particularly painstaking manner involving total area strippage that occupied some three to four weeks' examination of the relevant levels. None the less, the results remain not proven either way. The reason gradually became apparent across the whole site when it became clear that the latest Roman levels had been disturbed by agricultural cultivation. In the areas of the site where late Georgian intervention was not present, some 20–25 cm. separated the uppermost stratified Roman deposits from those associated with the development of housing round 1825–6. This was most clearly apparent in T.1 and T.2 to either side of White Lion Street where interference was minimal. The post-Roman levels in T.2, for instance, were represented by level 50, a dark reddish-brown loam with an admixture of medium-sized gravel and cobbles (fig. 11). On the south side of White Lion Street, the same deposit was represented by T.1, 70. The nature of these deposits gradually became apparent through the countless fragments of Roman pottery and tile, most of which had been heavily abraded or rounded through constant disturbance during cultivation. This had effectively truncated any possible trace of early mediaeval occupation, as well as removing stratified Roman levels of later than third century date except close to the exit road (p. 39). Thus any chance of settling this historical problem was removed.

Yet negative evidence has a value in archaeology. The cultivation level represents the archaeological evidence for the development of this particular area which is perhaps better known to history as a southward extension of the area of St. Peter's Fields, which lay in the area of the Free Trade Hall. The layer of cultivated soil above the Roman levels illustrates the history of the area throughout the later mediaeval and early modern period. In the earliest surviving map of Manchester and Salford, made about 1650 (partly shown on pl. 31a), actual settlement was limited to the area enclosed by the Hanging Ditch, the region of the Shambles, and linear development along Millgate, Market Street and, to the south-west, Deansgate. There, on the 1650 plan, houses are shown flanking the road running in the direction of Aldport

Lodge as far as the approximate position of Kendal Milne today. To either side of the ribbon development, however, there lay both pasture and arable running down towards the Irwell. The situation is depicted some seventy-eight years later in a south-western prospect of Manchester made in 1728 by S. and N. Buck. This shows (pl. 31b) that the area between Deansgate and the river was partly taken up by pasture which retained a few divisions but seemed to be used increasingly for recreational activities, and small plots of arable evidently fulfilling the role of market gardens. This particular etching does not quite reach the Castlefield area, stopping instead roughly in the position of the present Law Courts. The somewhat later etching of 1746 by R. Casson and J. Berry (partly reproduced in pl. 31a) moves the scene further south and shows, amongst other items, increased activity on the Irwell. There is a clearer view of the fields lying to either side of the antecedent of the present Quay Street. Lines of houses are shown running down from Deansgate, part of the way towards the river, but they are still separated by fields running up to the road itself, though the amount of arable appears to have been reduced. One of the important features of the particular map associated with this etching is that it fixes the name Aldport, now transformed to Alport, along the line of Deansgate to the south of Quay Street, i.e. in the area of the *vicus*, and in a position that tallies with references to it in pre-Norman sources (p. 170). More important for the actual Castlefield area is the evidence from two early maps of 1793 and 1820, reproduced as plates 32a and 32b. The earlier of these, drawn by Charles Laurent, is of particular importance. In the half-century separating this from the previous map, the face of Manchester had been transformed, and built-up areas extended across practically all the peninsula of land separating the Irwell from the Medlock. Extensive building, including the establishment of St. John's Church, had taken over much of the undeveloped area to the south of Quay Street, but Laurent's map is of particular importance in that it shows the area along the northern edge of Liverpool Road, then known as Preistner Street, as being devoted entirely to small market gardens that were intensively cultivated. The area of the actual excavation site immediately adjoins one of these patches and although it is shown as grassed over at this stage it is reasonable to suppose that it too was at times devoted to arable use. On that map of 1793 only one building, of unexplained purpose, is marked in the area of the excavation. The fort itself, marked as Castlefield, was also substantially clear although access tracks and enclosure walls were eroding its banks. Yet redevelopment must have been imminent because the whole area between Collier Street and Deansgate had been developed. This meant that the three blocks separating Collier Street from Deansgate, i.e. by means of Southern Street and Barton Street, had all been built up. The value of the map in question is that it shows the uses to which individual plots were put. The next map, dated to 1818–19, and made by William Johnson, who published it in 1820, is also of importance (pl. 32b). Although it does not show individual land utilisation, it is possible to see that now two buildings at least occupy the area of the excavation. Yet the bulk of the zone must have remained free as gardens. The evidence for the development of the area up to this date is borne out by that supplied by the clay pipes found on the site (p. 141, fig. 49).

The last two maps, spanning the last quarter of the eighteenth and the first quarter of the nineteenth century show that the whole area was in the grip of major social and industrial change. To the north-east, the Free Trade Hall was built in 1838, on the Fields of Peterloo; but elsewhere, particularly close to the confluence of the Irwell and the Medlock, development had an altogether seamier face. Behind the spacious late-Georgian façades of St. John's Street, there sprang up workers' houses, many of which remained in position until the cycle of urban renewal in the 1960's. It was houses of this kind that covered the excavation site and can still be seen standing on the air photograph of 1947 reproduced as plate 1. The date of their construction can be attributed with confidence to the year 1825, because the first recorded birth

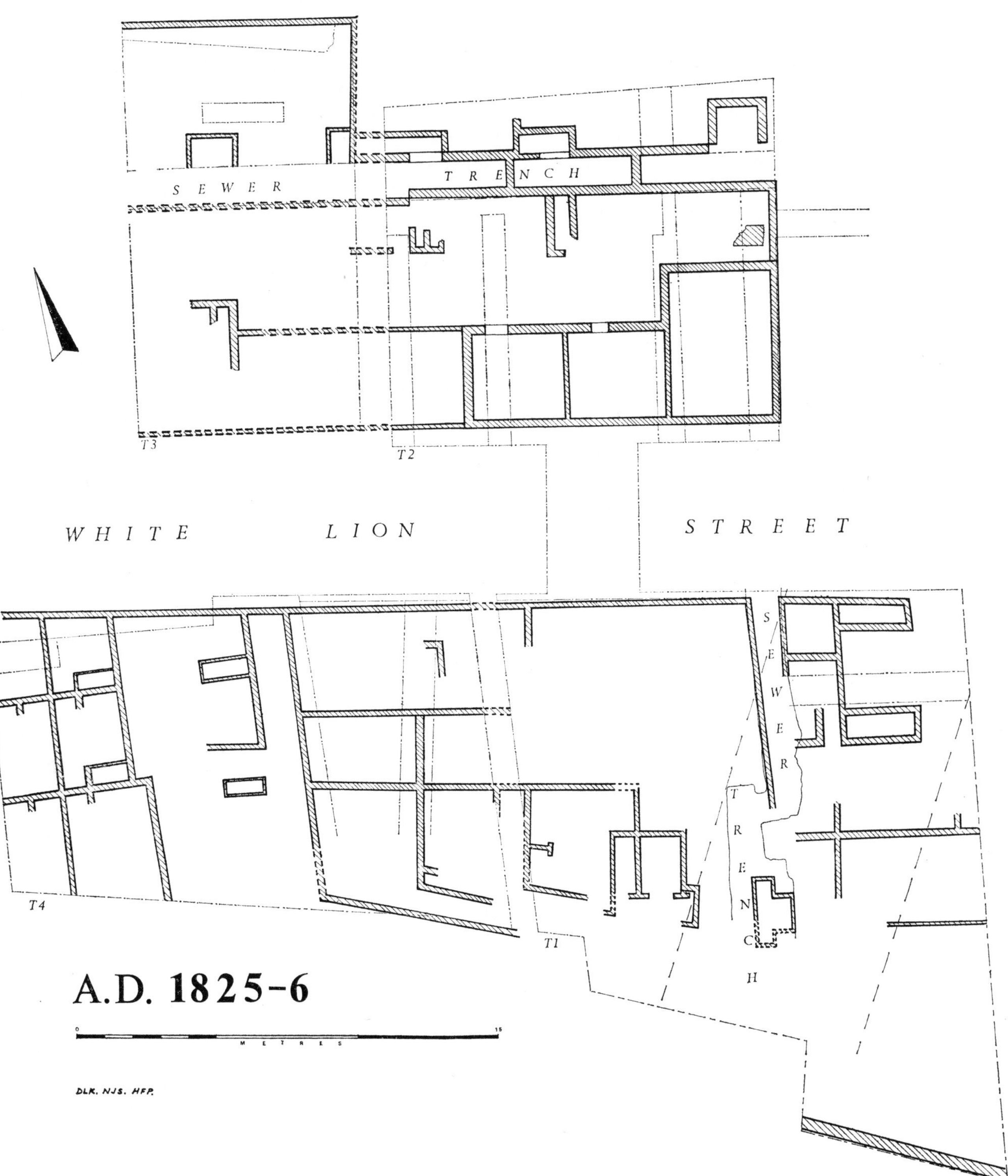

Fig. 29. General plan of late Georgian buildings built 1825–6 (p. 77).

certificates from the streets concerned—White Lion, Stone and Collier Streets—relate to the year 1826. The detailed plan of the foundations, excluding the front rooms, on Bridgewater Street and Liverpool Road (which all had cellars) is shown in fig. 29. The clearest indication of plan actually occurs in the houses on the north side of White Lion Street, particularly in the area of T.2. Structurally they were less substantial than their neighbours fronting the two major roads and the absence of cellars rendered them less destructive to the underlying Roman levels. Taking the plan as excavated in conjunction with the aerial photograph, it is possible to see that the houses were of the simple two-up, two-down variety, with access direct into the front room from the pavement. The back yards were minimal with a distance of some 7 to 8 metres separating the rear of houses in adjoining roads. There was no alleyway between the houses on Liverpool Road and White Lion Street but a major sewer ran roughly along the dividing line through the back yards. Considerations of lay-out suggest that an alley-way running off Collier Street did partly separate the houses on the south side of White Lion Street from those on the north side of Bridgewater Street. The alley was blocked, however, on the western side by buildings flanking the eastern edge of Stone Street. There is little else one can say of the plan as surviving in fig. 29, save to point out that it survived until the late sixties of the twentieth century, substantially without change apart from the addition of a few extra drains and sewers.

NOTES

1 See p.17.
2 See p.137.
3 See p.14.

II: The Finds

i: The Decorated Samian

PROFESSOR ERIC BIRLEY, M.B.E., M.A., F.B.A., F.S.A.

Form 29

1. Lower zone of decoration of continuous winding scroll in poor condition that prevents identification of the upper concavity. A pre-Vespasianic date is suggested. T.4(6)
2. Two conjoining fragments. The lower scroll inside the lower concavity shows part of a bird in a circular wreath. The concavity below the wreath is filled with a triangle of leaf tips. Of the upper zone part of a continuous winding zone survives and the contour of the carination appears relatively early, like the carination of a form 37 rather than the more developed shape of a Flavian form 29. The date could well be *c.* A.D. 70, or perhaps a little earlier. The vessel comes from a very worn mould. T.1(210)

As far as the other pieces of form 29 are concerned all would be appropriate in an Agricolan context.

3. Part of the upper zone. Vespasianic and the best glaze in the whole collection of samian ware from Manchester. T.1(3)
4. Slightly coarse upper zone of a later Flavian form 29. T.4(2)
5. A small piece of upper zone with hindquarters and tail of greyhound to right. The vessel has been broken and mended. Very large bead roll below the rim. T1.(65)
6. Part of lower zone in panel decoration. To right 'St. Andrew's Cross', to left part of concentric circles once enclosing a figure type and with corners of the panel occupied by leaves on curling stems. Rather angular profile suggesting a date of A.D. 80+. T.2(234)
7. Central division below which a straight wreath of grass tufts appears and under them a wavy line, below which in turn there was probably panel decoration. Profile not particularly late. T.1(28)
8. Smaller piece with a similar decorative layout. T.1(3) [Not illustrated]
9. Footstand with extreme end of potter's stamp, possibly with the first letter an A? Upper decoration formed by a series of striated sausages set vertically. T.1(+)
10. Rouletted rim. T.1(176) [Not illustrated]
11. Small fragment, very worn, close to No.8 in decorative arrangements. T.4(5)
12. Form 29, upper zone. T.2(115)
13. Form 29, lower zone partly survives. T.1(149)
14. Form 29, lower straight wreath. T.2(134)

Several other fragments of Form 29, too small to be worth illustrating, were also found from T.2(260) and T.2(198)

South Gaulish Form 37

15. A delightful piece assignable to GERMANUS, presumably made early in the seventies, when he had begun experimenting with form 37. Note the absence of horizontal line below the ovolo. T.3(63)
16. Three pieces. two of them conjoining, of a comparatively early example of a Flavian form 37, with its upper and lower zones of decoration separated from each other by a continuous series of large rosettes, bordered above and below by rather coarse wavy lines. T.2(260)

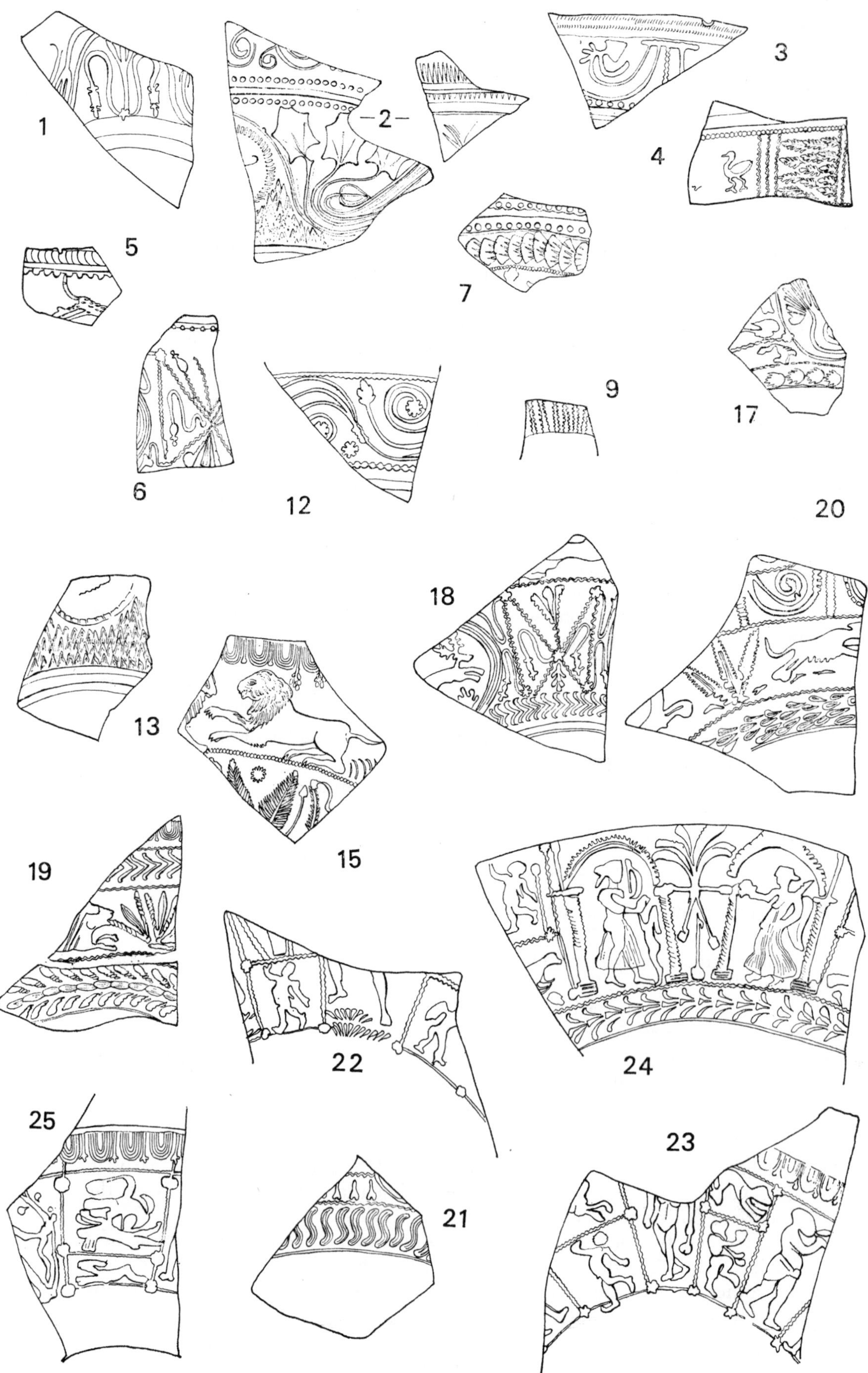

Fig. 30. Samian ware Nos. 1–7, 9, 12, 13, 15, 17–25 (scale ½).

17. A typical example of the style one might expect to find on a site occupied by Agricola. T.1(560)
18. *c.* A.D. 80. T.4(25)
19. Three conjoining fragments. A.D. 80–90. T.2(167)
20. A.D. 80–90. T.1(531)
21. An example of the S-type gadroon. ? Agricolan. T.4(140)
22. *c.* A.D. 90. T.4(47)
23. A.D. 90–100. T.4(68)
24. T.2(190)
25. T.3(+)
26. Typical late Domitianic piece, with irregular panels. T.4(29)
27. Domitianic. T.4(26)
28. Panel decoration with large 'St. Andrew's Cross'. This piece would be thought typical of an Agricolan context. T.2(52)
29. *c.* A.D. 80: note two zones of decoration divided by coarse wavy line. T.4(67)
30. *c.* A.D. 100. T.1(3)
31. *c.* A.D. 90–100. T.1(64)
32. *c.* A.D. 90. T.1(6)
33. *c.* A.D. 80. This piece would be thought typical of an Agricolan context. T.1(556)
34. *c.* A.D. 90. T.2(190)
35. *c.* A.D. 90. T.1(508)
36. ? *c.* A.D. 100. T.2(205)
37. *c.* A.D. 90—100. T.2(114)
38. [Not shown] T.1(510)
39. Large S-shaped gadroons. *c.* A.D. 90. T.2(134)
40. *c.* A.D. 90. T.2(126)
41. *c.* A.D. 90. This piece would be thought typical of an Agricolan context. T.2(134)
42. Another good example of one of the three-pronged ovolos which are characteristic of several South Gaulish potters working in the period A.D. 90–110. T.1(241)
43. [Not shown] T.2(25)
44. Similar ovolo and same period as No.83. This piece has been burnt black in a wood fire. T.4(162)
45. Badly abraded stamp below decoration, first letter probably O(F). T.2(182)

A few more fragments of South Gaulish form 37 not worth drawing were found in T.4(2), T.2(252), T.1(560) and T.1(577).

The impression given by the bulk of the South Gaulish form 37 is that much of it forms a collection such as has been found at Cannstatt, i.e. with a starting date of *c.* A.D. 90, but there are also enough pieces to indicate continuity of occupation from the time of Cerialis or even, just possibly, a few years earlier.

Miscellaneous South Gaulish Forms

46. Three pieces conjoining; a typical example of the rare Flavian form 67. T.2(260/262)
47. South Gaulish form 30. Worn fragment of late Flavian South Gaulish form 30. T.1/2(11)
48. Small fragment of form 78. Characteristically Flavian. T.1(41)
49. Small fragment of globular beaker with apparently appliqué decoration. T.2(205) [Not shown]
50. Small footstand and base of vessel of quite unusual form. T.1(41)

[Not shown] Two small pieces of a small, thin-walled bulbous beaker, undecorated. Probably Vespasianic. T.2(260/262)

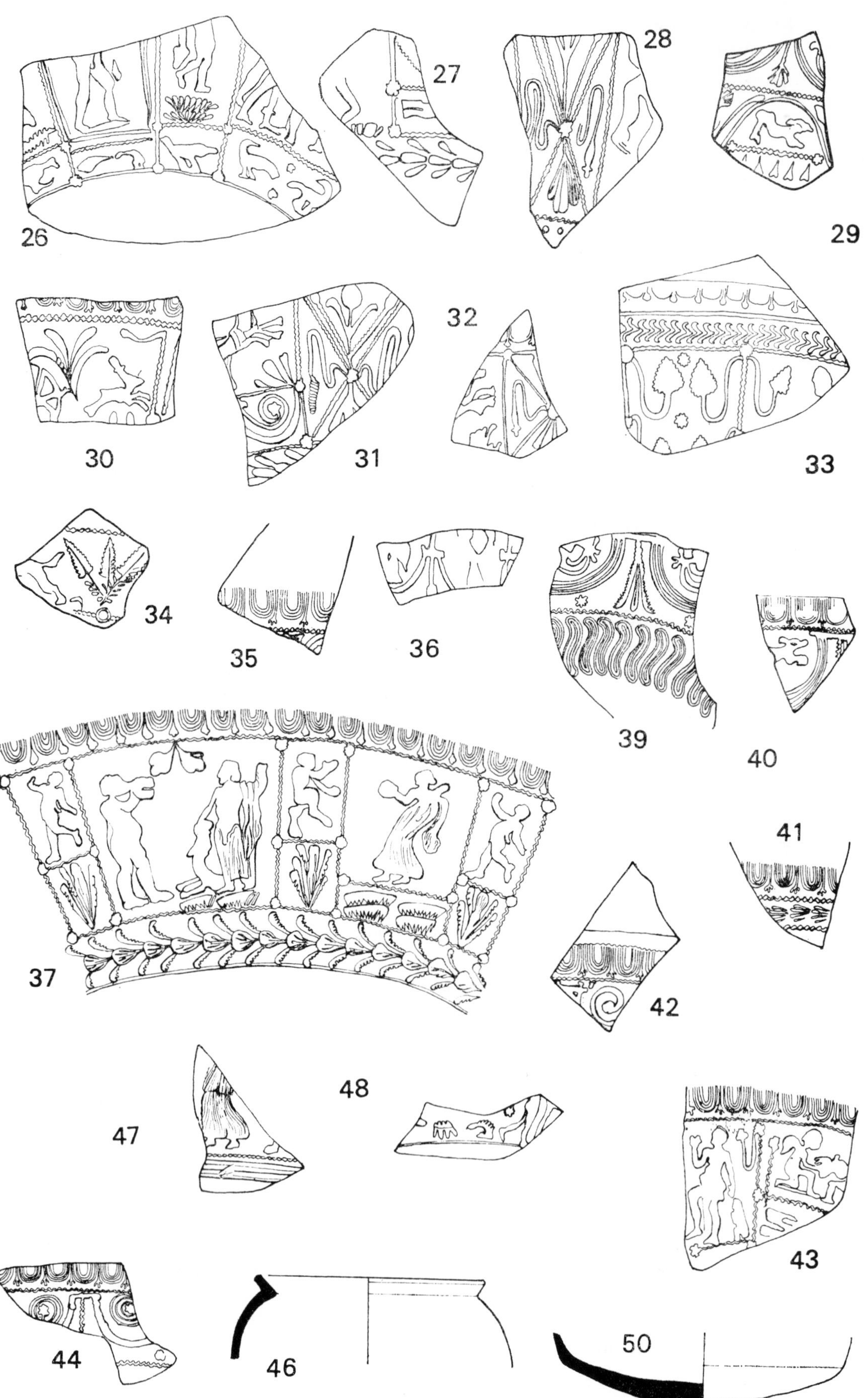

Fig. 31. Samian ware Nos. 26–37, 39–44, 46–48, 50 (scale ½).

Central Gaulish (except where specified otherwise, all of form 37)

The following eight pieces would all fit comfortably into the period A.D. 110–140, with the main weight towards the earlier part of that period.

51. Assignable to potter X-2, BILLICED(O). Trajanic. T.4(94)
52. Potter X-3, DRVSVS I. Trajanic. T.2(140)
53. Potter X-4, IGOTASCVS (shown on its side); *c.* A.D. 110–125. T.2(71)
54. Style of IOENALIS, with a botanical scroll instead of the more usual ovolo (cf. CGP, plate 37, 432); *c.* A.D. 110–120. T.4(171)
55. Three pieces from a bowl assignable to QVINTILIANVS or a member of his group; *c.* A.D. 120–135. T.2(69), T.2(55) and T.2(183)
56. Two pieces conjoining from a bowl assignable to PATERCLVS; *c.* A.D. 125–135. T.2(50), T.3(50)
57. Another product of the QVINTILIANVS group. Dating as no. 55. T.2(183)
58. Again, an association with QVINTILIANVS. Dating as nos. 55 and 57. T.2(134)

Next, four pieces assignable to the Antonine period.

59. *Form 30*. Three pieces from a bowl in the style of PATERNVS, in his characteristic free-style medley. After A.D. 150. T.3(30)
60. The ovolo and the different-sized circles in the field suggest an affinity with ADVOCISVS or LAXTVCISSA. Dating as no. 59. T.2(34)
61. Perhaps assignable to AVSTRVS (cf. CGP, plate 95, 19). Perhaps *c.* A.D. 150. T.4(140)
62. Also perhaps by AVSTRVS; the figure-type is 0. 124; *c.* A.D. 150? T.2(182)

The following three pieces provide a representative sample of the products of CINNAMVS yielded by the excavations. His firm was evidently in business for a very long period, but none of the Manchester pieces (also including no. 78, below) look to be earlier than *c.* A.D. 150.

63. Winding scroll, with large vine leaves in the upper concavity and an ornamental assembly capped by a hound to left in the lower concavity. T.1(511)
64. Similar winding scroll, with two contrasting leaves and bird in the upper concavity, figures in the lower one. T.2(52)
65. Design of arcades with caryatid supporters (cf. CGP, plate 161, 47). T.2(96)

The following six pieces are all assignable to CASVRIVS, who has one of the most distinctive styles of all the Antonine Central Gaulish makers of figured samian. A large number of bowls made by him is represented in the Corstopitum collection, but (for what it may be worth) they do not usually come from the destruction levels there which yield so many examples of the work of DIVIXTVS. Mr. B. R. Hartley has recently suggested that the work of CASVRIVS should be assigned to the period after A.D. 160 (*Britannia III*, 1972, 35f. and 53f.), in view of the fact that in Scotland it is at present only at Newstead and Cappuck that his products have been noted.

66. The small sea-horse to left is one of his favourite fillers of festoons. T.3(94)
67. [Not illustrated] T.2(115)
68. His version of Diana and the small hind, to left, is another of this potter's characteristic figure-types. T.2(181)
69. Fragment showing the smallest of his ovolos. T.2(134)
70. The same sea-horse as in no. 66, from a bowl in panel decoration (as are the majority of bowls by CASVRIVS). T.2(182)
71. Panel decoration, showing the reluctant beast to left, of which CASVRIVS was notably fond (cf. CGP, plate 137, 60). T.2(50)

The next five pieces are all assignable to PATERNVS. Of that potter Dr. Grace Simpson made the point (CGP, p.198) that his work is well represented on and south of Hadrian's Wall, but has not been noted anywhere in Scotland. Unless there are examples of his products among the unpublished Newstead material, to which Mr. Hartley has referred, the situation remains the same: one must therefore reckon on

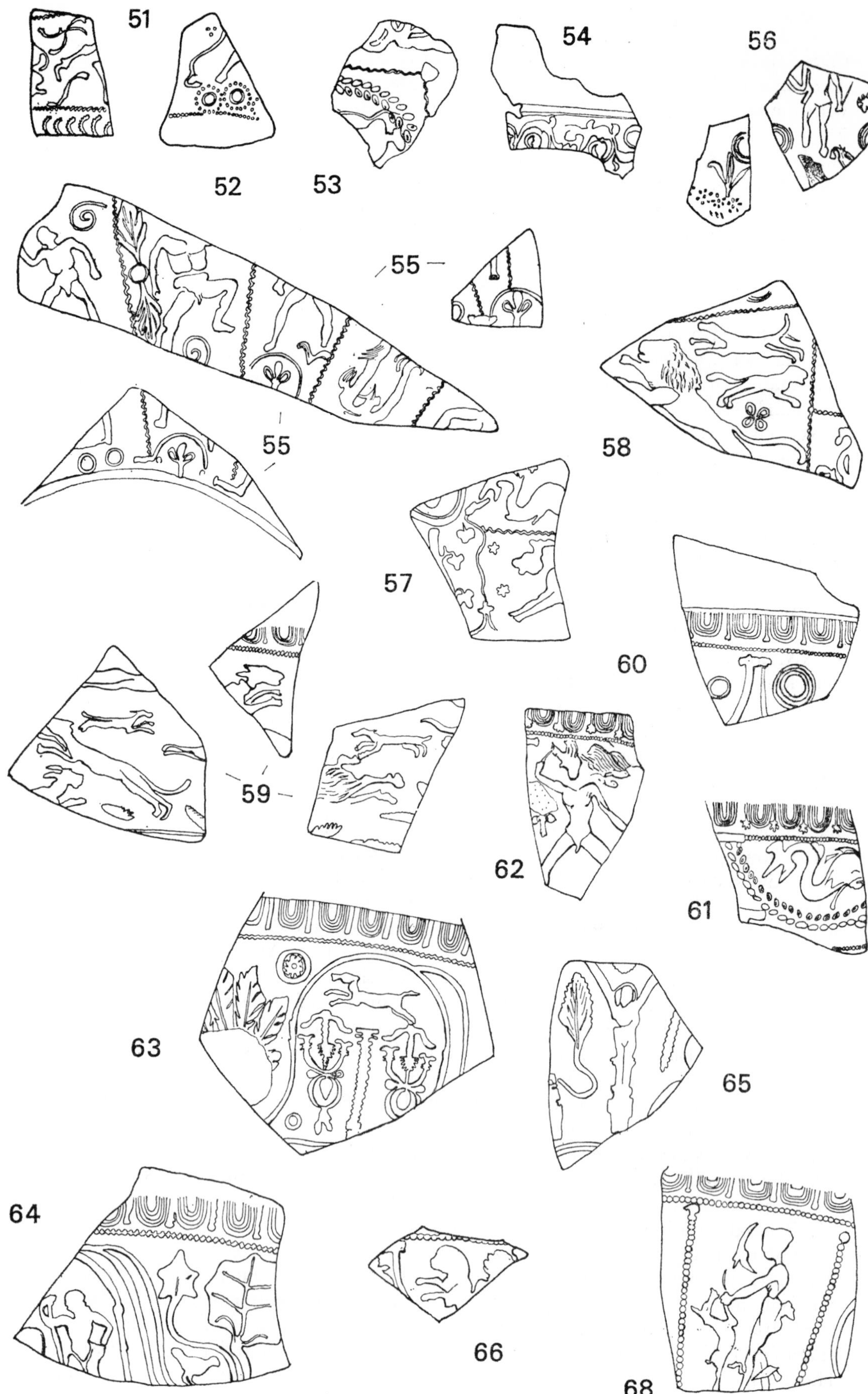

Fig. 32. Samian ware Nos. 51–66, 68 (scale ½).

the possibility that his products, like those of CASVRIVS, should be assigned to the period after A.D. 160.

72–74. [Not illustrated] Examples of his ovolos. T.3(94), T.1(516), T.3(25)

75. Panel decoration, with his characteristic corded dividing lines and satyr to front (when complete, standing on a mask, as in CGP, plate 104, 2 &c.). T.3(25)

76. *Form 30.* Free-style, from a bowl similar to no. 59, above. T.3(30)

Lastly, some more pieces assignable to the second half of the second century.

77. The ovolo with very thin tongue, and the coarse rosette which covers the junction of bead-rows subdividing a panel, combine to suggest that this is a product of the little-known potter BELSA. A stamped piece of his has recently been found at Vindolanda (Chesterholm), where by implication it should not be earlier than A.D. 160: it is to be published by Miss Louise Hird in the near future. T.3(2)

78. Free-style, assignable to CINNAMVS. T.2(91) and T.2(98)

79. Panel decoration, assignable to PATERNVS. T.3(40)

The next two pieces are assignable to DIVIXTVS, a potter whose decorated wares turn up regularly in the late second-century destruction deposits at Corstopitum, and also on the Antonine Wall and elsewhere in Scotland. Incidentally, the same can be said of the products of the Corstopitum mortarium makers, BELLICVS and SATV(RNINVS).

80. *Form 30.* Panel decoration with small plain rings masking the joins of the horizontal and vertical bead-rows; the ovolo with trifid tongue is one which DIVIXTVS used only occasionally. T.3(94)

81. Panel decoration showing several of this potter's characteristic details (cf. CGP, plate 116, 8 in particular). T.3(110)

Miscellaneous pieces

82. *Form 37.* Fragment showing crude circles and a vertical stroke, in effect a straight wreath below the (missing) decoration. I have no idea what the source of this piece may be. T.2(182)

83. *Form 37.* East Gaulish or German, probably later than A.D. 200. T.2(34)

84. *Form 67.* Profile of rim only shown as no. 46, above. South Gaulish. This form is virtually confined to the earlier part of the Flavian period. T.2(260)

Summary

The South Gaulish material and the Trajanic/Hadrianic vessels (nos. 1–58 and 84) give reasonable cover for the period *c.* A.D. 80–130, with a few South Gaulish vessels which might well be ten or twelve years earlier in date. The later Central Gaulish material seems to have its main weight after A.D. 150. In that connection, it may be worth while to point out that the current excavations at Vindolanda—where there is clear presumptive evidence for a gap in the site's occupation between *c.* A.D. 125–160—have already produced examples of the distinctive products of ADVOCISVS, CASVRIVS, DIVIXTVS and PATERNVS, and the pieces which are attributable to CINNAMVS help to suggest the dating for his Manchester material, given above. Judging by the figured samian, it seems that the part of the site examined in 1972 was not occupied between the governorships of Lollius Urbicus and Julius Verus or Calpurnius Agricola.

Stamped Samian

Full publication of the potters' stamps on Samian Ware is reserved for B. R. Hartley's forthcoming *Index of Potters' Stamps.* A total of seventeen stamps was found. Amongst these are included: on form 33 BIRAGILLUS (T.2.96), MICCIOMAN (T.2.50), REBURRI. OFF (T.1.69), SATURNINI (T.3.94), SEXTUSFE (T.2.206) and VINII; on form 31R PRITMANI. M (T.2.113); on form 18/31 DAGOMARUS; and on form 27 APOLINARIS (T.2.114).

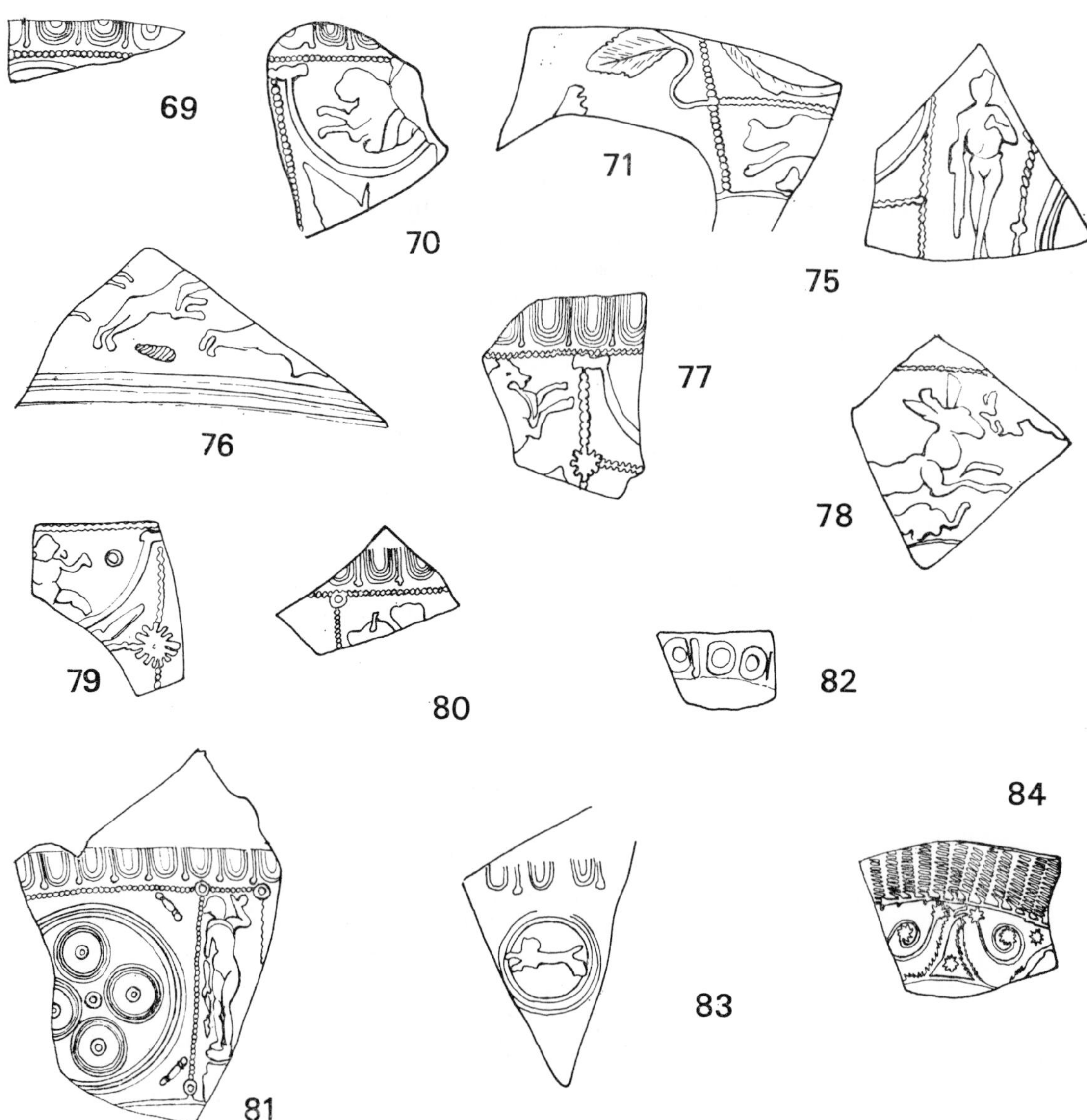

Fig. 33. Samian ware Nos. 69–71, 75–84 (scale $\frac{1}{2}$).

ii: The Coarse Pottery

PETER WEBSTER, B.A., M.Phil.

(*With contributions on the stamped mortaria by* MRS K. F. HARTLEY)

ACKNOWLEDGEMENTS

I should like to thank the large number of people who helped to arrange the pottery into some sort of order between my initial on-site sorting and the preparation of the final report. I should also like to thank Mrs. V. A. Jones for organising on-site drawing of pottery and Miss Shelagh Grealey who took charge of it once finds reached the Manchester University, Department of Archaeology; also the many people who prepared the drawings on which the final blocks are based. A number of the drawings (particularly those by Mr M. Snelgrove) betrayed considerable artistic talent and it is only with great reluctance that I have sacrificed these in order that the blocks should have an entirely consistent style and so that all vessels in the report should be capable of easy comparison one with the other.

ABBREVIATIONS USED IN THE COARSE POTTERY REPORT

AA_{1-4}. Archaeologia Aeliana 1st–4th Series.

Astley I. I. Walker, 'Excavations on a Romano-British site at Astley, 1956–8', *Trans. Worcs. Arch. Soc.* 35, (1958), pp. 29–57.

Balmuildy. S. N. Miller, *The Roman Fort at Balmuildy*, Glasgow, 1922.

Benwell 1926. J. A. Petch, 'Excavations at Benwell (Condercum)', *AA_4*, 4 (1927), pp. 135–92.

Bewcastle. I. A. Richmond, K. S. Hodgson, J. K. St. Joseph, 'The Roman Fort at Bewcastle', *C&W*, 38 (1938), pp. 195–239.

Birdoswald 1929. I. A. Richmond, E. B. Birley, 'Excavations on Hadrian's Wall in the Birdoswald–Pike Hill Sector, 1929', *C&W*, 30 (1930), pp. 169–205.

Brixworth. P. J. Woods, *Brixworth Excavations*, Vol. 1, Northampton 1971.

Caerleon Amphitheatre. R. E. M. and T. V. Wheeler, 'The Roman Amphitheatre at Caerleon, Monmouthshire', *Archaeologia*, 78 (1928), pp. 111–218.

Callender. M. H. Callender, *Roman Amphorae*, Durham 1965.

Camulodunum. C. F. C. Hawkes, M. R. Hull, *Camulodunum*, Report of the Research Committee of the Society of Antiquaries of London, No. 14, London 1947.

Carpow. R. E. Birley, 'Excavation of the Roman Fortress at Carpow, Perthshire, 1961–2', *Proc. Soc. Ant. Scotland*, 96 (1962–3), pp. 184–207.

Carrawburgh Mithraeum. I. A. Richmond, J. P. Gillam, 'The Temple of Mithras at Carrawburgh', *AA_4*, 21 (1951), pp. 1–92.

Castleshaw. F. A. Bruton, *The Roman Forts at Castleshaw* (1st & 2nd Report), Manchester 1908–11.

Chester: Deanery Field 1928. J. P. Droop, R. Newstead, 'Excavations in the Deanery Field, Chester, 1928. Pt. II. The Finds'. *Annals of Arch. & Anth.*, 18 (1931), pp. 113ff.

Chesterholm. E. and M. Birley, 'Fourth Report on Excavations at Chesterholm-Vindolanda', *AA_4*, 15 (1938), pp. 22–237.

Collingwood & Richmond. R. G. Collingwood, I. A. Richmond, *The Archaeology of Roman Britain*, Revised edition, London 1969.

Corbridge 1911. R. H. Forster, W. H. Knowles, 'Corstopitum: Report on the Excavations in 1911', *AA_3*, 8 (1912), pp. 137–263.

Corbridge 1937. E. Birley, I. A. Richmond, 'Excavations at Corbridge, 1936–38', *AA_4*, 15 (1938), pp. 243–94.

Corbridge 1954. I. A. Richmond, J. P. Gillam, 'Some excavations at Corbridge, 1952–4', *AA_4*, 33 (1955), pp. 218–52.

Crambeck. P. Corder, *The Roman Pottery at Crambeck, Castle Howard*, Roman Malton and District Report No. 1. York 1928.

C&W. Transactions of the Cumberland & Westmorland Antiquarian & Archaeological Society, New Series.

Droitwich: Bays Meadow. P. S. Gelling, 'Report on the Excavations in Bays Meadow, Droitwich, Worcestershire, 1954–5'. *Trans. Birmingham Arch. Soc.*, 75 (1957), pp. 1–23.

Farrar 1968. R. A. H. Farrar, 'A late-Roman Black-burnished Pottery Industry in Dorset and its affinities', *Proc. Dorset Nat. Hist. & Arch. Soc.*, 90 (1968), pp. 174–80.

Farrar 1973. R. A. H. Farrar, 'The Techniques and sources of Romano-British Black-burnished ware', pp. 67–103, in A. Detsicas (Ed.), *Current Research in Romano-British Coarse Pottery*, Council for British Archaeology Research Report No. 10. 1973.

Gillam. J. P. Gillam, *Types of Roman Coarse Pottery Vessels in Northern Britain*, Newcastle upon Tyne 1970.

Gillam 1973. J. P. Gillam, 'Sources of Pottery found on Northern Military sites', pp. 53–62 in A. Detsicas (Ed.), *Current Research in Romano-British Coarse Pottery*, C.B.A. Research Report No. 10. 1973.

Glenlochar. I. A. Richmond, J. K. St. Joseph, 'The Roman Fort at Glenlochar', *Dumfries & Galloway Nat. Hist. & Ant. Soc. Trans.*, 30 (1951–2), pp. 1–16.

Gloucester: Bon Marché. A. G. Hunter, 'Excavations at the Bon Marché site, Gloucester, 1958–9', *Trans. Bristol & Gloucs. Arch. Soc.*, 82 (1963), pp. 25–65.

Great Casterton III. Philip Corder (Ed.), *3rd Report on the Roman Sites at Great Casterton*, Nottingham 1961.

Heronbridge. B. R. Hartley, K. F. Kaine, 'Excavations at Heronbridge, 1947–8', *J. Chester Archit. Arch. & Hist. Soc.*, 39 (1952), pp. 1–20.

Holt. W. F. Grimes, *Holt, Denbighshire*, London 1930.

Kaye. W. J. Kaye, *Roman (and Other) Triple Vases*, London 1914.

Leicester: Jewry Wall. K. M. Kenyon, *Excavations at the Jewry Wall Site, Leicester*, Report of the Research Committee of the Society of Antiquaries of London, No. 15, 1948.

Leigh Sinton. P. L. Waters, 'A Romano-British Tile Kiln at Upper Sandlin Farm, Leigh Sinton, Worcs.', *Trans. Worcs. Arch. Soc.*, 15 (1963), pp. 1–5.

Littlechester Kilns. M. Brassington, 'A Trajanic Kiln Complex at Littlechester, Derby, 1968', *Ant. J.*, 51 (1971), pp. 36–69.

Manchester. F. A. Bruton (Ed.), *The Roman Fort at Manchester*, Manchester 1909.

Melandra Castle. J. A. Petch, 'The Date of Melandra Castle: Evidence of the Pottery', *Derbys. Arch. J.*, 69 (1949), pp. 1–40.

Milecastle 9. E. B. Birley, 'Excavations on Hadrian's Wall West of Newcastle upon Tyne in 1929', AA_4, 7 (1930), pp. 143–74.

Milecastle 48. J. P. Gibson, F. G. Simpson, 'The Milecastle on the Wall of Hadrian at the Poltross Burn', *C&W*, 11 (1911), pp. 390–461.

Mumrills. G. MacDonald, A. O. Curle, 'The Roman Fort at Mumrills near Falkirk', *Proc. Soc. Ant. Scotland*, 63 (1928–9), pp. 396–575.

Mumrills 1958–60. K. A. Steer et al., 'Excavations at Mumrills Roman Fort, 1958–60', *Proc. Soc. Ant. Scotland*, 94 (1960–1), pp. 86–132.

Newstead 1911. J. Curle, *A Roman Frontier Post and its People. The Fort of Newstead in the Parish of Melrose*, Glasgow 1911.

Northwich 1968–70. P. V. Webster, 'Coarse Pottery', pp. 66–73 in G. D. B. Jones et al., 'Excavations at Northwich (Condate)', *Arch. J.*, 128 (1971), pp. 31–77.

Northwich Kiln. W. S. Hanson, 'The Kiln Group', pp. 50–53 in the same report as *Northwich 1968–70* above.

O&P. F. Oswald, T. D. Pryce, *Introduction to the Study of Terra Sigillata*, London 1920.

Peacock 1973. D. P. S. Peacock, 'The Black-burnished Pottery Industry in Dorset', pp. 63–5 in A. Detsicas (Ed.), *Current Research in Romano-British Coarse Pottery*, C.B.A. Research Report No. 10. 1973.

Richborough IV. J. P. Bushe-Fox, *Fourth Report on the Excavations of the Roman Fort at Richborough, Kent.* Report of the Society of Antiquaries of London, No. 16. 1949.

Silchester. T. May, *The Pottery found at Silchester*, Reading 1916.

Slack. P. W. Dodd, A. M. Woodward, 'Excavations at Slack, 1913–15', *Yorks. Arch. J.*, 26 (1922), pp. 1–92.

Sutton Walls. K. M. Kenyon, 'Excavations at Sutton Walls, Herefordshire, 1948–51', *Arch. J.*, 110 (1953), pp. 1–87.

Turret 25b. C. Woodfield, 'Six Turrets on Hadrian's Wall', AA_4, 42 (1965), pp. 87–200. For *Turret 25b* see pp. 108–27; *Turret 26a*, pp. 128–50; *Turret 35a*, pp. 151–61.

Turret 26a. See *Turret 25b* above.

Turret 35a. See *Turret 25b* above.
Turret 50a. F. G. Simpson et al., 'Excavations on the Line of the Roman Wall in Cumberland during the years 1909–12', *C&W,* 13 (1913), pp. 297–397. For Turret 50a see pp. 350–1.
Verulamium I. S. S. Frere, *Verulamium Excavations.* Vol. I. Report of the Research Committee of the Society of Antiquaries of London. No. 28. London 1972.
Webster 1972. P. V. Webster, 'Severn Valley Ware on Hadrian's Wall', *AA_4*, 50 (1972), pp. 191–203.
Whitchurch. G. D. B. Jones, P. V. Webster, 'Excavations at Whitchurch, Shropshire, 1965–6', *Arch. J.*, 125 (1968), pp. 193–254.
Wilderspool Kilns. K. F. Hartley, P. V. Webster, 'The Romano-British Pottery Kilns near Wilderspool', *Arch. J.*, 130 (1973), forthcoming.
Wroxeter III. J. P. Bushe-Fox, *Third Report on the Excavations on the site of the Roman Town at Wroxeter, Shropshire, 1914.* Report of the Research Committee of the Society of Antiquaries of London. No. 4. London 1916.
Wroxeter 1923–7. D. Atkinson, *Report on Excavations at Wroxeter 1923–1927,* Birmingham 1942.
Wroxeter 1936–7. K. M. Kenyon, 'Excavations at Viroconium, 1936–7', *Archaeologia,* 88 (1938), pp. 175–228.
Wroxeter 'Pottery Factory'. A. W. J. Houghton, 'A Roman Pottery Factory near Wroxeter, Salop', *Trans. Shropshire Arch. Soc.*, 57 (1961–4), pp. 101–11.

Note: In the accompanying catalogue, the codes at the end of each item marked thus: 4.68 refer to the trench and layer numbers of the individual piece concerned.

INTRODUCTION

This report is intended primarily to present the detailed dating evidence for specific features on the site. The information thus provided is, however, capable of a more generalised interpretation, particularly in two much broader fields: the over-all dating of the site excavated and its economic links, as a market for pottery, with its sources of manufacture.

I. DATING

(a) *The Starting Date*

Flavian-Trajanic pottery is present in fairly large quantity and settlement certainly started in this period. The over-all assemblage is very similar to that from the Pennine Forts such as Ribchester, Slack and Melandra Castle all thought to have been founded at the time of the Agricolan advance of *c.* A.D. 79. From the coarse pottery alone it is not possible to be more precise as to the beginning of the settlement on this part of the site, but such evidence as there is agrees with a date in the later A.D. 70s suggested on the basis of the samian evidence.[1]

(b) *The Main Occupation*

As well as Flavian-Trajanic pottery already mentioned, pottery of a Hadrianic and Antonine date is also present in some quantities, suggesting continuous and extensive activity on the site excavated up to the close of the second century A.D. Pottery of the third century is somewhat less numerous, but still sufficient in quantity to suggest that activity continued without interruption well into that century. There is, however, an almost total lack of pottery types which can be reliably dated to the late third century and later. There are, for instance, none of the latest types of Black-burnished ware to reach Northern Britain, the jars with rims that flare well out beyond the line of the rest of the vessel (*Gillam* types 147–8) or the flanged and beaded bowls (*Gillam* type 228), all of which are characteristic of the close of Period II on Hadrian's Wall and of Period III. Thus extensive occupation on the site excavated must have ended before the last decade of the third century and a terminal date in the mid-third or, at most, the mid/late-third century seems best to fit the evidence.

(c) *The Latest Roman Activity*

There is no evidence for Roman occupation of the site later than the terminal date suggested above. It seems clear that both habitation and industrial activity on the site must have ended by this time. However, it would be surprising on a site so close to a fort which certainly continued in use up to the close of the Roman period in Britain[2] if there was not some indication of a Roman presence nearby. This is exactly what we have. Nos. 217–26 below, and the discussion which accompanies them, gather together pieces which *may be* of a later date than that suggested for the end of the main occupation of the site. Most can, however, be made to fit with the terminal date suggested, leaving only four pieces which *need be* later than mid-third century in date. These are all from vessels characteristic of the fourth and last occupation period on Hadrian's Wall and of the latest occupation period in the fort of Manchester itself. They almost certainly denote no more than the spreading upon derelict land of rubbish from the nearby fort at some time in the late fourth century.

(d) *The Post-Roman Period*

All the pottery from the excavation, whether stratified or not, was examined, but not a single sherd was identified as belonging to the period between the end of the Roman period and the seventeenth/eighteenth century. There was thus no evidence of occupation, or of anything but agricultural activity, on the site excavated between the Roman period and the Industrial Revolution.

II. THE SOURCES OF POTTERY REACHING ROMAN MANCHESTER

This section is intended to be a broad survey of the sources of pottery found on the site excavated in 1972, although a superficial examination of the material published in the 1909 report (cited below as *Manchester*) does not suggest any major differences between sources of pottery for the Fort and for the civil settlement. This is, of course, an attempt to discuss one site only. Many of the conclusions do, however, hold good for the whole of the Northern military zone. For a discussion of the sources of supply of this Northern zone as a whole, readers are recommended to J. P. Gillam's masterly reappraisal of the subject in the *CBA Research Report, No. 10* (1973).[3]

(a) *The Flavian-Trajanic Period*

The sources of this period are difficult to identify, probably because of their size and number—a mass of small centres many of which were producing broadly similar products, bulbous and pear-shaped jars, many with everted rims, flanged and often reeded bowls, etc. It seems likely that at a fort like Manchester, there would be a potter or potters operating in the vicus, as at nearby Melandra Castle,[4] even if the unit at Manchester did not possess its own pottery and tile kiln.[5] Whatever the sources in the immediate vicinity of fort and civil settlement, other local sources were probably also being drawn upon, as there is present at Manchester a class of pottery broadly characteristic of the whole Cheshire Plain area: self-coloured fabrics, many of them oxidised and high in a fine sand content.[6] Pottery was also being imported from elsewhere; the cheese strainer No. 6 is unlikely to be a local product, while the mortaria stamped by G. Attius Marinus (No. 50) and Albinus (Nos. 173 and 252) show that already by this period a trading connection with the Midlands had been established. As throughout the Roman period, vessels were also reaching the site as containers for its supply of oil, wine and perhaps other commodities; the globular amphorae (probably from Spain) are the most obvious example of this class of vessel but other vessels represented below may also have reached the site in this way (see, for example, No. 11).

(b) *A.D. 120–*c. *A.D. 250*

Evidence from elsewhere in the North suggests a major reorganisation of the supply of pottery at the time of the construction of Hadrian's Wall.[7] It is at this time that Black-burnished ware makes its first appearance in Northern Britain. In the Wall zone its introduction can be closely dated to the period A.D. 120–125 and there seems little reason to doubt that the ware first appears elsewhere in the military zone at approximately the same time. The North-West was certainly soon flooded with these wares[8] which drove off the market the jars and flanged bowls of the earlier period, replacing them with characteristic Black-burnished forms (see, for example, Nos. 235 and 242 below).

Black-burnished wares have been divided into two main categories (abbreviated for convenience to BB1 and BB2).[9] BB2 first makes its appearance in Northern Britain *c.* A.D. 140, but it does not appear on the West side of the Pennines in any significant quantity, if at all; certainly it is absent not only from Manchester but also from Ribchester and Lancaster;[10] it does not appear at Carlisle or in the Wall zone West of the Irthing (Turret 48a).[11] It therefore seems reasonable to assume separate supply routes for the two sides of the Pennines and probably separate contracts and store-distribution-centres as well. All the pottery described as 'Black-burnished ware' in the report below is in fact BB1 and the BB1 'factory'[12] remains one of the major sources of the Manchester pottery through the period of occupation of the site excavated in 1972. Taking this with the evidence from the Fort, it is clear that BB1 continued to reach Manchester, as elsewhere in the North, right up to the late A.D. 360's.

Other sources are apparent in the Hadrianic-Antonine period. Wilderspool products, including mortaria, attest local sources in the Cheshire Plain, and supplies could have come from more than one source here. Connections with non-local sources were still maintained, however, as the various Midlands mortaria (e.g. No. 254) attest and this connection appears to have been maintained into the third century.

There were, however, new sources (supplying fabrics other than BB1 to the site) which entered upon the scene during the course of the second century. In the mid/late second century Manchester began to receive pottery from the Severn Basin, the characteristic oxidised fabric known as Severn Valley Ware, much less sandy than the Cheshire Plain products and occurring in a series of readily identifiable forms.[13] The ware first appears at Manchester in levels associated with Building D (Nos. 57, 68–9) and is present throughout the remainder of the main occupation of the site excavated. Most of the standard Severn Valley ware classes of vessel are present: narrow-necked storage jars (e.g. No. 163), wide-mouthed jars (e.g. Nos. 171 and 206) and tankards (No. 68), although the latter is represented by only two examples. It seems likely that the sources of Severn Valley ware were scattered throughout the Severn Basin, and in this respect it is of interest to compare the Severn Valley ware at Manchester with that from the Hadrian's Wall area.[14] In the Wall zone Severn Valley ware was present from as early as A.D. 130 (tankards from Milecastle 50TW) and was present in small quantities up to about the close of the second century. The forms represented are predominantly tankards. The ware appears later at Manchester, but continues to reach the site for much longer. In addition, the forms represented are much more varied, with tankards forming a distinct minority. In this, Manchester resembles Whitchurch, Shropshire (where the ware was introduced in the (?)mid-second century and where tankards are completely absent) and to a lesser extent Wroxeter (where the ware was introduced in about the mid-second century but where tankards are plentiful). It seems likely that the potters producing Severn Valley ware had not moved into the Northern part of the Severn Basin until the mid-second century and that when they did, it was from this area that Manchester was supplied. The source of the Severn Valley ware on the Wall must, by contrast, lie further South as it is only there that kilns were in production at the required time. Export to the Wall zone via the Bristol Channel and the Solway seems possible, therefore.[15] The quantity of Severn Valley ware at Manchester is not great enough to suggest a source of supply nearer than the upper Severn Basin, it was certainly receiving neither the volume nor the variety of Wroxeter or Whitchurch and clearly lies outside the production area for the ware.

Towards the end of the second century colour-coated fabrics first made their appearance at Manchester (they do not appear in levels associated with Building D but are present in those associated with Building E). The ware never formed a very high proportion of the pottery reaching Manchester but it obviously fulfilled a demand for fine tableware, particularly beakers (virtually all of the Manchester colour-coated ware is from beakers), and it is present in sufficient quantity to add a distinctive character to the third-century deposits. Dr J. P. Wild has kindly examined all the colour-coated fragments from the excavations and confirmed that most, if not all, are of Nene Valley origin. This reflects the general dominance of Nene Valley products among colour-coated wares in the North (even on the Western side of the Pennines). It is notable that no imported colour-coated fabrics were identified.

(c) *The Latest Pottery*

There is so little pottery from the period after the mid/late third century that it is probably dangerous to generalise. However, the four definitely fourth-century pieces all conform to a single picture: they are Northern in origin and probably derived from kilns in East Yorkshire which provided the overwhelming bulk of the pottery in Northern England after the disaster of A.D. 367. In fact, in what is undoubtedly a random sample (from rubbish scattered from the final phase fort) one could hardly wish for a more representative collection.

CATALOGUE

The coarse pottery has been divided into sections below according to the supposed function of the features with which it was associated:

A. Military Activity.
B. Civilian Buildings.
C. Industrial Activity.
D. Roads.
E. Disturbed and Unstratified levels.

The material from the levels illustrated will shortly be deposited in the Manchester Museum (University of Manchester).

The *coarseness* of the vessels has been described according to the following criteria:

(a) A fabric has been described as *sandy* where it approaches the granular texture of Black-burnished ware Category 1.

(b) It has been described as *smooth* where it approaches the texture of samian ware.

(c) Where no description of coarseness has been offered, it can be implied that the fabric described has a texture which is either well known and described elsewhere (e.g. Black-burnished ware) or that it falls between the categories outlined above.

The nature of the subsoil at Manchester has not made it possible to make any meaningful description of *hardness* for most of the vessels, as soil action seems likely to have changed this radically since deposition. However, exceptionally well-fired vessels did sometimes survive unscathed and these have been described as *hard* where they could not be scratched by the fingernail (2.5 on Moh's scale of hardness) and offered reasonable resistance to a steel blade (6.5 on Moh's scale). In most cases they can be considered to have a hardness of about 4 on Moh's scale. The description of *soft* was reserved for those fabrics which seemed likely to have always been capable of being easily scratched by the fingernail, even allowing for the later action of the soil.

A. MILITARY OCCUPATION

From the palisade ditch/slot:

1. Amphora handle bearing the worn and fragmentary stamp QVTI. The letter Q seems more likely than the alternative letter O. This may be *Callender* No. 1512 (p. 233) belonging to Quietus. 3.139.

From the multiple ditches:

2. Jar in grey fabric; cf. *Gillam* type 101 (A.D. 70–110). 2.168.
3. Hemispherical bowl reminiscent of the samian form 37; cf. *Whitchurch*, 117. 2.168.
6. Cheese strainer in a smooth light buff fabric; cf. *Gillam* type 350. Gillam dates this type by its appearance at the Antonine fort of Mumrills but there seems no reason why a wider date range should not be possible for such a utilitarian object; cf. for example, a similar vessel of late 1st–early 2nd century date from Holt (*Holt*, 206). 2.262.

No. 6 above comes from the seal of ditch 2.248 as do the following items from demolished buildings pushed into the ditches.

7. Beaker in fawn fabric; cf. *Northwich 1968–70*, 18 (although our example is thicker than that from Northwich), late 1st–early 2nd century. 2.260.
8. Jar in soft pink-buff fabric; cf. *Whitchurch*, 133 (late 1st–early 2nd century). 2.260.
9. Rim of an everted-rim jar in smooth pink fabric; cf. *Gillam* type 101 (A.D. 70–110). 2.260.
10. Jar in fawn-buff fabric; cf. *Newstead 1911*, Fig. 25, 7 (A.D. 80–105); *Chesterholm*, 49 (A.D. 90–125). 2.260.

11. Neck of a jar in thick pink-buff fabric. This would appear to be part of a large storage vessel not unlike the *Dolia* which are a feature of storehouses, inns, etc., in such Italian towns as Ostia and Pompeii. 2.260.
12. Jar in grey fabric with rusticated decoration; cf. *Gillam* type 105 (A.D. 80–120); *Glenlochar*, 2 (A.D. 80–105), this latter has applied decoration as in our example. 2.260.
13. Flanged bowl in a hard fairly sandy grey fabric; cf. *Holt*, 90 (late 1st–early 2nd century). 2.260.
14. Flanged bowl in a sandy grey fabric; it is somewhat similar to *Gillam* type 215 (A.D. 80–125) and *Newstead 1911*, Fig. 26, 11 (A.D. 80–105); see also *Melandra Castle*, 2. 2.260.
15. Dish in pink-buff fabric, burnished externally; cf. *Holt*, 129 (late 1st–early 2nd century). 2.260.
16. Base of a bowl or dish in smooth orange fabric, with a circular groove around the base internally. It is perhaps intended to be reminiscent of one of the samian bowl/dish forms. 2.260.
17. Lid in hard mid-grey fabric. 2.260.

Nos. 7–17 seem uniformly to be of pre-Hadrianic date and the life of the buildings from which they derive must fall within the period later 1st to early 2nd century.

B. CIVILIAN BUILDINGS

(i) *Building A.*

18. Neck of a flagon in a fairly hard grey fabric; cf. *Whitchurch*, 143 (late 1st–early 2nd century). 1.286.
19. Jar in a light grey fabric with a darker grey exterior; cf. *Slack*, 15 (A.D. 70–140). The bulbous shape of the vessel suggests that it is most likely to be pre-Hadrianic in date. 1.286.

From the demolition of Building A or the construction phase of Building B:

20. Small jar in orange-buff fabric. 2.287.

(ii) *Building B.*

21. Flagon neck in orange fabric; cf. *Holt*, 114 (late 1st–early 2nd century). 1.182.

(iii) *Building C.I.*

22. Jar in dark grey fabric; cf. *Whitchurch*, 123 (probably late 1st–early 2nd century). 1.270.
23. Flagon neck in orange-buff fabric with a white slip; it is somewhat similar to *Holt*, 107 (late 1st–early 2nd century); see also *Newstead 1911*, Fig. 33, 5 (A.D. 80–105). From the construction trench 4.87.

(iv) *Layers contemporary with Buildings C.I and C.II.*

From a cobbled path:

24. Rim of jar in orange fabric burnt fawn on the rim. 3.55.

From the sandy loam and charcoal:

25. Flagon in orange fabric with a creamy white slip. The rim resembles that of *Holt*, 109 but lacks the lower ring of that example. In form, but not fabric, it resembles *Turret 26a*, 10. 3.53.
26. Jar in Black-burnished ware; cf. *Gillam* type 138 (A.D. 150–250). 3.53.
27. Dish in Black-burnished ware; cf. *Gillam* type 316 (A.D. 120–160). 3.53.

Probably associated with the sandy loam above:

28. Jar in smooth dark grey fabric, burnished externally and burnt fawn internally; *Gillam* type 65 (A.D. 140–300). 3.9.
29. Flanged dish in Black-burnished fabric; *Gillam* type 307 (A.D. 120–160). 3.9.
30. Jar in orange fabric. 3.42.

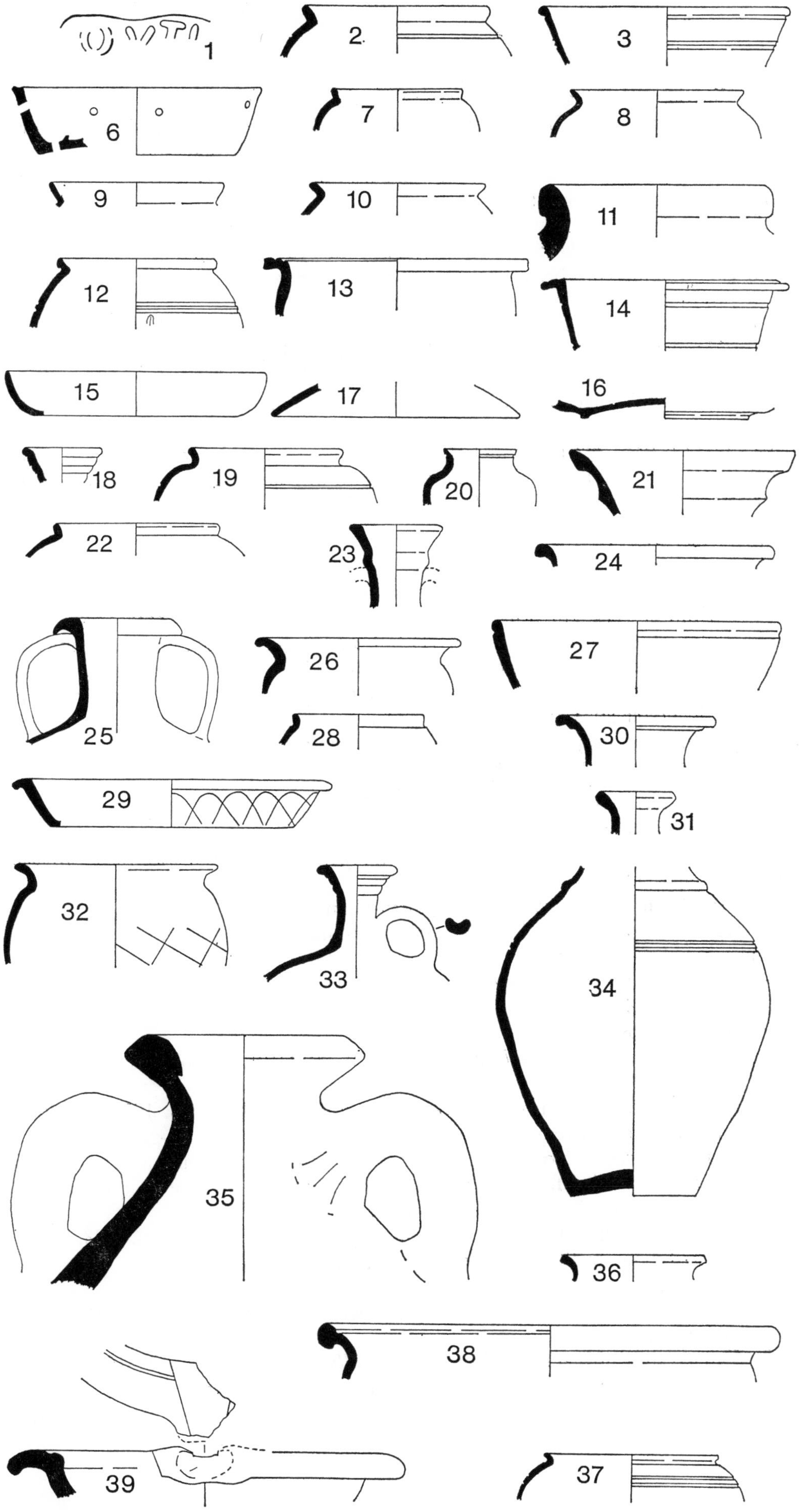

Fig. 34. Coarse pottery Nos. 1–39 (¼ scale).

From a pit:

31. Flagon neck in light orange with traces of a cream slip. 3.72.
32. Jar in Black-burnished ware; cf. *Northwich 1968–70*, 28 (early–mid-2nd century) *Slack*, 6 (the overall date of the site is A.D. 80–140 but Black-burnished ware is unlikely to have reached the area before A.D. 120). 3.72.

From the fill of ditch 3.91:

33. Flagon in smooth orange-buff fabric. The neck has been smoothed or burnished with vertical strokes; cf. *Gillam* type 5 (A.D. 110–150). 3.94.
34. Jar in light red fabric. The fabric has the high sandy content of many of the products of the Cheshire Plain area. 3.110.
35. Neck of a globular amphora of Dressel form 20 (cf. *Callender*, Fig. 1, 20, p. 281; also *Collingwood & Richmond*, Fig. 9, C). 3.110.

The layers contemporary with Buildings C.I and C.II produce pottery of which a fair proportion is Black-burnished ware. This suggests occupation until well after the introduction of this ware into northern England in the A.D. 120's. The total assemblage is not large but it includes a few types not introduced until the mid-2nd century (cf. Nos. 26 and 28.). Occupation until at least A.D. 140–160 seems likely. For associated samian see Nos. 72, 80–1 (p. 87).

(v) *Building D.*

36. Necked jar in grey fabric. 1.73.
    Layer 1.73 also produced a fragment decorated with wavy lines applied with a comb or very stiff brush. The style of decoration is very common in South Wales (cf. *Caerleon Amphitheatre*, 41) but uncommon in the North. The method of decoration was, however, used at the kilns near Littlechester, Derby (*Littlechester Kilns*, 193), and this fragment may perhaps be from there. The Littlechester kilns are Trajanic in date.
37. Jar in light grey fabric; the globular shape suggests a late 1st–early 2nd century date. 1.90.

(vi) *Contemporary with Building D.*

38. Wide-mouthed jar in orange buff fabric. The form is reminiscent of some of the 3rd–4th century jars in Severn Valley ware; cf. *Droitwich: Bays Meadow*, Fig. 8, 8. 3.33.
39. Mortarium in orange-buff. The spout-channel has been cut with a knife or wire; cf. *Wilderspool Kilns*, 83 (early–mid-2nd century). 3.33.

From a cobbled platform:

40. Flanged and grooved bowl in burnt Black-burnished ware; *Gillam* type 226 (A.D. 200–240). 3.5.

From the clay floor:

41. Jar in buff fabric; cf. *Gillam* type 101 (A.D. 70–110) probably a residual piece. 2.83.
42. Jar in burnt Black-burnished ware; cf. *Gillam* type 133 (A.D. 160–220). 2.83.
43. Jar; burning has removed the surface leaving a gritty fawn-grey fabric of a similar degree of coarseness to Black-burnished ware but which is more probably an allied fabric; the form is clearly related to that of the common Hadrianic-Antonine jars in Black-burnished ware. 2.83.
44. Jar in Black-burnished ware; cf. *Gillam* type 129 (A.D. 140–190). 2.83.
45. Flanged bowl in Black-burnished ware; cf. *Gillam* type 221 (A.D. 140–180). 2.83.
46. Flanged bowl or dish in Black-burnished ware; *Gillam* type 220 (A.D. 120–160). 2.83.
47. Flanged dish in Black-burnished ware; *Gillam* type 307 A.D. 120–160. 2.83.
48. Dish in a slightly sandy pink-buff fabric. It is reminiscent of the dishes in Black-burnished ware of the later 2nd century (e.g. *Gillam* type 318, A.D.

160–200) and is probably of a similar date; cf. *Turret 26a*, 32 (unstratified but probably A.D. 120–200) for a similar vessel. 2.83.

49. Dish in Black-burnished ware; cf. *Newstead 1911*, Fig. 32, 8 and 9 (Antonine). 2.83.

From the area not sealed by the clay floor:

50. Stamped mortarium. Mrs K. F. Hartley reports:
The vessel is in fine-textured, cream fabric tempered with fine mixed grit; there is a cream slip. The retrograde stamp reading FECIT, is a counterstamp of G. Attius Marinus, used in the later part of his career. This counterstamp, and particularly the name-stamp it is always coupled with, have degenerate lettering; indeed the name-stamp could not be read if it were not clearly a copy of his most commonly used stamp which was itself no more than tolerably literate.
G. Attius Marinus is, however, of particular interest since he began his career in the Colchester region *c.* A.D. 90–95, where he had some success selling mortaria as far afield as Caerleon. At this date, however, the potteries at Brockley Hill and Radlett were far more important and he soon moved to Radlett, where his work in local fabric was found at the kilns in 1898 (*V.C.H. Hertfordshire*, Pt. 5, p. 162 bottom line, stamps upside down). Since few of his stamps have been found on mortaria in Radlett fabric it is reasonable to suppose that he moved fairly soon into the Midlands to Hartshill, Warwickshire, where he is the earliest known potter. The Manchester example was made in the Midlands. There is good evidence to date his activity there within the period A.D. 100–130, and the die used suggests that this example could be more closely dated to A.D. 110–130 (for further details see *Verulamium I*, pp. 373–4, No. 12). 2.80.

Associated with the end of Furnace 21:

51. Flanged bowl in Black-burnished ware; a very small version of *Gillam* type 219 (A.D. 120–150). 2.96.
52. Mortarium in pale buff fabric bearing a fragmentary stamp reading R.R. The potter is Sarrius; cf. *AA_4*, 26, p.189, no. 47. For a recent summary of the work of this potter by Mrs. K. F. Hartley see *Verulamium I*, p.378, no. 35. Mrs. Hartley dates his production to the period A.D. 135–75 which goes well with the context of the Manchester piece. 2.96.
53. Flanged dish in Black-burnished ware; *Gillam* type 308 (A.D. 130–180). 2.158.
54. Flagon in hard cream fabric; this would seem to be a type with a fairly long life, cf. *Heronbridge*, 43 (Flavian-Trajanic); *Glenlochar*, 1 (A.D. 80–105) is similar but smaller and in a different fabric; *Corbridge 1954*, 8 (*c.* A.D. 200) 2.181.
55. Neck of a beaker (?) in hard dark grey fabric. 2.181.
56. Jar in burnt Black-burnished ware. The form is probably *Gillam* type 129 (A.D. 140–180) although it is more flared than the type-specimen; see, however, No. 44 above which is similarly flared but undoubtedly of 2nd-century date as it has wavy line decoration above the neck—a 2nd-century feature. 2.181.
57. Wide-mouthed jar in light orange Severn Valley ware, burnished on the rim and shoulder. For a discussion of Severn Valley ware see *Webster 1972*, p. 191. For the general type with rim tending to oversail the body cf. *Wroxeter* 1923–7, C5 (late 2nd–late 3rd century). 2.181.
58. Wide-mouthed jar in fairly sandy orange fabric with a grey core. 2.181.
59. Flanged dish in Black-burnished ware; *Gillam* type 307 (A.D. 120–160). 2.181.
60. Dish in Black-burnished ware; *Gilliam* type 318 (A.D. 160- 200) 2.181.
61. Mortarium in orange fabric with white and red trituration grits; cf. *Wilderspool Kilns*, 86 (early–mid-2nd century). 2.181.

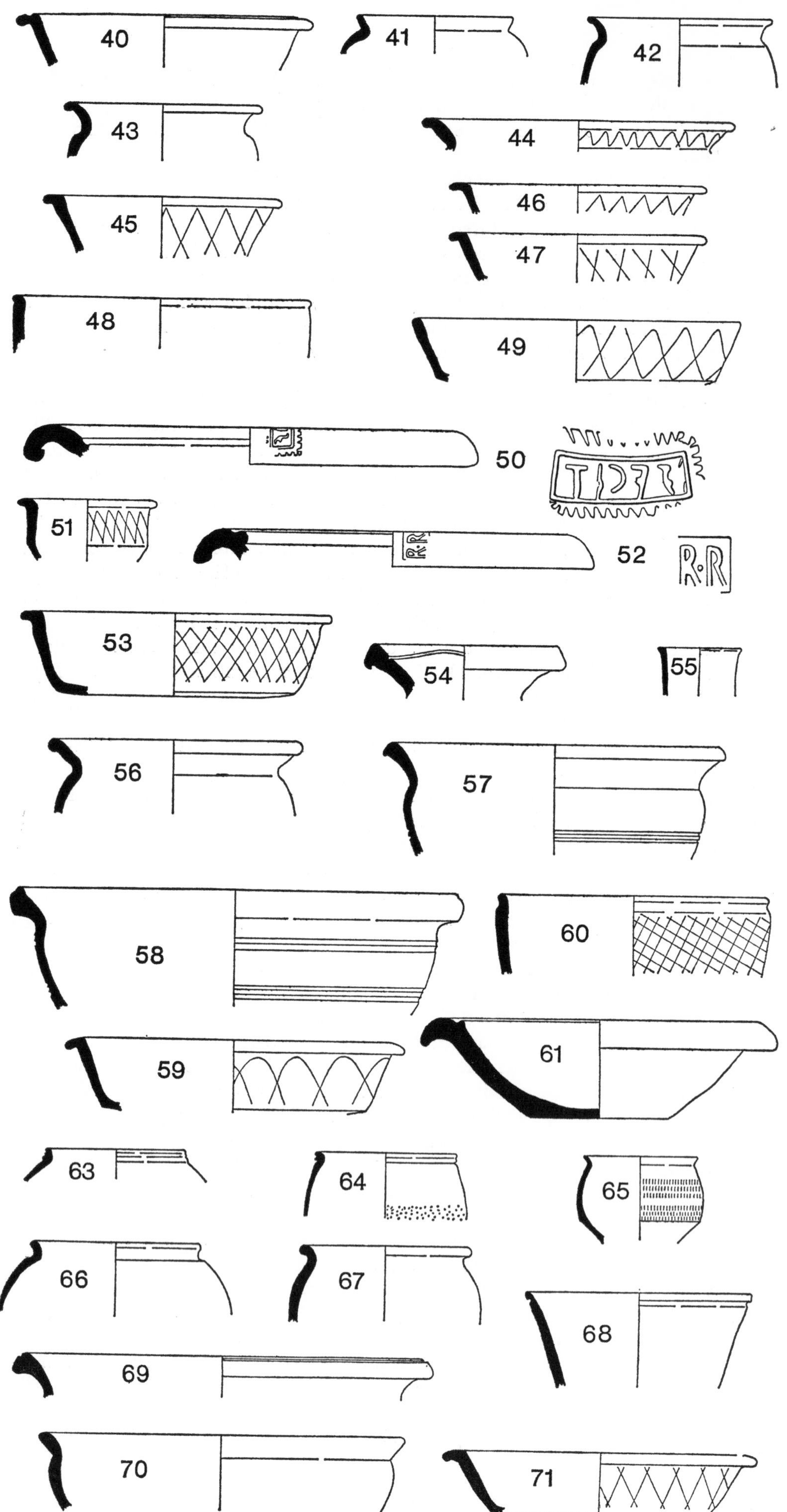

Fig. 35. Coarse pottery Nos. 40–71 ($\frac{1}{4}$ scale).

62. (Not illustrated.) Cylindrical neck probably of a flagon in orange fabric with a maroon/brown colour coat which has disappeared entirely from the exterior. It is very worn and lacks the rim. Length as preserved 8 cm., diameter 2.5 cm. 2.181.

From a general spread of this period:

63. Beaker in smooth fawn fabric with brown surface; cf. *Holt,* 78 (late 1st–early 2nd century); *Balmuildy,* Pl. XLVI, 10 (Antonine). 2.182.
64. Rough-cast beaker in pink-buff fabric with a maroon-brown colour coat; *Gillam* type 72 (A.D. 80–130). 2.182.
65. Beaker in light red slightly sandy fabric. 2.182.
66. Jar in Black-burnished ware; *Gillam* type 128 (A.D. 130–180). 2.182.
67. Jar in black calcite gritted fabric. 2.182.
68. Tankard in light red/buff Severn Valley ware with a lighter core; cf. *Sutton Walls,* fig. 20, 10 (a mixed 2nd–4th century deposit). The type also occurs in the Wroxeter Piscina deposit (an as yet unpublished late 2nd-century group from recent excavations by Dr. Graham Webster, who kindly made the material available for examination). Tankards were not common at Manchester but a further example came from 2.96, an approximately contemporary level with this example. 2.182.
69. Wide-mouthed jar in light red/buff Severn Valley ware with a grey core. The groove on the jar rim is unusual but otherwise this is one of the standard Severn Valley ware forms. Without the shoulder it is not possible to see how far, if at all the rim overhangs the body, but the date range is 2nd to 4th century; cf. *Astley I,* 48 (2nd–early 3rd century) and 121 (4th century). 2.182.
70. Bowl in light orange-buff slightly sandy fabric. There are traces of red colour coating, some of which appears to have been painted on with vertical strokes, rather than slipped, which is more common. 2.182.
71. Flanged dish in Black-burnished ware; cf. *Gillam* type 307 (A.D. 120–160). 2.182.
72. Amphora handle stamped LMVE (VE ligatured); cf. *Callender* p. 162, No. 898 (our stamp is not, however, identical to the one illustrated). 2.182.
73. Small jar in orange fabric. 2.68.
74. Bowl in Black-burnished ware with one or possibly two handles. It has not been possible to calculate the diameter from the fragment recovered, not only because of the distortion likely in the handle section but also because this type of vessel is frequently oval. Such handled vessels are relatively common in the South (cf. for example *Gloucester: Bon Marché,* fig. 12, 13 and fig. 14, 5) but very infrequent in northern Britain (for one of the few occurrences see *Northwich 1968–70,* 21). 2.68.
75. Bowl in mid-grey fabric. The form is highly reminiscent of the samian form Curle 15, made from the late 1st to the late 2nd century but common in the Antonine period. For similar 'imitations' cf. *Mumrills* fig. 105, 1 (Antonine); for another Antonine imitation of Curle 15 see *Gillam* type 338. 2.71.
76. Flagon in mid-grey fabric; cf. *Gillam* type 14 (A.D. 130–170). 2.84.
77. Jar in orange/light brown fabric. The form is reminiscent of Hadrianic-Antonine jars in Black-burnished ware and a similar date seems likely. 2.84.
78. Jar in pink-fawn fabric. 2.86.
79. Beaker in orange fabric; cf. *Wilderspool Kilns,* 33 (late 1st–mid-2nd century), an allied form but a different fabric; similarly *Gillam* type 75 (A.D. 130–180). 2.24.
80. Jar in grey fabric with a smoothed surface externally. It has been burnt orange in places. It is reminiscent of the common Hadrianic-Antonine jars in Black-burnished ware (e.g. *Gillam* type 122) and is probably of a similar date. 2.24.

Also from features of this period:

81. Jar in hard mid-grey fabric. 2.91.
82. Jar in Black-burnished ware; cf. *Turret 35a,* 2 (A.D. 120–140); *Turret 26a,* 19 (probably 2nd half of 2nd century); *Corbridge 1911,* 48 (A.D. 139–200). 2.91.
83. Flanged dish or bowl in Black-burnished ware; cf. *Gillam* type 309 (A.D. 160–200). 2.91.
84. Bowl in a slightly sandy light grey fabric. 2.91.
85. Dish in Black-burnished ware; cf. *Gillam* type 309 (A.D. 160–200). 2.91.
86. Dish in a grey fabric burnished. For a dish with similar decoration see *Gillam* type 328 (A.D. 150–200). 2.149.
87. A complete vessel in grey fabric with a dark grey burnished surface. There is some resemblance to the handled beakers *Gillam* type 65–6 (mid-2nd–mid-3rd century) and our vessel is probably of a similar date (although it can never have had a handle). 2.142.
88. Mortarium in orange fabric; cf. *Milecastle 48,* Pl. III, 2 (mid–late 2nd century). 2.108.
89. Jar in light grey ware. 2.111.
90. Amphora neck, probably of the same general type as No. 35 above. 2.114.

For samian evidence associated with these levels see Nos. 53,62,65,68,70,78,82(p.85ff). The material from Building D and its associated levels form a remarkably uniform collection. The great majority of it is 2nd century in date and much of this is mid-late 2nd century. The latest piece is likely to be No. 40 which must have been deposited at the very close of the 2nd century or later. All the rest of the material could have been made and used before the close of the century. Occupation and demolition of the building within the 2nd half of the 2nd century seems highly probable.

(vii) *Buildings E and F.*

91. (Not illustrated.) Flanged bowl in somewhat sandy orange-buff fabric; one of the Flavian-Trajanic flanged bowl series and clearly residual. 1.215.
92. Beaker in white fabric with a light red/brown colour coat. Too little remains to be certain of the form but cf. *Gillam* types 93 (A.D. 210–250), 94 (A.D. 200–270); also *Great Casterton III,* fig. 18, 3 (from a kiln *c.* A.D. 180–230). A late 2nd-century or more probably a 3rd-century date for the piece seems likely. 2.54.
93. (Not illustrated.) Everted rim jar in grey fabric, probably residual. 2.196.
94. Jar in Black-burnished ware; *Gillam* type 133 (A.D. 160–220). 2.95.
95. Flanged bowl in Black-burnished ware; cf. *Gillam* type 220 (A.D. 120–160). 2.95.
96. Bowl in pink-buff Severn Valley ware; cf. *Leigh Sinton,* 2. 2.95.
97. Beaker or small jar in Black-burnished ware; cf. *Gillam* type 65 (A.D. 140–300) 2.55.
98. Jar in Black-burnished ware; cf. *Gillam* type 129 (A.D. 140–180). 2.55.
99. Jar in Black-burnished ware, sooted externally; *Gillam* type 122 (A.D. 120–160). 2.55.
100. (Not illustrated.) Flanged bowl in light grey fabric with a reeded rim; one of the Flavian-Trajanic flanged bowl series and residual. 2.55.
101. Jar in grey burnished fabric. The vessel is most reminiscent of the common Hadrianic-Antonine jars and is probably of a similar date. 2.161.
102. Bowl in soft smooth pink fabric with traces of mica dusting. The vessel is most probably an imitation of the samian form 27 which itself was not produced after *c.* A.D. 150. cf. No. 154 above. 4.135.
103. Jar in mid-grey with dark grey surface. 4.85.

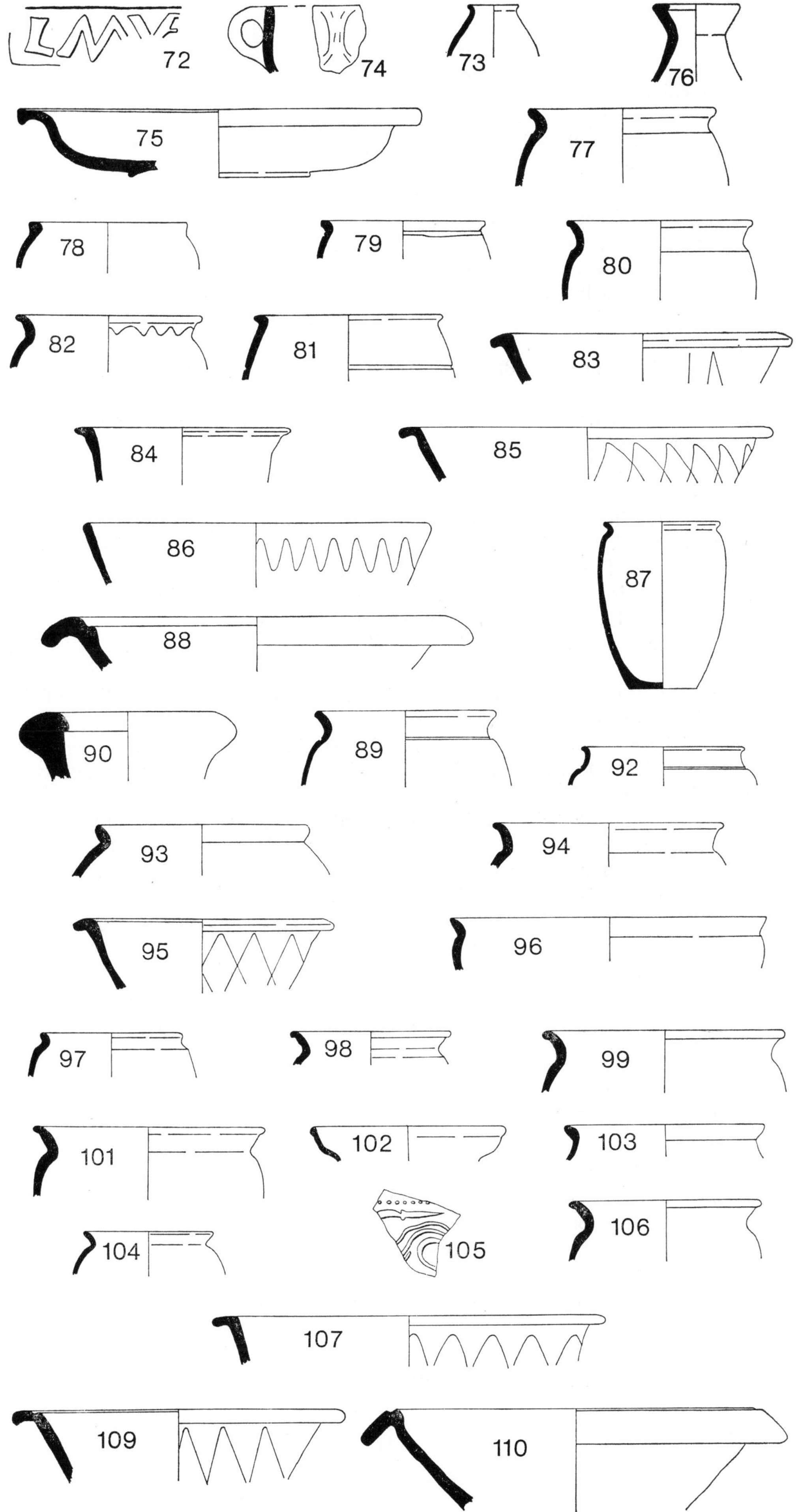

Fig. 36. Coarse pottery Nos. 72–110 ($\frac{1}{4}$ scale).

(viii) *Contemporary with Building E.*

From the cobbled path:

104. Jar in dark grey fabric. This vessel is reminiscent of some of the late 2nd–3rd century jars in Black-burnished ware (cf. *Gillam* type 143) and may be of a similar date. 2.72.

From the latest phase of the cobbled yard:

105. Fragment of beaker in white fabric with copper-brown colour coat. For a similar style of decoration see *Gillam* type 80 (A.D. 220–260). 2.74.
106. Jar in burnt Black-burnished ware; this type can probably be placed in the later 2nd or early 3rd century period; cf. *Newstead 1911*, Fig. 28, 8 (Antonine); *Balmuildy*, Pl. XLIV, 3 (Antonine); *Birdoswald 1929*, 18 (1) (A.D. 208–?296). 2.74.
107. Flanged bowl in burnt Black-burnished ware. One of the Hadrianic-Antonine bowl series. 2.54.
108. (Not illustrated.) Flanged bowl in Black-burnished ware. One of the Hadrianic-Antonine series. 2.74.
109. Flanged and grooved bowl in Black-burnished ware; *Gillam* type 314 (A.D. 220–360). 2.74.
110. Mortarium in white fabric with brown, white and grey trituration grits; cf. *Carpow*, fig. 7, 1 (early 3rd century, but it is noted that the type also occurs in the latter half of the 2nd century). 2.74.
111. Mortarium in creamy white fabric with grey and white trituration grits; cf. *Whitchurch*, 301 (late 2nd–mid-3rd century). 2.74.
112. Mortarium in white fabric with red grits; cf. *Gillam* type 279 (A.D. 210–320). 2.74.
113. (Not illustrated.) Flanged bowl or dish in Black-burnished ware. One of the Hadrianic-Antonine series. 2.45.

The material derived from Building E and its associated levels is clearly later than that from Building D. A number of residual pieces are present, but the majority of the material was current in the later 2nd century or early/mid-3rd century. The life of the structure must fit within this period. Furthermore, as a number of pieces are present which were not introduced before *c.* A.D. 210–220 (see Nos. 105, 109 and 112) the building must have continued in use until at least this time. Survival beyond the early/mid-3rd century is improbable.

C. INDUSTRIAL ACTIVITY

In this section has been placed the majority of the material derived from the furnaces and their associated levels. Presentation is by area, rather than as a chronological sequence.

(i) *Area 1.*

From Furnace 18:

114. An unusual wide-mouthed bowl in a light red fairly sandy fabric. 1.164.

(ii) *Area 2.*

From the road 2.165:

115. Amphora handle bearing a poorly impressed stamp O or Q. 2.165.

From the black charcoal area associated with furnace 2.158:

116. Rim of beaker or small jar in pink fabric. 2.220.
117. Rough-cast beaker in light red fabric with a dark brown colour coat; cf. *Gillam* type 72 (A.D. 80–130). 2.220.
118. Beaker in white fabric with a dark brown colour coat; cf. *Gillam* type 93 (A.D. 210–250). 2.220.
119. Jar in Black-burnished ware; cf. *Mumrills* fig. 96, 1 (Antonine); *Milecastle 48*, 22 (3rd century). 2.220.

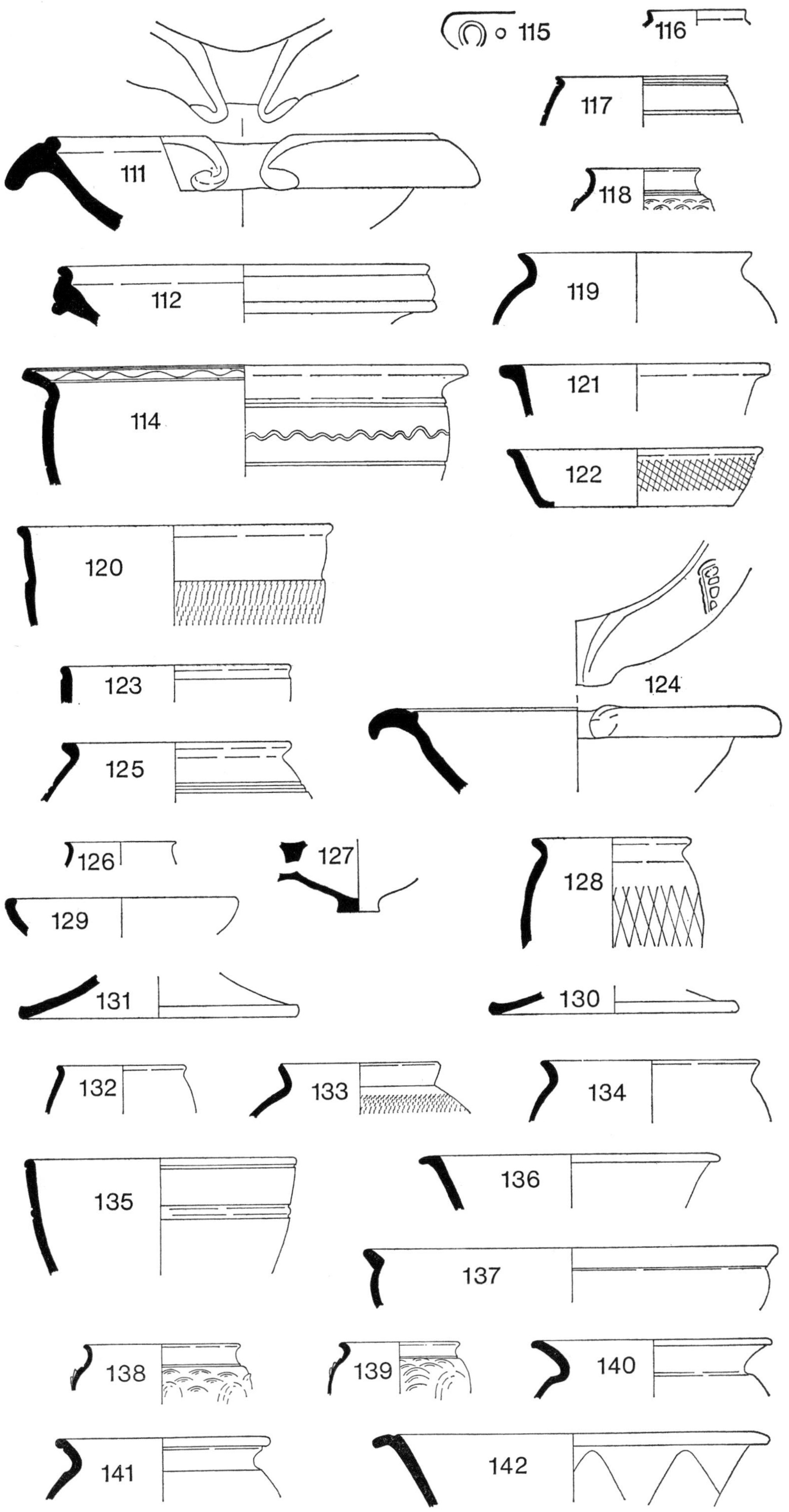

Fig. 37. Coarse pottery Nos. 111–142 ($\frac{1}{4}$ scale).

120. Bowl in grey fabric with a darker grey surface and rouletted decoration. The vessel is reminiscent of the samian form 37. 2.220.
121. Flanged bowl in grey fabric. 2.220.
122. Flanged dish in Black-burnished ware; one of the Hadrianic-Antonine bowl series. 2.220.
123. Dish in Black-burnished ware; *Gillam* type 318 (A.D. 160–200). 2.220.

The charcoal area thus produces a rather mixed collection of pottery. The latest pieces are, however, consistent with deposition in the late 2nd–early 3rd century.

From Furnace 32 and associated layers:

124. Mortarium in cream fabric bearing an incompletely impressed stamp which has not been deciphered. 2.190.
125. Jar in grey fabric; somewhat similar to *Ilkley*, 6 (pre-Hadrianic). 2.69.
126. Rim of a beaker in white fabric with a dark grey colour coat. Too little remains to be certain of the form but the possible parallels suggest a 3rd-century date; cf. *Gillam* type 50 (A.D. 200–260); *Gillam* type 93 (A.D. 210–250). 2.206.

From the probable Furnace 22:

127. Fragments of a triple vase, of *Kaye* Class 1. Triple vases were being produced at the Wilderspool kilns in the period *c.* A.D. 90–160 (cf. *Wilderspool Kilns*, 70) and it is probably to this source that the Manchester example can be attributed. For discussion of the distribution of triple vases in the North-West see *Wilderspool Kilns*, 69–70, and *Northwich 1968–70*, 45. 2.70.

From pit 2.198 containing slag, etc.:

128. Jar in Black-burnished ware; cf. *Gillam* type 132 (A.D. 140–220). 2.198.
129. Bowl or possibly a lid in dark grey fabric smoothed externally. 2.198.
130. Lid in grey fabric. 2.198.
131. Lid in grey fabric. 2.198.

From Furnace 31:

132. Jar in Black-burnished ware; cf. *Milecastle 9*, 46A (A.D. 122–140); *Turret 50a*, 44 (2nd half of 2nd century). 2.224.
133. Jar in smooth orange fabric with rouletted decoration; cf. the complete vessel No. 152 below. 2.224.
134. Jar in smooth light grey fabric smoothed externally. 2.224.
135. Bowl in light red fabric. It is reminiscent of the samian form 37 but production of this type beyond the terminal date of the samian original is possible as the form was also produced by the potteries producing colour-coated wares. 2.224.
136. Flanged bowl or dish in Black-burnished ware; cf. *Gillam* type 220 (A.D. 120–160). 2.224.

This furnace would seem to have gone out of use by the early–mid-2nd century.

From Furnace 30:

137. Bowl in orange-buff fabric. 2.246.

From the fill associated with Furnace 22:

138. Beaker in white fabric with a chocolate brown colour coat. The lower part of the beaker was evidently indented; cf. *Gillam* type 93 (A.D. 210–250). 2.52.
139. Indented beaker in white fabric with a colour coat which appears maroon internally and brown externally. See No. 138 above (A.D. 210–250). 2.52.
140. Jar in Black-burnished ware. The currency of this type would seem to fall within the period mid-3rd to mid-4th century; cf. *Benwell 1926*, 13 (A.D. 205–296); *Bewcastle*, 38 (A.D. 300–343/360); *Carrawburgh Mithraeum*, 29 (late 3rd century). 2.52.
141. Jar in light grey fabric, burnished in the inside of the rim. 2.52.
142. Flanged and grooved dish in Black-burnished ware; *Gillam* type 314 (A.D. 220–360). 2.52.

143. Mortarium in smooth creamy white fabric; cf. *Carpow*, fig. 7, 1 (later 2nd–early 3rd century). See No. 110 above. 2.52.

144. Mortar-like bowl in pinky white fabric. A similar form but in a different fabric occurs in early 3rd-century levels at the Jewry Wall site, Leicester (*Leicester: Jewry Wall*, fig. 22, 21). 2.52.

145. (Not illustrated.) A further fragment of vessel No. 58. 2.52.

Assuming that the fill from this feature denotes the period when it went out of use and was filled in, the material illustrated above suggests that this event took place in the early–mid-3rd century.

(iii) *Area 3.*

From Furnace 25:

146. Double-handled flagon in light red/orange fabric. The upper end of the handle survives on one side and the lower end on the other, allowing an approximate restoration of the position of both. For a similar rim cf. *Northwich 1968–70*, 10 (late 1st-early 2nd century). 3.68.

From Furnace 26:

147. Jar with a frilled, flanged rim in smooth light red fabric with a thin cream slip. Jars with a 'double' rim such as this were made, among other places, at Wilderspool (*Wilderspool Kilns*, 11–16). The 'pie-crust' frill was also popular with the Wilderspool potters; this, combined with the fabric of the vessel, is sufficient to suggest that it is from the Wilderspool kilns which were in production *c.* A.D. 90–160. 3.108.

From pit 3.38:

148. Jar in Black-burnished ware; cf. *Gillam* type 145 (A.D. 230–300). 3.38.

149. Hammer-head mortarium in white fabric with red and black trituration grits; cf. *Gillam* type 283 (A.D. 250–350). 3.38.

From pit 3.92:

150. Jar in orange-buff Severn Valley ware; cf. *Astley I*, 28 (2nd–early 3rd century). 3.92.

(iv) *Area 4.*

From Furnace 1:

151. Jar in smooth light red fabric. 4.67.

From Furnace 2:

152. Complete jar in light red fabric. For the general rim-shape cf. *Castleshaw*, Pl. 36, 9 (A.D. 80–140). The over-all shape of the vessel also suggests a late 1st–early 2nd century date (cf. *Gillam* types 97–8). 4.41.

153. Mortarium in a fabric which has probably been turned light brown as a result of burning. There are signs of a light coloured slip (?cream); cf. *Melandra Castle*, 22–5 (A.D. 80–140). 4.41.

154. Vessel in imitation of the samian form 27 in light red fabric with traces of mica dusting. It is likely to have been made before *c.* A.D. 150 when the samian original went out of production. See No. 102 above. 4.41.

From the furnace spread 4.142:

155. Flanged bowl in light fawn/brown fabric; cf. *Corbridge 1937*, Level IV, 17 (A.D. 79–125). 4.42.

156. Bowl in hard dark grey fabric, decorated internally on the base and with a small fragment of a potter's name-stamp still extant on the centre-base. Three concentric grooves decorate the base internally with further decoration between the inner and middle grooves. This decoration has been impressed with some object twisted into a spiral (possibly a piece of cord or even a few strands of wire wound together as in a twisted wire bracelet, e.g. *Richborough IV*, Pl. XLIX, 11). The fabric may be an attempt to imitate Terra Nigra but is much coarser. It may perhaps be an attempted copy of a Terra Nigra dish such as *Camulodunum*, Pl. XLIX, 16Ac. For a not dissimilar vessel but lacking the

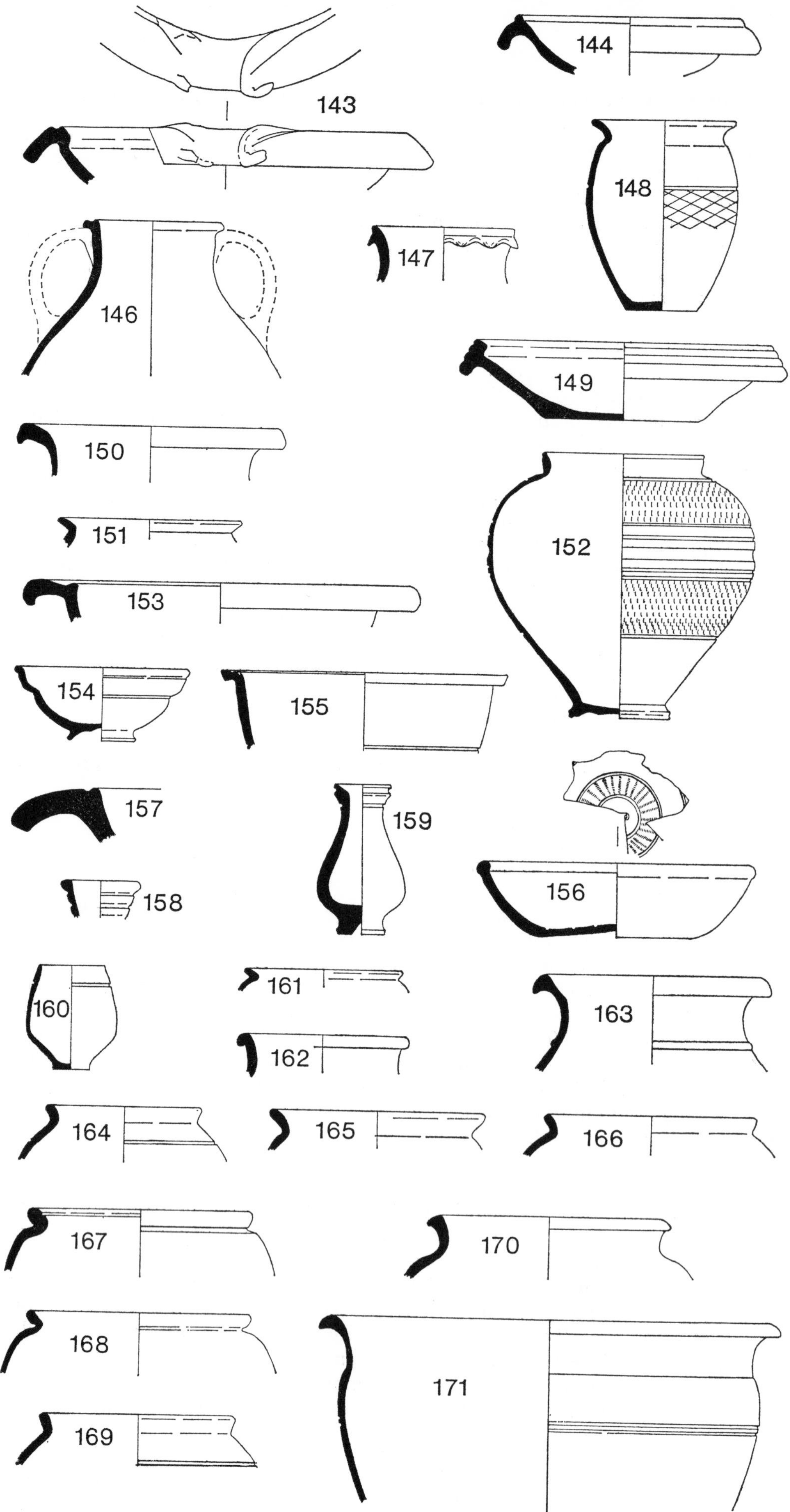

Fig. 38. Coarse pottery Nos. 143–171 ($\frac{1}{4}$ scale).

internal decoration (although with the concentric rings) see *Gillam* type 337 (A.D. 70–110); a similar date for our piece seems probable. 4.142 with other joining fragments from 4+.

From the area of burnt clay equivalent to 1.278:

157. Mortarium in soft light buff fabric. The fragment found is from near the spout and an accurate measurement of the diameter was not, therefore, possible. The diameter was, however, clearly in excess of that of the average domestic mortarium and use in a commercial bakery seems possible. The form is somewhat similar to *Gillam* type 238 (A.D. 70–110). 4.131.

Nos. 158–180 form one of the largest groups from the site. They are from the pit 4.68, and associated layers.

158. Flagon neck in orange-buff fabric with a grey core and with traces of a cream slip; cf. *Gillam* type 5 (A.D. 110–150). 4.68.
159. Small flask in orange-buff fabric; cf. *Turret 25b,* 15 (A.D. 122–140); the vessel is also somewhat similar to *Corbridge 1911,* 64 (A.D. 139–200). 4.68.
160. Small cup in white fabric with grey-brown colour coat; cf. *Gillam* types 80–81 (A.D. 220–260). 4.68.
161. Jar in light grey fabric. 4.57.
162. Jar in light grey fabric; cf. *Chester: Deanery Field 1928,* 11a (Flavian-Trajanic). 4.68.
163. Jar in reddish-buff Severn Valley ware with a grey core; cf. *Astley I,* 26 (2nd–early 3rd century); *Wroxeter 1936–7,* fig. 10, 25 (late 2nd–mid-3rd century). 4.68.
164. Jar in grey fabric. 4.68.
165. Jar in grey fabric. 4.68.
166. Jar in grey fabric. 4.68.
167. Jar in light grey fairly sandy material. 4.68.
168. Jar in dark grey fabric smoothed externally. The vessel has been severely pitted by burning; cf. *Northwich 1968–70,* 13 (late 1st–early 2nd century). 4.68.
169. Jar in smooth light grey fabric. 4.61.
170. Jar in light grey fabric. 4.68.
171. Jar in orange Severn Valley ware; cf. *Astley I,* 49 (2nd–early 3rd century); *Sutton Walls,* fig. 20, 27 (probably 2nd–3rd century). 4.68.
172. Neck of a wide-mouthed jar in smooth orange-buff Severn Valley ware, similar to No. 171 above but with a more flared rim; cf. *Wroxeter 1923–7,* C5 (late 2nd–late 3rd century); *Sutton Walls,* fig. 17, 6 (late 2nd century). 4.68.
173. Mortarium in granular cream fabric. Mrs K. F. Hartley reports:

    The stamps read ALBINUS and VIANVACAE? respectively. Albinus was by far the most prolific potter stamping mortaria in Britain or indeed elsewhere. More than 300 of his stamps are now recorded including 11 from Scotland. Securely dated stamps have been found at Inchtuthill (*c.* A.D. 83–7), the Neronian-Flavian fort at Baginton, Warwickshire (3 examples), Verulamium (*Verulamium* I, p.371). This evidence and the rim forms fit well with a date of A.D. 65–95. His kilns are not known but the fabric and distribution are entirely appropriate for the important potteries between Verulamium and London (including Radlett and Brockley Hill where his son Matugenus worked). In common with a few other potters he used counterstamps (F. LVGVDV) indicating manufacture at a place presumably named Lugudunum. This Lugudunum undoubtedly lay fairly near to Verulamium. The second type of counterstamp used by him alone, probably reads VIANVACAE retrograde, as suggested above. This could either be a place name or conceivably one of Albinus's workmen (for a longer discussion of Albinus's work see *Verulamium I,* pp. 371–2). 4.140B.

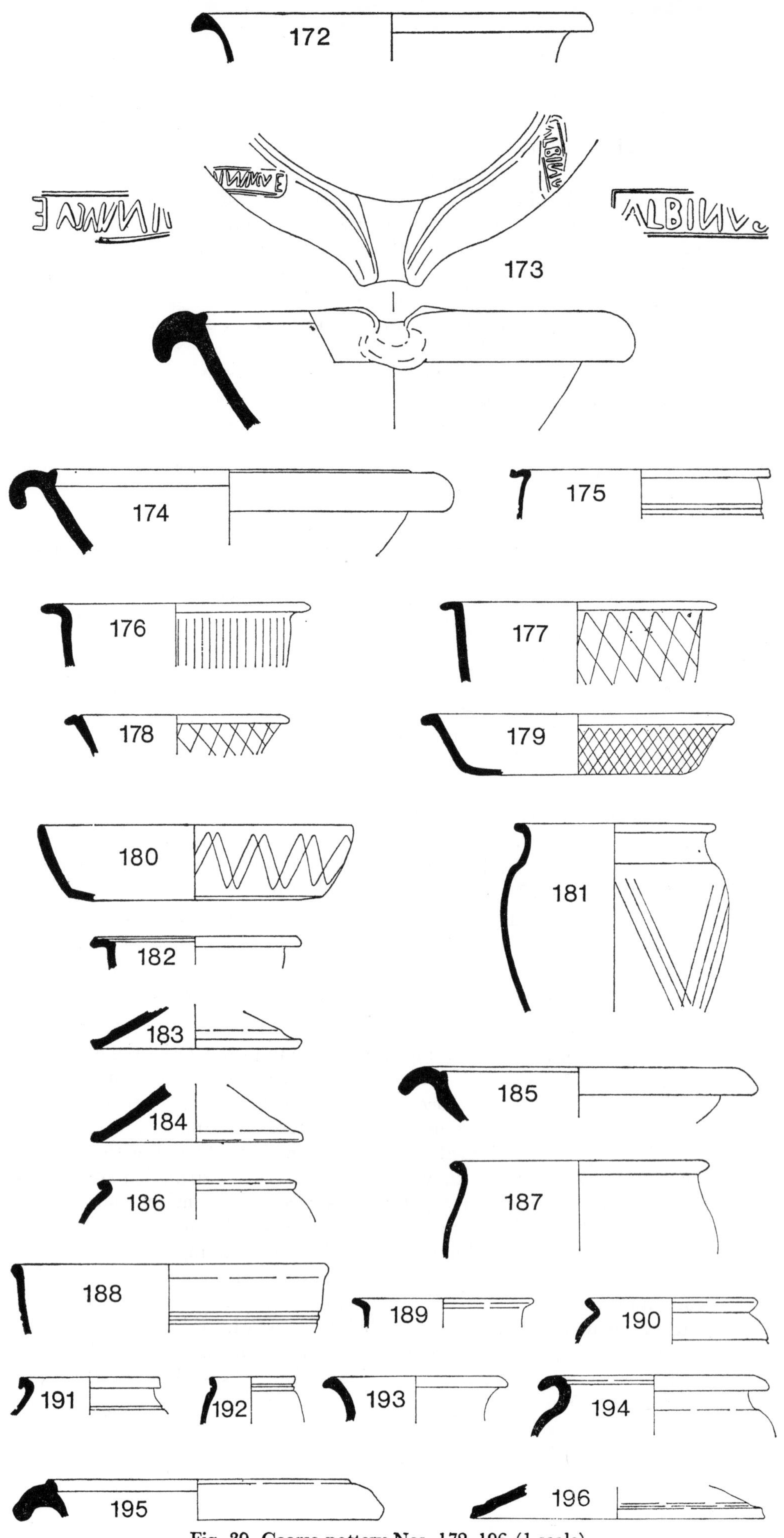

Fig. 39. Coarse pottery Nos. 172–196 (¼ scale).

174. Mortarium in light red fabric with a cream slip and grey and red trituration grits; cf. *Mumrills*, fig. 91, 20 (Antonine). 4.68.
175. Flanged bowl in orange fabric with a grey core; one of the late 1st–early 2nd century flanged bowl series. 4.68.
176. Flanged bowl in grey fabric. 4.68.
177. Flanged bowl in Black-burnished ware; one of the Hadrianic-Antonine flanged bowl series. 4.68.
178. Flanged and grooved bowl in Black-burnished ware; *Gillam* type 226 (A.D. 200–240). 4.68.
179. Flanged dish in Black-burnished ware; *Gillam* type 307 (A.D. 120–160). 4.68.
180. Dish in Black-burnished ware; cf. *Newstead 1911*, fig. 13, 8 (Antonine). 4.68.

This group is evidently a very mixed collection of material derived from all periods of occupation of the site up to the 3rd century. It may well be the result of filling in the pit with material from elsewhere on the site and is probably largely redeposited and therefore residual. The latest pieces present may, however, be derived from vessels only recently discarded at the time of the infilling operation. These (Nos. 159, 160, 163, 171, 172, 178) suggest final deposition of the group in the first half of the 3rd century.

From Pit 4.69 and associated levels:

181. Jar in mid-grey fabric. 4.71.
182. Flanged bowl in light grey fabric; one of the late 1st–early 2nd century flanged bowl series. 4.99.
183. Lid in dark grey fabric. 4.94.

D. ROADS

As might be expected, the road surfaces produced little in the way of pottery.

From the third road surface:

184. Lid in grey fabric sooted externally; cf. *Chester: Deanery Field, 1928*, 39b (A.D. *c.* 120–180); *Holt*, 101 (late 1st–early 2nd century); *Manchester*, Pl. 72, R.13 1.556.

From the fourth road:

185. Mortarium in light red fairly sandy fabric; cf. *Wilderspool Kilns*, 84 (*c.* A.D 90–160). 1.503.
186. Jar in grey fabric; it is somewhat similar to *Gillam* type 105 (A.D. 80–120) and *Chesterholm*, 38 (A.D. 90–125) and is probably of a similar date. 1.551.
187. Jar in grey fairly sandy fabric; somewhat similar to *Newstead 1911*, fig. 25, 3 (A.D. 80–105). 1.551.
188. Bowl in mid-grey fabric; when complete it was probably intended to be reminiscent of the samian form 37. Such bowls were fairly popular in the North-West at such sites as Chester, Holt, Heronbridge and Northwich, within the period A.D. 90–160. 1.551.
189. Flanged bowl in fawn fabric. 1.551.
190. Jar in grey fabric; cf. *Northwich 1968–70*, 13 (late 1st–early 2nd century). 1.535.

The material from this road level appears to be uniformly pre-Hadrianic in character.

From the fifth road:

191. Jar in dark grey fabric; cf. *Gillam* type 96 (A.D. 80–130); *Corbridge 1911*, 25 (A.D. 79–125). 1.504.

From the ditch associated with the fifth road:

192. Beaker in pinky-grey fabric much abraded; the rim with a double groove is reminiscent of that on many of the rough-cast beakers and a similar date (late 1st–early 2nd century) may be suggested for this piece. 1.502.
193. Jar in light red slightly sandy fabric. 1.502.
194. Jar in black calcite gritted fabric; *Gillam* type 163 (A.D. 360–400). 1.502.

195. Mortarium in hard cream fabric, burnt grey in places; cf. *Whitchurch*, 301 (late 2nd–mid-3rd century). 1.502.

196. Lid in dark grey fabric; cf. *Whitchurch*, 157 (2nd century?). 1.503.

The material from this ditch covers almost the whole period of occupation at the site. It seems likely from the presence of 3rd- and 4th-century pieces that the ditch stood open or remained as a depression up to the very close of the Roman occupation at Manchester.

E. DISTURBED AND UNSTRATIFIED MATERIAL; OTHER MATERIAL

From the great mass of material from disturbed levels I have selected a number for inclusion in this report, either because of their general interest or because of their bearing on the history of the site. These have been divided into three sections:

(i) A collection from the post-Roman plough-soil in Area 2.

(ii) The latest pieces of Roman pottery from the site.

(iii) Material included for its general interest in demonstrating the range of pottery available on the site.

(i) *The Post-Roman Plough-soil.*

197. Beaker in white with a dark grey colour coat; it is difficult to identify the exact type without more of the vessel, but see *Gillam* types 87 (A.D. 200–240), 89 (A.D. 210–260), 90 (A.D. 220–280). A 3rd-century date is highly probable. 2.50.

198. Beaker in hard grey fabric. 2.50.

199. Beaker in white fabric with a colour coat varying between red and brown; too little remains to be certain of the form but see *Gillam* types 92 (A.D. 180–250) and 94 (A.D. 200–270); also *Brixworth*, 304 (3rd century) and *Great Casterton III*, 54 and 55 (*c.* A.D. 200). A late 2nd–mid/late 3rd century date for our piece seems highly likely, therefore. 2.50.

200. Jar in orange-buff Severn Valley ware; cf. *Wroxeter 1936–7*, 25 (late 2nd–early 3rd century); *Astley I*, 91 (late 3rd–early 4th century). The type seems most likely to fall within the range late 2nd–late 3rd century. 2.50.

201. Jar in Black-burnished ware; cf. *Gillam* type 135 (A.D. 170–250). 2.50.

202. Jar in Black-burnished ware; cf. *Gillam* type 145 (A.D. 230–300). 2.50.

203. Jar in hard light grey fabric; it is reminiscent of the 2nd–3rd century jars in Black-burnished ware (cf. *Gillam* type 138, A.D. 150–250; *Gillam* type 142, A.D. 190–280) and is probably of a similar date. 2.50.

204. Jar in light grey fabric; it is reminiscent of 3rd-century jars in Black-burnished ware (e.g. *Gillam* type 145, A.D. 230–300) and is possibly of a similar date. 2.50.

205. Wide-mouthed jar in a pink-buff fabric which may be Severn Valley ware. 2.50.

206. Wide-mouthed jar in orange Severn Valley ware; cf. *Astley I*, 117 (late 3rd–early 4th century); *Sutton Walls*, fig. 20, 26 (mixed 2nd–4th century); *Wroxeter III*, 79 (Bushe-Fox implies a date in the 3rd century or later); *Wroxeter 'Pottery Factory'*, fig. 26, 14 (3rd–4th century). A mid 3rd–4th century date would suit the type. 2.50.

207. Cup in grey fabric with a smooth dark grey surface. The drawing is a reconstruction from two non-joining fragments. The piece is an imitation of the samian form Dragendorf 33. 2.50.

208. Mortarium in cream fabric; the body of the vessel includes a number of fragments of broken stone up to 7 mm. in diameter; the trituration grits are dark grey; cf. *Carpow*, fig. 7, 1 (late 2nd–early 3rd century). 2.50.

209. Mortarium in cream fabric; *Gillam* type 282 (A.D. 230–340). 2.50.

210. Mortarium in light buff fabric; cf. *Gillam* type 272 (A.D. 190–300). 2.50.

211. Bowl in dark grey smooth fabric, burnished; the vessel is reminiscent of the samian bowl form Curle 15 and its associated types from East Gaul, such as Ludovici type To[1] (cf. *O&P*, Pl. LVI, 9 and Pl. LXIX,4). It may be an attempt

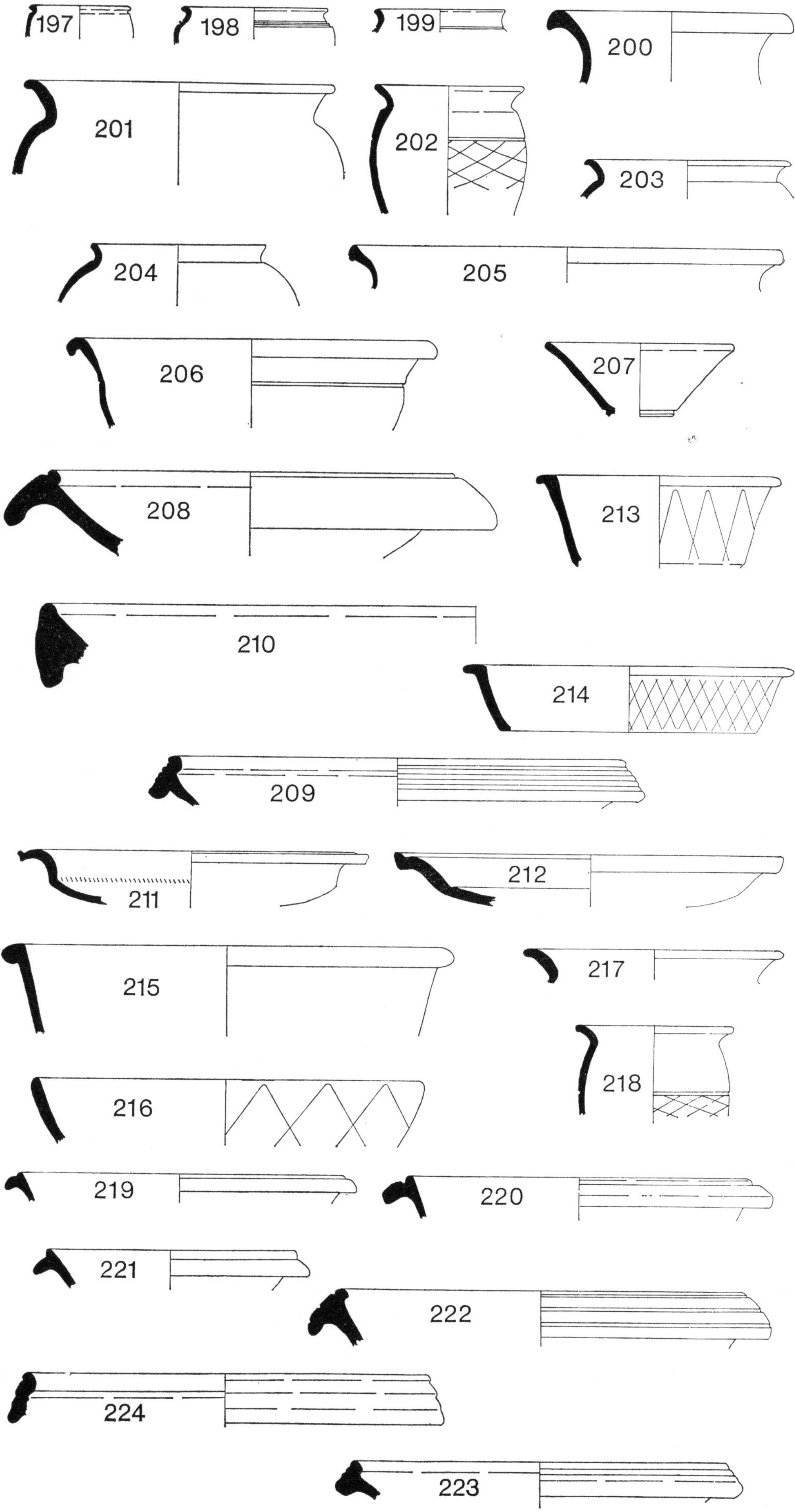

Fig. 40. Coarse pottery Nos. 197–224 ($\frac{1}{4}$ scale).

to imitate the samian original or it may be derived from later colour-coated imitations of that form. 2.50.

212. Bowl in grey fabric; it is a much coarser product that No. 211 above but again some similarity to Curle 15 is discernible; cf. *Mumrills*, fig. 105, 1 (Antonine). 2.50.
213. Bowl in Black-burnished ware; cf. *Gillam* type 219 (A.D. 120–150). 2.50.
214. Dish in Black-burnished ware; possibly *Gillam* type 309 (A.D. 160–200). 2.50.
215. Bowl in light grey sandy fabric; the form is reminiscent of certain late 2nd–3rd century bowls in Black-burnished ware (cf. *Gillam* type 225, A.D. 200–250, but also *Mumrills* fig. 101, 18, which suggests that the type may first have been produced in the late 2nd century); our vessel may be of similar date to these Black-burnished bowls. 2.50.
216. Dish in Black-burnished ware. 2.50.

The significance of this collection is twofold. It would seem to represent the tilth built up by ploughing and cultivation in the post-Roman period. It is likely to be derived, therefore, from the latest Roman occupation of the site. As such it is useful corroboration of the impression gained from study of the material from Building E and the industrial areas: that there was little activity on the site after the mid/late 3rd century (although as we shall see from section (iii) below, occupation of a later period *nearby* can be implied from scattered finds). In addition the collection could be expected to reflect any immediately post-Roman occupation on the site and there is none discernible.

(ii) *The Latest Roman Pottery.*

217. Jar in Black-burnished ware; cf. *Gillam* type 145 (A.D. 230–300). 3.25.
218. Jar in Black-burnished ware; cf. *Bewcastle*, 61 (A.D. 343/360–367); this vessel is a slightly less developed example of *Gillam* type 147 (A.D. 290–370). 2.38.
219. Flanged and beaded bowl in light grey fabric with a darker grey surface; cf. *Crambeck*, 10; this type of vessel in this fabric (which is probably of East Yorkshire origin) is certainly 4th century in date and could well belong to the period A.D. 360–400. 3.30.
220. Flanged and beaded bowl in grey-buff fabric with a worn mid-dark grey surface; cf. *Crambeck*, 8. Of similar date to No. 219 above. 3.1.
221. Flanged and beaded bowl in light grey fabric with a mid-grey surface; cf. *Crambeck*, 5; of similar date to No. 219 above. 4.+.
222. Mortarium in off-white fabric. The form is apparently typologically a little earlier than the hammer-head mortarium. Late 2nd–early 3rd century? 1.41.
223. Hammer-head mortarium in smooth creamy buff fabric; cf. *Gillam* type 281 (A.D. 230–340). 2.34.
224. Mortarium in hard cream fabric; one of the hammer-head mortarium series (3rd–early 4th century). 3.+.
225. Mortarium in a fairly sandy, light red fabric; cf. *Turret 35a*, 22 (unstratified). 4.2.
226. Mortarium in off-white fabric, very abraded; cf. *Gillam* type 272 (A.D. 190–300) for a somewhat similar piece. 3.15.

This small collection includes nearly all the pieces which were selected as being possibly of a later date than those published from the stratified levels. It will be seen, however, that most could belong to the mid/late 3rd century, the date suggested for the end of the main occupation of the site. Only Nos. 219–21 must belong to a later period than this. To these three can be added No. 194 above from the road ditch. These four pieces are the only ones identified from the site which are likely to belong to a late 4th-century occupation, and indeed the only certainly 4th-century sherds. They are most likely a scatter from the nearby fort rather than an indication of any occupation on the site examined.

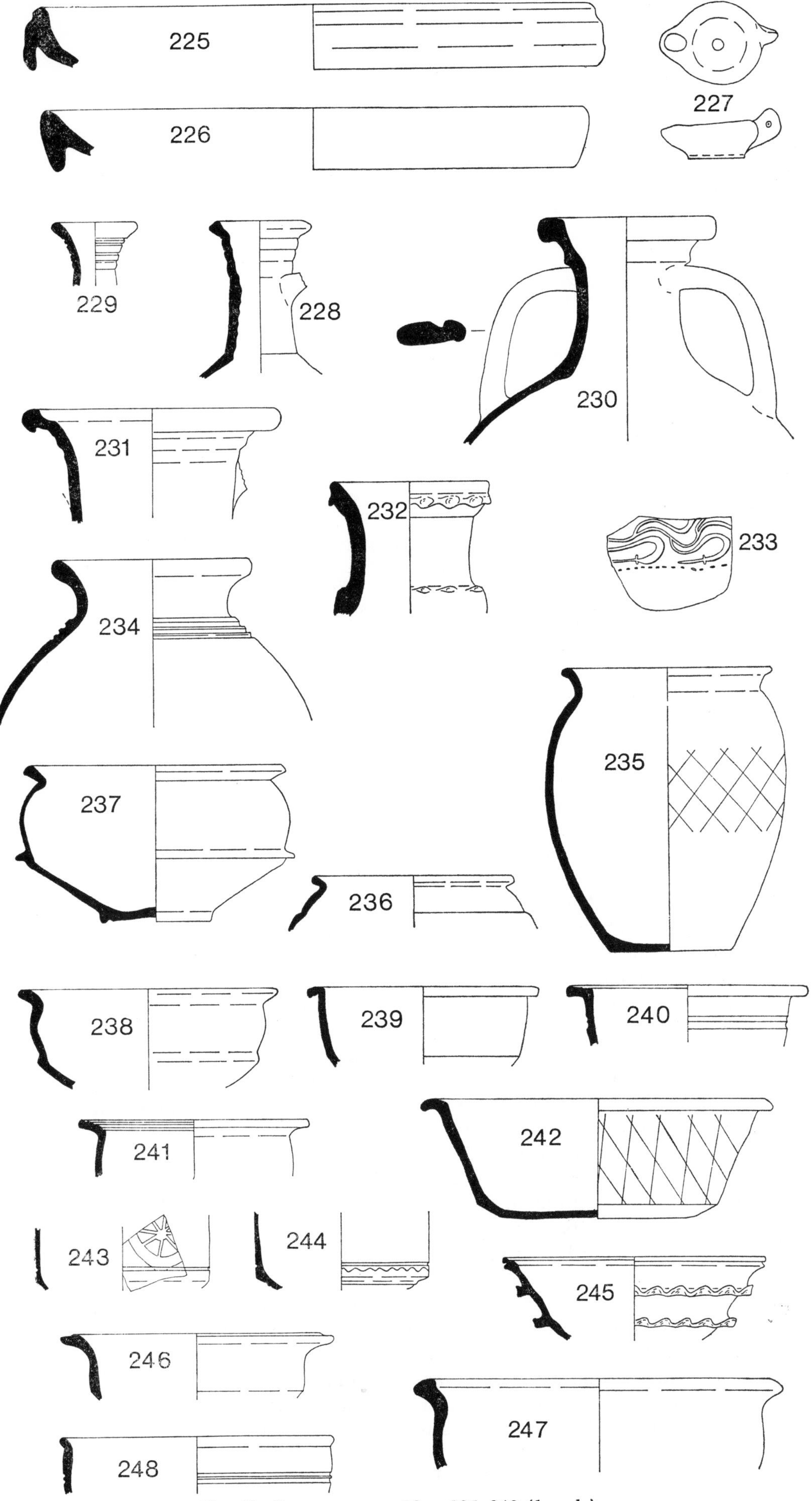

Fig. 41. Coarse pottery Nos. 225–248 (¼ scale).

(iii) *Material of general interest.*

A number of complete vessels have been included in this section, together with a number of others which it was felt would add something to the general picture of Roman ceramics at Manchester gained from the preceding sections.

227. Lamp in pink/fawn fabric, sooted around the spout. Simple lamps were being made at Wilderspool in the period A.D. 90–160 (*Wilderspool Kilns*, 71–3) and although this particular type cannot be paralleled at Wilderspool, it remains a likely source for the vessel. 4.5.
228. Flagon neck in hard sandy buff fabric; a variation of *Gillam* type 5 (A.D. 110–150). +.
229. Flagon neck in light red fabric with a creamy white slip; 2.+.
230. Double-handled flagon in light red fabric with traces of cream slip; cf. *Holt* 114 (probably late 1st–early 2nd century). 2.227.
231. Flagon in sandy buff fabric; cf. *Gillam* type 7 (A.D. 130–200). 1.116.
232. Jar in a somewhat sandy light red fabric with traces of white slip; cf. *Wilderspool Kilns*, 18 for a somewhat wider version of the same type. +.
233. Fragment of a beaker in white fabric with brown colour coat; cf. No. 105 above. 2.47.
234. Jar in soft light red fabric. 2.47.
235. Complete jar in Black-burnished ware; *Gillam* type 125 (A.D. 120–160). 2.93.
236. Jar in grey fabric; late 1st–early 2nd century. 1.131.
237. Wide-mouthed jar in smooth fabric with a dark grey core and an orange surface fired grey in parts. The drawing is a reconstruction from numerous fragments, many of which overlapped but did not join. There is a certain resemblance to the samian forms 44 and 81 (cf. *O&P*, Pl. LXI) both popular in the Antonine period. +.
238. Bowl in fawn/grey fabric with a darker grey surface; cf. *Wilderspool Kilns*, 53 (*c* A.D. 90–160). 2.32.
239. Flanged bowl in light grey fabric. This vessel together with Nos. 240–1 below are included to add to the range of late 1st–early 2nd-century flanged bowls already illustrated. 4.25.
240. Flanged bowl in light grey fabric with a dark grey surface; see No. 239 above. 2.28.
241. Flanged bowl in light orange-brown; see No. 239 above. 1.28.
242. Flanged bowl in Black-burnished ware; *Gillam* type 220 (A.D. 120–160). 2.183.
243. Bowl in pink fabric with white painted decoration; the form is reminiscent of the samian form 30. 1/2.2000.
244. Bowl in light grey fabric; the upper zone above the groove was probably originally rouletted in several bands but the fragment is too worn to be certain of this; the form is reminiscent of the samian form 30. 3.2.
245. Tazza in orange fabric; tazzas were being made at Wilderspool in the period *c.* A.D. 90–160, but this does not look like a Wilderspool product and a source at greater distance from Manchester seems likely. Fragments from 1.45 and 1.20.
246. Bowl in light orange fabric. 2.39.
247. Bowl or wide-mouthed jar in a fairly sandy light red fabric. 2.+.
248. Bowl in light red Severn Valley ware with a grey core. 3.25.
249. Bowl or dish in light red fabric with traces of a white slip. The decoration has been rouletted. 1.516.
250. Dish in Black-burnished ware burnt to a buff colour; cf. *Newstead 1911*, fig. 32 9 (Antonine). 4.5.
251. Fragment of mortarium in granular light yellow fabric bearing a stamp. Mrs. K. F. Hartley reports that this is a die A of Doinus; see *Arch. J.*, **129** (1972), pp. 77–82, for full discussion. 1.209.
252. Stamped mortarium. Mrs K. F. Hartley comments:
    Mortarium in hard cream fabric. The stamp reads F. LVGVDV and is a counterstamp of Albinus. For a discussion of Albinus see No. 173 above. 4.66.

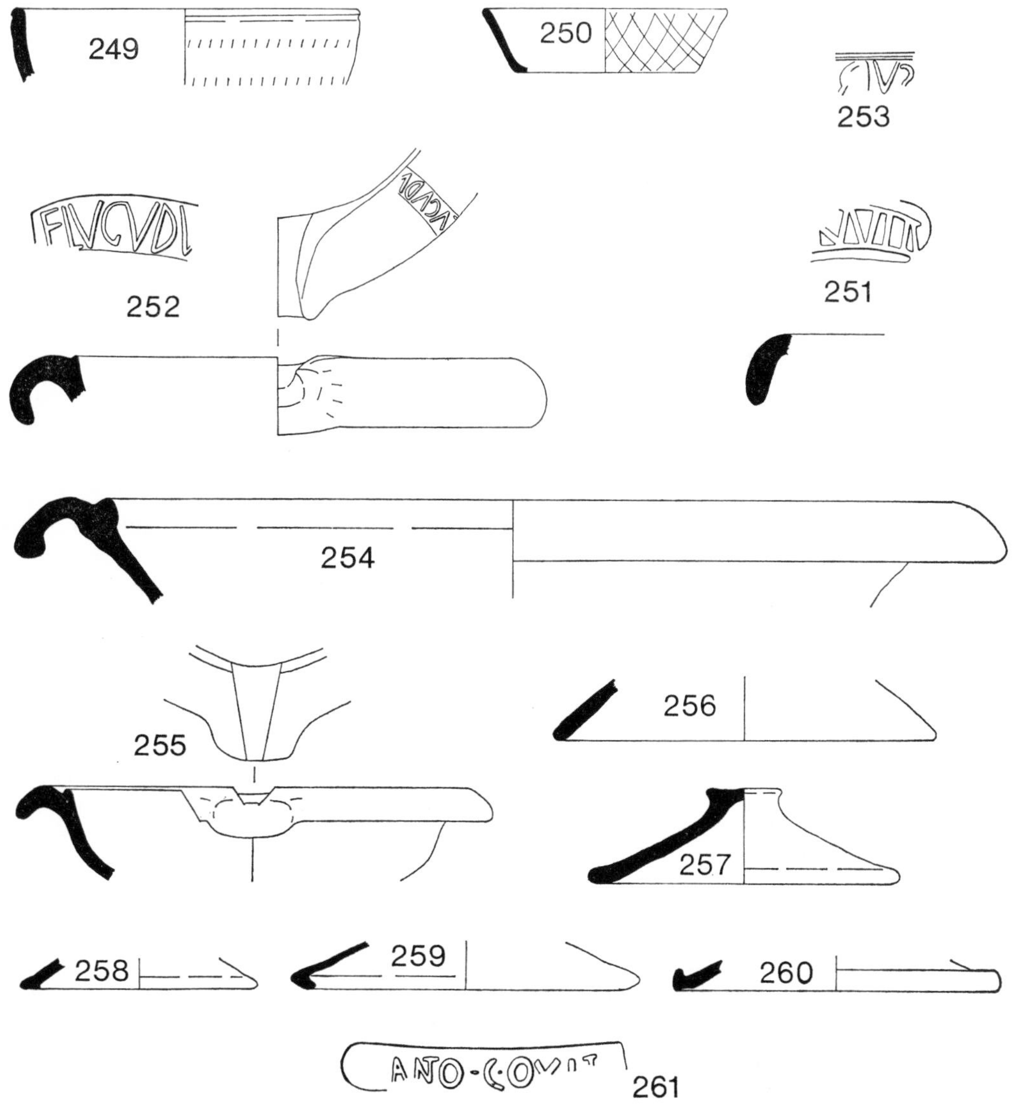

Fig. 42. Coarse pottery Nos. 249–261 (¼ scale).

253. Small fragment of mortarium rim in pale buff fabric bearing a poorly impressed stamp reading SVR . . . retrograde. 2.47.

254. Mortarium with faint traces of a stamp. Mrs K. F. Hartley comments:
The mortarium is in fine-textured cream fabric, liberally tempered with fine grey and brown grit. The tiny portion of a potter's stamp surviving is insufficient for certain identification but it is likely to be from one of the dies of Iunius who worked in the Hartshill and Mancetter potteries. The mortarium can be dated *c.* A.D. 150–185. 3.74.

255. Mortarium in light red fabric with white and red trituration grits. The spout has been cut with a knife or wire; cf. *Wilderspool Kilns*, 102 (A.D. 90–160). +.

256. Lid in a black gritty fabric similar to Black-burnished ware; cf. *Gillam* type 340 (A.D. 100–140). 3.2.

257. Lid in light grey with a darker grey surface externally. 1.132.

258. Lid in grey fabric. 1.1000.

259. Lid in light grey fabric with a darker grey surface externally; a similar form at the Jewry Wall site, Leicester, occurs predominantly in the 1st and 2nd centuries (*Leicester: Jewry Wall*, fig. 31, 4–7). 4.47.

260. Lid in hard mid grey fabric; cf. *Gillam* type 339 (A.D. 80–140). 3.2.

261. Amphora handle bearing the stamp AN͡TO. C. O[v]IT. 1.527.

262. (Not illustrated.) Fragment of a 'wine strainer' in smooth white-buff fabric. The type of vessel from which it was derived may be that illustrated and discussed as *Heronbridge* 65 (for a more complete example see *Silchester* type 71). All we have of our vessel is a pierced surface joined to the vessel wall which certainly extended both above and below the joint. The piercings have been made in a series of triangular panels. The purpose of the vessel is obscure but use as a strainer or as an incense burner has been suggested. Fragment from 4.62 with a further fragment from what may be a coarse example in mid-grey fabric from 4.25.

REFERENCES

[1] See above, p. 41. [2] See below, p. 139, for examples.

[3] Cited below as *Gillam 1973* (see list of abbreviations for full reference). It should be noted that Gillam here accepts the scheme of dating for Hadrian's Wall Period Ib and Antonine Wall Period II proposed by B. R. Hartley (*Britannia*, 3 (1972), pp. 1–55). This is not the scheme on which parts of his typology (*Gillam* q.v.) are based and minor variations in the dating of some types is, therefore, necessary. This may marginally affect the date of certain vessels below, although it does not affect the overall dating of the various features at Manchester.

[4] See: P. V. Webster, 'Melandra Castle, Derbyshire. Excavations in the Civilian Settlement, 1966–9', *Derbys. Arch. J.* for 1971 (forthcoming).

[5] Tile stamps of *Cohors III Bracaraugustanorum* occur at both Manchester and Melandra Castle (at the latter and probably at both, within the period A.D. 80–140). A tile kiln is at least a possibility. I am grateful to Mr J. Broadbent and Mr R. P. Wright for information about the stamps.

[6] The pottery from the *Wilderspool Kilns* (q.v.) the *Northwich Kiln* (q.v.) and some of the Holt products (see *Holt*, p. 144) fit into this category and there may well be other kilns awaiting discovery.

[7] cf. *Gillam 1973*, pp. 54–5.

[8] The dramatic nature of the change can be seen by comparing two groups from Northwich (*Northwich 1968–70*, 8–17 and 23–40) or indeed the pottery associated with the earlier occupation at Manchester (Nos. 1–21) with that from Buildings CI and CII (Nos. 24–35). The rapidity of the change may have been assisted by the closing down of many of the military potteries.

[9] See *Mumrills 1958–60*, pp. 126–130, and *Gillam 1973*, pp. 55–61.

[10] This statement is based partly on the published evidence, but mainly on extensive examination of the pottery from the two sites, much of it from recent and as yet unpublished excavation.

[11] *Gilliam 1973*, pp. 57–8.

[12] The source of BB1 is still problematical. Farrar has produced good evidence for production in above-ground bonfire 'kilns' which leave little archaeological evidence (*Farrar 1968*) and has argued for a major production centre in Dorset (*Farrar 1973*, pp. 86–97) backed by the evidence of mineral analysis (*Peacock 1973*). Despite the difficulties of distribution throughout Western Britain without either shipping the pottery around Land's End or taking it for long distances overland, this is clearly a major step forward in identifying the source or sources of the ware.

[13] For a discussion of the fabric see *Webster 1972*, p. 191, and P. V. Webster, 'Severn Valley Ware: a Preliminary Chronology', *Trans. Bristol and Gloucs. Arch. Soc.* (forthcoming).

[14] For full details on Severn Valley ware from the Wall zone see *Webster 1972*.

[15] As seems possible with BB1, see Note 12 above.

iii: The Small Finds

JANET WEBSTER, B.A.

ABBREVIATIONS

Abergavenny 1962–9: L. Probert, J. L. Davis, H. N. Savory, G. C. Boon, K. T. Greene, M. G. Spratling, 'Excavations at Abergavenny 1962–1969 (i) Prehistoric and Roman Finds', *Monmouthshire Antiquarian*, Vol. II, pt. iv, pp. 163–98.

Caerleon: Myrtle Cottage Orchard 1939: A. Fox, 'The Legionary Fortress at Caerleon, Monmouthshire: Excavations in Myrtle Cottage Orchard 1939', *Archaeologia Cambrensis*, 95 (1940), pp. 101–52.

Camulodunum: C. F. C. Hawkes and M. R. Hull, *Camulodunum: First Report on Excavations at Colchester* 1930–39, Report of Research Committee of Society of Antiquaries of London, no. XIV, 1947.

Cranborne Chase (iii): A. Pitt-Rivers, *Excavations in Cranborne Chase* (iii), 1892.

Fishbourne (ii): B. Cunliffe, *Excavations at Fishbourne 1961–69*, vol. ii, The Finds; Report of the Research Committee of the Society of Antiquaries of London, no. XXVI, 1971.

Hod Hill (i): J. Brailsford, *Hod Hill*, Vol. i; *Antiquities from Hod Hill in the Durden Collection* 1962.

Housesteads 1934: Eric Birley and John Charlton, 'Third Report on Excavations at Housesteads', *Archaeologia Aeliana*, 4th series, XI, 1934, pp. 185–205.

Jewry Wall: Kathleen M. Kenyon, *Excavations at the Jewry Wall Site, Leicester*; Report of the Research Committee of the Society of Antiquaries of London, no. XV, 1948.

Maiden Castle: R. E. M. Wheeler, *Maiden Castle, Dorset*; Report of the Research Committee of the Society of Antiquaries of London, no. XII, 1943.

Mumrills: Sir G. MacDonald and Alexander O. Curle, 'The Roman Fort at Mumrills near Falkirk'. *P.S.A.S.* 63 (1928–9), pp. 396–575.

Newstead: J. Curle, *A Roman Frontier Post and its People—The Fort of Newstead in the Parish of Melrose*, 1911.

Nor'nour: Dorothy Dudley, 'Excavations on Nor'nour in the Isles of Scilly 1962–66', *Arch. J.*, CXXIV (1967), pp. 1–64.

Richborough IV: J. P. Bushe-Fox, *Fourth Report on the Excavations of the Roman Fort at Richborough, Kent*; Report of the Research Committee of the Society of Antiquaries of London, no. XVI, 1949.

Richborough V: B. Cunliffe, *Fifth Report on the Excavations of the Roman Fort at Richborough, Kent*; Report of the Research Committee of the Society of Antiquaries of London, no. XXIII, 1968.

Roman Cheshire: F. H. Thompson, *Roman Cheshire*, 1965.

Shakenoak (ii): A. C. C. Brodribb, A. R. Hands, D. R. Walker, *Excavations at Shakenoak Farm, near Wilcote, Oxfordshire, Part II*; Sites B & H, 1971.

Frere, Verulamium (i): S. S. Frere, *Verulamium Excavations*, Vol. 1; Report of Research Committee of Society of Antiquaries of London, no. XXVIII, 1972.

Wroxeter, The Defences of Viroconium: Graham Webster, 'The Defences of Viroconium (Wroxeter)', *Trans. of the Birmingham Archaeological Society*, vol. 78 (1962), pp. 27–39.

Note: In the accompanying catalogue, the codes at the end of each item marked thus: 1 (66) [135] refer to the trench, layer and small find numbers of the individual piece concerned.

I. BRONZE OBJECTS

(a) *Brooches.*

1 & 2. Severely abraded fragments of a Hod Hill brooch with fragments of what is probably an identical brooch, the latter not illustrated.

Most of the head of the brooch is extant. The pin is hinged and the pivot bar is of iron. Across the upper part of the bow is a transverse ridge. A longitudinal ridge, flanked by grooves, runs down the centre of the bow and there were probably two further such ridges, one down each outer edge; traces of one such ridge remain.

The foot and catchplate are lost.

The fragments of the second brooch comprise a small part of the bow decorated with transverse and longitudinal ridging in apparently identical pattern to the first brooch. It seems probable that the two brooches formed a pair.

cf. *Camulodunum*, pl. XCVII, no. 140ff.; *Hod Hill* (i), fig. 8, nos. C53ff.

Hod Hill brooches were popular in Britain in the Claudio-Neronian period with occasional survivals into the early Flavian period. 1 (260) [302]

3. The flat, tapering bow and catchplate are all that remain of this brooch. The pin arrangement and the head of the brooch are missing. A line of ornament runs down each side of the bow close to the edge. Each line of decoration comprises a light ridge, defined by indented lines and crossed by fine, closely spaced, zigzag incised lines. Some attempt seems to have been made to produce mouldings at the foot.

The brooch is similar to a group of flat, tapering bow brooches from Hod Hill, derived, according to Brailsford, from the Langton Down type (the latter pre-Conquest and Claudian in date); cf. *Hod Hill (i)*, fig. 7, nos. C33–C39, p. 8, also *Maiden Castle*, p. 260, fig. 84, nos. 23 and 25, both dated A.D. 25–70.

In the absence of the pin arrangement and the head it is difficult to be certain that the fragment belongs to this pre-Flavian group of brooches. 1 (241) [277]

4. Dolphin brooch, badly corroded. The spring arrangement is obscure. There is no means of securing the external chord. An axial bar to the spring probably passed through the pierced disc terminals of the short side-wings. There is a broad, pronounced, probably knurled margin at the outer edge of each side-wing. The catchplate is lost but its ridge is carried up the back of the brooch to the spring.

The Dolphin form appears at Camulodunum in the early part of the second half of the first century A.D. and is current into the second century. 1 (66) [135]

5. Dolphin brooch, considerably corroded. The hinged pin is secured by an iron bar which passes through a long cross-bar decorated on the front with ridges. A ridged line decorated with tiny knobbed dots runs down the centre of the thick, faceted bow. There is no foot-knob. The catchplate is solid.

cf. *Richborough IV*, pls. XXVII and XXVIII, nos. 28 and 31.

The hinged form of the dolphin brooch is generally thought to be later than the earliest spring forms. Late first to early second century A.D. 4 (71) [111]

6. The spring is secured by means of an axial bar which passes through the pierced disc terminals of the short side-wings and there is a broad hook at the crest to secure the chord. The side-wings terminate in sharp, ridged margins. The bow is humped at the broad head and tapers slightly. The head is flanked by moulded, semi-circular plates. These features indicate that the brooch is one within a general category discussed by Mackreth (Shakenoak II, p. 118–9, no. 70) with a distribution mainly in the West Midlands and South Wales. The decoration of brooches of this type varies considerably. In this case, an elongated V-shaped panel of enamel ornament extends from the plain head over the upper part of the bow. The enamel decoration consists of two lines of alternating rectangular blocks of colour, yellow and ?green. The two lines are separated from each other by a fine bronze wall but there are no such walls dividing the alternating rectangular blocks from each other. The panel terminates in a triangular sinking from which the enamel has been lost.

The bronze margins which flank the ornamental panel taper to a point at its lower end and continue as a medial ridge down the lower part of the bow. Much of the lower bow is lost.

Mackreth suggests a date range of A.D. 75 into the second century for this category of brooches. Compare also a brooch from Wilderspool, Cheshire (*Roman Cheshire*, p. 82, fig. 20, no. 4). Although the profile of the head of the bow is sharper than the Manchester example the brooch is closely similar and the spring arrangement appears to be the same. Thompson suggests that the form of enamelled decoration seen on the Wilderspool brooch may perhaps be regarded as characteristic of the Wilderspool workshops and it therefore seems not unlikely that the Manchester brooch is a Wilderspool product, too. The date range of the general type and the date range of the Wilderspool workshops between them suggest an early second century A.D. date for this brooch. 1 (156) [163]

7. The brooch has a spring pin. The axial bar of the spring is secured through pierced discoid projections which form a case for the spring behind the U-shaped plate at the head. There is an internal chord. At the top of the U-shaped plate is a cast loop, now broken. The upper part of the bow is decorated with two rows of enamel ornament. The two rows are separated from each other by a bronze wall but there are no such walls separating the alternating rectangular blocks of colour which comprise each row. There are two lobed mouldings below the enamelled panel. The lower part of the bow has slight marginal flanges. The foot is moulded.

Compare a very similar brooch from Willoughby-on-the-Wolds (*Trans. Thoroton Soc. of Notts.*, 1966, pp. 9–10). Mackreth discusses the origins of the type and lists other examples of similar brooches. On stylistic grounds he dates the type to the first half of the second century A.D. MC. 72 (+) [331]

Nos. **8** to **12** are trumpet brooches. The date range for such brooches is Flavian to late second century.

8. The brooch has a spring pin, part of the spring being intact. The trumpet head rises to a central point to form a stop for the wire loop. The half-round moulding at the waist comprises a plain button flanked by acanthus mouldings, and a transverse groove and plain moulding lie to either side of the waist-knob separating it from the upper and lower sections of the bow. The foot is missing. 1 (531) [158]

9. Part of the spring remains. There is a stop for a wire loop set back from the trumpet head and a catch for the internal chord at the rear base of the trumpet head. The upper section of the bow has a slight medial ridge. The mouldings at the waist are now severely damaged. The button is flanked by crude derived-acanthus mouldings. There is a slight transverse moulding, flanked by grooves, separating the upper bow from the waist ornament. Below the waist knob is a broad knurled transverse moulding. The waist mouldings are not carried fully round the back of the bow. The lower part of the bow is flattish with a light medial ridge and with very narrow flanged margins. There is an abraded foot-knob.

cf. *Richborough V*, pl. XXVIII, no. 30, for a brooch combining similar decorative elements. 4 (148) [299]

10. The pin was sprung. There is a marked chordhook at the rear base of the trumpet head. A pronounced moulding defines the outer edge of the front face of the trumpet head. There is elaborate moulding at the waist all of which is carried right round the bow. The button itself is very pronounced and is ornamented with a zigzag pattern of raised lobes. It is defined by a very thin transverse moulding above and by a similar moulding below. Broader, knurled transverse mouldings, defined by narrow ridges lie to either side of the button, separated from it by grooves. The lower bow is rounded to the front. There is a foot knob with knurled ornament, flanked by narrow mouldings. There are traces of silvering or tinning. MC.72(+)[332]

11. The brooch is severely corroded and much of the lower bow is lost. The pin is sprung. A pronounced marginal moulding, flanked by an inner groove, encircles

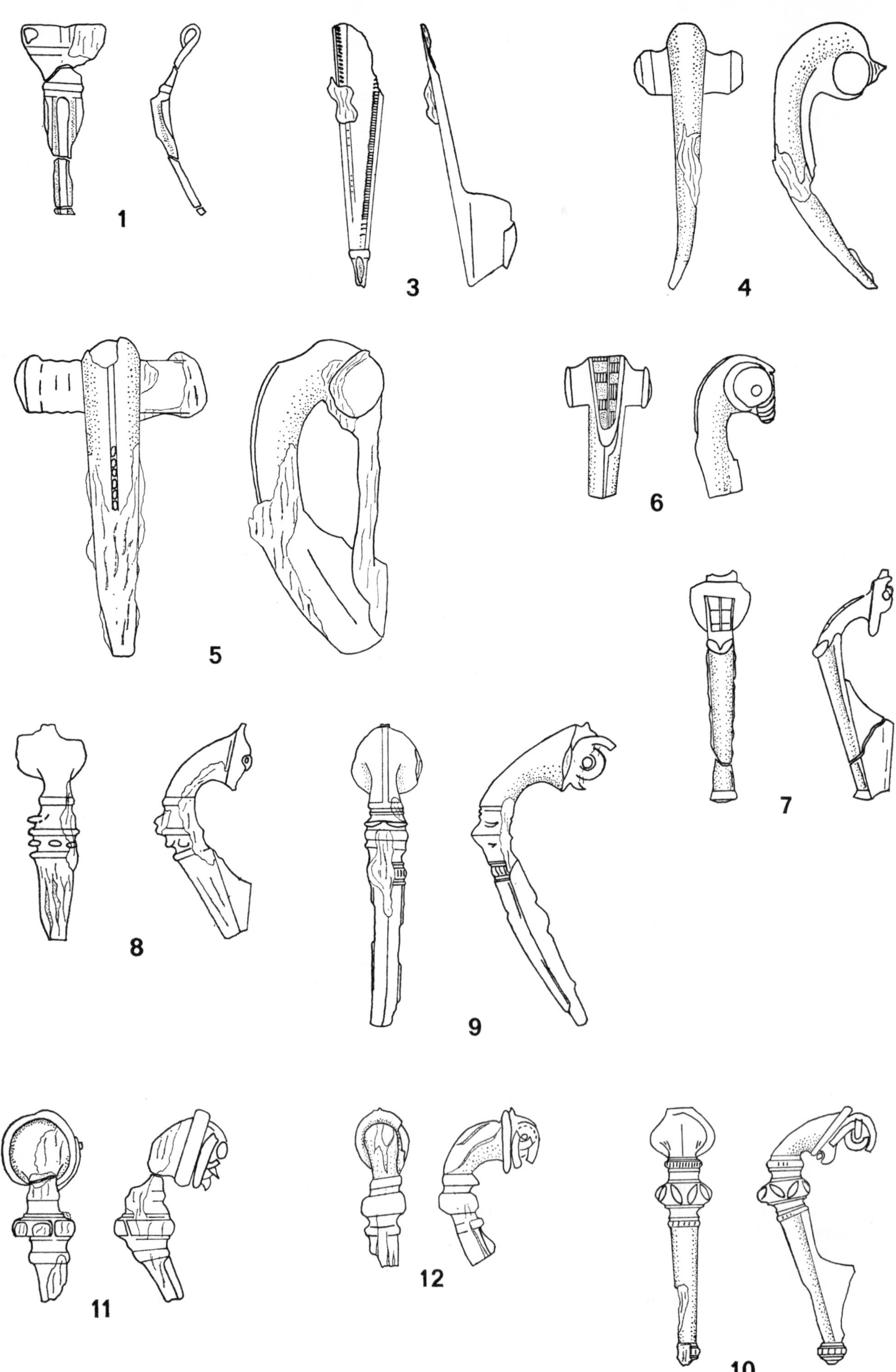

JW

Fig. 43. Small finds Nos. 1–12 ($\frac{1}{1}$ scale).

the outer edge of the trumpet head. There is a pronounced button apparently ornamented with knobs which are now abraded away. A slight moulding defines the upper and lower edges of the button. There is a further broad, transverse moulding, below the waist knob. The mouldings are carried fully round the bow and it is only at the back that the moulding above the waist knob can now be seen.

cf. *Nor'nour*, p. 45, fig. 17, no. 110, a variant of the trumpet brooch but with similar waist knob. T1/2 (15)? [328]

12. The brooch is badly corroded. The pin is sprung. The trumpet head is reduced to a flat oval plate. There are remains of a small loop-stop to the rear of the trumpet head. The mouldings at the waist are carried round to the rear but are flattened at the back of the brooch. The waist knob is plain and there are plain mouldings flanking the grooves to either side of the waist knob. The lower part of the bow is largely lost. 2 (52) [48]

(b) *Other Bronze Objects.*

13. Harness link. The roundel is flat with a projecting central knob and with a pronounced projecting margin with dot decoration. The rings, cast in one piece with the roundel, whereby the various leather straps were secured to it, remain only as fragmentary projections. cf. an almost identical harness link from Newstead. *Newstead*, pl. LXXIV, no. 6. 4 (+) [325]

14. Roundel for attachment to the leather straps of horse harness. The roundel has two projecting rectangular loops to the rear, through which the leather strap passed; one of these loops is now damaged. The roundel is similar in appearance to the harness link above but has an additional moulding around the central knob. Two slight projections indicate that this roundel, too, was equipped probably with a ring for securing a further leather strap which must have lain at right angles to that which passed through the rectangular loops at the back of the roundel. 4 (148) [273]

15. ?Harness attachment. There is a rectangular loop at the rear of the object for a leather strap to be attached to or pass through. The object is severely abraded; cf. *Newstead*, pl. LXXVII, no. 14. 1 (265) [305]

16. Small terret; cf. a very similar example from Wilderspool, *Roman Cheshire*, p. 82, fig. 20, no. 24. 4 (71) [110]

17. Fragment of flat bronze ring with red enamel ornament. Perhaps from horse trappings. 4 (99) [115]

18. Plain bronze ring, probably from horse harness. 2 (79) [88]

19. Plain bronze stud or roundel with pronounced projecting margin and slight central knob. The arrangement at the back of the roundel is not now intelligible. Possible harness attachment. 4 (162) [275] (not illustrated)

20. Stud with triskele decoration inlaid with turquoise and yellow enamel. The device is common; cf. brooches from Wroxeter, *The Defences of Viroconium*, p. 38, fig. 6, no. 22, and Nor'nour, *Nor'nour*, p. 55, fig. 21, no. 193, and p. 63, fig. 25 no. 257. 1 (133) [90]

21. Stud with concentric rings and star design in enamel. Traces of blue and yellow enamel remain.

cf. *Housesteads* 1934, pl. XXIXe, no, 1, p. 203–4, no. 49 dated to Wall Period I; *Newstead*, pl. LXXXIX, no. 10. 2 (134) [196]

22. Lion head attachment. The features are crudely rendered. There is a large triangular raised patch for the nose and two horizontal ridges represent the eyes or eyebrows. There is a small pointed beard. The mane is represented in groups of clustered locks with individual hairs sketchily shown by indented lines. The metal extends back from the mane as though to form a cylinder. Inside the boss, underneath the nose, is a projecting portion of bronze, presumably for attachment.

cf., for example, *Frere, Verulamium* 1, p. 136, fig. 43, no. 141, and pl. XXXVIIId, no. 108. 1 (502) [56]

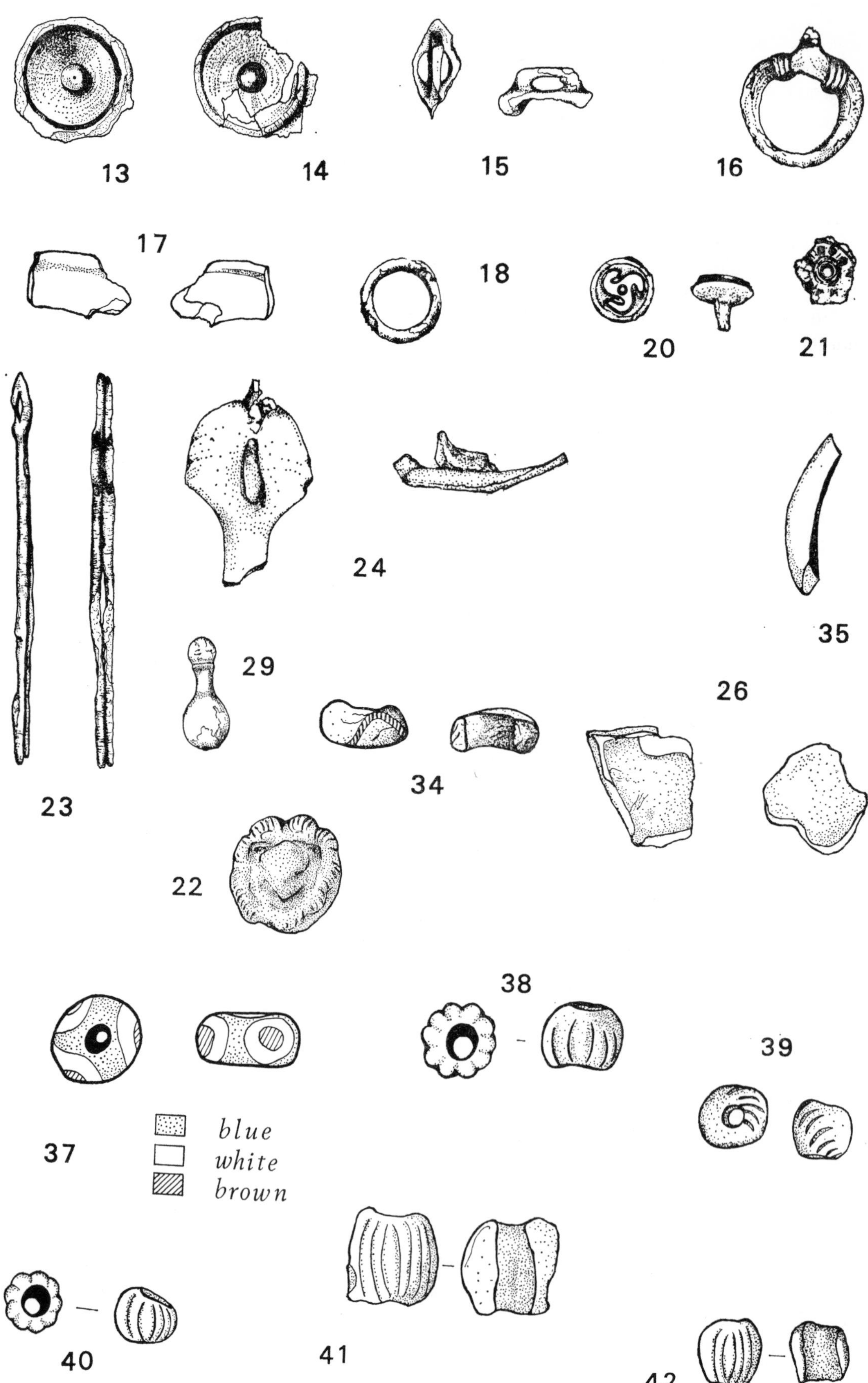

Fig. 44. Small finds Nos. 13–18, 20–24, 26, 29, 34, 35, 37–42 (all at ½ scale except Nos. 17, 22, 26, and 35–42 which are actual size).

23. Folding foot-rule?; cf. *Roman Cheshire*, p. 82, fig. 20, no. 1. 1 (265) [307]

24. The hinged lid of a bronze vessel. The handle for lifting the lid was probably in the form of a stylised dolphin with a tall, upward-pointing tail. cf. *Abergavenny* 1962–9, Fig. 10, no. 6, and p. 195. 4 (162) [282]

25. Fragments of sheet bronze with wood attached. Perhaps part of a bronze cased wooden box. 2 (258) [298] (not illustrated)

26. Fragments of a lozenge-shaped seal box. 2 (?) [192]

27. Bronze binding. 1 (510) [178] (not illustrated)

28. Strap end?; cf. *Newstead*, pl. LXXVI, no. 13. 2 (168) [309] (not illustrated)

29. Bronze knob ornament. Traces of attachments at either end. cf. *Jewry Wall*, p. 259, fig. 87, no. 5—identified tentatively as the head of a linch pin; and *Mumrills* p. 554, fig. 115, no. 16—unidentified. 1 (35) [237]

30. Head of pin or nail. 2 (95) [67] (not illustrated)

Nos. **31–33** are not illustrated because of their poor condition.

31. Stud in the form of a solid boss. The boss is *c.* 2 cm in diameter and *c.* 0.9 cm in height. 3 (142) [243]

32. Fragment of a pair of tweezers. 2 (115) [197]

33. Fragments of sheet bronze folded together, perhaps for melting down and reworking. 2 (108) [143]

II. OBJECT OF OBSIDIAN

34. Bead in ring form of reddish volcanic glass (obsidian) with twisted white and blue glass pressed into a channel. Very possibly found as a pebble and drilled as the inclusion bubbles are still in their spherical state. The object is clearly a bead not a finger ring. The internal diameter is too narrow to be worn on the finger and the ring itself is too thick to be capable of lying between the fingers.

1 (286) [327]

III. GLASS OBJECTS

35. Part of a bracelet of opaque white glass. 2 (115?) [223]=Glass object No. 90.

36. Glass counters. Eight from one deposit, one from elsewhere. cf., for example, *Maiden Castle*, pl. XXXII, A, nos. 1–10.

1 (286) [329] 8 counters; 4 (66) [57] 1 counter

37. Glass bead with eye decoration. The bead is dark blue. The eyes are white with large amber-coloured centres. cf. *Newstead*, pl. XCI, nos. 16–19. 1 (22) [27]

Nos. **38–42** are melon beads and may be compared, for example, with those from *Caerleon, Myrtle Cottage Orchard 1939*, p. 133, fig. 7, nos. 22, 23, and Newstead, *Newstead*, pl. XCI, nos. 2, 4, 7–11, 13–15, 21–22, 27–29, 33–34.

38. Complete grey/turquoise in colour. 1 (531) [181]

39. Small green bead. 2 (188) [170]

40. Damaged. Turquoise in colour. 4 (137) [185]

41. Half a bead. Turquoise in colour. 4 (29) [77]

42. Half a small bead of turquoise colour. 2 (181) [133]

There were three other complete, turquoise-coloured melon beads and fragments of fifteen others of pale green, green, turquoise and opaque and clear dark blue shades.

1 (209) [200]; 2 (167) [203]; 1 (169) [140]; 1 (241) [256]; 1 (600) [177]; 1 (209) [219]; 1 (560) [278]; 4 (47) [145]; 2 (260) [324]; 1 (156) [141]; 1 (260) [301]; 1 (176) [157]; 4 (112) [152]

IV. LEAD OBJECTS

43. Spindle whorl. 1 (38) [53]

44. Spindle whorl. 4 (148) [263]

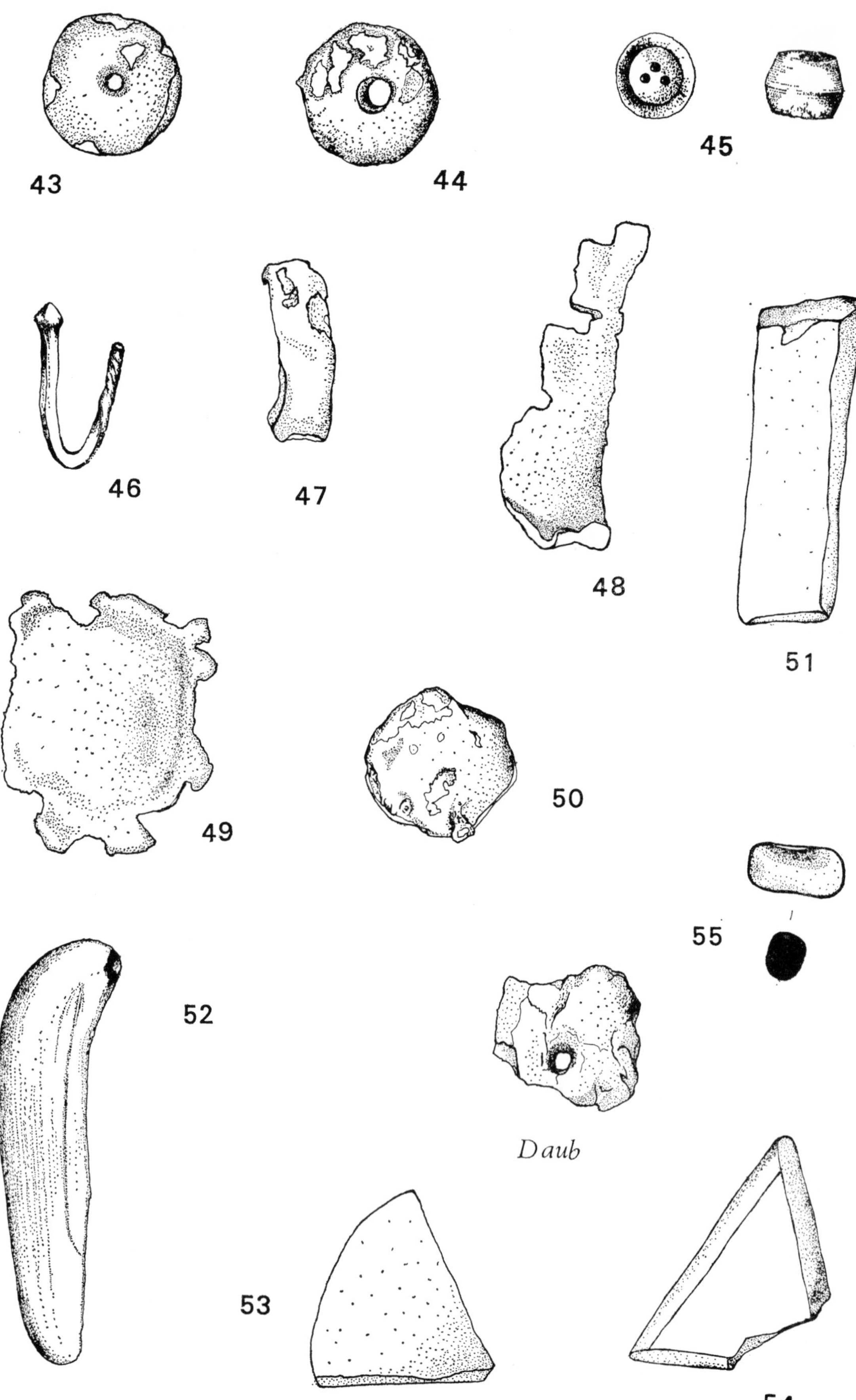

Fig. 45. Small finds Nos. 43–55 (all at ½ scale except Nos. 43, 44 and 48–50 which are actual size).

45. Weight. One face has three circular depressions, probably designed to show at a glance the weight of the object. 1 (186) [244]

46. Lead rod with a knob at one end. The part nearest the knob is of square cross-section and this gives way to a twisted portion. cf. a similar rod, of iron, *Cranborne Chase III*, pl. CLXXIV, no. 25. 1 (29) [51]

47. Binding. 2 (53) [37]

48. Binding. 1 (565) [314]

49. Fragment of sheet lead. 3 (94) [211]

50. Disc with one flat face and one irregular surface. 4 (96) [187]

Twenty-one other fragments of lead were recorded from the site, none illustrated.

V. STONE OBJECTS

51. Whetstone. 1 (176) [166]

52. Whetstone. 1 (83) [58]

53. Worked stone, apparently part of a disc. 2 (50) [97]

54. Worked stone, perhaps an architectural fragment. 2 (182) [280]

55. Stone object shaped like a knuckle-bone and possibly used for a game.

VI. IRON OBJECTS

56. Ballista bolt. 1. 212B (not illustrated)

57. Massive ring and tie; cf. *Fishbourne (ii)*, p. 130, fig. 57, no. 22. 2 (72) [82] (not illustrated)

58. Chisel; cf. *Hod Hill I*, fig. 13, G26. 2 (128) [122]

59. Fragments of a hob-nail boot. 3 (110) [206]

60. Fragments of a hob-nail boot. 3 (117) [272]

61. Iron hob-nails from a boot. 3 (92) [238]

62. Similar hob nails. 3 (126) [233]

63. Bracket or hook. 3 (81) [189]

64. Hook. 4 (53) [47]

65. Knife. 4 (68) [254] (not illustrated)

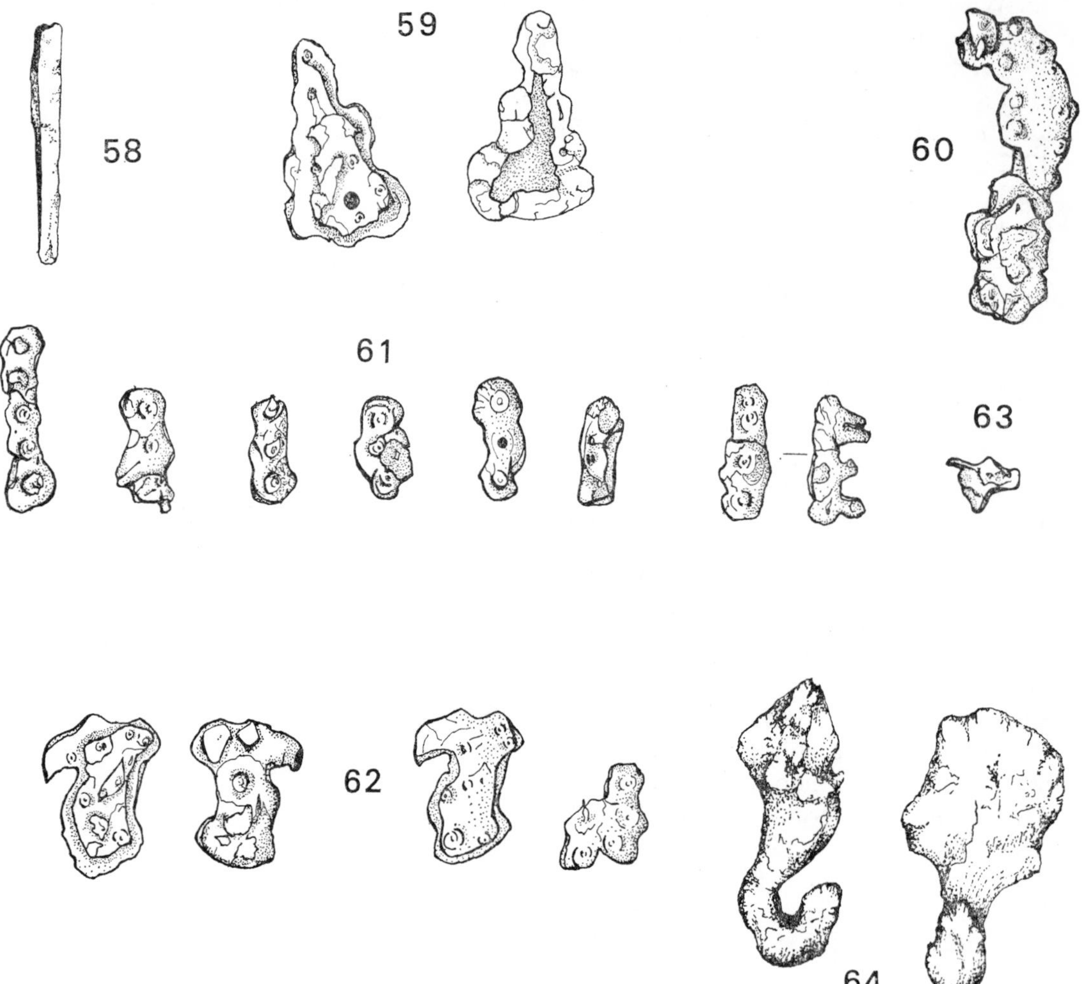

Fig. 46. Small finds Nos. 58–64 (scale ½).

VII. QUERNS[1]

SHELAGH GREALEY, B.PHIL., M.A.

The quern fragments fall into two categories, those of basalt certainly alien to Britain and presumed to derive from the Andernach lava series in Germany,[2] and those of millstone grit. There are abundant sources for the latter in the nearby Pennines while imported Andernach querns are attested at Chester, Melandra and Brough-on-Noe.

66. Leucitic basalt. Diameter 27 cm. Depth 3 cm. Slot for handle (fig. 47). 4 (140) [248]

67. Leucitic basalt. Broken. Diameter approx. 28 cm. Depth 14 cm (fig. 47). 4 (110) [?]

68. Leucitic basalt. Broken. Diameter approx. 29 cm. Depth 15 cm. Concentric grooves on upper face (fig. 47). 4 (140) [246]

69. Leucitic basalt. Maximum diameter 32 cm. Depth 8 cm. Grooves radiate from central perforation on upper face (fig. 47). 4 (140) [247]

70. Leucitic basalt. Broken. Depth 4 cm. Grooves radiate from central perforation on upper face (not illustrated). 4 (83) [80]

71. Leucitic basalt. Broken. Depth 5 cm. Grooves visible on upper face (not illustrated). 1 (531) [168]

72. Millstone grit. Broken. Depth 4 cm. Grooves visible on upper face (not illustrated). 2 (+) [171]

73. Millstone grit. Broken. Depth 6 cm (not illustrated). 4 (96) [190]

74. Leucitic basalt. Broken. Depth 8 cm. Grooves visible on upper face (not illustrated). 1 (510) [222]

75. Leucitic basalt. Broken. Depth 5 cm. Grooves visible on upper face (not illustrated). 1 (165) [229]

76. Millstone grit. Broken. Depth 5 cm. Grooves visible on upper face (not illustrated). 4 (68) [253]

77. Leucitic basalt. Broken. Diameter approx. 25 cm. Depth 5 cm (plate 28a). 1 (69) [65]

78. Leucitic basalt. Diameter 25 cm. Depth 6 cm. (plate 28b)

REFERENCES

1 E. C. Curwen, 'Querns', *Antiquity*, XI (1937), 133–152.
2 L. West, *Roman Britain: The Objects of Trade* (1931), s.v. querns.

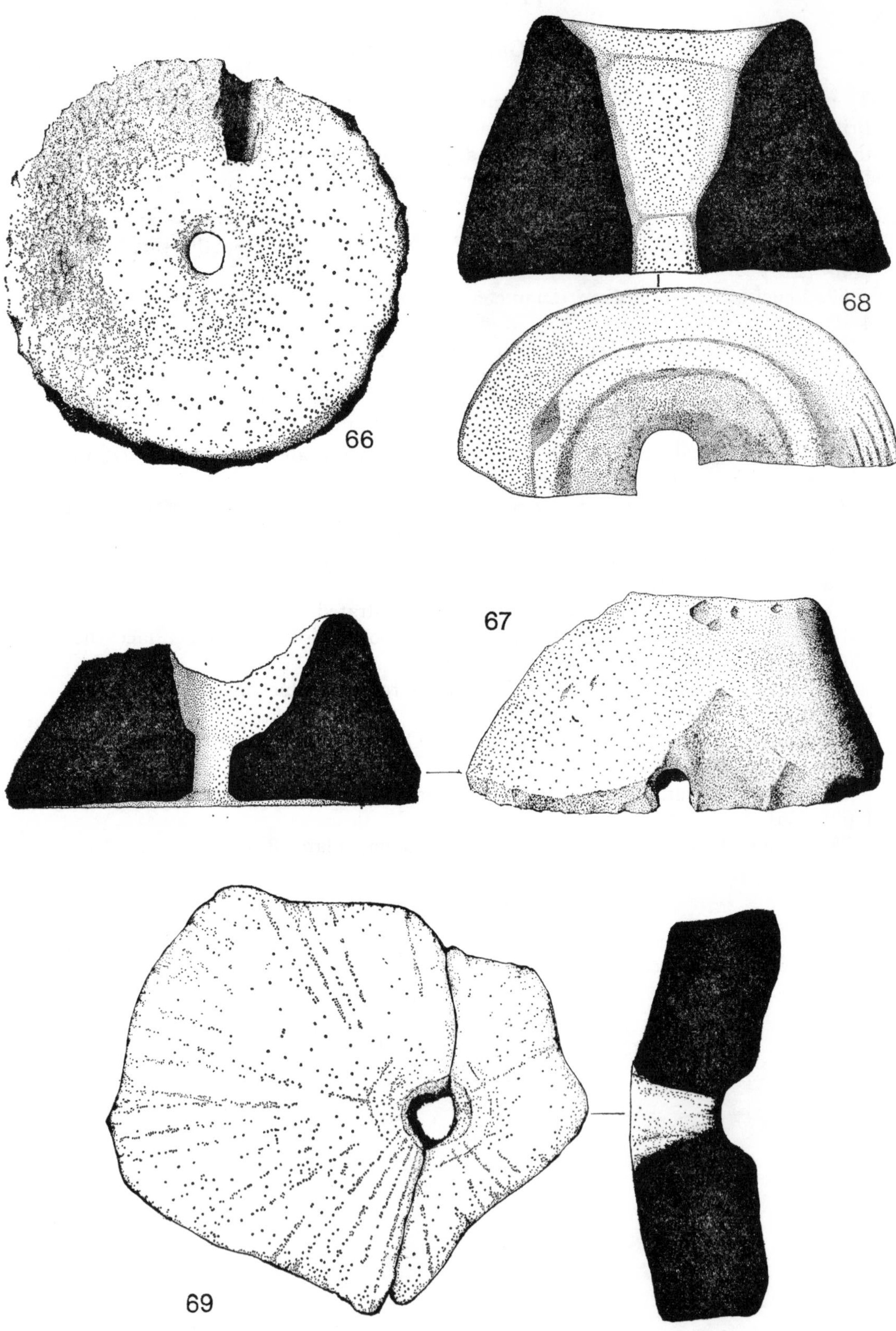

Fig. 47. Quern-stones, Nos. 66–69 (p.129). Drawn by M. J. Snelgrove

VIII. THE GLASS

JENNIFER PRICE, B.A.

The excavations produced 110 fragments of Roman glass. Ten of these were window glass, all of the matt-glossy type,[1] 73 were from square and cylindrical bottles, 25 were from other glass vessels (including 4 fragments distorted by fire) and 2 were glass objects. All of the vessel glass is free blown, with the exception of the square bottles and the cylindrical bottle with horizontal ribs ('Frontinus' bottle.).

The report lists the interesting and uncommon fragments. I have not included the fragments which provide no information about the date, form or decoration of the vessel.

79. Fragment, curved shoulder and body; dark blue with opaque white marvered blobs; blobs gathered on paraison and marvered flush before final inflation of vessel; 3.1 × 4.6 cm. 4 (79).

The form of the vessel is uncertain, but may be a jug similar to one from the Aegean islands now in the British Museum.[2] Coloured glass with opaque white marvered decoration was probably manufactured in North Italy in the middle of the first century A.D., and is quite rare on Romano-British sites. There are fragments from Camulodunum,[3] Silchester, London, Canterbury,[4] and Usk.

80. Fragment, blue; straight-sided vessel; one optic blown vertical rib (first blown into a ribbed mould then into a plain mould, thus depressing the ribs through the wall of the vessel); 2 × 2.5 cm. 1 (539) [232].

This fragment perhaps belongs to a conical jug,[5] or carinated bowl.[6] Both forms are quite commonly found on Romano-British sites in later first and second century contexts.

81. Two fragments; light green; curved side; one optic blown rib on each fragment; 2.2 × 2.3 cm. and 1.6 × 2.2 cm. 2 (245) [268].

It is not possible to identify the form of this vessel. Optic blown ribs were a fairly common form of decoration in the Roman period; jugs, jars, cups, unguent bottles and bowls were decorated in this manner.[7]

82. Fragment, rim; bluish green; horizontal rim, edge rounded and thickened in flame; raised ridge at junction with body, formed by S-fold in wall of vessel; diameter (rim) 19 cm. T 1 (56) [28].

The form of the vessel is not certain, but it may have been a one-handled cup.[8] S-folds in the walls of vessels are comparatively rare, though they were sometimes employed as foot-rings in shallow plates and bowls. A very similar rim fragment was found during excavations at the Holbrooks site at Harlow, Essex, in 1970, and a body fragment with a similar fold was found at Verulamium in 1949.[9]

83. Fragment, rim; bluish green; flattened hollow tubular rim formed by bending edge out and down; diameter (rim) 9 cm. 2 (102) [292].

The fragment probably comes from a small jar, either square or ovoid.[10] Both forms are found in later first and second century contexts. Similar rims occur on bowls, which are more commonly found on Romano-British sites, but these tend to be much larger in rim diameter.

84. Fragment, rim and upper body; bluish green; rounded tubular rim, edge rolled up and inwards, conical upper body; diameter (rim) 9.4 cm. Height of fragment 2 cm. 3 (25) [106].

The fragment may come from a conical cup, but the rim form is most unusual. It might also be part of a vessel with a deep funnel mouth, perhaps a jar, similar to one found at Verulamium.[11]

85. Fragment, lower body and base-ring, indented cup; colourless; outsplayed tubular pushed-in base-ring with domed base (mostly missing); parts of two indents on lower body; diameter (base-ring) 4.6 cm. present height 1.6 cm. 2 (182) [217].

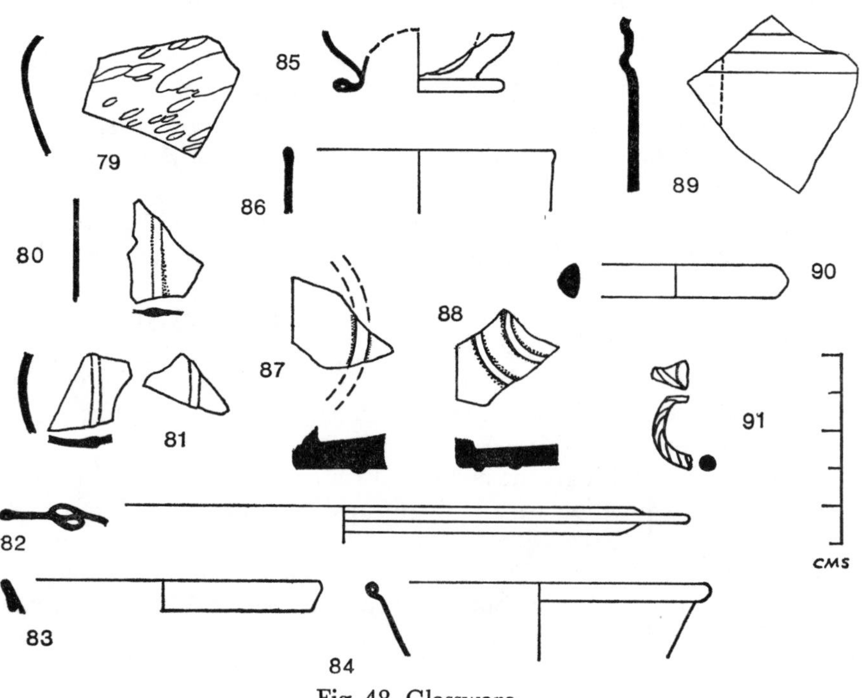

Fig. 48. Glassware.

Cups and beakers of this form occur in first and second century contexts.[12] A similar cup was found in Well I at Richborough.[13] and another example, from a stone coffin on The Mount, York, may date from the third century.[14]

86. Fragment, rim of cup; colourless; rim vertical, rounded and slightly thickened in flame; cylindrical upper body; diameter (rim) 7.4 cm.; present height 1.8 cm. 2 (34).

This is from a cup with low cylindrical body and double base-ring, the outer being tubular and pushed-in, and the inner formed by an applied coil. These cups are very common in Britain and the Rhineland in the second and third centuries.[15] There is a complete example from a cist grave at Airlie, Angus,[16] and another was found in a well at Verulamium.[17]

87. Fragment, base of prismatic bottle; bluish green; mould blown; base and body angle; decorated with part of raised arc; 1.8 × 3 cm. 4 (32) [83].

This almost certainly comes from a square bottle. These were widely used in the first and second centuries, as containers and sometimes as cinerary urns. They are extremely common throughout the Roman Empire.[18] The commonest form of basal decoration is a series of concentric circles, but other designs often occur. I know of no parallel for this arc, though arcs within a square are fairly common. The designs on the base are thought to be the 'trade mark' of different bottle manufacturers.

88. Fragment, base of prismatic bottle; bluish green; mould-blown; part of base and angle with body; two raised concentric circles on base; 2.8 × 3.3 cm. 2 (100).

This is probably from a small square bottle; however, a rectangular bottle from Linz in Austria has two sets of concentric circles on the base, with an inscription in raised letters between them.[19]

89. Fragment, body of barrel-jug; bluish green; mould-blown; cylindrical body, with two horizontal raised ridges on upper part, and undecorated below; vertical scratch marks; mould-seam visible; 4.8 × 4.6 cm. 4 (96).

Barrel-jugs, often called Frontinus bottles because some of the bases have this maker's name in raised letters, are mainly found in third to fourth century contexts, though some are said to come from first and second century sites.[20] They are common in Gaul and the Rhineland, but few have been found in Britain. Examples are known from Faversham, Dorchester (Oxon.), Silchester, Kenchester, Park Street villa (Herts.), and Corfe (Dorset). The scratch marks indicate that the vessel has been lifted in and out of a closely-fitting case.

90. Fragment, bangle; opaque white; D-shaped section; plain surface; diameter 6.2 cm. 2 (115)? [223].

Glass bangles of this and other types[21] are found on sites in Roman Britain, especially on Roman and native sites in Scotland, but not elsewhere in the Roman empire. Dated examples of this form are few, but a late first to early second century date is indicated. There is another fragment of a glass bangle from Manchester, found during the excavations in 1907,[22] but this is from a Kilbride-Jones Type 2 bangle.

91. Fragment, finger ring; colourless with marvered opaque yellow spiral trails; circular glass rod with part of flattened bezel; diameter 2.2 cm. 2 (220) [241].

A fragment of a very similar ring was found during recent excavations at Gloucester, and a complete ring of yellow glass with opaque white spiral trails was found in Köln in 1927 in a first–second century context.[23]

REFERENCES

1 For this technique see G. C. Boon, 'Roman Window Glass from Wales', *J. Glass Studies*, VIII, 1966, 41–7.

2 D. B. Harden et al., *Masterpieces of Glass*, London, 1968, 58, No. 71.

3 D. B. Harden, 'The Glass', in C. F. C. Hawkes and M. R. Hull, *Camulodunum;* Report of the Research Committee of the Society of Antiquaries of London, XIV; London, 1947; 295-6 and Pl. LXXXVII.

4 D. B. Harden, 'Objects of Glass', in F. Jenkins, 'Canterbury Excavations June–December 1947', *Archaeologia Cantiana*, LXV, 1952, 130, Pit R1,3a.

5 J. W. Brailsford, *Antiquities of Roman Britain*, 2nd edn., London, 1958, 44, Nos. 9 and 10, Pls. XI and XII.

6 J. W. Brailsford, op. cit., 43, No. 6, Pl. XII.

7 C. Isings, *Roman Glass from Dated Finds*, Archaeologica Traiectina, II; Groningen 1957; 52, form 37; 60, form 44b; 70, form 52b; 72-4, form 55; 88, form 67c.

8 C. Isings, op. cit., 52–3, form 37.

9 D. B. Harden, in M. A. Cotton and R. E. M. Wheeler, 'Verulamium, 1949', *Transactions of the St. Albans and Herts. Architectural and Archaeological Society*, 1953, 42 and fig. 1,12.

10 C. Isings, op. cit., 81, form 62, and 87, form 67b.

11 D. Charlesworth, 'The Glass', in S. S. Frere et al., *Verulamium Excavations. Vol. I*; Report of the Research Committee of the Society of Antiquaries of London, XXVIII, London 1972; 205 and fig. 76,30

12 C. Isings, op. cit., 49, form 35.

13 J. P. Bushe-Fox, *First Report of the Excavation of the Roman Fort at Richborough, Kent*; Report of the Research Committee of the Society of Antiquaries of London, VI, London 1926; 49 and Pl. XIX,8.

14 D. B. Harden, 'Glass in Roman York', in *An Inventory of the Historical Monuments in the City of York: Volume I Eburacum. Roman York;* R.C.H.M., 1962; 140 and Pl. 66 (HG 180).

15 C. Isings, op. cit., 102, form 85b.

16 J. Davidson, 'Notice of a small cup shaped glass vessel found in a stone cist at the Public School, Airlie', *Proceedings of the Society of Antiquaries of Scotland*, XX, 1886, 136-8.

17 R. E. M. and T. V. Wheeler, *Verulamium. A Belgic and Two Roman Cities*; Report of the Research Committee of the Society of Antiquaries of London, XI, London 1936; 186 and fig. 29,24.

18 C. Isings, op. cit., 63–6, form 50.

19 D. B. Harden, 'Ancient Glass, II: Roman', *Archaeological J.*, CXXVI, 1970; Pl. IV,B.

20 C. Isings, op. cit., 107, form 89, and 158, form 128.

21 H. E. Kilbride-Jones, 'Glass Armlets in Britain', *Proceedings of the Society of Antiquaries of Scotland*, LXXII, 1937–8, 376-81 and fig. 4; Type 3,A.

R. B. K. Stevenson, 'Native Bangles and Roman Glass', *Proceedings of the Society of Antiquaries of Scotland*, LXXXVIII, 1954–6, 208-221.

22 F. A. Bruton (ed.), *The Roman Fort at Manchester* (Manchester, 1909), 126 and Pl. 42,5.

23 F. Fremersdorf, *Römisches Buntglas in Köln*: Die Denkmäler des Römischen Köln, III; Köln, 1958; 55. (Pl. 123, middle right, and pl. 123, middle left.)

iv: Roman Coins from the Manchester Vicus 1972

P. J. CASEY, B.A.

THE CONDITION of the coins at the moment of loss has been indicated by a notation of the wear displayed by the coins, where this can be ascertained. This is a subjective matter and has no absolute chronological value. The system is thus:

UW/UW—unworn obverse, unworn reverse. A virtually uncirculated coin.
SW—slightly worn. The highest parts of the design a little flattened by wear.
W—worn. The design well abraded but the legends quite visible.

Small find no.	*Issuer*	*Denomination*	*Type*	*Issue Date*	*Condition*
4	Illegible	*As/Dupondius*			
6	Antoninus Pius	*Sestertius*	poss. RIC 549	A.D. 139+	SW/SW
7	Domitian	*As*	Illegible	A.D. 81–96	
20	Trajan	*Dupondius*	as RIC 505 —SPQR OPTIMO PRINCIPI. S.C.	A.D. 103+	W/W
21	Domitian	*As*	Illegible	A.D. 81–96	
44	Vespasian	*As/Dupondius*	Illegible	A.D. 69–79	
45	Domitian	*As*	as RIC 248 —MONETA AUGUSTI. S.C.	A.D. 84+	SW/SW
54	Illegible	*Denarius*			
55	Titus	*As*	as RIC 82 —SECURITAS AUGUSTI. S.C.	A.D. 79+	
79	Domitian	*As*	Illegible	A.D. 81–96	
81	Trajan	*Dupondius*	Illegible	A.D. 98–117	
121	Domitian	*Quadrans*	RIC (Anon. Quads.) 21 —Trophy. S.C.	A.D. 81+	
142	Illegible	*As/Dupondius*			
159	Domitian	*As*	as RIC 301B —Mars adv. left. S.C.	A.D. 85+	SW/—
160	Illegible	*As/Dupondius*			
184	Vespasian	*Denarius*	Illegible	A.D. 69–79	
191	Domitian	*As*	as RIC 305A —VIRTUTI AUGUSTI. S.C.	A.D. 85+	SW/SW
221	Domitian	*As*	as RIC 248 —MONETA AUGUST . . . S.C.	A.D. 84+	SW/—
234	Illegible	*Denarius*			
235	Domitian, Caesar	*As*	as RIC (Titus) 170C —Minerva adv. S.C.	A.D. 80–81	
250	Domitian, Caesar	*As*	Illegible	A.D. 73–81	
250B	Domitian, Caesar	*Denarius*	RIC (Vespasian) 238 —Pegasus adv. Cos. IIII	A.D. 76	
262	Vespasian	*As*	as RIC 528 —Eagle on globe. S.C.	A.D. 72+	

Small find no.	*Issuer*	*Denomination*	*Type*	*Issue Date*	*Condition*
267	Illegible	*As/Dupondius*			
274	Illegible	*Denarius*			
286	Illegible	*As/Dupondius*			
290	Domitian	*As*	Illegible	A.D. 81–96	
291	Domitian	*Dupondius*	RIC 357 —IMP. XIIII COS. XIII CENSOR PERPETUUS P.P. S.C.	A.D. 87	SW/SW
293	Domitian	*As*	as RIC 298 —FIDEI PUBLICAE. S.C.	A.D. 85+	UW/UW
294	Vespasian	*Dupondius*	prob. RIC 744 —SECURITAS AUGUSTI. S.C.	A.D. 72+	W/W
295	Illegible	*As/Dupondius*			
304	Illegible	*As/Dupondius*			
312	Domitian	*As*	Illegible	A.D. 81–96	
317	Illegible	*As/Dupondius*			
326	Nero	*Dupondius*	as RIC 225 —ROMA. S.C.	A.D. 64–68	
330	Domitian	*As*	Illegible	A.D. 81–96	

Ref.: Mattingly, H., and Sydenham, E. A. *The Roman Imperial Coinage*

v: Some Roman Coins from Manchester found *c.* 1820–1907

RICHARD HIGGINBOTTOM, F.R.N.S.

THE INFORMATION gathered in the following coin lists is derived from the catalogue of Roman coins published in F. A. Bruton's *Roman Manchester* (1909). The bulk of the coins in Bruton's catalogue were found in or near Manchester during the nineteenth century and in 1909 were dispersed among a number of private and public collections in the Manchester area. Most of these coins are now deposited in the Manchester Museum.

One would like to know exactly how many Roman coins were found in Manchester in the nineteenth century and just where each was uncovered, but this is impossible. Bruton's catalogue is not comprehensive for the period (about 1821 to 1907) which it covers, and there are hints that many coins were dispersed or lost immediately after their discovery, or at least before Bruton composed his lists. The Trafford Street hoard of 200 coins is just one known complete loss. With the distribution of the coins into various collections, further loss may have occurred, but confusion of the record is the main factor, since in the process the actual find-spots of particular coins or groups of coins may have been mixed up.

Further problems in the analysis of Bruton's coin lists arise regarding the division into the two categories of hoards and individual site finds. Many of the coins were discovered in the mid-1840s during railway construction work in the vicinity of Knott Mill. Apart from the haphazard nature of such discovery, the proportion of dispersal and the lack of adequate recording of amount or denomination, there is extreme difficulty in trying to differentiate between hoard and non-hoard material. Moreover, the value of such finds is diminished if it cannot be determined whether a coin or coins were found within the area of the Roman fort or outside it. One is confronted in Bruton's catalogue by vagueness over certain collections—for instance, part of a collection may be described as having been found 'in or near Castlefield'; the technical difference here is considerable, since 'Castlefield' roughly represents the area of the fort. In the case of the Worsley Collection, there are indications in Bruton's record that many of the coins came from a hoard, possibly deposited in a wooden box. The Charlton Collection originally appears to have formed part of the Knott Mill hoard. But the most hopeless situation is that of the so-called 'Rosicrucian Collection', which is now lost and for which there is only fragmentary information. Of course, none of these gaps in the record are necessarily Bruton's fault—he was describing coins which in many cases had been found more than fifty years earlier and he admits, from his own researches, that some relevant coins had been lost or detached from private collections.

Due to the general lack of information about many of the coins which Bruton describes, it would be meaningless to try to produce accurate statistics for the coin series, say in the form of a histogram. The inclusion of hoard material would distort such statistics ridiculously, since hoards do not relate directly to occupational periods in archaeological terms; but such inclusion would be inevitable in attempting a histogram since, as has been said, it is difficult to distinguish categories among the Manchester coins. However, in the lists which are here presented, an attempt has been made, where evidence permits, to sort out some of the hoard material from the rest—so, the Charlton Collection has been included in the Knott Mill hoard, while the Rosicrucian Collection, although it may have included a small hoard or hoards, has been included in the site finds category, due to its dubiousness. An attempt has also been made to distinguish between coins found inside and those found outside the fort, although the tag 'Castlefield' has been accepted usually as implying a find-spot within the fort, so some discrepancies probably remain. Thus caution should be used in trying to evaluate the lists and a check should be made with Bruton's catalogue. Denominations are not supplied, again due to patchy evidence. Where there is doubt over the identification of certain coins, they have been assigned either to a general period, e.g. first to second century, or to the most likely reign or dynasty.

In general terms, hoard material predominates, as may be expected, but the total number of coins from Manchester in these lists (about 2,300) is quite small compared with other sites, e.g. Richborough (58,000). It has been noted already that a great many coins must have been lost without trace after discovery. With reference to the site finds, there appears to be a pattern of steady continuity in ancient coin loss (implying occupation) from the Flavian to the Antonine period, with a marked decline, both inside and outside the fort, in the coins from about A.D. 180 to the mid-third century. But once again, it must be remembered that new material or probable inaccuracies, due to paltry evidence, in the lists, might drastically alter such a pattern, which, as it is, is based on a very small number of coins. At the same time it can be said of the hoards (principally the Knott Mill hoard) that the House of Constantine is well represented. Deposition of the Knott Mill hoard very likely took place between A.D. 375 and 380. The Worsley hoard was probably deposited in the reign of Pius.

APPENDIX

ROMAN COINS FOUND IN THE FORT AREA *c.* 1820–1907

(although most of these coins are described as coming from 'Castlefield', this very probably implies that they were found within the fort area).

Date	*Site finds*	*Hoards*
Period I (to A.D. 69)		
Republic	15	1
Augustus	2	
Tiberius	1	
Claudius	—	
Nero	—	2
Galba	2	
Vitellius	1	1
Period II (70–96)		
Vespasian	8	7
Titus	5	1
Domitian	7	6
Period III (96–117)		
Nerva	3	3
Trajan	12	6
Period IV (117–138)		
Hadrian	6	11
Sabina	1	1
Aelius	1	
Period V (138–180)		
Pius	8	5
Faustina I	2	1
M. Aurelius	1	
Faustina II	5	
Antonine period		4
Period VI (180–235)		
Commodus	—	—
Severus	—	—
J. Domna	1	—
Caracalla	1	—
Geta	1	—
Julia Maesa	1	—
Severus Alexander	3	—
Illegible 2nd/1st century A.D.	14	44
Period VII (235–305)		
Gordian III	1	—
Gallienus	—	—
Salonina	1	—
Postumus	1	—
Victorinus	1	—
Tetricus I	2	—
Tetricus II	—	—
Period VII (continued)		
Claudius II	3	—
Tacitus	1	—
Probus	3	—
Maximian	4	—
Period VIII (305–337)		
Galerius	1	—
Maximinus II	1	1
Licinius I	1	—
Licinius II	—	—
Constantine I	30	34
Fausta	—	1
Helena	—	10
Constantine I or his sons	2	11
Delmatius	—	1
Crispus	2	—
Constantine II (Caesar)	5	22
Constans (as Caesar)	—	11
Constantius II (as Caesar)	4	18
Divus Claudius	—	1
Period IX (337–364)		
Constantine II	1	2
Constans	26	473
Constantius II	17	393
House of Constantine	—	600
Magnentius	3	—
Gallus	—	2
Julian	—	17
Jovian	—	1
Period X (364–402)		
Valentinian I	3	10
Valens	1	25
Gratian	3	1
Valentinian II	1	—
Honorius	1	—
Illegible 4th/3rd century A.D.	5	72
Uncertain, but Roman	4	—
TOTALS	229	1799
SUM TOTAL	2028	

ROMAN COINS FOUND OUTSIDE THE FORT AREA, IN OR NEAR MANCHESTER, *c.* 1820–1907

Date	*Site finds*	*Hoards*
Period I (to A.D. 69)		
—	—	—?
Period II (70–96)		
Vespasian	—	—?
Titus	—	—?
Domitian	3	?
Period III (96–117)		
Nerva	—	—?
Trajan	5	—
Period IV (117–138)		
Hadrian	8	
Sabina	—	?
Period V (138–180)		
Pius	3	
Faustina I	1	?
M. Aurelius	3	
Faustina II	1	
Period VI (180–235)		
None	—	—
Illegible 2nd/1st century A.D.	4	
Period VII (235–305)		
Trajan Decius	1	
Gallienus	4	1
Valerian II	1	
Postumus	2	
Victorinus	2	6
Tetricus I	1	12
Tetricus II	—	2
Claudius II	2	2
Aurelian	1	—
Florian	1	—
Probus	2	—
Period VII (continued)		
Numerian	1	—
Carausius	1	—
Diocletian	1	—
Illegible late 3rd century	2	9
Period VIII (305–337)		
Maxentius	1	—
Licinius I	4	—
Licinius II	1	—
Constantine I	10	—
Constantius I (consecration)	1	—
Helena	—	—
Crispus	1	
Constantine I or sons	1	
Constantine II (as Caesar)	2	
Constans (as Caesar)	—	—
Constantius II (as Caesar)	1	
Period IX (337–364)		
Constantine II	1	
Constans	3	
House of Constantine	5	
Period X (364–402)		
Valentinian I	—	
Valens	3	
Gratian	1	
Uncertain Roman	2	
TOTALS	87	232*
SUM TOTAL	319	

* (Including 200 of Trafford Street hoard)

vi: Clay Pipes

P. S. MIDDLETON

THE collection of clay pipes from Manchester well reflects the use of Castlefield as parkland until its encompassment by the spread of Victorian Manchester in 1835, both in the wide time-spread of the material, and its relative paucity compared to an occupation site. It is interesting to speculate on the causes of the grouping of the material into two periods around the latter half of the seventeenth century and the early part of the nineteenth century. Whilst the first group is supported by an analysis of the stem bores, some 25.6% being dateable by the Walker method to the late seventeenth century, it is of course possible that the eighteenth century is represented by the number of unidentifiable pipe bowl fragments and in the large percentage of stem fragments (72.6%) which under the present state of knowledge must be regarded simply as eighteenth/nineteenth century, the Walker method of stem bore analysis not being sufficiently developed to differentiate between the two. It is also possible that Nos. 8 and 9 may date from late eighteenth century, these particular designs coming into use about 1750 and spreading rapidly in distribution. Of the nineteenth-century material, no example can be dated with certainty past 1850 and this is a clear reflection of the fact that with the erection of houses, the parkland went out of use, and the citizens of Manchester were obliged to go further afield for their recreation.

Examples illustrated in Fig. 49 (overleaf)

1. Small bulbous bowl with spur of York type; cf. Oswald[1] type 9 *c.*1640–60, Parsons[2] type 2 *c.*1630–60.
2. Slightly bulbous bowl with rouletting below lip; cf. Parsons type 14 *c.*1650–80.
3. Slightly bulbous bowl; cf. Parsons type 5 *c.*1670–90.
4. Overhanging bowl with flat base; cf. Parsons type 9 *c.*1680–1720.
5. Late spur type; cf. Oswald type 19 *c.*1690–1710.
6. Narrow brittle bowl; cf. Parsons type 6 *c.*1680–1710.
7. Early nineteenth century; cf. Parsons 13/14 *c.*1780–1840.

8 & 9. Common decorative designs—Masonic and floral, late eighteenth century/early nineteenth century.

10. Squat, slightly bulbous bowl; cf. Parsons 18/34 post-1840.
11. Irish type—although stamped Dublin, these were made at several centres in Britain from a type mould; cf. Oswald type 33 post-1840.
12. French nineteenth century.

REFERENCES

1 Atkinson and Oswald, 'London Clay Tobacco Pipes', *Journal of the Archaeological Association*, Vol. XXXII, 1969.

2 Parsons, 'Archaeology of the Clay Tobacco Pipe in N.E. England', *Archaeologia Aeliana*, 1964.

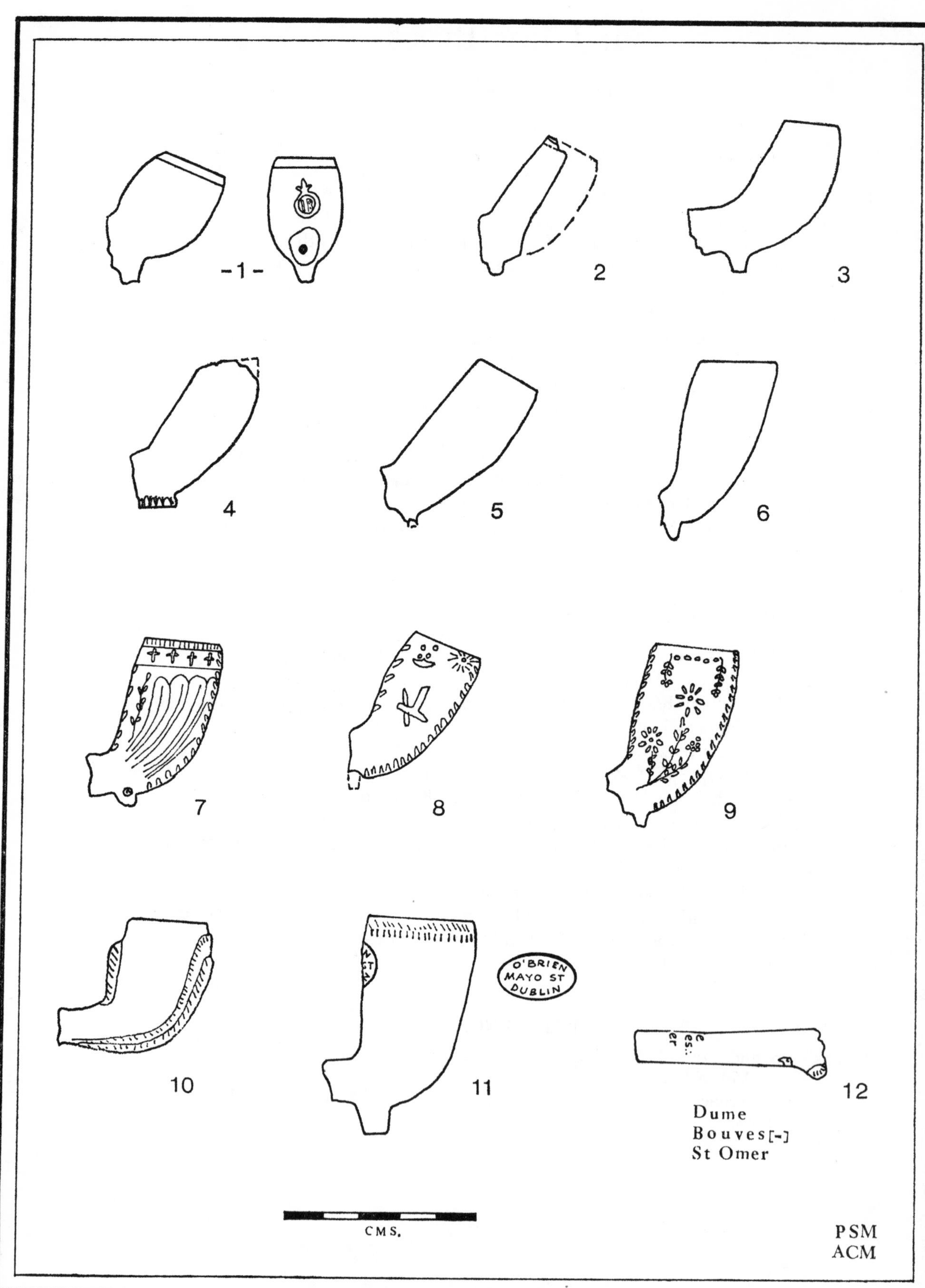

Fig. 49. Clay pipes Nos. 1–12 (p.141).

C: Metal Working in the North-West

J. D. BESTWICK, B.A., and J. H. CLELAND, B.Sc., Ph.D.

INTRODUCTION

Iron-working furnaces used in Roman Britain may be classified as either smelting furnaces or smithing hearths[1] according to their primary function. In the last two decades smelting furnaces have received a great deal of attention and two classifications have been proposed, one based upon shape, the other on function. In addition, several field and laboratory trials using reconstructed furnaces have yielded valuable information with regard to such problems as (a) the furnaces themselves, (b) mode of operation, (c) the products, and (d) the logistics of operation. The second class of furnace, however, has not received a similar amount of critical attention. This is due mainly to the nature of the structures themselves, for smithing hearths did not require an amount of fabrication comparable to that necessary for smelting furnaces. Unlike smelting furnaces no great temperature had to be attained, no reducing zone was necessary and there was no need to have a local supply of raw materials, viz. suitable iron ore, a good refractory clay and a source of fuel.

From this it is evident that a smithing hearth could be constructed anywhere, as and when required, and thus many such hearths were of an essentially temporary nature.

In the North-West few examples of Class I, the smelting furnaces, have been located. May, however, excavated a sufficient number at Wilderspool to allow classification into three types[2] while in recent (1972) excavations at Northwich, Jones produced evidence to link some of the excavated furnaces with iron smelting.

However, the great majority of furnaces located in the North-West appear to belong to Class II, the relevant sites being Wilderspool, Middlewich, Northwich and Manchester. Such is the number of these furnaces that one of the purposes of the present paper is to propose a tentative classification of smithing hearths.

THE ROASTING PROCESS AND CARBONATE ORES

Roman metal-working is a subject fraught with misconceptions and over generalisations. In view of this, although the present paper proposes to discuss only one aspect of this wide-ranging topic, it is felt essential to start from first principles.

Prior to the actual smelting it was beneficial to roast the ore in order to remove carbon dioxide and water to increase its reducibility* and to weaken the nodules so that they broke down into smaller pieces, or at least were liable to fracture when struck after removal from the roasting furnace (see table I).

Table I. *Effect of roasting on a carbonate ore.*[3]

	Unroasted	Roasted	Improvement %
Wt.% of iron	48.3	69.9 max.	45% max.
Reducibility index	1.05	1.34	27%

It has been argued that roasting could have been performed in open fires without the construction of a furnace of any kind, as a moderate temperature (300–400°C) suffices, and the conditions must be oxidising. Sound archaeological evidence exists, however, to indicate that roasting was carried out in shallow troughs or pits and that an artificial draught was applied.[4] Such an arrangement would have allowed control to be exerted over both the degree of roasting and the physical boundaries of the process. Control over the roasting process was necessary on two points: (a) over-roasting would produce too great a quantity of fines unsuitable for smelting, and (b) under certain conditions some reduction and partial slagging of ore may occur. The reducibility of this material would have been inferior to that

* The reducibility of an ore is its ease of reduction to metallic iron.

of the raw ore. The choice of fuel for the roasting pit is not critical and most combustibles would have sufficed. The roasting process may be represented by the equations

$$Fe\,CO_3 \rightarrow FeO + CO_2 \qquad \text{Thermal decomposition}$$

and $$4FeO + O_2 \rightarrow 2Fe_2\,O_3 \qquad \text{Oxidation}$$

The roasted ore is typically magenta-coloured and is itself the main evidence for the roasting process. It is probable that many of the larger 'bowl' furnaces cited in the literature were, in fact, roasting pits.

THE SMELTING PROCESS

The chemistry of the smelting process is represented by

$$Fe_2O_3 + 3CO \rightarrow 2Fe + 3CO_2$$

the carbon monoxide being produced by the interaction of the charcoal fuel and the oxygen of the air draught. The non-metallic part of the ore, gangue, is slagged off mainly as the compound fayalite $2FeO\ SiO_2$, 70 wt.% = FeO. This will be referred to as tap-slag. Tap-slag has a distinctive dense appearance and is the main evidence for smelting activities. The second type of slag produced is that portion which remains in the furnace and will be referred to as cinder. Again this is mainly fayalite but has a definite 'cindery' appearance which makes it most difficult to distinguish from smithing cinder—the by-product of smithing the bloom of iron.

The iron produced in the process was, generally, never liquid since the reduction of iron oxide to iron is possible at temperatures in excess of 800°C. The slag so formed, however, had a free-running temperature of *c.* 1150°C, and this was the minimum operating temperature at which a reasonable separation of the slag from the reduced iron could have been achieved by liquation of the slag. The iron produced is thus a mixture of iron and residual slag, in the form of a 'bloom'.

As stated in the introduction, there have recently been several simulations of iron-making in a furnace of typically Roman type. Experiments by Cleere[4] have reconstructed the use of shaft furnaces in antiquity. After ignition of a primary charcoal charge, iron and charcoal in ratios of either 1:1 or 2:1 were charged into the shaft and the temperature was raised by an induced draught at the base of the furnace using bellows and tuyère. In the experiments the rate of draught was found to be a critical factor in the process and had a direct effect upon the amount of iron obtained from the ore. As reduction of the ore proceeded, slag was formed from the gangue part of the ore and collected at the bottom of the shaft. Experiments have shown that it was essential to allow this slag to flow out of the shaft at regular intervals or, if possible, continuously. Simultaneously, small additional charges of ore and charcoal, 1:1, were added to the stock in the shaft. At the bottom of the shaft the iron bloom, consisting of a spongy mass of iron and entrapped slag, was formed above the waste slag. At the base of the shaft furnace a temperature of at least 1200–1300°C would have had to be maintained.

Initially Cleere concluded that at least ten men would have been required to run the process efficiently. Recent examination of the structure of slag and waste heaps on Wealden iron-making sites has, however, suggested that a manning figure of five to six men per furnace may be more probable.[5] The most successful trial by Cleere had a yield of 10% in terms of weight of iron from weight of ore charged. Calculation shows that if one assumes a furnace efficiency of 100% the percentage yield should be approximately 20% (see Appendix I). This allows a rough estimate of the total efficiency of Cleere's furnace to be 34%, though naturally it must be stressed that such figures can only be approximate.*

* For those wishing to pursue the question of early iron-making technology to depths beyond the scope of the present paper the following references may be welcome: Tylecote[1,6]; Wynne and Tylecote[7]; Tylecote, Austin and Wraith[8]; Straube, Tarmann and Plöckinger[9]; Pleiner[10,11]; Thomsen[12]; Gilles[13]; Mazur and Nosek[14]; Morton and Wingrove[15].

CLASSIFICATION OF SMELTING FURNACES

Coghlan suggested that furnaces for iron smelting in the Roman period fell into three categories.[16] The bowl furnace was the most primitive kind and comprised a simple hollow lined with clay cut into the surface of the ground. This furnace was operated by filling the bowl with charcoal and iron ore while a draught was supplied artificially by bellows that were probably portable and could be directed from any direction. This method would most likely produce small pieces of iron mixed with a pool of slag. The metal would have to be separated by hand after cooling, then re-heated and worked into a larger bloom by hammering.[2] The draught of air was introduced into the mixture of charcoal and ore by means of a nozzle or tuyère over the edge of the bowl. The bellows were probably provided with wooden nozzles which could be applied to the outer end of the clay tuyère to avoid burning. As the temperature of the bowl furnace was raised to around 1200°C, the ore was reduced and on obtaining that temperature, slag collected at the bottom of the bowl. This slag consisted of non-metallic ore and iron oxide.[17] The iron formed in this process did not become molten, but formed as a spongy mass above the slag. It has been suggested that this type of furnace was covered with turves to reduce heat loss.[17]

The second class of smelting furnace suggested by Coghlan was the domed furnace. The hearth was flat and the furnace covered by a permanent dome of clay with a hole in the top to allow for escaping gases. This use of a permanent dome can be seen as a development from the turf-covered bowl, and allowed access to the top of the charge of charcoal and ore, which would mean that by the addition of more materials a larger bloom could be obtained. As the hearth was flat, the slag could be allowed to run out, leaving more room in the furnace for iron to form.[17] The draught was probably natural, but arguments have been put forward for the use of bellows and it is likely that both systems were used. These furnaces are usually found to have had an average diameter of 1 metre.[17]

Coghlan's third type of smelting furnace was the shaft furnace. This consisted of a cylindrical shaft of clay which originally stood to a height of 1.2 m. The internal vertical shaft was, on average, 30 cm in diameter, widening near the base. An opening at the bottom of the shaft, 30 cm square allowed the air for the vertical draught to be drawn in, the slag to be removed and the finished bloom of iron to be pulled out without destroying the clay shaft. Examples of this type of furnace have been found at Ashwicken, Norfolk.[18]

Cleere has suggested a new classification for the three types of smelting furnace described above.[17] He has divided the furnaces into two basic groups, A and B, the former being furnaces with hollow hearths from which the tap-slag cannot run, and the latter with flat hearths from which the slag could be removed by raking into a channel through the lower aperture. Sub-sections of A include (1) bowl furnaces (2) furnaces with a superstructure. Sub-sections of B are: (1i) cylindrical furnaces with a forced draught; (1ii) conical superstructure and forced draught; (2i) as in section 1 but with natural draughts. This classification is based on the function of the furnaces rather than on the apparent shape and may be preferred to a purely morphological approach.

EVIDENCE OF SMELTING IN THE NORTH-WEST

Traces of iron smelting have been noted with certainty only at Wilderspool, Middlewich and Northwich. Bowl furnaces of the type described above are often found in settlements of the Roman period and too readily ascribed to the iron smelting process without proof. In the North-West, a group from Wilderspool were described by their excavator, Thomas May, but these seem to have been used as smithing furnaces and will be discussed later. May also found some more complex furnaces which he ascribed to ore roasting and smelting. Little or no evidence of the roasting process seems to have been discovered but smelting would appear to be the only explanation of the structures described and drawn[1] (May, fig. 1). Tylecote describes the three furnaces illustrated as shaft furnaces of varying complexity. Furnace A was a single shaft, but had two clay channels leading from the base aperture, one being perhaps a separate slag-tapping channel at right-angles to the main channel. This cannot be ascribed certainly to the same process, as the two channels were possibly not contemporary. Furnace B comprised two oval shafts with axes 46 cm and 75 cm with a semi-circular clay hearth in front. The shafts were found standing to a height of 31–46 cm and were similar to furnaces found at Ashwicken. Furnace C was a simple shaft with a flared limb terminating in a brick or tile floor. The base of the internal shaft was slightly lower than the floor, probably due to wear which would have been repaired by the addition of new clay.

The sizes of the axes of the Wilderspool furnace B were intermediate between the diameters of typical English furnaces and those of typical German examples (see table II).

TABLE II. *Comparative sizes of shaft furnaces.*

Site (ref)	Diam./axes (cm)	Wall thickness (cm)
Bardown[4]	30.5–38	23–30.5
Ashwicken[18]	30.5	30.5
Wilderspool[1]	46 × 75	
Silberquelle (Siegen)[13]	90	36–45
Minnerbach (Siegen)[19]	60–80	33 approx.

The recent excavations at Northwich have produced large pieces of iron slag of the type found in smelting furnaces. This slag was not associated with all of the furnaces found but provides evidence of possible iron-smelting (see Appendix II for further details).

TABLE III. *Comparison of %FeO, %MnO, %SiO_2 and %Al_2O_3 between Wilderspool slag, Northwich slag and modern experimental slag.*

	%FeO	%MnO	%SiO	%Al_2O_3	$\frac{\%(FeO + MnO)}{\%(SiO + Al_2O_3)}$
Wilderspool	51.8	0.33	28.1	5.2	1.56
Northwich B	56	0.18	30.6	3.7	1.63
Cleere[4]	44	2.4	32	3.4	1.34

It is probable that the three shaft furnaces found at Northwich in 1972 form the remains of three smelting furnaces. As may be seen from table III, Appendix II and fig. 52, the slags fall within the correct composition range of early slags. Furthermore, microscopic examination revealed their structure to be large grains of fayalite, containing acicular anorthite and wüstite—FeO. Additionally, they contained small particles of entrained charcoal and the fayalite grains showed random orientation. The nature of the fayalite grains indicates slow-cooling as would be the case of cinders collected at the bottom of a furnace during smelting. Thus the weight of scientific evidence points to their being smelting cinder, and *casu quo* the furnaces being smelting furnaces. Of the three furnaces found only one was sufficiently undisturbed in fact to allow measurement of its dimensions to be made. These are given in table II. It can be seen that they are close to the dimensions of the Wilderspool furnaces. The fired clay of the furnaces was of a deep pink colour and the method of construction can be seen clearly from fig. 28 to be sectional. This method of furnace construction has been tentatively reported from Romano-British sites in Kent and Sussex. The cobbles would appear to have formed part of the foundations of the furnaces.

The importance of this group of furnaces is great, in that they are the first smelting furnaces, in this area, to be identified by strict palaeotechnological techniques. No other traces of smelting furnaces or tap-slag have been found in the North-West but metal-working furnaces or slags have been found at Heronbridge and Holt,[1] Middlewich,[20] Holditch[21] and Whitchurch.[22] *

SMITHING HEARTHS

When a bloom of iron had been produced in the smelting furnaces it was necessary to reheat it by forging to a high temperature (*c.* 900°C). This would permit removal of the entrapped slag, which would have caused the iron to be brittle. Thus the conditions in a smithing hearth were essentially oxidising.

Smithing would have produced slag but not in such large quantities as smelting since no tap-slag was produced. Smithing slag resembles smelting cinder in appearance but, whereas cinder may occur in massive lumps, it is unlikely that smithing slag would do so. It is also possible that the FeO fraction of the fayalite could have oxidised to Fe_3O_4, or even to Fe_2O_3. Further chemical action would have led to $Fe(OH)_2$—a moderately soluble salt. Thus a site producing smallish lumps of slag, perhaps slightly magnetic and appearing to be high in silica, may *in the absence of any tap-slag* be described as a smithing site. After the smithing stage, final treatment would have been effected on a forging hearth, for which process such a temperature would not have been necessary. The by-product of forging was a scale of iron oxides.

At Wilderspool, May found over thirty furnace or hearth structures, many of which fell into the category of bowl furnaces. Two of the furnaces were of particular interest and possessed unusual features (May, fig. 2). Furnace A took the form of an elongated bowl of figure-of-eight form with a permanent bellows nozzle or tuyère inserted in the wall at one end. Tylecote[2] postulates that for the smithing of small pieces of iron, only the right-hand end of the furnace would be fired, but for larger pieces of iron or even beams the whole length could be fired and a draught applied to the left-hand end by means of portable bellows. It may also be argued that smithing could have been performed in the right-hand end of the furnace, where the draught from tuyerès would have permitted the attainment of high temperatures, and that forging could have occurred in the less severe conditions of the left-hand end. Forging at high temperature would have led to excessive oxidation of the iron.

Also from Wilderspool (May, fig. 2B) a smithing furnace of advanced form, consisting of a clay pot standing almost 61 cm high, showed how a permanent air supply from beneath the pot could achieve high temperatures. Only a small amount of slag was associated with this furnace and it would appear to have been fired with charcoal although a piece of coal was found near by. In the light of new evidence from Manchester it is not improbable that this furnace could have been used for crucible melting of non-ferrous metals and/or alloys.

At Middlewich, although ten furnaces have been found since 1963, only one can, with any certainty, be attributed to iron smithing (Bestwick, fig. 3). The Middlewich example took the form of a clay-lined bowl with an average diameter of 3.35 m and a maximum depth of 0.61 m. Traces of iron slag together with charcoal were found at the centre, and the base of the hearth had been relined with clay three times. On the west side, a cobbled area was attached to the hearth which appeared to have been connected with its use, but this was not clear. Two other suspected bowl furnaces were located within 1.52 m of the first, one only 46 cm in diameter, the other 1.22 m in diameter. The clay construction of these latter furnaces was similar to the large example and charcoal was found at their centres, but no traces of smithing slag were found, so their use remains in doubt.

Excavations at Northwich in 1968 revealed three bowl 'furnaces' in Trench I and traces of two others of a different type.[24] Furnace 1 had an average diameter of 1.83 m and was 0.75 m deep, cut into the natural clay. Furnace 2 had an average diameter of 1.3 m and was also 0.75 m deep, while Furnace 3 was 1.52 m long and

* At the time of going to press, conclusive evidence of iron smelting, in the form of smelting slag, has been noted at Middlewich.

0.75 m deep. Furnace 1 had a shallow channel leading away on its west side which the excavators suggested was a flue. All three furnaces had a dense charcoal fill but lacked any signs of a high degree of firing. With hindsight it is probable that they were ore-roasting pits.

All the smithing hearths so far described were of the plain circular or irregular form of bowl or flat-hearth type. At Wilderspool,[25] Middlewich, Holditch,[21] Northwich[24] and Manchester,[21] however, a more complex furnace type has been found in which the clay base was perforated by holes with an average diameter of 50 mm. These hearths have given rise to much speculation concerning their use, but the weight of evidence and more particularly the detailed material from Manchester now points to the working of iron. The holes have been explained as the footing of tables or benches in clay floors that were in some cases later fired accidentally.[21] Alternatively they have been described either as holders for crucibles for lead casting (due to small fragments of lead having been noted by the excavators in the perforations) or as marks left by either small anvils or some kind of bellows supports. They could also be thought of as holes for the collection of slag, but the clay of these hearths has not been fired to a temperature at which the slag would have been fluid. A further suggestion that they were ventilation ducts leading into the hearth, capable of producing a draught underneath the charge is improbable since many of these holes were blind (see below, p. 150).

Interim Classification.

The excavations at Deansgate, Manchester and at Northwich have produced good examples of perforated hearths from which it is possible to draw up the following interim classification based on the shape of the hearth and the distribution of the holes. (P—perforated.)

P.I An irregular clay area containing random perforations with no recognisable pattern of distribution.
- A. Highly fired clay.
- B. No sign of firing.
- C. The entire feature lying on a foundation of packed stones.

P.II A fired clay hearth with a recognisable elongated trough or channel; perforations situated on either side of the trough.

P.III A circular fired clay hearth in the form of a bowl with a circle of perforations around the bowl, sometimes a double circle.

P.IV A circular fired clay hearth in the form of a bowl with perforations around and within the bowl. In some cases the perforations may be confined to the interior of the bowl only.

The importance of this interim classification is that it facilitates the following discussion. It must be emphasised, however, that it is based upon material taken from a relatively small geographical area and doubtless will require amendment as more information becomes available.

Table showing classification of hearths of the perforated type from Manchester and Northwich.

Class		Manchester	Northwich	Class	Manchester	Northwich
P.I	A	F 21		P.III	F 2	
		F 1	F1		F 6	
		F 27			F 8	? F2
					F 11	
	B				F 10	
					F 26	
	C	F 23		P.IV	F 4	
		F 28			F 3	
P. II		F 17			F 5	F3
					F 24	

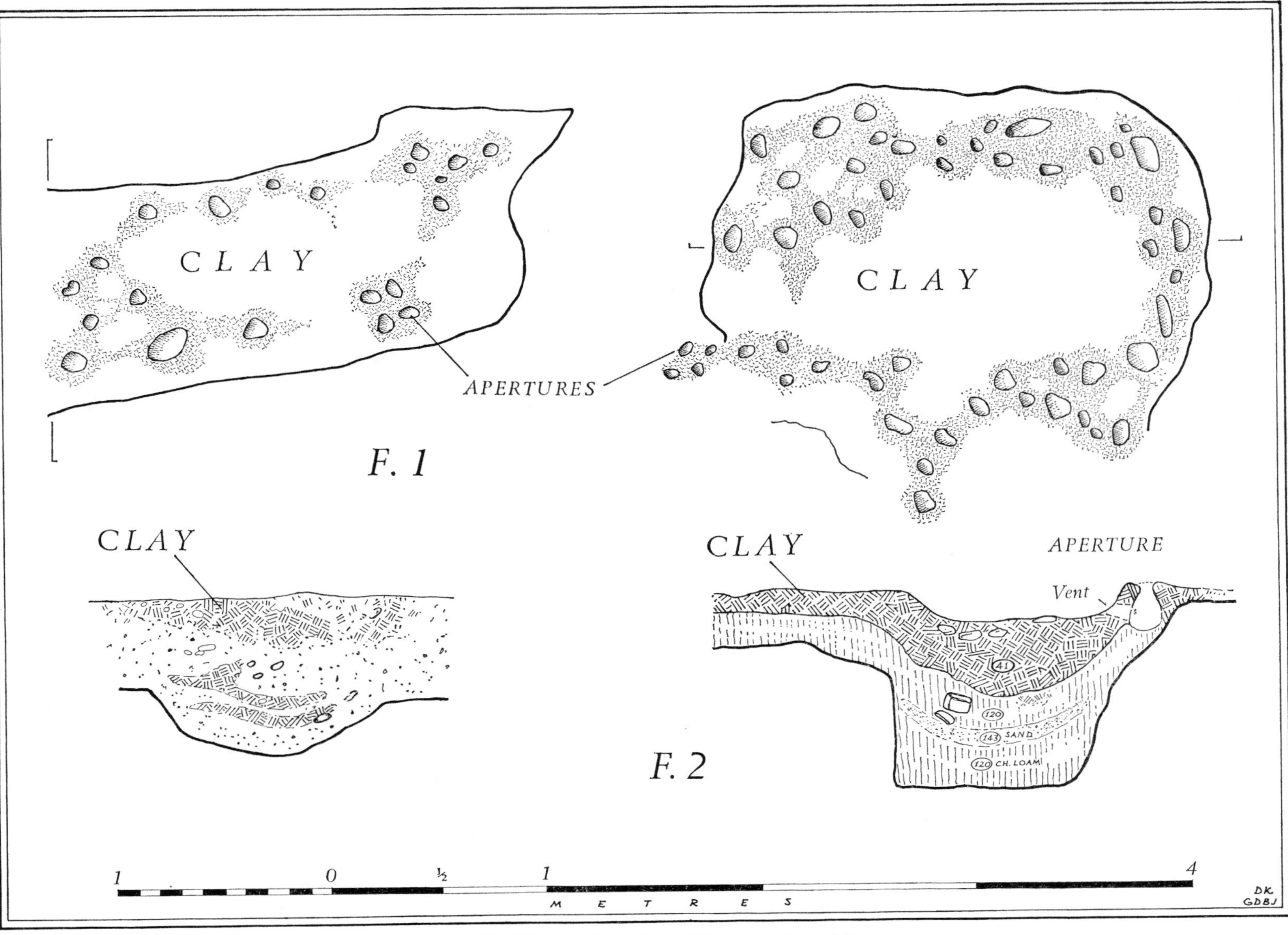

Fig. 50. Plan and section of furnaces 1 and 2.

Although iron smithing is usually suggested as the use for these perforated hearths, it is still uncertain, especially as the perforations themselves cannot be explained satisfactorily as a functional part of the structures. The pattern which the holes form around the hearths of type P.III suggests that they formed part of a domed frame, perhaps in the form of branches as used in Roman pottery kilns. These perforations could also be explained as footing holes for portable bellows which could be moved around the hearth to give the required draught from any direction. Such bellows were probably mounted on a wooden frame with two or more legs which could be fitted into the holes, thus giving the bellows stability while the operator worked the bellows with both hands. In type P.IV, however, where the holes actually lie in the hearth, it is possible that they were connected with lower ventilation and may be explained as air ducts, although evidence in the form of a continuation beneath the hearth floors is completely lacking at present.

Yet again, in type P.I(C) the perforations and the clay hearth were built over a close-packed stone foundation which would seem to discount the possibility of the holes forming air ducts beneath. In type P.I(A) both the clay hearth and the perforations have no recognisable form. In this case only the texture of the fired clay points to it being a furnace or hearth at all. Perhaps the most difficult type to interpret is P.I(B) where the clay was not fired and it is possible that the perforations had an entirely different origin.

At Manchester, a large number of perforations were found in the area between recognised hearths, for example, in Trench IV between hearths 8, 10 and 11. A similar scatter was noted between hearths 2 and 3 in the same trench, and also between hearths 5, 7 and 10. This random distribution may have been due to earlier or unrecognised furnaces, or because the perforations were part of a light structure or rack associated with furnaces in the vicinity.

To sum up the present conclusions on the perforated hearths, it is probable that they were iron smithing hearths (types P.II, P.III, and P.IV), and that the perforations were either part of a covering structure or some form of subfloor ventilation, or represent the position of portable bellows stands. The absence of slag and the temperature to which the furnaces had been fired rules out their use in the iron smelting process. Type P.I is difficult to fit into any metallurgical context but this may be due to the absence of other parts that had been destroyed in antiquity.

Hearths of the type P.III, of which F2 is a good example, sometimes show a coupling of the perforations. F5 (P.IV) shows doubling and elongation of the perforations. This elongation is not consistently radial to the centre of the hearth nor in line with the circumference. The clay between the holes may have been removed accidentally when timber was being pulled out during demolition of a superstructure. Some other holes in F2 show signs of this type of enlargement but it is also possible that this occurred when the clay was wet during construction. It does not seem likely that the coupling of the holes served any functional purpose.

An examination of the degree of firing of the hearths was made to determine if there was any correlation with the interim classification but, apart from a higher incidence of highly fired hearths in P.III, the distribution of lightly and highly fired hearths appeared to be random. Again no size distribution against the interim classification could be detected nor could any relation between the size of hearth and incidence of perforations be discerned.

Before proceeding to examine some of the more interesting hearths individually it must be stated that the problem of smithing hearth classification is in its infancy, but it should be apparent that more recording of details is necessary when hearths are excavated. Many such hearths have been excavated but have been summarily dismissed as 'hearths' or 'bowl-furnaces'. Consequently there is a grave lack of material in so far as classification is concerned. Also the waste-products of smithing —slag and scale—appear to have received even less attention (see Appendix III).

Hearth F2 (P.III), had a deep pit with vertical sides beneath the hearth, 0.8 m in diameter and 0.8 m in depth below the hearth centre. The hearth did not show signs of having been fired, but fired clay and daub together with brown loam soil were found in the lower pit. This pit may have been cut to form a suitable foundation for the bowl of the hearth or it could have been an earlier pit used conveniently as a foundation. An example of the latter has been found at Middlewich.[20] The lower pit can also be postulated as a functional part of the whole structure, forming a cavity beneath the hearth. The lack of charcoal, signs of heating and the absence of any kind of hearth support, as in some types of pottery kilns, renders this postulate unlikely.

F26 (P.III) is an important structure in this group. Here it is possible to see perforations running from the rim of the bowl into the interior. However, the walls of the bowl were not fired but the infill was composed of highly fired clay, which sealed the lower end of the perforations. No trace was noted of further perforations coming up through the fired clay fill of the bowl. This means that the bowl and perforations may have been part of a lower chamber over which a clay hearth had been constructed. This hearth could now be represented by the fired clay fill, after it had collapsed into the lower chamber.

F23 and F28 are hearths of type P.I(C), having random perforations in a clay hearth which is convex and is set on a foundation of packed stones. The depth of the centre of the clay hearth is around 20 cm. The perforations appear random but the angle at which these holes enter the clay remains a right-angle. This is a characteristic of all the perforations so far examined. Thus in the case of hearth types P.II or P.III, where the hearth is a shallow concave bowl, the holes appear to run away from the centre. In the case of F23 and F28, where the edges of the hearths curve down, the holes run inwards towards the foundation. In view of the heavy stones lying beneath the hearth, it is not very likely that the perforations, in this case, can be regarded as ventilation holes.

The Deansgate excavation also produced a group of plain bowl hearths probably used in the smithing of iron. These were furnaces 7, 9, 12, 14, 16, 22, and perhaps 13. In the case of F9 the bowl of fired clay was packed with small stones. This probably occurred after the hearth was abandoned in an effort to level the floor of a later working area. If the stones had been *in situ* when the hearth was in use, the clay beneath would not have been fired. A similar stone-filled hollow has been noted at Northwich. In general, the bowl hearths seem to have been in use alongside the perforated types and they may thus represent different aspects of the smithing process.

A group of furnaces consisting of F18, F19 and F20 on the Deansgate site seems to have been later in date than the examples mentioned above. This group shows a small technical superiority over the others with respect to shape and structural finish. F20 is of the perforated type P.III but the central hearth is almost a shaft rather than a bowl. F18 and F19 are clay-lined shafts about 90 cm diameter and 60 cm and 40 cm deep respectively.

The mode of construction of F18 and F19, being unlike any other in the Deansgate site, is worthy of mention. F19 was removed for laboratory tests. The shaft appears to have been built partially into a small retaining bank. The wall thickness changed regularly from 10 cm at the top to 5 cm at the base, and the wall and the base do not appear to have been continuous. The clay of the wall had been fired to a definite red colour whilst the base had been fired to a blue-grey colour indicative of firing under reducing conditions. This latter point is consistent with the finding of a 1.5 cm layer of powdered charcoal on top of the base. The clay of both the wall and the base showed signs of intentional reinforcement by the inclusion of small pieces of already fired clay as filler material while the layered nature of the clay indicated vigorous ramming during construction.

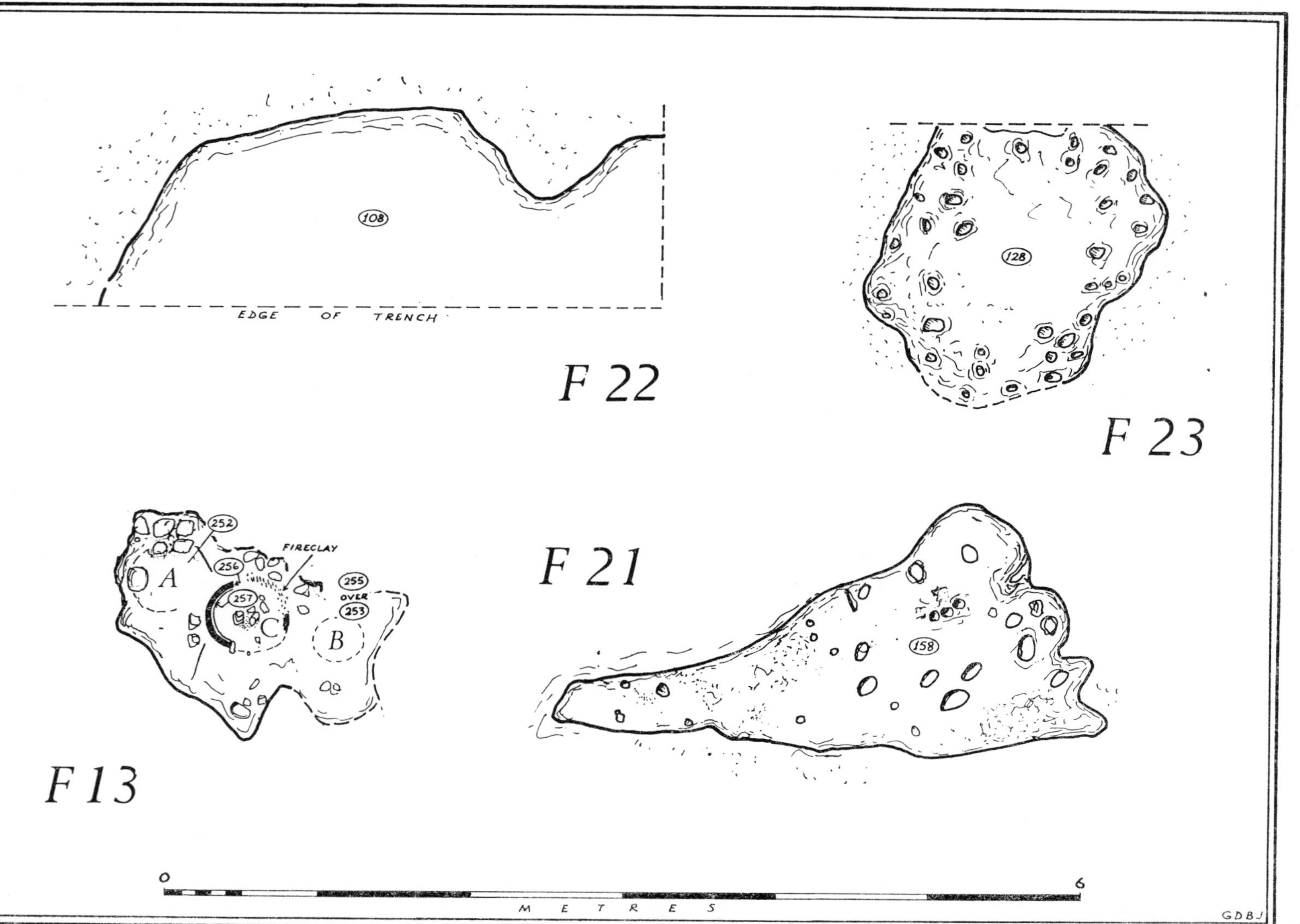

Fig. 51. Plan of furnaces 13, 21, 22 and 23.

The absence of any sign of slag attack on the linings of either F18 or F19, the absence of slag and the finding of small pieces of lead in their vicinity suggest that F18 and F19 were used for the crucible melting of lead prior to casting. Unfortunately no crucible remains were found to substantiate this theory. The resemblance of one of the cited hearths from Wilderspool (May, fig. 2B) to these hearths is the basis of the postulate that perhaps this hearth was also used for non-ferrous crucible melting.

F20 is thought to have been a contemporary iron-smithing hearth, possibly used for the repair of iron tools used with furnaces F18 and F19. As indicated in the text, there is a definite *modus operandi* for Roman iron-working which may be described as roasting, smelting, smithing. Yet we have concluded that the Deansgate hearths were smithing hearths and that no traces of the preliminary processes exist either in the form of tap-slag, roasted ore, heavy charcoal deposits or furnaces themselves. This conclusion should perhaps be seen only as due to the physical boundaries of the site and does not preclude roasting and smelting operations from having taken place in the neighbourhood. Definite conclusions on the processes must await further excavation and greater knowledge of the location of ores.

THE LOCATION OF IRON ORES

There are three possible ore types which may have been used in the North-Western smelting furnaces and these will be examined from the point of view of availability. A more satisfactory approach would be to attempt to correlate the chemical composition of ores found at furnace sites to specific ore deposits but this has not been possible; thus no absolute source of ores may be cited.

The first type of ore is the carbonate ore so common in most of the British coalfields. It is represented by the formula $FeCO_3$, contains 48.3 % iron, and occurs as nodules. The type is found below the coal seam itself and can be obtained easily where surface outcrops occur, e.g. hillsides and river valleys. This ore type is obviously very common in the area of North-East Cheshire and South Lancashire. The second type of ore is the limonite; represented by the formula $2Fe_2O_3{-}3H_2O$ and containing 60% iron. The most important deposits of limonite occur at some distance from the area of interest; the possibility of small local deposits cannot, however, be ignored. The third type of ore is the haematite ore, represented by the formula Fe_2O_3 and containing 70% iron. The principal source of this ore is in the west and south of the Lake District and it is unlikely that it would have been transported to the smelting sites in view of the local availability of the carbonate ores.

Obviously the geographical factors make it evident that the carbonate ore was the most likely to have been used. As previously stated, no absolute source of ore may be cited but a consideration of local coalfields, stretching as they do from Warrington to Ruabon, yields a great number of possible sources. On a purely local point there are outcrops of coal and associated ore in the Manchester area. There were extensive small mediaeval workings in this area and attention may be drawn to a recent newspaper report[28] on the finding of a pit shaft underneath a city restaurant. The ore types associated with these deposits would be a carbonate ore occurring as nodules below the coal seams and commonly known as Blackband Ironstone. Similar nodular ores were exploited in Kent and Sussex during the Roman period and, although found in clay beds, belong to the same geological period: the Carboniferous.

Indeed it is even possible that ore may have been brought from the North Staffordshire coalfields with greater ease of transportation. By the twelfth century, opencast coal working occurred in North Staffordshire, probably in the Biddulph Valley, which would have formed a readily accessible source of ore if known in the Roman period.[29] It may be stated that there is no certain evidence to indicate that the iron ores associated with the copper deposits of Alderley Edge were known in the Roman period.[30]

CONCLUSION

The only evidence of iron smelting south of the Mersey comes from Wilderspool and perhaps Northwich. Such a small smelting industry does not accord with the wide distribution of iron objects in the North-West during the Roman period or with the number of secondary smithing hearths. It is possible that iron was brought into the region in the form of smelted blooms from a production centre near the source of the ore, perhaps in South Lancashire. This supposed movement of iron implies the existence of a suitable means of transportation by road and river from a centre, which was organised on a larger scale than the local artisan traders of small settlements. The organisation of such an industry, from a military and economic standpoint, can perhaps be compared either with the Roman lead industry[1] or the Wealden iron industry.[4] The latter example demonstrates well one of the roles of the *Classis Britannica*: in this instance the role of a supplies arm concerned with the manufacture and distribution of iron. Here the subject rests until further information can be located by excavation.

REQUEST

On the matter of recording smithing hearths the authors intend to compile a register of details of smithing hearths with the ultimate aim of providing a satisfactory classification. With this in mind they would welcome details not only of newly-excavated hearths but also of any previously excavated hearths which may be of interest.*

ACKNOWLEDGEMENT

One of the authors, J.H.C., takes pleasure in acknowledging the encouragement of Professor K. Entwistle of the Metallurgy Department of the University of Manchester Institute of Science and Technology, and Messrs R. W. Adams and R. I. Smith of the same department for undertaking the chemical analyses of the slags. He also wishes to thank Mr A. Williams of the Department of History of Science at the U.M.I.S.T. for introducing him to the Deansgate excavations.

APPENDIX I

All samples for analysis were taken from the unoxidised core of the slag specimens, and the analytical method was atomic absorption spectrophotometry performed in a borofluoride medium.

In this calculation of efficiency three main assumptions are made:

(i) the roasting is carried out to an efficiency of 9–100%;

(ii) only fayalite, $2FeO\ SiO_2$, and anorthite, $CaO\ Al_2O_3\ 2SiO_2$, are formed in the slag;

(iii) manganese oxide, MnO, replaces FeO in the fayalite if it is present.

Let a typical carbonate ore be examined, which on roasting has the following composition:

$$\%FeO = 62,\ \%MnO = 3.4,\ \%SiO_2 = 9.6,\ \%CaO = 5.7 \text{ and } \%Al_2O_3 = 3.9$$

Considering anorthite, 3.9% Al_2O_3 will combine with 2.1% CaO and 4.6% SiO_2 leaving 5.0% of 'free' silica to be reduced

$$\%Fe \text{ in } FeO = 54$$
$$\%Fe \text{ in 'free' } FeO = 0.54\ (53.5)$$
$$= 28.9$$

Thus with the above assumptions, a maximum of 28.9 lb. of iron could be obtained from 100 lb. of roasted carbonate ore, or from 149 lb. of unroasted ore. This calculation again demonstrates the advantages of a preliminary roast.

* The authors can be contacted c/o Department of Archaeology, The University, Manchester, M13 9PL.

Cleere's most successful trial yielded almost 20 lb. of iron from 201 lb. of roasted ore, giving an efficiency of approximately 34%.

Percent efficiency is sometimes quoted[26] as

total iron extracted/total amount of iron in ore,

but it is proposed that a more realistic efficiency index would be

total iron extracted/total amount of 'free' iron in ore.

The model slag produced by this ore would have the following composition:

18% SiO_2, 43.5% FeO, and 38.5% anorthite

and would have a liquidus temperature of *c.*1180°C (see fig. 52). The unusually high anorthite percentage is due to the high CaO content of the ore. There is evidence to suggest that CaO may react to form compounds other than anorthite[4] thus lowering the anorthite content of the slag, and the liquidus temperature.

Point M1 represents the model slag and the arrow indicates the effect of lowering the anorthite content.

A similar calculation on a typical coal-measure carbonate ore yields the figure of a maximum of 28 lb. of iron from 100 lb. of roasted ore. The slag produced, M2, would have a liquidus temperature of *c.*1150°C.

APPENDIX II

Calculations on Slags.

The approximate compositions, in terms of the FeO, SiO_2 and anorthite contents, and the approximate liquidus temperatures have been calculated for four slags, other than the two model slags, M1 and M2.

Table A gives the slag compositions as analysed, and Table B gives the slag compositions in terms of the major phases.

TABLE A

%FeO	%MnO	%SiO_2	%CaO	%Al_2O_3	
65.1	0.2	30.3	1.0	3.2	Northwich A
58.5	0.2	31.9	0.9	3.8	Northwich B
60.1	0.3	29.2	3.1	5.4	Wilderspool
44.0	0.8	32.0	7.6	3.4	Cleere[7]

TABLE B

%(FeO+MnO)	%SiO_2	% anorthite	Liquidus °C.	
66.2	28.4	5.3	*c.*1150	Northwich A
62.9	32.1	5.0	*c.*1177	Northwich B
61.5	23.3	15.0	*c.*1150	Wilderspool
54.6	34.1	11.3	*c.*1160	Cleere[7]

From fig. 52 it is clear that the Northwich slags fall within the limits of composition of Roman bloomery slags, and that M2 is also a reasonable estimate. However, it is apparent that the simplifying of a slag into the constituents FeO, SiO_2 and anorthite is not valid for either ores or slags of a high CaO content. The proximity of M2 to the dashed line leads to the proposal that 1.4% CaO be considered as the limiting CaO content for this simplification to be valid.

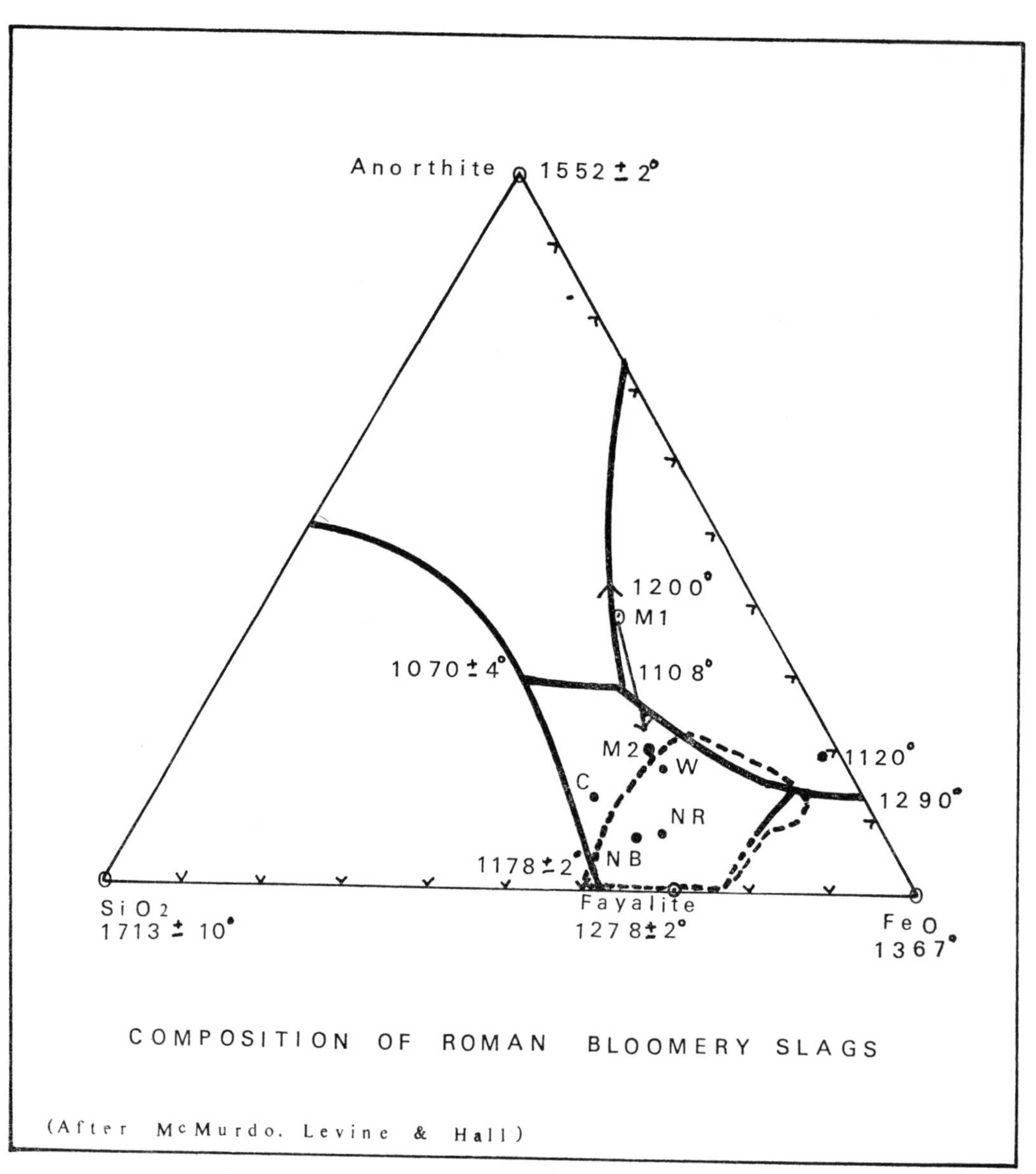

COMPOSITION OF ROMAN BLOOMERY SLAGS

(After McMurdo, Levine & Hall)

Fig. 52

Key: NR = Northwich A W = Wilderspool
NB = Northwich B C = Cleere[5]

Dashed line is limit of composition of Roman bloomery slags.

APPENDIX III

Smithing slag and Hammer scale.

Implicit in what has been written is the assumption that there were at least two stages of smithing: a preliminary de-slagging of the iron and a final forming treatment which is termed forging. Thus there are two by-products which demand attention: smithing slag and forging, or hammer, scale.

The latter has received attention in the literature (Tylecote, 254); but the former has no specific mention. The Manchester site, however, yielded large quantities of iron slag which, by virtue of the arguments expressed in the text, must be smithing slags, and two analyses are given on p. 157. In this case the iron is expressed as $\%Fe_2O_3$ rather than $\%FeO$ since the slag is the product of a process carried out in oxidising conditions.

	Sample I	Sample II
$\%Fe_2O$	56.0	53.7
$\%Al_2O$	8.76	8.41
$\%SiO_2$	34.3	40.7
$\%CaO$	0.19	0.15
$\%MnO$	1.025	0.025

From these analyses it is clear that the point expressed on p. 154 about the higher silica content is borne out. If the transformation of the haematite to wüstite, FeO, is made and the iron oxide percentage is expressed in terms of %FeO, then this figure is found to be lower than that obtained for a simple smelting slag.

To conclude these appendices on slags and analyses a cautionary note must be written. No absolute conclusion can be made from a slag analysis alone as to whether a site was for smelting or smithing since no definite division can be made between such slags. However, when taken together with other points, e.g. furnace shape and temperature of firing, the absence or presence of roasted ore, the incidence or the slag itself, etc., slag analyses do provide a powerful pointer to the particular use of a site.

REFERENCES

1 R. F. Tylecote, *Metallurgy in Archaeology*, Arnold (1962), Chs. 6 and 7.

2 F. H. Thompson, *Roman Cheshire*, Cheshire Community Council (1964), pp. 67–87 fig. 19.

3 H. F. Cleere, private communication.

4 H. F. Cleere, *Britannia* II (1971), pp. 203–17 (1971).

5 H. F. Cleere, *Bull. Historical Metallurgy Group* V (1971), pp. 74–75.

6 R. F. Tylecote, *J.I.S.I.* 203 (1965), pp. 340–8.

7 E. J. Wynne, R. F. Tylecote, ibid. 190 (1958), pp. 339–48.

8 R. F. Tylecote, J. N. Austin and A. E. Wraith, ibid. 209 (1971), pp. 342–63.

9 H. Straube, B. Tarmann and E. Plöckinger, 'Erzreduktionsversuche in Rennöfen Norischer Bauart', *Kartner Museumschriften* XXXV (1964).

10 R. Pleiner, *Pamatky archaeologické* LX (1969), pp. 458–87.

11 R. Pleiner, *Základy Slovanského Železářského Hutnictví v Českých Zemích*, Prague (1958).

12 R. Thomsen, *Kuml* (1963), pp. 60–74.

13 J. W. Gilles, *Unser Werk* 12 (1957); *Stahl u. Eisen* 12 (1958), pp. 1690–5; ibid. 14 (1960), pp. 943–8.

14 A. Mazur and E. Nosek, *Materialow Archaeologicznvch* 7, pp. 19–38.

15 G. R. Morton and J. Wingrove, *J.I.S.I.* 207 (1969), pp. 1556–64.

16 H. H. Coghlan, *Pitt Rivers Museum Occasional Papers in Technology* 8, p. 86.

17 H. F. Cleere, *Ant. J.* LII (1972), pp. 8–23.

18 R. F. Tylecote and E. Owles, *Norfolk Arch.* 32 (1960), pp. 142–62.

19 H. Behagel, *Germania* 23 (1939), pp. 228–37.

20 J. D. Bestwick, *Roman Middlewich* (at press).

21 J. M. T. Charlton, *N.S.J.F.S.* 2, p. 65 and Plate IVa.

22 G. D. B. Jones and P. V. Webster, *Arch. J.* CXXV (1968), p. 193.

23 J. S. Wacher, *Britannia* II (1971), pp. 200–202.

24 G. D. B. Jones, *Arch. J.* CXXVIII (1971), pp. 31–77.

25 J. H. Williams, *J.R.S.* LVII (1967), p. 179; LVIII (1968), p. 182.

26 G. R. Morton and J. Wingrove, *J.I.S.I.* 207 (1969), pp. 1556–64.

27 G. R. Morton and J. Wingrove, *Bull. Historical Metallurgy Group* 311 (1969), pp. 66–7.

28 *The Daily Telegraph* No. 36655, Saturday, 24 March 1973.

29 J. D. Bestwick, *Biddulph Historical Society Transactions* I (1966), p. 6.

30 C. Roeder, *Transactions of the Lancs. and Ches. Ant. Soc.* 19 (1901), pp. 77–118.

D: The Roman Name for Manchester

JOHN HIND, M.A., Ph.D.

I. FORMER AND PRESENT THEORIES

THE ROMAN NAME for the fort and settlement at Manchester is an old problem which has intrigued many scholars since Camden down to the early years of this century. During the last fifty years or so the puzzle has been allowed to rest, with the general acceptance of a name form which nevertheless was first suggested with some diffidence, and also was received with a certain amount of caution, when the matter was most fully discussed in the years around 1900–9. In some ways, the matter might still be summed up in the words of Haverfield, quoted by James Tait in 1909:

> 'The question of the name of *Mancunium* . . . does not seem to me at present to be answerable. On the whole the simplest course seems to be to avoid using any Roman name for the place. That is quite easy and cannot be wrong.'[1]

There is, of course, always the temptation to do better than this, and the early attempts to establish the name have led to the version MANCUNIUM which is well-nigh indelible in the public mind. This was based on the version of the name given by the Antonine Itinerary (*Iter* X). The majority of manuscripts read MANCUNIO (manuscripts ABCFGUV), although other variants are MAMCUNIO (L), MANCUMO (M,O,R.T.), MANCOMO (Q), MACOCUNIO (N), and COACCIUNIO, COACOCUNIO (J).[2] The consensus of readings in *Iter* X should give a version, then, approximating to MANCUNIO or MAMCUNIO, especially as B. and L. are considered to be among the earliest and best manuscripts. The wilder corruptions of the name found in N. and J. are to be completely discounted, in spite of Charles Roeder's ill-founded attempts to find an old Celtic root word in COACC ('red'),[3] similar to that in the Roman name for Wigan (COCCIUM).

So far, the version MANCUNIUM might seem to be preferable to the others, which are to be seen as corruptions in the manuscripts. The Celtic root from which the Latin name was derived has been said to be 'MAEN' for 'rock, hill' (as in Mona, Isle of Man, or Coniston Old Man), or a word MAN, MANN meaning 'place'.[4] Tait in 1909 was against these derivations on philological grounds, but, as the idea was first proposed by Camden in 1586, and was last found in W. H. Thompson's *History of Manchester* in 1967, it obviously dies hard.[5] Tait's philological arguments against the form MANCUNIUM have some weight since, even though the first factor in the toponym might be explained as akin to MONA, MAEN, it ought, in a compound word, to end in a vowel, as perhaps MANACUNIO or MANDACUNIO. Further, the second element in the name -CUNIO is not easily to be explained. Roeder thought it connected with the Celtic root -COCHION 'red', meaning 'red stones', but this has not found favour with anyone.[6] Another explanation is that -CUNIO may be from a Celtic root meaning 'height', but the linguistic probability of this is dubious and the meaning 'stony height' is doubtfully applicable to the low stony outcrop of Castlefield by the Medlock where lay the Roman fort.

Perhaps the gravest objection to these speculations is the fact that they purported to take the best readings of the manuscripts as their basis, yet they failed absolutely to take into account the quite different version to be found in the same manuscript but in a different section. In *Iter* II of the Antonine Itinerary the name form is MAMUTIO in eleven out of fifteen manuscripts, MANUTIO in one, and MAMUCIO in the remaining three. This last version is given in B. and L. which are the oldest manuscripts, dating to the eighth century. The collation of the manuscripts was made by Parthey and Pinder in a definitive edition of the *Itinerarium Antonini*[7] and their preference for the manuscripts B.L. in general and (in the case of MANCHESTER) for the form MAMUCIO has been followed by most serious scholars of the twentieth century.

The name MAMUCIUM has found its way into the Ordnance Survey Map of Roman Britain, and (as the received version) into such authoritative works as Crawford and Richmond's, 'The British Section of the Ravenna Cosmography', and Rivet and Jackson's 'The British Section of the Antonine Itinerary', which came out in 1949 and 1970 respectively.[8]

The form MAMUCIUM, then, has as strong manuscript support as has MANCUNIUM, although popular tradition still holds to the latter. When one considers what the popular mind is capable of making of names ('Manchester' was in Camden's day locally supposed to be the 'city of Men', or of the 'good burghers and true' who fought back the Danes)[9] this particular consideration gives the received form no real advantage. Those who accept the form MAMUCIUM as the original Latinised Celtic name have the problem of finding a satisfactory derivation. Indeed this did not prove too difficult, since the word MAM, MAMM, is to hand. This means in Irish or Welsh 'breast', 'mother' or 'womb'. To the specialist scholar, then, the name means 'breast-like hill' and is compared to CICUTIO, a place-name with similar meaning of a fort sited in Wales (Y Gaer).

Within the last forty years the form MAMUCIUM seems to have become accepted among specialists at least, as the original name. It is so treated in Ekwall's *Place Names of Lancashire*, by K. Jackson in his *Language and History in Early Britain*, and by Richmond and by Rivet and Jackson in the articles mentioned above.[10] Yet there are reasons for doubt to remain. Professor Tait's discussion of the name, written in 1909, remains the fullest to date. A professional philologist, he voiced the rhetorical query thus: 'in view of the possibility of corruption in the manuscripts of the Itinerary to which reference has already been made, can we even be certain that the true form of the name has been preserved? The number of variants and the strange form of one of them suggest caution at the outset'. Elsewhere he adds, 'The first syllable at all events of *Mancunium* cannot be correct, while the form *Mamucium* lies under some suspicion'.[11]

Tait, in the concluding section of his article, did himself prove to be cautious. He tentatively accepted the form MAMUCIUM, but considered Bradley's suggestion MAMMIUM (locative case MAMMIO) also within the bounds of possibility. The Celtic root meaning would be the same, but the form suggested by Bradley might go some way to explain still other corrupt versions of the name found in an early Byzantine geographer (the so-called *Ravenna Cosmography*) which reads MANTIO, MANCIO, MAVTIO.[12] Bradley and Tait believed that a shorter original version MAMMIUM might more easily become corrupted into the Ravenna versions of the name than the longer MAMUCIUM.

Finally, an important consideration to Tait and to any historian seeking to establish the original name form is the fact that the Saxon and early mediaeval records seem to prefer a form with 'M' rather than 'N'. 'Mameceaster' appears in the Anglo-Saxon Chronicle under the year A.D. 923. In Domesday Book of 1183 the name is 'Mamecestre' and several times in subsequent years it is 'Mammecestre'. In 1310 and 1384 it becomes 'Mancestre', but in 1385 it is still 'Mamchestre'. In 1330 and 1480 it is 'Manchestre' and 'Manchester'. It has been suggested that the use of 'n' in the mediaeval records may be a scribal slip, and the version 'Manceaster' does not appear to become regular until the Court Leet Records of 1572.[13] Is all this, then, sufficient evidence that the original Roman-Celtic name was spelt with an 'm'? It may be so, and the modern scholars quoted seem to believe so. Yet the Anglo-Saxon Chronicle for A.D. 923 seems to have a manuscript variant 'Manigeceaster', so the version with 'n' may be a variant found in local speech, rather than a corruption by scribal hands.[14] Certainly the modern name has settled down to the form 'Manchester', and there is an exact parallel development in the case of Mancetter (see below).

To sum up the present state of the question, modern scholars give preference to the form MAMUCIUM over the traditional one of MANCUNIUM. They do so maybe correctly, since the majority of mediaeval texts prefer a form in 'm'. However, the original proponents of the name form were a good deal less dogmatic on the matter than the current writers on the subject, and were inclined to accept that MAMMIUM was also a possibility, or that the original form has been lost and is masked by the variants in the Roman and Byzantine Sources (*Iter* X, II, and *Anon Ravennas*). Yet another possibility was mooted by Charles Roeder, that *Mancunium* and *Mamucium* were different sites. This is so unlikely that it can be discounted, although it is possible that the compilers of the Itinerary obtained their two variants from different sources. A parallel here would be Colchester which appears in *Iter* V as *Colonia*, but in *Iter* IX as *Camulodono*.[15]

II. *MAN(N)U-VICIUM* (PONY VILLAGE?)

Doubts of the sort expressed by Haverfield and Tait embolden me to make two observations, which may, perhaps, allow us to establish an *Ur-Mancunium*. In the first place there is a Roman site in the English midlands, whose modern name is very similar to that of Manchester. This is Mancetter in Warwickshire. The name is made up of what seem to be identical factors, 'Man', and 'cetter'. The latter element is from Anglo-Saxon 'ceaster', 'chester'—the normal word for a place formerly occupied by the Romans, meaning 'a walled fort', or 'town'. It so happens that the Roman name for Mancetter is known to have been MANDUESSEDUM.[16] The latter element means 'chariot', and the former probably means a 'small draught horse'. A similar place name derived from a Celtic root, and situated in the Alps was TARVESSEDUM ('bull-drawn cart'). The historical reasons why a place should be named the 'place of horse chariots' may not be clear, but the fact seems to be so. If MANDUESSEDUM became 'Mancetter', the complicated latter part of the word being dropped and MANDU (MANNUS) becoming 'Man',[17] a similar development could have occurred at Manchester. Here the full name may have been MANDU (MANNU) VICIUM. Such a form would be easily shortened to MANUICIUM, which in turn through corruption in the manuscripts could become the versions found in the two routes of the Antonine Itinerary II and X (MAMUCIO, MANCUNIO) and even shortened to the Ravenna's MANCIO, MAUTIO, MANTIO.[18]

The second observation is that *-vicium* (loc. *-vicio*) is a regular suffix in Romano-British place names, represented at such northern sites as *Borcovicus*, *Vercovicium* (Housesteads), *Delgovicia* (Millington, east of York) and *Langovicium* (Lanchester). Certainly a name form ending in *-vicium* is preferable, other things being equal, to versions ending -UCIO, -UTIO (locative case) since the parallel offered for these forms (CICUTIO) ends in *-o* in the nominative, while *Mamucium* has the second declension ending *-ucium*.

The present suggestion amounts to the following. The root word contained in the first factor of Man-chester may go back to a Celtic original MANDU, MANNUS, a word which is now (by the most recent authorities) said to mean 'a small draught horse'. A parallel line of development in the toponym can be observed in the Roman name *Manduessedum* which became Mancetter. There seems in fact to have been some confusion in the Middle Ages between Manchester and Mancetter, reflected in Canon Raine's list of the rectors of Manchester. For instance Hugh de Manchester is in the Patent Rolls of 1294, 'de Mamcestre' or 'de Maunnecestre'.[19] Mancetter was also called Mamecestre or Maumecestre (1196, 1234). In the case of MAN(N)-

UICIUM, the word contains a second factor meaning 'village', 'settlement', instead of a factor meaning 'chariot'. The corruption in Latin manuscripts from MANUICIUM to MAMUCIUM or MANCUNIUM would involve a mere stroke of one letter in the first instance and little more in the second.

The proposal made above may seem to fall on the stumbling block of the Anglo-Saxon variants of the name with 'm'. Yet Mancetter also has similar variants and even in the case of Manchester the version with 'n' appears earlier than has sometimes been claimed, notably in the Anglo-Saxon Chronicle for A.D. 923 (*Mameceaster, Manigeceaster on Norþhymbrum*). This might be the Saxon corruption of 'Manuic-ceaster'. Gradwell, whose theories on the meaning of the name have long been supplanted, may have been not far off the mark in regard to the second factor. He suggested 'Man-wicken'—'Stone village'.[20] If we set aside the old derivation from 'stone' and substitute *Mannu* (*Mandu*) then we are left with an original *Man(n)uvicium*, 'Pony-Village', perhaps a place where the small Celtic chariot horses were bred. It would be appropriate if this derivation for the name of Roman Manchester were accepted in the very year (1972/73) when archaeological evidence for the site of the *vicus* (settlement) outside the fort at Manchester is beginning to be found.

NOTES

1 James Tait, *apud* F. Bruton, *The Roman Fort at Manchester*, 1909, p. 16.

2 G. Parthey and M. Pinder, *Itinerarium Antonini* (Berlin, 1848), Iter II, Iter X. 223, 230. For discussion see Tait, loc. cit. pp. 9–19. See also *Itineraria Romana* Vol. I, ed. O. Cuntz (Leipzig, 1920).

3 C. Roeder, *Roman Manchester*, 1900, p. 1ff.

4 W. B. Dawkins, 'Manchester in Prehistoric Times', *Archaeological Journal*, 1909, p. 173.

5 Camden, *Britannia*, 1695, p. 746ff. Camden thought the name stemmed from the Celtic, 'maen'—stone, rock. W. H. Thompson, *History of Manchester*, 1967, pp. 2–3.

6 Roeder explained the whole name as derived from Meini-cochion, meaning 'red-rock'. But this is not convincing (cf. Tait, p. 19) and Roeder had a very odd theory that there were two Roman Manchesters, one with the name Meini-cochion (*Mancunium*) and one *Mamucium*. C. Roeder, op. cit.

7 See n. 2.

8 O. G. S. Crawford and I. A. Richmond, *Archaeologia* 93, 1949, p. 40; K. Jackson, *Britannia* I, 1970, p. 76. Jackson explains the Anglo-Saxon name as Mamec-ceaster. See also Jackson, *Language and History in Early Britain*, p. 487, n. 4.

9 Camden, *Britannia*, 1695, p. 746ff.

10 Ekwall, *Place Names in Lancashire*, p. 34, n.; Crawford and Richmond, loc. cit.; Jackson *Britannia* I, p. 76. The suffix *-ucio* is explained as *-ūc* in the same sense as *-āc* (adjectival).

11 Tait, loc. cit. pp. 12, 16.

12 H. Bradley, *English Historical Review*, 15, 1900, p. 495.

13 J. Tait, loc. cit.; Tait, *Mediaeval Manchester and the Beginnings of Lancashire*, 1904, pp. 1–2.

14 The Parker MS. of the Anglo-Saxon Chronicle for A.D. 923. *Manigeceaster* (G). In 1861 John Reilly used the name form 'Manigeceaster' regularly, *History of Manchester*, pp. 17–18.

15 I owe the observation concerning *Camulodunum* to Dr J. P. Wild.

16 For *Manduessedum*, Jackson, *Britannia* I, 1970, p. 76; *Victoria County History, Warwickshire* I, p. 233.

17 Lucretius, *De Rerum Natura* 3, 1063; Pliny, *Ep.*, 4, 2, 3; *Alt-Celtische Sprachreste* (ed. Holder) 1896–1904. D. Ellis Evans, *Gaulish Personal Names*, 1967, p. 222ff. An earlier interpretation of the *Mandu* element was that it meant 'thinking about', 'concerned with', d'Arbois de Joubainville, *Noms Gaulois chez Cézar*, pp. 127, 132.

18 Dr Wild reinforces my view a little with the observation that MANCIO in *Ravennas* might arise more easily through a ligature of N with V (from MANVCIO) than by syncope of M with V (from MAMUCIO).

19 *Victoria County History, Lancashire,* Vol. IV, p. 193, n. 289. For variants in the name of Mancetter including Mannecestre, Mamecestre, Maunchester (A.D. 1247, 1196, 1551), *English Place Name Society, Warwickshire* (1936) pp. 84–85.

20 R. Gradwell, 'Origin of the Name Manchester', *Lancashire and Cheshire Archaeological Society* 9, p. 195. He thought that 'Man-wicken' became *Mancenion, Mancunium.* Another suggestion which may have been on the right track with the second factor is that of Professor Strachan, MAMMIOVICIUM—which is condemned by Tait as 'too long', *Roman Fort at Manchester* 1909, p. 16, n. 16.

E: The Problem of post-Roman Manchester

J. D. BU'LOCK, B.A., PH.D., F.S.A.

HOW DID Roman Mamucium, with which this book is concerned, become modern Manchester? Some sort of answer to this question is quite properly part of any study of the Roman site, which at its fullest might aim at a description of its origins and destinies as well as of its centuries of active existence, but this present chapter is a more modest postscript intended to bring the story through to the Norman manor of *Mamecestre* and so into contact with times regarded by historians as fit and proper for their attention. Though the resulting account may be brief, for lack of material, the problem is a difficult and intriguing one. We start where the archaeologists leave off, with the fourth-century *castrum* over at the junction of the Irwell and the Medlock and its associated *vicus* extending some way to the north between the Irwell and the main highway, modern Deansgate. There follow seven dim centuries during which British, English, and Scandinavian travellers and settlers come and go mysteriously, upon a darkened stage on which we realise that the scenery is somehow being rearranged. When the lights go up we find the mediaeval manor-house, precursor of modern Chetham's, standing at the other end of Deansgate where the Irk joins the Irwell, with its chapel and the tenements of its dependants surrounded by fields, wastelands, and woods. The walls of Mamucium are an overgrown ruin, while the *vicus* is now called Aldport and woods and coppices stretch from modern Quay Street to Knott Mill (fig. 54). From this transformation scene onwards the story is fairly clear, and the next act in particular was studied very fully by Professor Tait many years ago,[1] but accounts of the intervening centuries are another matter.

The coin series from Castlefield runs down (with a relative drop in numbers after A.D. 180) to *c.* A.D. 402, which is certainly later than that at Chester, but we do not know how much of the late fourth-century activity upon the site was military, or directly dependent upon military needs, and how much was due to independently viable civilian activity. At least two, and probably more, hoards further distort the chronological picture. There is no sign of the presence of Germanic auxiliaries in the vicinity, and with the end of formal military occupation the whole site may well have been abandoned. For the ensuing two centuries we must presume that the area was at least frequented by communities about whom we know little more than that they were British, speaking a language ancestral to mediaeval Welsh. The population would in any case be much smaller than it had been in the days when the Roman Army had provided security, employments, and a money economy, for in this area of Britain the Roman administration had not developed the endogenous economic potential much beyond that of prehistoric times. For post-Roman Manchester the local resources were the woods, with wild game and domestic pigs, the river for fishing, and a very modest area of tillage. The most permanent vestiges of Roman Manchester were to be the line of highway which is modern Deansgate and the location of the river crossings which it defines, by Knott Mill on the Medlock and at Hunt's Bank, under Victoria Station, on the Irk.

Whether the Roman name of the site was Mamucium or Mancunium is an old and perhaps unfruitful controversy—the concentration of vertical strokes in *mucium* or *ncunium* was always confusing—but the first element of the name was in either case Celtic and from our viewpoint it is interesting that it remained locally current for long enough to give the English a name for the place; they called it *Mameceaster.*[2] Post-Roman speakers of a British dialect also remained in the area to transmit to English incomers topographic names for the hilly woods which circle Manchester—*cateir* (*cader*) in Chadderton to the north, *pen* in Pendlebury and Pendleton, *cēto* (*coed*)

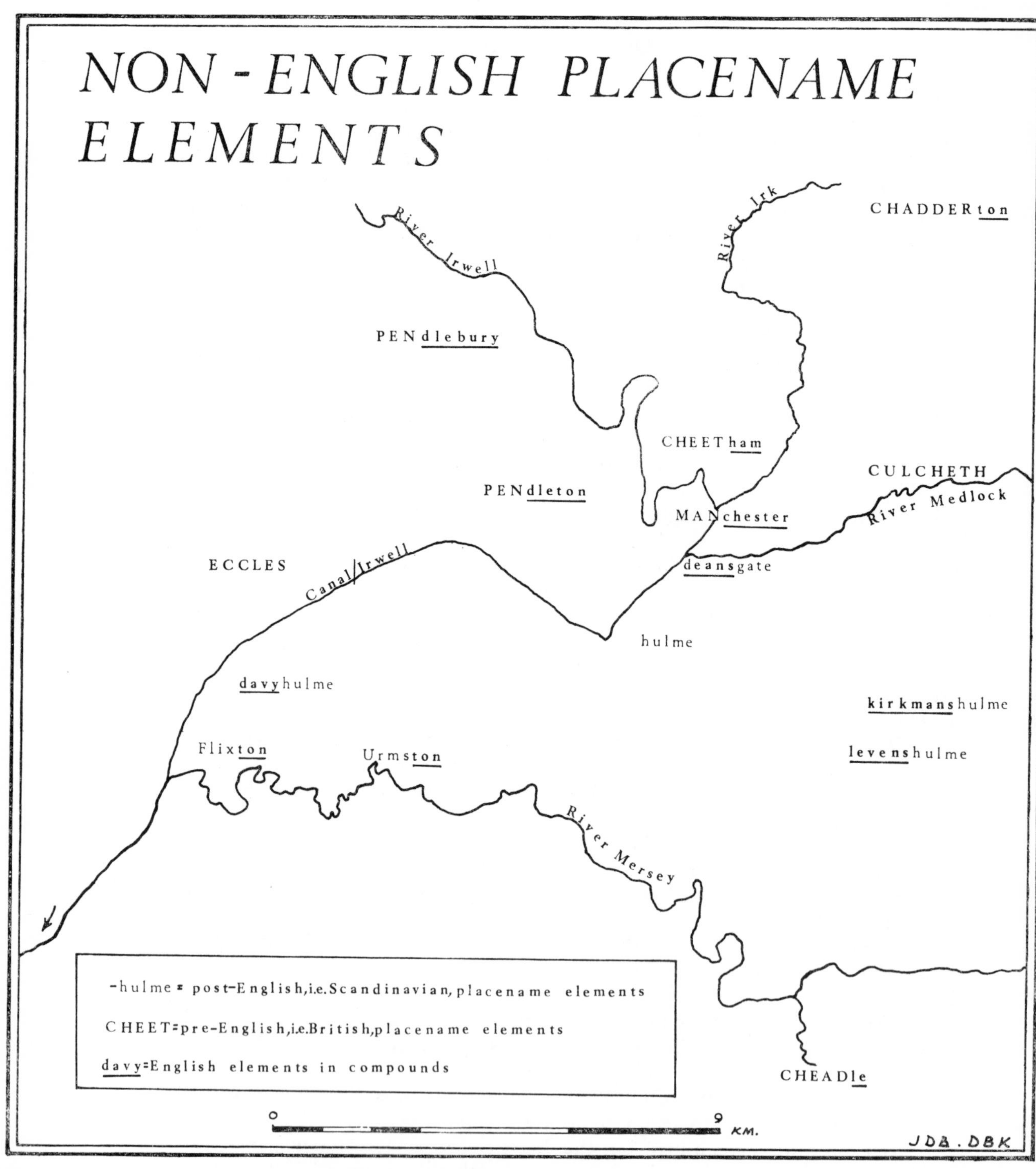

Fig. 53. Non-English place-name elements in the Manchester area.

in Cheetham to the north and Cheadle to the south—all hybrid names compounded with English terminations. Completely British is Culcheth (Welsh *cil coed*, the 'back wood'). Since all these names are purely topographic they carry no implication of British settlements at the spots designated, but only of contact between British and English settlers in the vicinity, perhaps around A.D. 550–650. Such contacts may have been rather limited, moreover, for the British failed to pass on their own names for the local rivers, and Irk, Irwell, Medlock and Mersey all have English names (unlike Etherow, Goyt and Thame). One place-name, Eccles, is rather different; the name comes from Latin *ecclesia* through British to old Welsh *eccluys*, modern *eglwys*, and it implies a pre-English church hereabouts, and so by extension a local British community (fig. 53).

We do not know to which rulers these British occupants of the Manchester area owed their allegiance. Just as in Wales, the North British had divided themselves amongst a number of kingdoms and sub-kingdoms, but the boundaries of these, and even the locations, are sometimes uncertain, and there were almost certainly some small kingdoms of which even the name has been lost. The Cumbrian kingdom of Rheged may have extended at least as far south as Rochdale, if place-names are evidence, while the best-known of the Pennine kingdoms was Elmet (otherwise Loidis, cf. Leeds); I have argued elsewhere that at least until A.D. 617 the Welsh kingdom of Powys extended well into modern Cheshire.[3] Between Rheged, Elmet, and Powys there may have been some unknown petty kingdom, or Manchester may have been marginally in one of the three known ones.

Perhaps the first record of an English incursion into the Manchester area tells of the passage of a Northumbrian army under Æthelfrith in A.D. 616–17, when their route to the battle of Chester may have used either the Manchester or the Warrington river-crossing. Older writers took this event also to imply a Northumbrian conquest and subsequent settlement, but the more recent view of this campaign as a temporary incursion is perhaps preferable.[4] However, we also know that Æthelfrith had already reduced the British kingdom of Elmet to client status[5] and when its last king, Ceretic map Guallauc, died[6] we must presume that Elmet at least was opened to Northumbrian settlement. Meanwhile the first half of the seventh century also saw the emergence and expansion of the midland kingdom of Mercia, and a series of campaigns and raids, ranging from the Severn to the Forth, between Northumbrians on the one hand and an alliance of Mercians and Welsh on the other. From the historical accounts it is quite impossible to deduce whether the Manchester area was settled by Mercians or by Northumbrians, and indeed the first English settlers were probably pioneer families who cared little for either. For them the Mersey was a boundary of some kind, hence its Old English name, *mǣres ēa*, the border river. However, the dialect boundary between Northumbrian and Mercian forms in place-names lies well to the north of Manchester (for example, in *Ribchester* the Mercian *-ch-* form where *Lancaster* has the northern hard *-c-*), coinciding with the later boundaries of the Lichfield diocese and of Chester shire.

The general pattern of place-names in the area makes it clear that effective settlement was not begun until the seventh century was well advanced, and this is confirmed—in a negative way—by the absence of English pagan burials in Lancashire and Cheshire generally. However, there is one notable exception to this generalisation; about 1850 an Anglo-Saxon cremation urn was dug up at Red Bank, on the north side of the Irk crossing (i.e. under modern Victoria Station).[7] Only illustrations of it survive (pl. 30b); it was wide-mouthed with grooved and stamped decoration in typical English style, but it is scarcely profitable to discuss its stylistic affinities on the scanty evidence now available. For us it clearly demonstrates the presence of at least one group of early seventh-century English settlers at Manchester, significantly located at the northern end of the Deansgate axis and in sight of the later manor house.

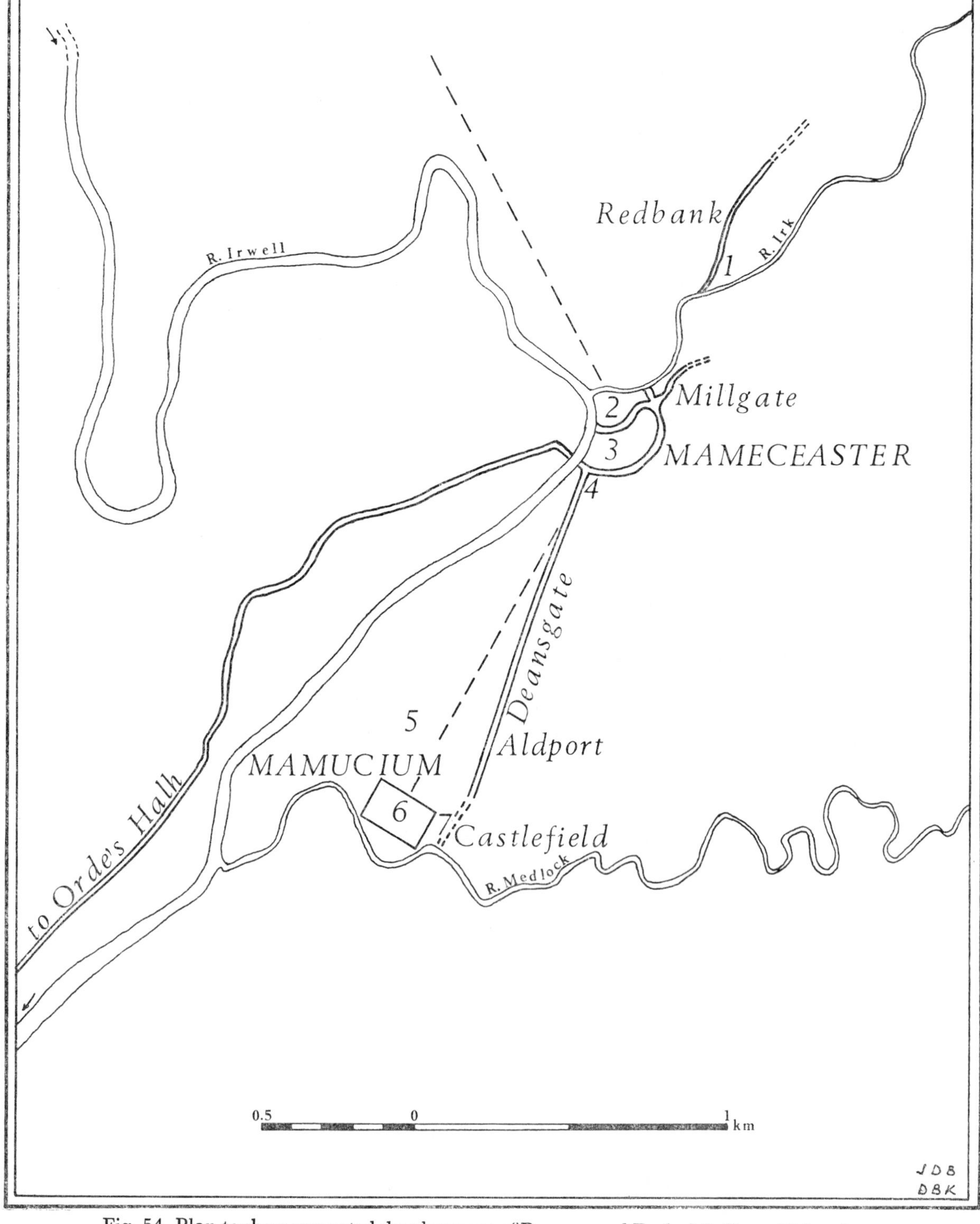

Fig. 54. Plan to show suggested development of Roman and Early Mediaeval Manchester.

1. Find-spot of Anglo-Saxon urn.
2. Hunt's Bank.
3. Cathedral.
4. Hanging Ditch
5. Find-spot of Saxon *sceattas*.
6. Roman fort.
7. Approximate find-spot of Viking-style brooch.

Whatever the character and origin of the first English immigrants in the area, their settlements were really consolidated during the period of Mercian supremacy in the eighth century. This was also, in all probability, the period when the boundary of the diocese of Lichfield was set on the Ribble. This was a phase of extensive colonisation of previously afforested land, and around Manchester there are plenty of 'clearance' place-names to attest this phase—Astley, Blackley, Kearsley or Worsley, for example. By this time the area of the Roman *vicus* was probably overgrown with scrub, but along the adjacent length of Deansgate some kind of trading or market centre seems to have persisted, in Anglo-Saxon terms as *port*, which eventually became *Aldport*, the 'old market' (presumably when a new market area was established nearer the manor, as discussed later). Modern excavations have not encountered any trace of this phase, but around 1820 a hoard of eight or nine silver *sceattas* was found in digging the foundations for St Matthew's church in Tonman Street.[8] The *sceattas* were Mercian coins of the early eighth century which mark the beginnings of a return to a coinage economy such as had not existed since Roman times, and it it pleasant to record the Tonman Street hoard as tangible evidence (now most unfortunately lost) of the beginnings of Manchester's commercial history!

Perhaps during the eighth or early in the ninth century we should suppose the establishment of a manor farm on a strong enclosed site at the *northern* end of Deansgate, on the rock headland between the Irwell and the Irk. The enclosure bound was the later 'Hanging Ditch', probably a ditch, bank, and wooden stockade; the fifteen-acre site thus defended was to become the centre of mediaeval Manchester. It overlooked the Irk crossing to the north and a crossing of the Irwell to '*Ord's halh*', Ordsall; the latter became the centre of Salford Hundred but Manchester was to become its principal manor, and within its enclosure was established the principal church of the area (see map, fig. 54). This river and road junction already had some importance in Roman times, to judge from reports of 'quantities' of Roman coins, etc., found when the adjacent stretch of river was cleared for a while in the last century,[9] though the theories of a second Roman *castrum* here are quite superfluous as well as unfounded.

Arguing back from the evidence about later mediaeval Manchester,[1] we can deduce an outline of the layout of the pre-Norman manor. The hall stood at the northern end of the enclosed area where later that of the de Grelleys, now Chetham's, stood; possibly it had its own inner palisade. To its south stood the church and buildings for the priest and his household; immediate dependants of the manor and the church lived within the line of Hanging Ditch. Outside lay the fields of the manor—some land was part of the endowment of the church—and beyond these the still uncleared woods, marshlands, heaths and moors, for large areas within what is now Manchester were still uncultivated waste in the fourteenth century.

Our only direct archaeological evidence comes from the church, ancestor of today's Cathedral. Here, when a thirteenth-century porch was taken down in 1871, was found the fragment of sculpture, which is still preserved in the Cathedral.[10] Artistically it is a rather poor piece of Mercian figure-sculpture, probably dating from the late ninth century and showing an angel bearing a scroll. The inscription is badly cut and crowded but still takes up more space than the carver allowed on the scroll. It reads

INMANVST / VASDMECO / MMEDOSP / X

that is, *in manus tuas, Domine, commendo spiritum* (*meum*), clearly a memorial inscription and using what were said to be the last words of (among others) the Emperor Charlemagne. The sculpture is intrinsically hard to date but most authorities would probably agree to place it not far from A.D. 900, and this would be in good agreement with some peculiarities of the epigraphy; it is important to note that it provides rather earlier evidence about settled community life in Manchester than the first historical reference to the place.*

This comes in the entry in the Anglo-Saxon Chronicle for the year 919:

> 'In this year after autumn King Edward went with the army to Thelwall and ordered the *burh* to be built, occupied, and manned; and while he stayed there he ordered another army, also from the people of Mercia, to occupy Manchester in Northumbria, and repair and man it.'
>
> [*D. Whitelock's translation*]

At this time Northumbria had fallen under Scandinavian rule, effectively from York; Mercia was no longer independent but part of the non-Danish 'England' which Alfred of Wessex had founded, and the phrase 'Manchester in Northumbria' probably means no more than that it had not been under Mercian control for some time. It is more of a problem to know what was being repaired and manned there. Edward's objective at this time was to contain the northern Vikings and in particular to obstruct contact between the two Scandinavian kingdoms of York and Dublin by way of East Lancashire and the Wirral, where Scandinavian colonies were firmly established. This involved extending the network of fortified strongpoints, the *burhs*, begun by Alfred. At Thelwall the fortification was a new construction, but at Manchester an old one was repaired. Professor Tait[1] argued that it was the old Roman station which was refurbished, and wrote:

> 'As part of the walls were still standing to a height of ten feet as late as 1765, there is no good reason to suppose that eight centuries earlier, before it was used as a quarry for the town bridges, it could not have been very easily made defensible enough to serve as one of those advanced military posts with which Edward secured and extended his conquests. The point, however, is not one on which it is possible to speak with much confidence.'

We cannot pretend to any greater confidence upon this issue today than was possible in 1904, and though we may be more convinced that the defended site at Hanging Ditch was also in existence when Edward's levies came to Manchester in 919 this does not exclude the possibility that Castlefield may still have been the more suitable site for military purposes. In that event, subsequent development of Manchester around Hanging Ditch would reinforce the idea that settlement around the manor site existed before 919 so that the refurbishing of the *burh* nearly a mile away did not have any permanent effect on its future development. The name Aldport, already noticed, cannot have come into use particularly late and it implies that a *new* market area just outside Hanging Ditch had come into use; whatever renovations had taken place at Castlefield had not materially changed the historical course upon which the town was set.

One piece of evidence independently brings the Castlefield area into the tenth-century picture; this is the little brooch from the Ellesmere collection.[11] This object is of Viking style and moreover it is almost certainly of Baltic (Swedish or Danish) rather than Norse origin, and it is presumed to come from the vicinity of the Castlefield site though the exact find-spot is not known. We should consider it along with the place-name evidence that shows that, whatever the political consequences of Edward's strategy, the *burh* at Manchester did not prevent Danish settlers from coming into the area, particularly into what is now the southern part of the city. Just across the Medlock from Castlefield is Hulme, a Scandinavian farming settlement from which lesser ones like Davyhulme, Cheadle Hulme, and Levenshulme were distinguished. In all these the element *hulm*, for a waterside settlement, is distinctively Danish. So too are the personal names compounded in Urmston and Flixton and the

* Other pre-Conquest carvings from the Manchester area, Bowdon and Cheadle in Cheshire, Barton (Eccles) in Lancashire, belong to the Anglo-Scandinavian period.

Middle English word *gate* for a road (Scandinavian *gata*) seen in Deansgate and Saltersgate (the old name for Burnage Lane/Slade Lane, the road by which mid-Cheshire salt came north) (map, fig. 53). To such Scandinavians as the founders of these settlements we must also ascribe the use of their own systems of land-measurement in the area, which was found by the clerks who drew up the Domesday account of the area for William the Norman.[12] What they wrote in 1086 tells us little more about pre-Norman *Mamecestre* than that it was a head manor belonging to the king and that St Mary's church also held lands there, but with their record the continuous historical record of Manchester begins.

REFERENCES

1 J. Tait, *Mediaeval Manchester* (Manchester, 1904).
2 On regional place-names, see G. Barnes, *T.L.C.A.S.*, **63** (1952), 131–55; F. T. Wainwright, ibid., **58** (1945), 71–116; E. Ekwall, *The Place-Names of Lancashire* (Manchester, 1922).
3 J. D. Bu'lock, *Pre-Conquest Cheshire* (Chester, 1972).
4 J. D. Bu'lock, *T.L.C.A.S.*, **72** (1962), 47–56.
5 Bede, *Ecclesiastical History* IV, 23.
6 *Annales Cambrensis, sub anno* 616.
7 *T.L.C.A.S.*, **5** (1887), 295.
8 *T.L.C.A.S.*, **3** (1885), 269.
9 C. Roeder, *T.L.C.A.S.*, **23** (1905), 83–84.
10 J. J. Phelps, *T.L.C.A.S.*, **23** (1905), 172–81.
11 J. D. Bu'lock, *T.L.C.A.S.*, **67** (1957), 113–4.
12 cf. the *Victoria County History of Lancashire, etc.*

F: System Planning in Urban Archaeology

B. E. L. LONG, M.A.

How was the Manchester excavation set up? How did it make an impact in an area where little was known of archaeology before? Largely by recognising from the outset the changed circumstances surrounding excavation today. Not simply in archaeology itself with the advent of major urban rescue excavations but also in public and local government opinion where archaeology increasingly appears as one of many potential environmental or planning constraints. With few exceptions, excavations can no longer be regarded as isolated academic forays conducted by distinguished, if remote academics, and there are good indications that many archaeologists are already aware of this fact. Rescue, for example, can be regarded as a pressure group which attempts to impose some influence upon the contemporary political, social and economic environment, and which takes a somewhat militant stand against those factors in the environment which work against the interests of archaeology. Whilst it must be admitted that an excavation in a remote rural area does have several constraining influences, these are miniscule when compared with contemporary urban rescue archaeology. The planning of an urban excavation is an act of political intervention in the life of a community which has economic, social and educational overtones as suggested by the diagram of overall activities surrounding an excavation (fig. 60). As this is the case, until the first spadeful of earth is removed from the proposed site, archaeology, as such, is fairly low down on the scale of priorities.

This may well be a strong statement for many archaeologists to accept for, as a group, archaeologists often display a curious naiveté about matters other than their subject. It is surely obvious that contemporary archaeology is wholly bound up with current environmental and conservational interests to such an extent that archaeological factors are now firmly represented in the political arena. Given such a situation, academic innocence has to be replaced with some clear-minded business thinking. Two terms are of significance in this context. The first of these is 'reaction'. To what extent is archaeology still in a state of 'reacting' to events? We often hear spokesmen telling sad tales about how archaeologists arrived on a site, where some other activity (such as building) was taking place only to find that they are too late to perform any meaningful investigation of the situation. Contractors have moved in and have already invested considerable time, money and effort in pursuing their own interests.

To understand the situation let us try to put ourselves in the position of the developer. Once he moves on to a site he has already invested men, machines and effort in the development of that site. The contracting business is competitive and profit margins can be very thin. If the work is stopped, because some archaeologist is 'reacting' to something which the builder has uncovered, it does not mean that the outflow of cash from the developers' pockets also ceases. Archaeologists must be aware of this fact. If an archaeologist hires a bulldozer for two weeks, and only uses it for two days, he is still liable for the two weeks hire of that machine. Thus asking a developer to halt development is asking him to amend his work schedules. As these are closely related to his profit calculation, one is really asking him to put his potential profit at risk for an apparently worthless piece of pottery.

The other significant term is 'proaction'. Proactive simply means acting before one is managed by events. This is a concept of some importance. Most urban excavation is governed by constraints inherent in some system that is not archaeologically orientated. The archaeologist is thus at the mercy of events over which he has had no control. The archaeological potential of most urban sites is usually apparent before developers arrive on a site. If it is known that a site is to be developed, and

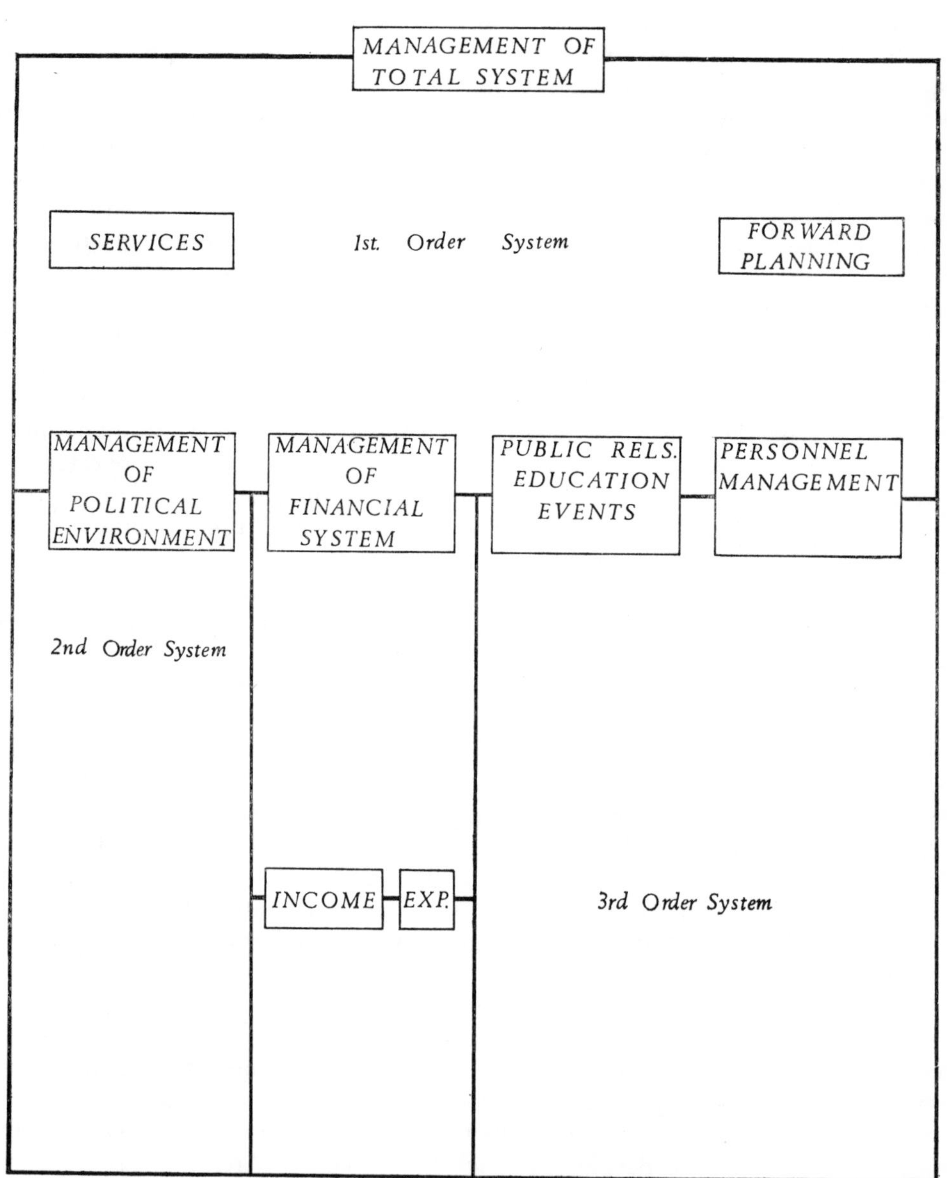

Fig. 55. Suggested system design to illustrate pre-excavation organisation.

there is a clear date for the start of that development, it is thus possible to ensure that the archaeologist is planning his own intervention in such a way that he, and not the developer, will manage events. If a developer can be sure that certain activities are going to take place before he can actually develop a site, he is then in a better position to plan his development accordingly. His costs and profit margins can be more accurately calculated and his work scheduling can be planned accordingly.

There is also a further point to be made in this context which some may consider cynical. Currently great pressures are being placed upon developers to become more sensitive to environmental and conservational issues. It has not been our unique experience to discover that a proactive approach to the issue of excavating a site prior to development, produces a high level of interest and occasionally a financial commitment from those who are eventually to develop the site. It is all too easy to classify all developers as archaeological philistines. Such an attitude, however, only fits a small percentage of those involved in such work. The vast majority of managers involved in a development company would probably exhibit an honest interest in archaeology, as long as it did not conflict with the objectives they have to achieve in order to survive in their own companies.

If one is talking about proactive organisations one is talking largely about a system in which, for a long time, archaeology is only a minor task. System identification is crucial to this chapter. It is also precisely the point that is sometimes ignored by archaeologists. Hitherto, when archaeologists have dealt with such topics, the focus has been on the internal organisation of an excavation, i.e. the micro-view.[1] While valid within its own terms we must recognise that it is the pre-excavation organisation system that controls the actual outcome in most ways. And controls it, moreover, in a manner not unique to esoteric archaeological interests but common to most organisation systems.[2]

Let us begin with the concept of time management. If it is known that a particular site is scheduled for redevelopment in just over seven months time, one has two hundred days in which to plan, organise, finance and execute an excavation. Within that sort of time-scale probably a hundred and fifty days will be spent on preparation and only fifty days actually spent on the site. The hundred and fifty days will be spent organising a system which will create a situation whereby for the last fifty days a totally different system can achieve maximum objectives. The hundred-and-fifty-day system has a series of objectives, none of which has much to do with archaeology *per se*. These objectives have an order and that order is to some extent predictable.[3]

First let us examine a possible system design which can be used to explain the hundred-and-fifty-day organisation (fig. 55). It will be observed that this hundred-and-fifty-day system has little about it which is concerned with archaeology. It has come into being as a result of a decision to examine a site prior to the arrival of the developers. The first order system contains the overall direction of the activity. This body is responsible for deciding upon policy for the total system and then assigning tasks within that system. The objective of this system is to prepare for fifty days of archaeology. It therefore decides upon the various tasks required to be achieved prior to the fifty days and to ensure that these tasks have been executed.

The first order system is aided in its function by a services group, namely administration, and a forward planning group which is concerned with events at least one month away. At the initial stage 'forward planning' is the only agency which might be concerned with problems of the actual site itself. The real work is being performed by the second order systems. There we have identified four critical functions. Managing the political environment, financial management, public relations, etc., and personnel management. The personnel function may well have started its life as part of forward planning, in so far as some agency has to recruit members for all the second order systems. When this model is operational, however, it is concerned with the recruitment, selection and training of labour for the actual site itself.

What tasks are assigned to these various second order systems? Starting with the management of the 'political environment', this second order system is a recognition of the facts of life in urban archaeology. All local authorities have some sort of redevelopment plan. The authority is the body responsible for determining what sort of redevelopment will take place, when it will take place and, to a large extent, how it will take place. In order to achieve these tasks the authority has a democratically elected group of people (councillors) who are responsible for making these important decisions. The councillors are assisted by a group of experts (officials) who give advice on specialist matters, and are largely responsible for interpreting the decisions of the council in order that those decisions may be executed. Officials are also responsible for ensuring the execution of decisions, except in such cases where another party is allocated that responsibility (e.g. a land developer).

Like all human organisations there is a great difference between the apparent and the real organisation. The 'family tree diagram' so rarely reflects the true system of communication and decision making, that it is often an irrelevance. In some local authorities, for example, it is possible to find that a particular official is more important than any single councillor. In one famous case involving a Midland county prior to World War II there was a Clerk to the Council who was renowned for his ability to act independently of his elected council. In his heyday he was quite capable of making decisions without reference to the council, and equally would only implement those decisions of the council which met with his approval. Whilst such characters are not quite so common today, there is, almost inevitably, a pecking order of council officials, and occasionally that order is headed by one individual who exercises considerable power. In other local authorities one finds that there exists an 'inner ring' of councillors who control, through caucuses and whips, the behaviour of the rest of the council. In a few cases, one can make a good case to prove that real power lies not in the council or the officials, but in a party office which controls a majority.

Anyone wishing to move into this world must first undertake a little research to discover what sort of power system is to be found in the local authority. There are various ways of gleaning this information. One might, for example, co-opt on to the first order team an elected member of the local authority and simply apply his particular knowledge. Alternatively a study of the local press might reveal certain names which appear more often than others. Equally local pressmen have all sorts of information which can be useful. The whole point of this exercise is to ascertain where power lies, because sooner or later, the archaeologist is going to have to contact the local authority.

The contact with the political environment needs to be carefully managed. In order for this second level system to work effectively it needs to consider its 'sales' approach. The archaeologist must realise that he is trying to sell someone an idea. A product cannot be sold unless the *customer* is made to feel that he has need of it. No archaeologist would buy an encyclopaedia simply because the salesman needed to sell it. It is scarcely necessary to say that the archaeologist has a great deal in his favour when trying to sell archaeology. Our generation has now made terms such as 'conservation' and 'environment' a fashionable preoccupation. Archaeology is about conservation of the environment. Equally a concern of this generation is man's use of his leisure. Archaeology is a creative use of leisure. The product to be marketed thus has a degree of fashionableness about it.

More important to the functioning of the second order system concerned with the management of the political environment is the old adage about politicians being creatures of the ballot box. Towns, be they prestigious or otherwise, like a volume of good publicity, a commodity which is appreciated by councillors and officials alike. A rescue excavation can produce good publicity. An excavation must therefore be sold, as a product to a consumer in such terms that he appreciates the benefit to him.

The second part of the second order system, is the financial aspect. As will be observed, this is broken down into two further third order systems, namely income and expenditure. During the early life of the hundred-and-fifty-day system, the prime task will be income generation, but as the end of the period approaches then expenditure will begin to loom large as a priority. This system has the task of generating the cash for the excavation. In addition it has to generate some cash simply to sustain the hundred-and-fifty-day system. This system has obvious links with the political management system, but their functions ought not to be confused. Whilst some of the finance may well be derived from the local authority, finance will also be derived from several other, non-political sources. The first order system will have to determine how much finance actually has to be raised and then set a goal for the second order system. As a large portion of the finance will be obtained from governmental sources the inclination is often to combine this with other functions. An analysis of the task, however, will reveal the enormous amount of work performed by this function and thus the need to maintain fairly clear boundaries between this financial and the political functions.

Management of the public relations system can also be easily confused with the political system. This is a great mistake. Public relations is concerned with the public and not with the private world of politics. It requires regular contact with the various media which are available and the management of a campaign aimed at promoting the idea of an excavation. Here, we are talking about excavations which take place within a town or a city. Whilst the political function will be working with the various political bodies involved in the control of the actual site, this body should be easing the task of dealing with the politicians by providing a good groundswell outside in the electorate. Good public relations and publicity will also ease the task of the finance system in raising money from the public.

Public relations, in this context is not just concerned with the careful manipulation of the environment. There are other important objectives such as the preparation of an educational campaign which ought to be one of the important by-products of any excavation. People will always come and stare at holes being dug in the ground. If they can be provided with information about the hole they will tend to take a greater interest.

Archaeology is also an educational activity and thus is of interest to schools and other educational bodies in the region. Schools do not simply turn up at sites without any preparation and somebody has to take responsibility for organising a proper schools information system. One might even, in a large excavation, consider a number of third order systems within this system, e.g.

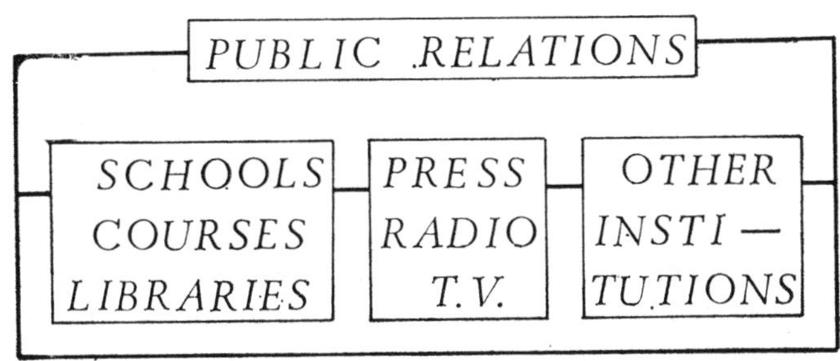

Fig. 56. Public relations systems.

Each of these functions is fairly well self-contained and can be assigned to an appropriate individual for development. In this context one must also provide liaison with one important local body, namely the library. It is estimated that 25% of the population use library services in one form or another. Libraries are not simply places where people borrow books. They are information dissemination systems. One might even go so far as to suggest that the sort of person who uses a library might well be the sort of person who visits an excavation.

The final second order system is concerned with the personnel management aspect of the excavation. Excavations take place when people finally start to work a site. For a large excavation there will be a problem of selection and recruitment. Some excavations never have a problem of recuitment because teams are always in existence to work with certain archaeologists. This may well be a convenient policy for some archaeologists to manage, but it does little for the local community if no opportunity is offered for local participation. Whilst one recognises that many well-meaning but untrained volunteers on a site is an unsatisfactory situation, one also has to recognise that in any urban community there are a lot of people who would dearly love to work on a site, if only they could get some sort of training in simple techniques. Thus a system has to be established for training potential labour and incorporated within the actual excavation system.

Towards the end of the hundred and fifty days, preparation must be made for the development of a totally new organisation. If the work has been well prepared then there will be adequate political involvement, more than adequate finance, good local information and a well-prepared labour force. The system then has to reconsider its tasks and priorities. The priority now in fact is archaeology. The new system may well be drawn as follows.

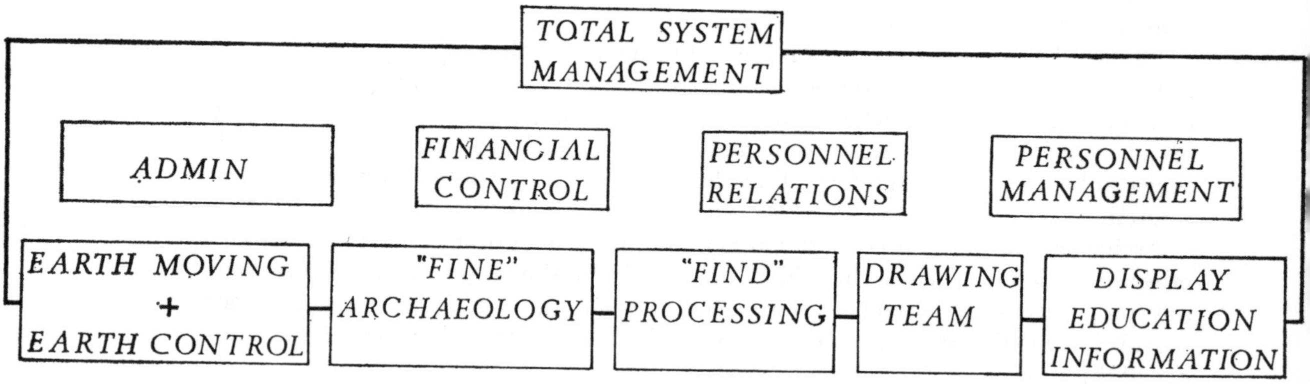

TOTAL SYSTEM MANAGEMENT

ADMIN | FINANCIAL CONTROL | PERSONNEL RELATIONS | PERSONNEL MANAGEMENT

EARTH MOVING + EARTH CONTROL | "FINE" ARCHAEOLOGY | "FIND" PROCESSING | DRAWING TEAM | DISPLAY EDUCATION INFORMATION

Fig. 57. Suggested system for excavation period.

This new system recognises that the important second order systems are concerned with the productive processes of archaeology and these have received extensive coverage elsewhere.[4] In this case only one issue stands out as being odd and that perhaps is the management of earth-moving and earth-control. Unlike archaeology conducted in a remote field, the question of earth-control is critical on an urban site. As the upper layers are removed the disposal of the debris is a prime decision. An earth dump may well occupy a quarter of the area available to the archaeologist, thus any site is only going to be 75% efficient. The placing of the debris and the control of the dump rates considerable attention.

The service systems to the first order system are important in that, apart from some of the educational functions, all are the residue of the hundred-and-fifty-day second order systems. Administration apart, financial control is the carry-over of the financial management system; public relations, dropping some of its educational functions, continues to work in a support role, and personnel management is now largely concerned with people who are on site. On a dig of fifty days it is important that attention be paid not just to the provision of archaeology, but also to the provision of events and activities which serve to maintain the morale and interest of the whole group. The personnel function, in addition to its labour-control role, should also be ensuring that events take place which will bring the whole team together, if only for talks or tea.

One may well ask why these particular methods of describing systems have been used. People are much more used to the familiar picture of a tree, albeit an inverted tree. We might, for example, have described our organisation as follows:

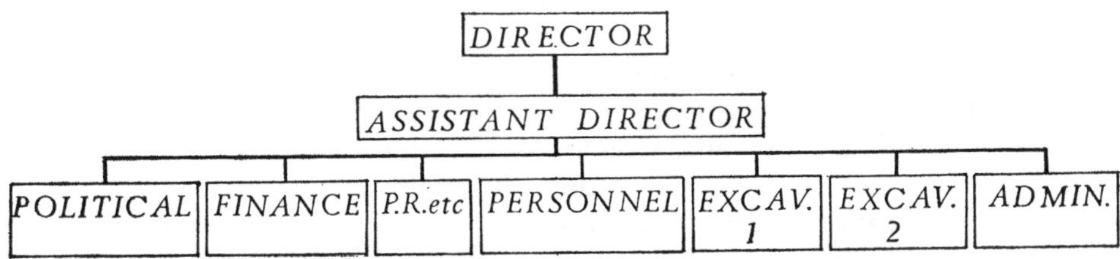

Fig. 58. Conventional diagram of excavation structure.

This type of organisation description takes no real account of the reality of the situation because linkages exist in this system that make a nonsense of the theoretical pattern. Take the example we are going to examine—Manchester. There existed a link between the Director and the head of the political function which had been cemented long before this system came into being. To describe that link a dotted line would have to be introduced to explain away the special status of this particular man. Continuing the analysis further we would discover that the whole system is covered with a series of dotted lines which would nullify the apparent system. This type of description also fails to distinguish between operational functions and service functions. Administration, for example, cannot be of the same order as one of the productive functions, e.g. earth-moving and control. The description also fails to take account of the changing nature of this organisation. We are, in fact, dealing with two quite different organisations. The first is there simply to prepare the ground for the second. The first organisation will have priorities of function which have nothing at all to do with the priorities of the second system. Also, once the tasks of the hundred-and-fifty-day organisation have been accomplished there still remains one more task, namely the facilitation of the second system—and the peaceful demise of the first system. In order to achieve all this the hundred-and-fifty-day system changes its form from an operating system into a service system.

These concepts of organisational form were very much in the minds of those responsible for establishing the Manchester excavation. We began by trying to apply some simple systems concepts to the activity. The best known example of a system is probably that shown below:

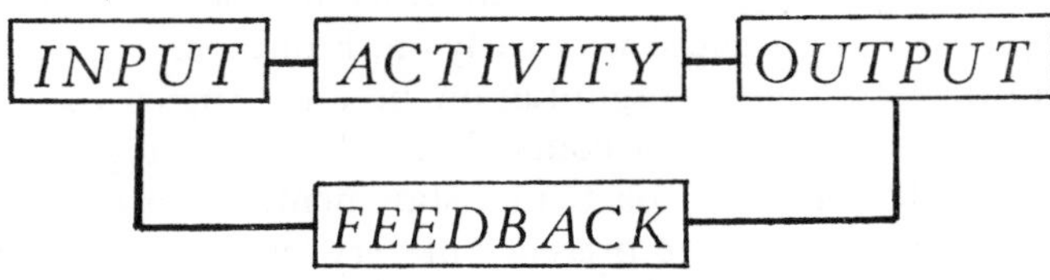

Fig. 59. Input-output model.

This model presupposes that all activities have inputs and outputs. As the inputs are designed to achieve some desired output, it is important to check, through feedback, that the outputs match the intention of the inputs.

In terms of the inputs for Manchester we had:

1. A site.
2. Personnel.
3. Finance.
4. Materials.

The activities were:

1. An excavation.
2. Environmental management.
3. Data processing.
4. Site and personnel management.

The outputs were designed to be:

1. Organised data concerning Roman Manchester.
2. A museum collection to replace the existing unstratified collection.
3. Public education in the broader sense, through on-site guiding and post-excavation lectures.
4. Publications, both interim and final.
5. Team satisfaction.

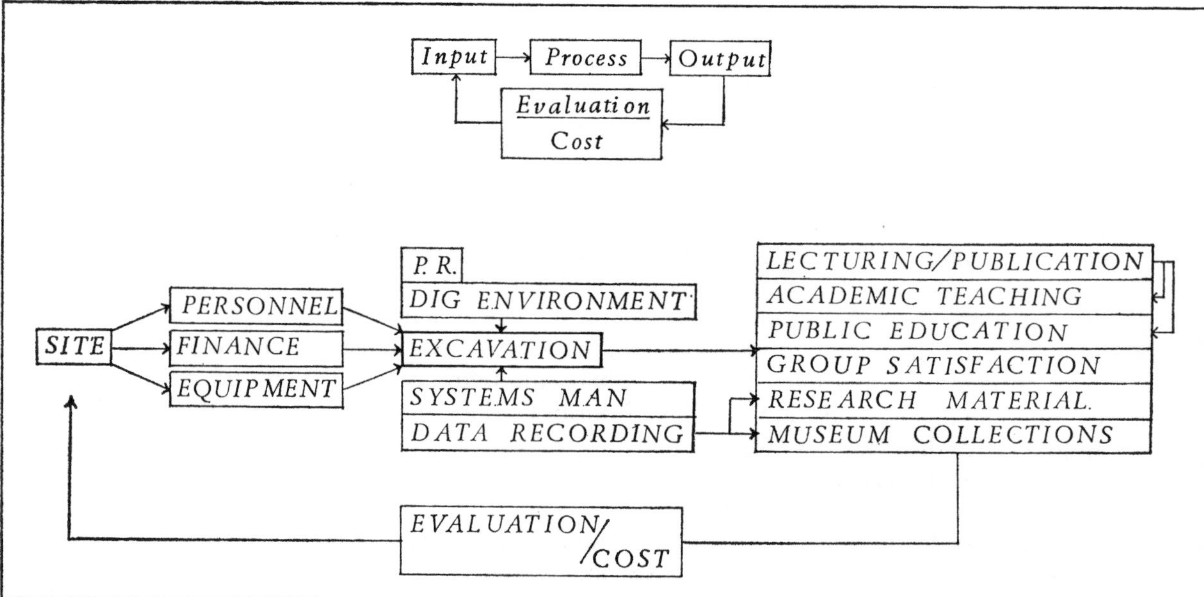

Fig. 60. System of overall excavation strategy.

These were all rather simple views of what transpired to be a much more complex system. We had an adequate time span within which to work, in that the information on site redevelopment was produced very early on. From then on, however, the need for two quite distinct systems of organisation became apparent. There is an old management adage about 'horses for courses' and the sort of organisation produced at Manchester seems to verify that particular statement. An examination of the pre-excavation organisation reveals the presence of very few archaeologists. Apart from one member of the first order directing system and one or two others in second order systems most of the staff of the hundred-and-fifty-day system were specialists in quite different fields. Indeed, to emphasise this point, the four committees covering the various second order functions set out in fig. 55 all liaised through a co-ordinator with no previous archaeological experience whatsoever, as shown in the diagram below:

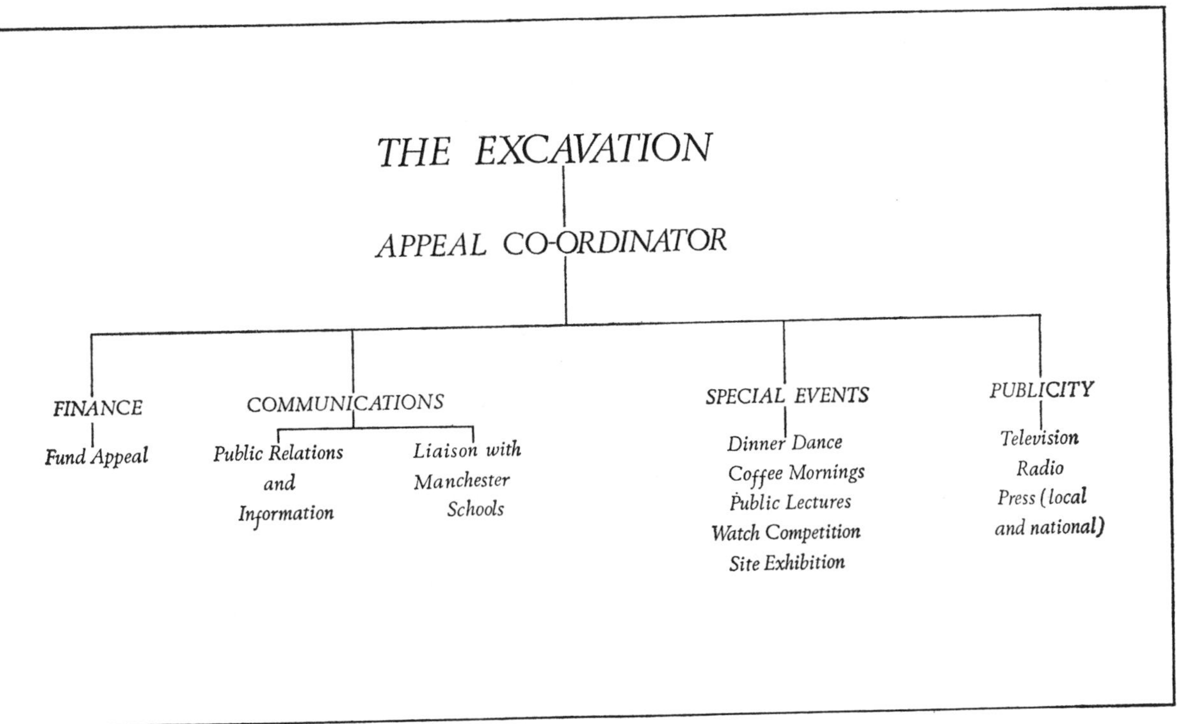

Fig. 61. Committee roles in the Manchester project.

The two major priorities of the pre-excavation system were the political management system and the finance management system. The political management system began by examining the nature of Manchester City Corporation and quickly it uncovered certain types of power structure at both councillor and official level. Simultaneous approaches made to both levels produced encouragement rather than actual results at this stage. The value of this groundwork was not realised until the financial organisation started to move towards the pursuit of funds from the local council. This was a major step because Manchester had not previously been noted for its involvement in rescue archaeology. What was amazing was the willingness with which properly briefed councillors and officials offered help. One important lesson was learned from all this. Councillors and officials are not over-anxious to spend public money (despite popular opinion). They will, however, spend money when they can see some value or legitimacy in such an expenditure. The presentation of the case for funds must therefore be couched in terms which are meaningful to the purchaser and not to the salesman. Publicity, tourism, sight-seeing, are all of value. So is educational value. The intrinsic values of academic archaeology. however, are not.

Once the groundwork was completed there was an opportunity to begin the publicity campaign two months prior to the excavation proper. This campaign was planned in such a way that the initial impact would be substantial and the interest generated would then be sustained at a lower level until a few days before the excavation was open to the public when the second campaign would take place. Local and national press, as well as the other news media, were contacted and well briefed. The result of this was that reporters took a special interest in the activity and provided much more cover than was expected. Granada TV agreed, at this point, to make a film about the excavation. All these factors then begin to feed into each other. The publicity produces a greater awareness of value inside the local corporation. The media also awaken interest in schools and colleges and thus the public relations/educational activity could start to operate. Equally, recruitment of labour could begin because the excavation was by now certain. An example of the use of our systems approach concerns the relationships between the excavation site and the media. It was apparent that the TV crews would need somewhere to film. The forward planning service accordingly planned to accommodate this constraint on the site by setting out part of the site plan with a camera stand in mind. When the fifty-day organisation came into being it already had a site plan which could accommodate such a space.

As the hundred-and-fifty-day system drew to a close there was the problem of establishing the fifty-day system. This was facilitated by the fact that the overall director of the hundred-and-fifty-day system was also the overall director of the fifty-day system. As it happened, the transition phase lasted about ten days because the fifty-day system required a starting phase of two weeks completely free of interference. Thus the finance, political and public relations activities continued as a major system until the actual excavation was about two weeks old. The reasoning for this was not difficult. The site itself had to be cleared and prepared. The team itself had to be organised and trained. During this time members of the public would have been an embarrassment, if only because the sub-system concerned with their management had not been fully organised. After two weeks of this preparation, however, the hundred-and-fifty-day system came to a halt and turned itself into a service sub-system for the fifty-day period.

It is important, however, to recognise that the hundred-and-fifty-day system did not come to an abrupt halt once excavation began. There were still problems relating to the political and social environment which had to be handled. If archaeologists wish to pursue their primary task then some other agency or person has to manage those tasks which still exist, but are not wanted. Public figures, who have been responsible for financing part of the exercise, will at least wish to visit the site and possibly wish to be photographed there. The press and other media have to be managed and informed. The administrative functions still have to be performed and a strict financial control has to be exercised. No excavation is ever going to be over-endowed with funds to the point that it can become profligate. Some system must exist for the careful management and disposition of funds. In a hierarchical system, financial decisions tend to be made by those responsible for finance (often accountants) and senior managers. In our sort of system those persons responsible for second order systems are also involved in financial allocation decisions relating to their systems. Thus a decision to spend X pounds on one second order system can be made with the senior direction plus all the second order system managers. This enables a more adequate information flow through the total system and prevents many of the unpleasant management issues which can occur over undeclared reasons for cash allocation.

A point which may be made, in reply to all this, might be the fact that much archaeology is in fact bound to be reactive. One cannot predict what a motorway excavation will unearth. Hopefully, agencies such as RESCUE will be able to provide a form of hundred-and-fifty-day organisation which can react instantly. On the other hand, any reputable archaeological or antiquarian society should be able to recognise the fact that it too might well become involved in some sort of rescue operation. Sadly, most of these societies have antiquarian forms of organisation which are related to the internal needs of the system to run itself, rather than to the external needs created by the environment. If this is the case then it is perhaps time that local organisations set up sub-systems capable of proacting rather than relying upon reactive systems.

It is a measure of the public impact of the 1972 Manchester excavation that the next phase of rescue work in Manchester, in the area of the Cathedral, is currently being planned at the express invitation of the City Corporation and with its financial support.

NOTES

1 The earliest comprehensive work dealing with the internal organisation of an excavation from a modern standpoint is R. E. M. Wheeler, *Archaeology from the Earth* (Pelican edition, 1956), especially 153ff and 209ff. Many further works on the same subject have since been published, the most recent being J. Alexander, *The Directing of Archaeological Excavations* (London, 1970), especially 21ff and 49ff. While giving coverage to the internal running of an excavation, none of the volumes available deals analytically with the question of archaeological forward planning in its broader sense.

2 G. Hutton, *Thinking about Organisation* (1972); A. Etzioni, *Modern Organisations* (1964); T. Lupton, *Management and the Social Sciences* (1970); E. Schein, *Organisational Psychology* (1965).

3 Hutton, *op. cit.*, 95–104.

4 Alexander, *op. cit.*, note 1.

Summary

THE PROGRAMME of work conducted on the one-acre site immediately north of the known Roman fort at Castlefield, Deansgate, produced the first excavated evidence for the plan and development of part of the civil settlement associated with the Roman fort at Manchester. The area concerned lay on the south side of Liverpool Road and its eastern sector was principally taken up by the line of the road leaving the north-eastern gate of the fort. The earliest discoveries, dating to the seventies of the first century A.D., comprised an extensive ditch system that formed the outer defences of the auxiliary fort. These included a small annexe on the north-western side of the excavation site, an annexe that extended north-westwards under the present City Exhibition Hall. This ditch system was abandoned at some stage in the Flavian period and deliberately filled in to allow the creation of timber-built shops and houses close to the fort in the very late first and early second centuries. Excavation revealed the position of several rapidly changing timber structures the layout of which was mainly controlled by the axial line created by the Roman road. Amongst these buildings was in fact a furnace shed designed to provide cover for a series of iron working furnaces. By the end of the second century this concentration on the industrial process of secondary iron working was reflected across practically the whole of the area examined. Thirty-three furnace areas, both large and small, were discovered within the site, some inside buildings, others in open spaces to the rear. The metallurgical evidence suggests that they operated at differing temperatures ranging between 400 and 1400 degrees Centigrade and form the largest group so far examined in this country. The last surviving buildings on the site belong to the early years of the third century. Any trace of later buildings was destroyed by the intensive cultivation that characterised this area around the core of late mediaeval Manchester. The site was then converted to accommodate high-density working-class housing in 1825–6.

The centre of Manchester has been undergoing major redevelopment for the last decade. In the last few years in particular the pace of redevelopment has accelerated with the complete rebuilding of much of the area around the mediaeval buildings surviving as the Shambles at the northern end of Deansgate. The creation of an inner relief road linking the northern and southern ends of Deansgate formed the principal reason for the rescue work involved in 1972. The north-western alignment of the new relief road running from the proposed roundabout at Knott Mill Bridge forms the basis for a possible further series of investigations across the next few years as more elements along the line become available for examination. Of these the most important single site is perhaps that formed by the City Exhibition Hall directly opposite the present excavation site. This massive Victorian wrought-iron building is known to overlie a site that yielded a Roman altar and also nine Saxon coins. Despite its massive size, the structure in fact contains no cellars and would form an important area for further exploration of the Roman *vicus* at some greater distance from the actual line of the defences. The hint of the religious nature of part of the area concerned certainly encourages examination in the next few years. How far this applies to the next section of the road is difficult to assess because as the line approaches Quay Street east of the Granada Building the extent of cellarage is not at all clear. This problem affects the whole onward course of the inner relief road towards the area of the old Exchange Station and the complexities provided by the course of the River Irwell. The road itself is designed to link with the A57 route towards Bury at the lower end of Great Ducie Street. This development brings us into the key area of the Cathedral and Victoria Station.

As already shown in a section of this book, it is in this area, incorporating the Cathedral and Chetham's School, that there is evidence for Saxon occupation, related to the problematical monument known as Hanging Ditch and Hunt's Bank. In fact the line of this feature may be represented by the semi-circular road on the eastern side of the Cathedral and Chetham's School. In this area, therefore, the archaeological evidence of early mediaeval Manchester theoretically exists. The extraction of archaeological information depends on the speed of redevelopment and the problems of access and finance. The zone is one that is in fact due for partial redevelopment in the seventies and it is here that rescue excavation must principally occur within the city by the end of this decade. A programme of work in this area is the logical successor to the present archaeological situation within the city. It would throw potential light on the development of early mediaeval Manchester just as the work at Castlefield at the opposite end of Deansgate has illuminated the development of the Roman predecessor of Manchester. Indeed, as this predominantly Roman volume goes to press, it is a measure of the success of the Deansgate excavation that the City Corporation and the North-Western Water Board have provided both the opportunity and the finance for the first archaeological investigation of mediaeval Manchester.

MANCHESTER EXCAVATION APPEAL COMMITTEES

Appeal Co-ordinator
H. F. PARTRIDGE, Esq.

Finance
W. BROCKBANK, M.D. (Chairman)
A. R. ARMOUR, Esq., Honorary Auditor
G. ARNOLD, Esq., Press Officer, The Rescue Trust
Miss D. CHARLESWORTH, Inspectorate of Ancient Monuments, Dept. of the Environment
Mrs H. CLARKE
D. HEPPELL, Esq., Assistant Chief Architect, Manchester City Corporation
Alderman A. LOGAN, Chairman, Cultural Committee, Manchester City Council
B. E. L. LONG, Esq., Dept. of Adult Education, Manchester University

Special Events
Mrs A. CHALMERS (Chairman)
D. KENNEDY, Esq.
Mrs E. McPHERSON
M. MILNER, Esq.
Dr M. TAYLOR
Dr J. P. WILD

Publicity
B. E. L. LONG, Esq. (Chairman)
G. ARNOLD, Esq.
Mrs A. CHALMERS
D. I. COLLEY, Esq., Chief Librarian, Manchester Public Libraries
M. J. JONES, Esq.
A. J. N. W. PRAG, Esq., Manchester University
Mrs G. W. PRICE
Dr J. P. WILD, Dept. of History, Manchester University

Communications
Miss C. BRIDE
Dr W. H. CHALONER, Dept. of History, Manchester University
R. CLARKE, Esq.
Miss J. CROMACK
D. HILL, Esq., Staff Tutor in Archaeology, Dept. of Extra-Mural Studies
Miss D. KENYON
I. S. D. MOLL, Esq.
Mrs C. ROSE
S. ROWE, Esq.

CONTRIBUTORS TO THE MANCHESTER UNIVERSITY EXCAVATION FUND

Miss A. R. Adamson
Hon. Mrs M. Adderley
Mr Ainsworth
Dr J. J. G. Alexander
Mr E. W. Allen
Dr Marjorie Allen
Mrs D. A. Allman
Alpha Engineering Services
Miss Lucy Alston
Mr W. E. Anderson
Mrs R. G. Armstrong
Mr E. Arnold
Mr H. L. Ashby
Mr Ashton
Dr H. W. Ashworth

Dr Douglas G. Bagg
J. S. Bailey Ltd
Mr H. J. Baker
Mr Hugh Baldwin
Mr John Ball
Mr W. Bannatyne
Dr D. N. Barber
Dr G. W. R. Bartindale
Mr J. V. Baskerville
Bass Charrington (N.W.) Ltd
Mr H. Bassett
Dr Eric Batley
Mr E. L. Behrens
Sir Leonard Behrens
Mr A. A. Bennett
Miss D. Bernard
Miss E. Berry
Mr James Bethell
Miss M. M. Binns
Miss N. H. Binns
Mr T. Birchall
Mrs J. P. Birley
Constance Bishop
Mr M. G. Bishop
Prof. D. A. K. Black
Dr D. M. Blamires
Boardman, Woolrich & Partners
Dr D. R. & Mrs C. A. Bodey
Bolton Smithills Townswomen's Guild
Miss D. C. Booth
Drs M. S. & L. J. Bourne
Mr A. M. Boyd
Mr E. Boyle
Dr C. J. Bradfield
Mrs K. Bradshaw
Betty Brady
Dr M. J. Brayshay
Miss Claire Bride
Mrs S. L. R. Bride
British Engine Boiler & Electrical Insurance Co
Dr William Brockbank
Dr A. A. Brown
Drs A. M. & A. B. Brown
Mr C. S. Brown
Mrs R. C. Brown
Mr J. A. Browne
Miss Ruth Brownson
Mr F. F. Bruce
Mr F. H. Buckley
Building Design Partnership
Miss A. L. Bullough
Mr R. A. Burchell
Mrs H. Burd
Dr C. B. Burdett-Smith
Mr M. A. Burton
Dr E. Blanche Butler
Mr S. N. Butterworth
Miss G. E. Busby

Mrs N. Caiger
Prof. A. C. P. Campbell
Mr V. R. Cane
The Hon. Mr Justice Cantley
Mrs G. M. Carrington
Miss D. Carty
Mr S. A. Casstles
Dr Florence Cavanagh
Mr T. H. Chadwick
Mr K. Challinor
Mr R. Challoner
Mrs Ann Chalmers
Mr W. Chalmers
Mr Randell Champion
Ciba-Geigy Ltd
Dr A. D. Clarke
Mr R. V. Clarke
Mr T. H. Cleworth
Mr W. Clough
Dr I. Cogan
Mr Caspar Quas-Cohen
Mr H. Cohen
Mr S. J. Cohen
Prof. Patrick Collard
Mr G. F. B. Collins
Mr and Mrs G. L. Conlan
Mr Colin Cooke
Miss Joan Cooper
Dr and Mrs C. Corbett

Mr & Mrs L. Corbett
Mr A. Cornelius
Mr T. Cornish
Miss M. G. Coutts
Dr H. J. Crewe
Dr S. N. Cristea
Miss Andrea Crook
Mrs J. Crook & Pupils, Forest School, Timperley
Prof. D. W. J. Cruickshank
Cruickshank & Seward
Mr & Mrs J. Cubban
Mr T. D. Culbert

Dr K. S. Daber
Miss Helen Dare
Mr John Dark
Miss I. M. Davidson
Prof. John Davis
Drs Davison and Myers
Mr S. R. K. Dawber
Dr Annie M. Dawson
H. Day & J. J. Hodgson, also R. Davies, J. H. Lord, J. C. Bailey, T. D. Hart, J. K. Burke & Colleagues
Alfred G. Deacon & Co
Mr J. F. Delany
Mr D. Devine
Prof. R. Beresford Dew
Dr B. M. Dick
Mr Frank Dickinson
Mr H. Diggle
Mr Tom Dinsdale
Dr C. S. D. Don
Mrs E. Donavan
Mr W. J. Driver
Mr G. H. H. Dwyer
Mr E. B. C. Dyckhoff

Mrs E. Eastwood
Eccles Adult Education Centre
Mr G. A. Elder (Price, Forbes (Northern) Ltd)
Mr Cecil Ellison
Mr P. Ellwood
English Calico Ltd
Dr B. Epstein
Mr & Mrs Eroch
Miss Elizabeth A. E. Evans

Failsworth Townswomen's Guild
Harry S. Fairhurst & Son
Fallowfield Church High School for Girls
William Fearnhead & Son
Miss C. I. Fell
Ferranti Ltd
Field Cunningham & Co
Mr J. W. Firth
H. R. Fitton & Butler
Mr T. B. Fitzgerald
Dr B. Flacks
Miss Ann Fort
Dr B. Foster
Mr D. J. Fox
Mr F. V. Fox
Dr S. Fox
Fram Gerrard Ltd
Mrs C. Francis
Mr Nicholas J. Frangopulo
Dr H. Freeman

Mr R. L. Gadd
Miss E. Garbutt
Mr A. E. Gardiner
Mr J. B. Garland
Dr M. Garretts
Mr J. Garstang
Miss E. M. Gath
Miss E. Gent
Dr P. W. Gilman
Dr D. M. Ginever
Mr Marcello Giobbe
Mr Alan Glass
Mr S. L. Goodman
Miss Florence M. Goodyear
Goulty & Goodfellow
Dr A. H. Gowenlock
Dr A. J. Graham
Mr T. H. Graham & Colleagues
Granada Television Ltd
Mr A. Gratrix
Greenall Whitley & Co
A. Grierson, Thompson, Carter & Co
Mr D. Ll. Griffiths

Prof. W. Haas
Miss E. Hadfield
Mr R. M. Hadfield
Mrs G. Haigh
Prof. Basil Hall
Drs W. S. Hall & A. Fox
Dr I. M. Hallack
Mr Colin Harding & members of Extra-Mural Classes, Bolton
Mr R. H. Hargreaves
Mr G. R. Harlow
Mr J. Harrington
Sir Cyril Harrison
Mr K. Harrison
Sir Geoffrey & Lady Haworth
Miss M. E. Haworth

Mr Richard Haworth
Dr G. E. Heald
Dr K. Heap
Mr L. A. Hemming
Miss V. N. Henstock
Mrs E. M. Heslop
Mr James F. Heslop
Mr T. Stewart Heslop
Mrs K. S. Heywood
Mrs N. Heywood
Mr S. N. Heywood
Miss Rosa Higginbotham
Mr J. S. Higham
Mr D. M. Hindson
Mr W. C. Hockenhull
Miss Caroline Hodgetts
Mr David Hodson
Mr K. G. Holden
Mr R. Holmes
Mr R. L. Holt
Mr Arthur H. Hope
Mr C. Horrox
Mr B. Horsley
Dr I. B. Houston
Dr H. T. Howat
Dr G. Howitt
Mrs K. W. D. Hull
Mr & Mrs S. Hulme
Mr M. Hulse
Dr A. R. Hunter
Hydes Anvil Brewery Ltd

Ian Hunter & Partners
I.C.I. Ltd
Mr A. T. S. Ife
Mr G. A. Illingworth
Dr Ian Isherwood
Mr R. Isherwood
Prof. M. C. G. Israels

Dr A. H. Jackson
Dr P. W. Jackson
Mr L. S. H. Jackson
Miss Marjorie Jalland
Miss Vera A. Jaques
Dr R. F. Jennison
Mr K. E. Jermy
Mr D. W. Johnston
Mr J. B. Jones
Mr R. Jones
Mr A. Jolleys
The Very Revd A. Jowett

Mr Nigel C. Keddie
Prof. R. E. Keller
Miss A. A. Kellett
Prof. J. H. Kellgren
Mrs A. D. Kelly
Mr C. J. E. Kempster
Mr G. H. Kenyon
Mr W. E. Ker
Dr D. F. Kerr
Miss Kiernan
Miss Elizabeth Kinsey
Mr D. C. Kirby
Mr Noel F. Kirkman
Miss Kathleen Knibb
Miss B. M. Knight
Mr Stephen Knight
Dr G. M. Komrower

Mr E. W. Lambert
Prof. V. Lambert
Lancashire Hygienic Dairies Ltd
Dr & Mrs Roger W. G. Lancashire
Prof. R. E. Lane
Mr Leahy
Dr Basil Lee
Dr J. Lee
Misses P. M. & A. B. Leech
Dr S. A. Leslie
Miss Margaret Lever
Levenshulme High School
(Upper School)
Dr David Lewis
Mrs V. Lewis
Miss Betty Lilly
Prof. H. Lipson
Mr F. C. Lofts
Mr Harold Lomas
Lomax, King & Rothmer
Mr E. Low
Dr A. Lowe

Mrs P. Macdonald
Dr R. I. Mackay
Miss E. R. L. Makin
Manchester Geographical Society
Dr & Mrs H. D. Manderson
Marks & Spencer Ltd
Marple Antiquarian Society
Mr H. B. Marton
Mather & Platt Ltd
Sir William Mather
Mr R. G. Maxwell
Maydella Manufacturing Co Ltd
Dr J. McCracken
Mr G. D. McLeish
Mr G. J. McLeish
Mr N. McLeish
Mr M. S. Metcalfe
Midland Bank Ltd
Dr Stanley Miles
Mr J. M. Miller

Mr J. Mills
Prof. G. A. G. Mitchell
Mr I. S. D. Moll
Mr Thomas Moore
Mr C. E. Morris
Prof. W. I. C. Morris
Morris & Yeaman Ltd
Mr A. W. Moule
William A. Muir Ltd
Mr & Mrs J. H. Mulholland
Dr P. B. Mumford

Mr M. H. Nash
National Vulcan Engineering Group Ltd
National Westminster Bank
Mr R. M. Naysmith
Miss J. S. Nixon
Mr Brian D. Norris
Mr John O. H. Norris
North Manchester Federation of Townswomen's Guilds
Notre Dame High School

Dr Agnes S. O'Brien
Dr C. A. O'Connor
Dr S. Oleesky
Mr C. M. O'Hora
Dr Barbara Oldham
Colonel R. & Dame K. Ollerenshaw
Mrs H. Oswald
Ove, Arup & Partners

Mr Alan Parker
Dr J. S. Parkinson
Mr & Mrs H. F. Partridge
Mr J. Ellis Paul
Mr N. G. C. Pearson
Peat, Marwick, Mitchell & Co
Mr B. E. Peers
Dr C. D. R. Pengelly
Mrs Janet H. Phillips
Mr R. S. Phillips
A. S. Pigott & Son
Pochin Ltd
Mrs K. Poplawska
Mr Stanley Pollitt
Dr B. Portnoy
Dr D. W. Preston
Price Bros Ltd
Mr G. W. Price
Price Waterhouse & Co
Dr & Mrs R. N. Priestland
Mrs Florence Printy

H. & J. Quick Group Ltd

Rank Xerox Ltd
Mr V. I. Rawlinson
Mr John Reed
Dr M. M. Reekie
Refuge Assurance Co Ltd
Miss E. Reiss
Renold Ltd
Dr & Mrs A. Roberts
Miss J. Roberts
Mr M. Robinson
W. H. Robinson & Co
Mr R. Robinson
Mr C. A. Rodewald
Mr S. S. Rose
Prof. J. S. Roskell
Royal Insurance Group
Mrs A. M. Royle
Mr George C. Royley
Miss Lorna A. Ruff
Russell's (of Didsbury) Ltd

Saddleworth Historical Society
St Peter's Grammar School, Prestwich
Sale Co-op Guild
Neville Sassoon & Co
Mr F. W. Saunders
Canon Eric Saxon
Scherrer & Hicks
Dr D. Scragg
Seal Arnold & Co
Mrs K. M. Seddon
Mrs W. L. Seddon
Dr P. G. Seed
Mrs R. Segal
Mr Winston B. Senior
Drs J. & S. Shafer
Mr D. B. Shaw
M. E. Short & Co
Mr P. J. Short
Mr G. K. Siddall
Dr Brian A. Sides
Mr S. Sidebotham
Mr N. H. Simmonds
Mr J. R. Simmons
Mr C. G. H. Simon
Sir Frederick Snow & Partners
Sir James Farmer Norton & Co Ltd
Mr A. Sladen
Mr F. Slater
Slater, Heelis & Co
Alwyn Smith
Dr F. Wemyss Smith
Miss K. A. Smith
Prof. R. E. Smith
Mr L. Solloman
Spicer Pegler & Co
Mrs Phoebe Standart
Miss Helen Stanhope

Mr R. F. T. Stepto
Mr P. C. Steptoe
Stockport Historical Society
Dr R. V. Stone
Mr R. C. Stones
Mr T. B. Stretton
Prof. F. E. Sutcliffe
Miss Joan Sutcliffe

Dr M. J. Tarsh
Mr J. Tasker
Mr Eric Taylor
Taylor, Kirkman & Mainprice
Taylor, Whalley & Spyra
Miss N. Templar
Dr B. D. Tennant
Tesco Stores Ltd
Wm Thorpe & Son Ltd
Miss E. J. Timpson
Dr P. Tingley
Dr A. Tognarelli
Torkington Engineers Ltd
Mr L. R. G. Treloar
Mr D. J. R. Turner
Turquands, Barton, Mayhew & Co
Dame Mabel Tylecote

Mr H. B. Vanstone
Miss E. Verity
Mr C. Vickerman

Dr Geoffrey Wade
Dr Henry Wade
Dr M. W. P. Wade
Miss May Walmsley
Mr & Mrs J. Walsh
Dr M. Ward
Mr & Mrs J. Warmisham
Mr D. W. Warrell
Mr F. Warwick
Mr N. Waterfall
Dr G. H. Watson
Dr R. J. Alan Webb
Miss I. A. Webster
Mr S. Weinholt
Prof. & Mrs D. Welland
Dr J. M. Weller
Major & Mrs R. D. West
Prof. H. D. Westlake
Miss Christine M. Wheat
Whinney, Murray & Co
Mr A. Whitehead
Mr N. D. Whitehouse
Mrs Vivien M. Whiteman
Mr A. J. Whittam
Mrs Helen Wickham
Dr & Mrs J. F. Wilde
Dr J. M. Wilding
Miss B. J. Wilkinson
Prof. T. S. Willan
Williams & Glyns Bank Ltd
Dr Rhys Williams
Dr A. Wilson
Mr R. M. Winston
Dr W. H. Wolstenholme
Mr D. Woodhall
Mr M. I. Wright

Mr & Mrs E. Yates
Dr M. L. M. Young
Mr T. M. Young

Index

1

1947 aerial photograph showing site of 1972 excavations. Central Station is in the foreground.

2

1970 aerial photograph showing site of 1972 excavations. Central Station lies lower left.

3
Aerial view of the Roman fort at Castleshaw from the west.

4a

Portion of south-eastern gateway, the only upstanding remain of the Roman fort at Manchester.

4b

General view of site from south-west during 1972 excavations.

5a

The southern part of the site at an early stage of excavation.

5b

Floor make-up of Georgian houses built over excavation site *c.* 1825 (pp.77–80). Scale in feet.

6a

Removal of Furnace 2 for examination.

6b

The military ditch system. Arrows indicate the line of the ditch (fig. 12).

7a

Military ditch T.3.148 after removal of fill.

7b

Section across sump of military ditch after excavation (p. 43).

8a

Ditch of military annexe after excavation (p. 45).

8b

Palisade trench running parallel to ditch of annexe (p. 47). Scale 15cm. long.

9a

Lateral view of section through exit road showing over 1m. of metalling involved in at least eight re-surfacings (p. 33).

9b

East face of north-south section across T4 showing clay bases for smithing hearths (fig. 25, Furnace 10). Scale in feet.

10a

View across exit road with paving slabs in foreground (p. 39).

10b

General view of road and associated paving with gutter to left (E.).

11a
Wheel-rut surviving in road surface.

11b
Close-up of wheel-rut.

11c

Section through exit road showing the earliest surface with rut (see above) (p. 39).

12a

General view of minor road from west (p. 53).

12b

As above from east, with truncated clay floor to centre left.

13a

Construction trench of west wall of timber building A (p. 46; fig. 17).

13b

Construction trench of timber building B (indicated by arrow) cutting that of building A (p. 46; fig. 17).

14a

Construction trench (on right) of Building E running towards associated post-hole (p. 59). Furnace 16 appears in the foreground at a preliminary stage of excavation.

14b

Construction trenches of two phases of furnace sheds Ci and Cii (p. 52; fig. 17).

15a
General view of Furnace bases (2 and 3) found at Northwich (p. 146). Horizontal scale in feet.

15b
Base of Northwich Furnace 3 and associated section.

15c

Furnace base 33 found at Manchester (T4.113) closely parallel to the Northwich example (p. 146). Scale 30cm long.

16a
Northwich Furnace 1 when first discovered (pp. 147–8).

16b
Northwich Furnace 1 in half-section.

16c

Northwich Furnace 1 fully exposed.

17a

General view of Furnace 15 and surrounding area from north (p. 71; fig. 27).

17b

Floor of Furnace 15 from south.

18a

Furnace 2 and area showing scatter of external perforations (p. 151).

18b

Furnace 2 after excavation (p. 151; fig. 50).

19a

General view of Furnace 21 from south.

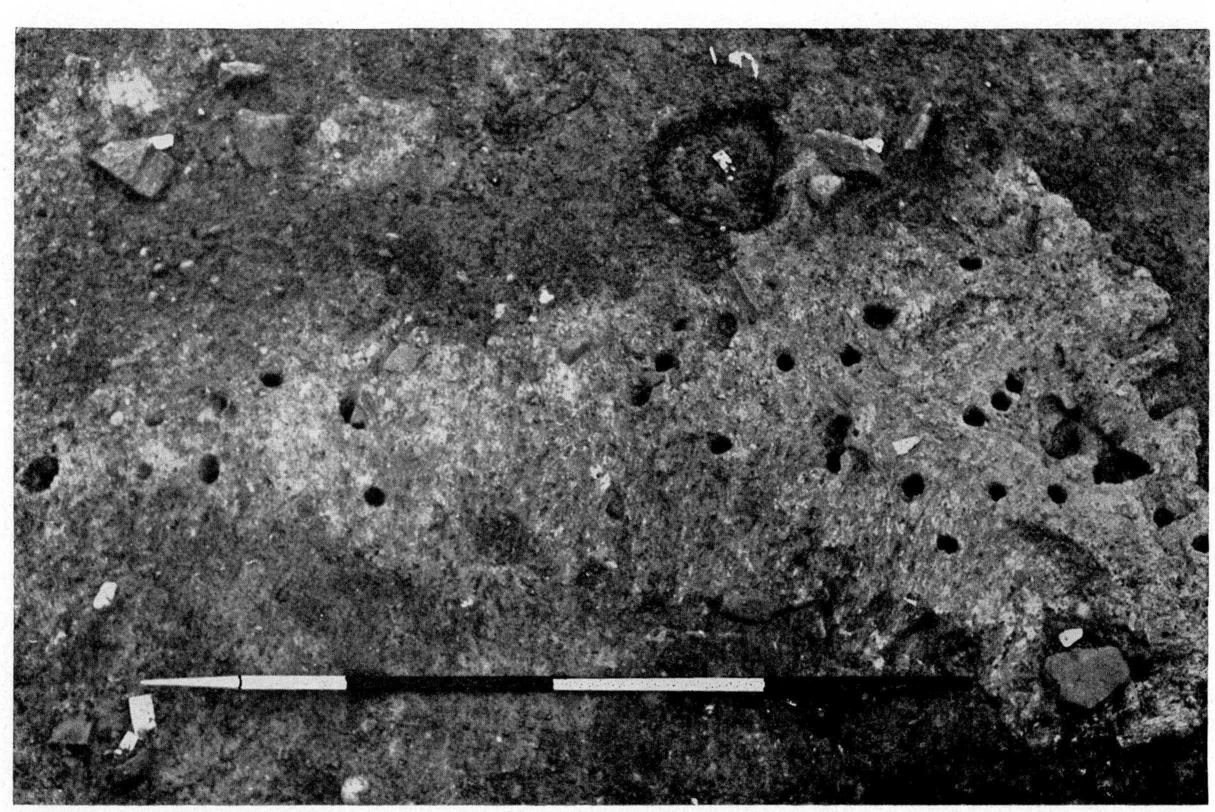

19b

Close-up view of Furnace 21 (p. 150; fig. 51).

20a

Section through Furnace 19 after removal of fill (fig. 22).

20b

Section through Furnace 18 showing internal build-up (fig. 28).

Section through Furnace 18 showing clay lining.

1b

Furnace 20 after excavation.

22a

Section through Furnace 23 showing cobble foundations (fig. 51).

22b

Furnace 17 cut by later construction trench (T1.519) of Building J (fig. 22).

23a

General view of furnaces and furnace bases in T4, east side (fig. 23).

23b

Furnaces at north end of T4 (fig. 23).

24a

Removal of Furnace 19 for examination at U.M.I.S.T. Department of Metallurgy.

24b

General view of pits 68 (right) and 69 in T4.

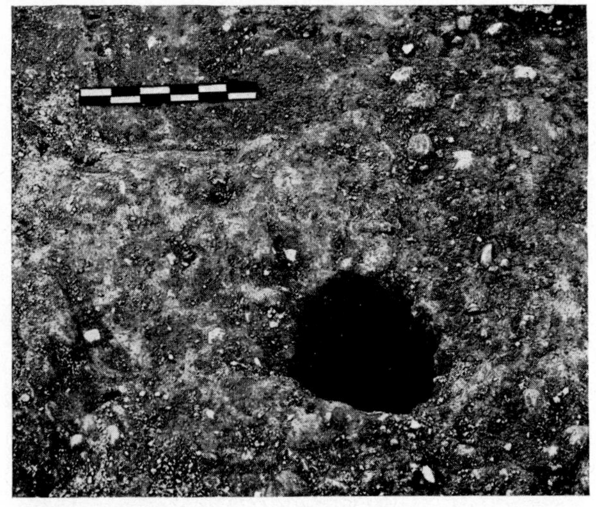

25a
Building D post-hole set in clay-packed post-pit (T1/2), (fig. 21).

25b
Building D post-hole (to right) of clay-packed post-pit into which a stone-packed post-pit of Building E has been inserted (p. 59; fig. 21).

25c
Post-holes for timber uprights of Building E.

26a
Stone-packed post-pit (T2.191) of Building E.

26b
Stone-packed post-pit (T1.61) of Building E.

26c
Section of post-pit (T1.113) belonging to Building E.

26d
Black-burnished jar *in situ* (T2.93).

27a

Clay floor on north side of Building E showing lay-out of post-holes for timber uprights (p. 59).

27b

Quern-stones used for grinding of corn, as found in preliminary stage of excavating pit T4.68 (pp. 55, 129–30).

28a

Quern-stone no.77 (p. 129).

28b

Quern-stone no.78 (p. 129).

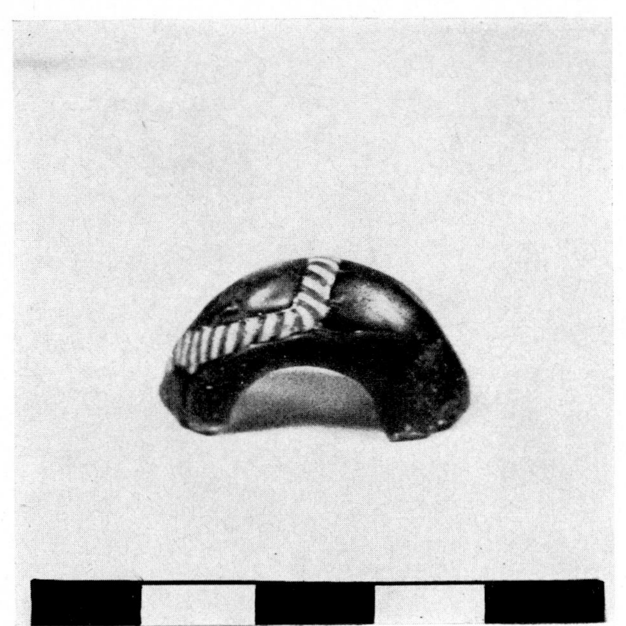

29a
Obsidian bead (p. 125; fig. 44).

29b
Obsidian bead (p. 125; fig. 44).

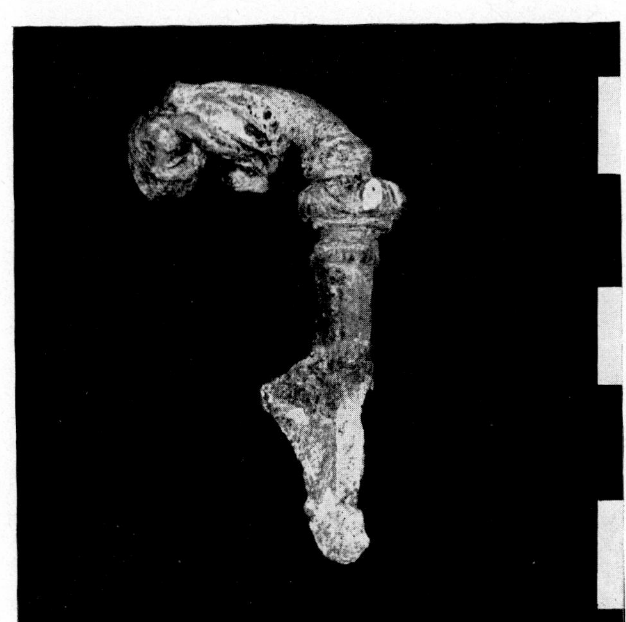

29c
Trumpet brooch (p. 121; fig. 43).

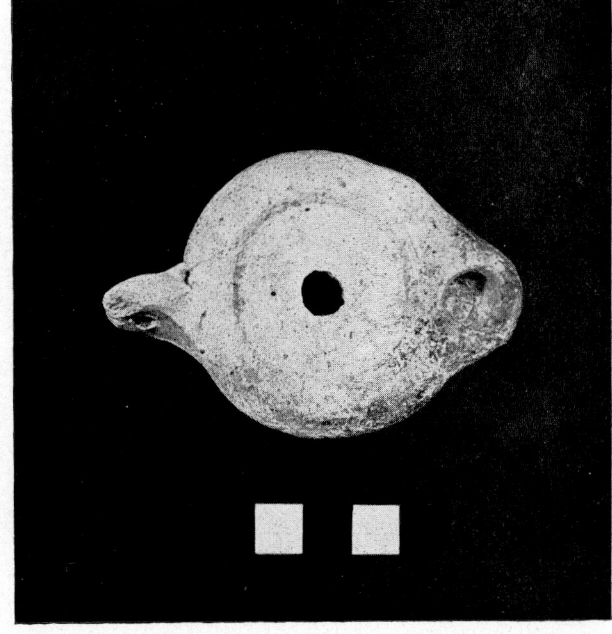

29d
Lamp (p. 116; fig. 41).

30a

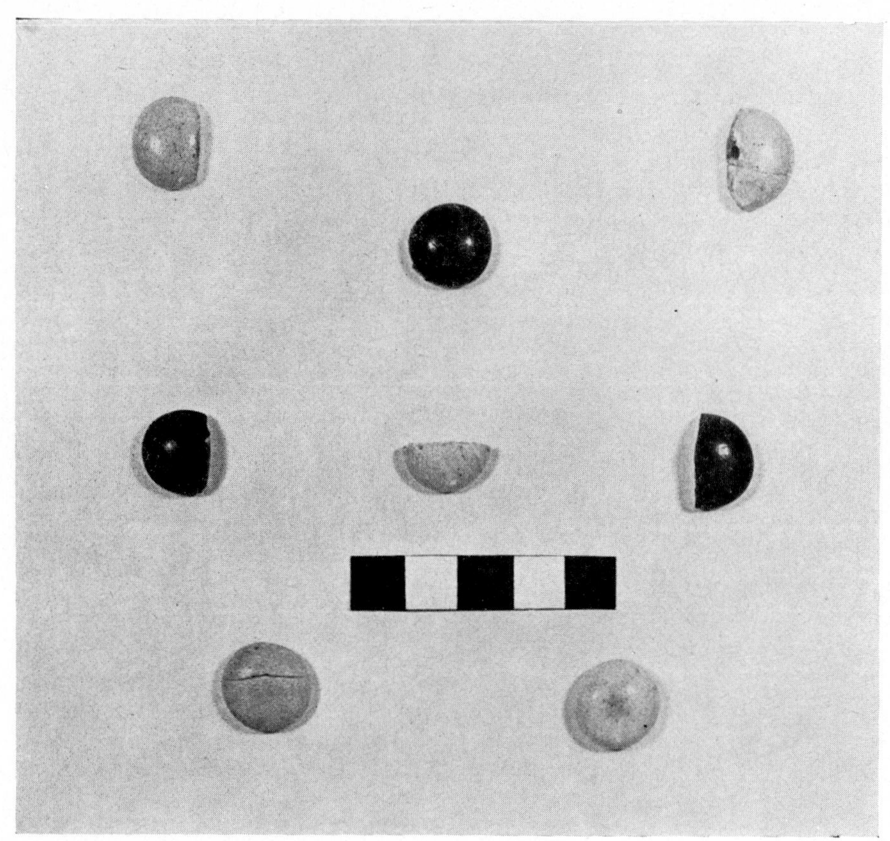

Glass gaming counters found in Building A (p. 125).

30b

Anglo-Saxon burial urn found at Red Bank in 1850 (p. 167).

31a 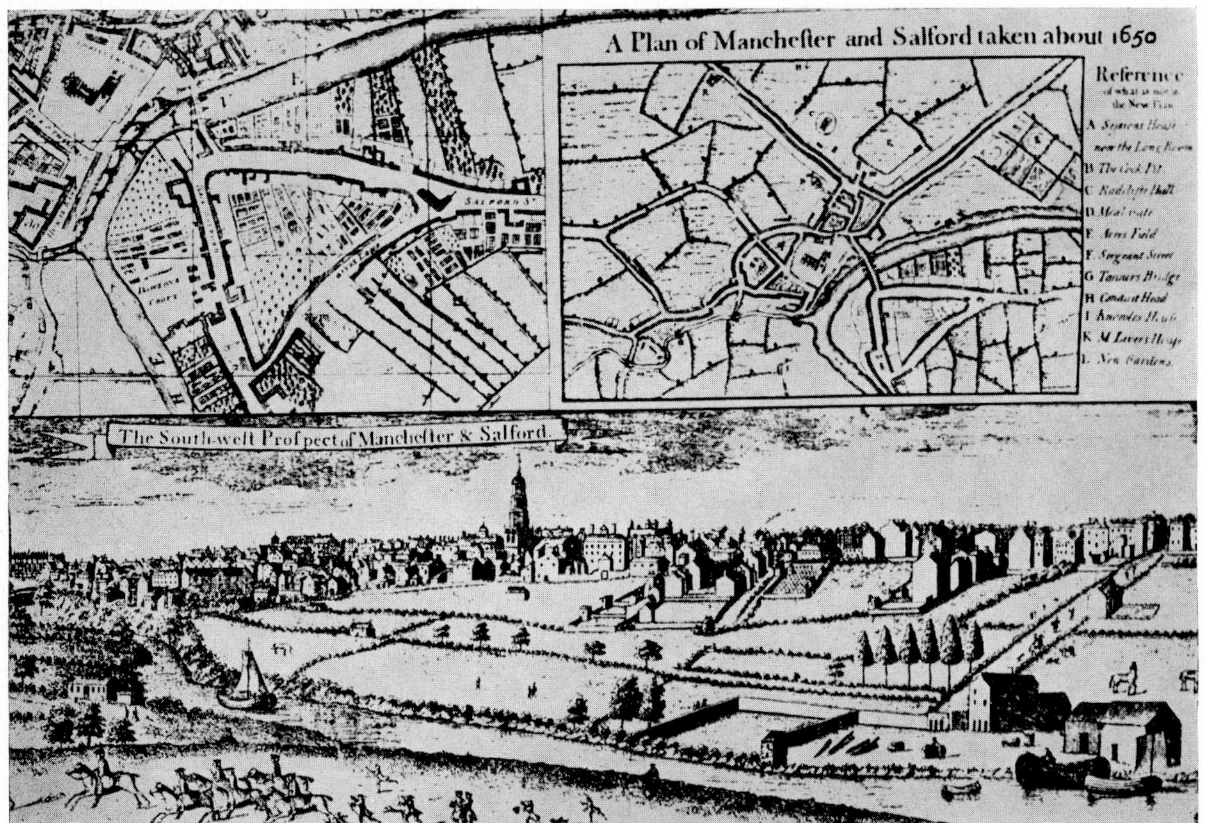

Plan of Manchester and Salford in 1650 superimposed on part of 1746 plan of R. Casson and J. Berry and including south-west prospect of Manchester and Salford.

31b 

South-west prospect of Manchester in 1728 (S. and N. Buck).

31c 

Detail of plate 31b showing the fields bordering the R. Irwell on the west side of Deansgate.

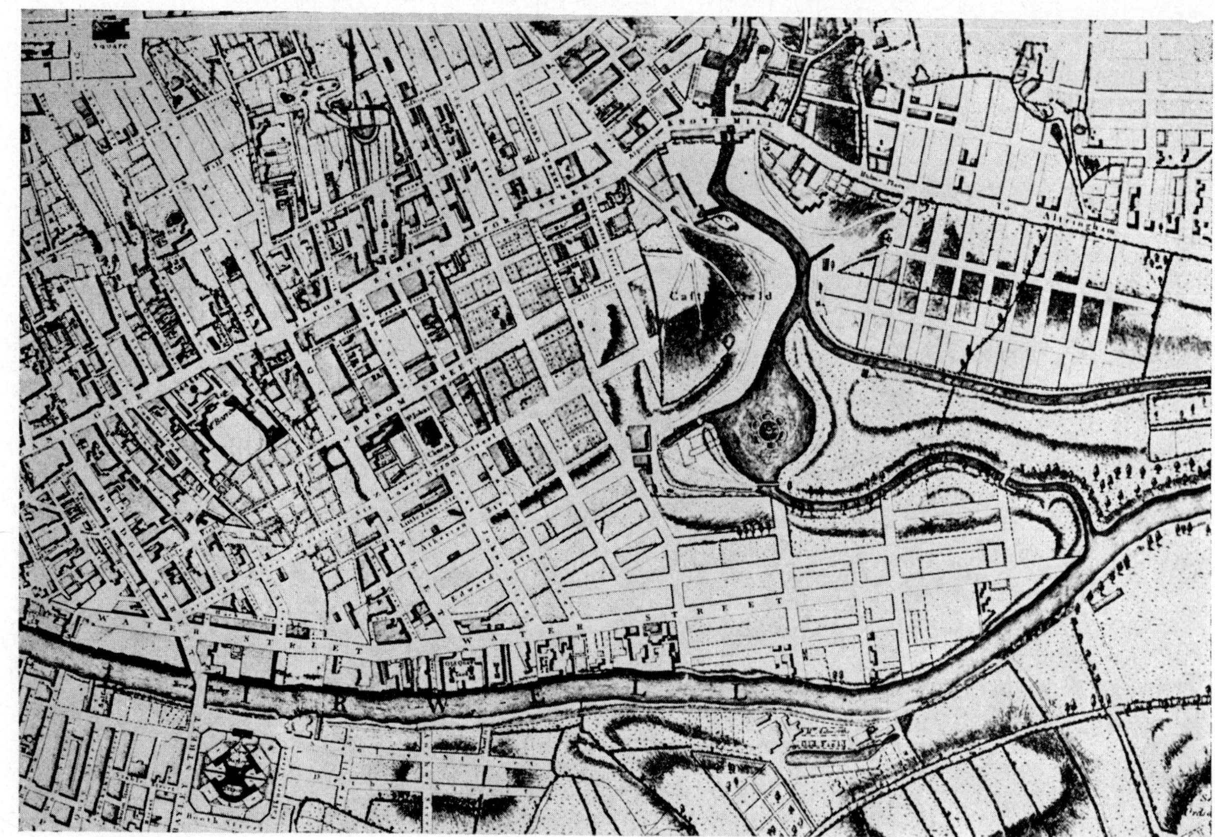

32a Detail from plan of Manchester and Salford in 1793 (C. Laurent).

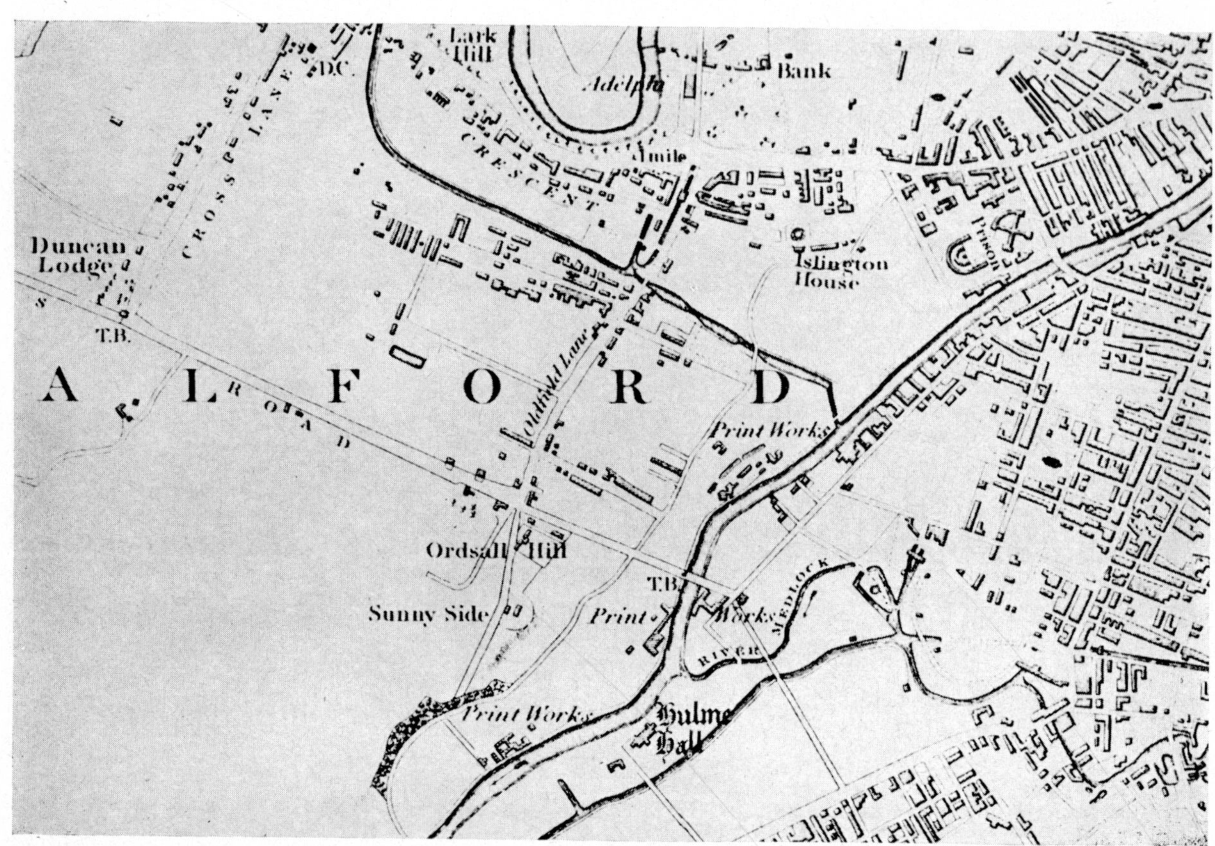

32b Detail from plan of Manchester and Salford in 1820 (William Johnson).